Guido delle Colonne

Historia Destructionis Troiae

Guido delle Colonne

TRANSLATED WITH
AN INTRODUCTION
AND NOTES

by Mary Elizabeth Meek

INDIANA UNIVERSITY PRESS
BLOOMINGTON · LONDON   1974

Published in Canada by Fitzhenry & Whiteside, Ltd., Don Mills, Ontario
Library of Congress Catalog Card No. 72-85603   ISBN 0-253-32740-7

This volume is No. 71 in the Indiana University Humanities Series.

MANUFACTURED IN THE UNITED STATES OF AMERICA

Translator's Note

This is a translation of the only modern edition of the *Historia Destructionis Troiae,* that of Nathaniel Edward Griffin, published by the Mediaeval Academy of America in 1936. It is a literal translation, intended to facilitate use of the Latin text as well as the vernacular works stemming from it. In the case of proper names, it has seemed best to use the conventional Anglicized Latin forms, as *Aeneas* for *Heneas,* especially for the characters and places familiar to us from classical literature. Occasionally the textual form is kept, as in the catalogues of the heroes in which all kinds of garbled readings occur, or as in the case of Briseida, whose name and character have almost nothing to do with the classical Briseis.

I should like to express my appreciation for the inspiration of the three teachers under whom the translation was begun: Professors William Alfred, F. P. Magoun, Jr., and B. J. Whiting; for the assistance and advice of my friends and colleagues Alfred David, James W. Halporn, Jack F. Kottemann, Clarence H. Miller, Paul Strohm, and Ian Thomson; and for the grant from Indiana University which financed the work in its later stages. I am also much indebted to Professor Graydon W. Regenos for calling my attention to some oversights in the translation and for suggesting many improvements. Finally, I am most grateful to my mother, Elizabeth Woodward Meek, for the help that she gave me in the preparation of the manuscript.

Pittsburgh, Pennsylvania   *Mary Elizabeth Meek*
May, 1973

Contents

Introduction

The *Historia Destructionis Troiae* by Judge Guido delle Colonne of Messina[1] was completed, as its author tells us in his epilogue, in November of 1287. Guido states that it is the authentic history of the Trojan War based upon the eyewitness accounts of Dictys of Crete and Dares the Phrygian. However, as has long been known, it is actually a Latin prose paraphrase, and in many instances a fairly close translation, of the *Roman de Troie,* a French romance in octosyllabic couplets written more than a hundred years earlier by Benoit de Sainte-Maure.[2] Despite this fact, the *Historia* was immediately accepted for what it purported to be, was widely copied and translated, and did not lose its reputation for authenticity until the eighteenth century, when its supposed sources fell into discredit. There may be as many as one hundred and fifty manuscripts of it, and one of them, in the Saltykov-Shchedrin Library in Leningrad, bears the signatures of the English kings Richard III, James I, and Charles I, as well as the signature of Oliver Cromwell.[3] Eight printed editions appeared in the last quarter of the fifteenth century. During the fifteenth and sixteenth centuries it was translated several times into French, German, and English. There are also versions in Spanish, Flemish, and Bohemian; one German version appeared as early as 1392, and an Italian one as late as 1665. A French translation of it was made by Raoul le Fèvre for his *Recueil des Histoires de Troie,* an English version of which was the first English book printed by Caxton and served as a source for Shakespeare's *Troilus and Cressida.* Boccaccio's *Filostrato,* while derived principally from the *Roman de Troie,* also shows use of the *Historia;* Chaucer's *Troilus and Criseyde,* adapted from the *Filostrato,* is indebted to both the *Roman* and the *Historia,* and Lydgate's *Troy Book* is a metrical paraphrase of the *Historia* with occasional use of the *Roman.*[4]

The *Historia* is not only the chief means by which the medieval Troy story was transmitted to later times; it is also the culmination of the

development of that story. In medieval Europe, when Greek was no
longer read, Homer's work was known only through the *Ilias Latina,* a
Latin abridgment of the *Iliad* attributed to Pindar, but it played no real
part in the creation of the medieval concept of Troy. Western Europeans
were more interested in the Trojans than the Greeks because they believed
that Europe had been colonized by Aeneas and other Trojan refugees.
Accordingly, the preferred sources for Troy material were the *Aeneid,* of
which Guido makes appropriate use on several occasions, and, more
important, Dictys' *Ephemeris Belli Troiani* (despite its Greek bias) and
Dares' *De Excidio Troiae Historia,* both of which Guido claims to have
followed, and upon which his principal source, Benoit's *Roman,* was
based.[5]

The versions of the *Ephemeris* and the *De Excidio*[6] available in the
Middle Ages are Latin and date from the fourth and sixth centuries
respectively. Nevertheless both have prefatory letters stating that they are
translations of Greek originals composed by participants in the Trojan
War. Evidence does exist that there were Greek originals but that they
can be no earlier than the first century A.D.[7] The letter at the beginning
of the *Ephemeris* states that it is a translation made by one Lucius
Septimius of the journal written by Dictys, a follower of Idomeneus of
Crete. The journal is said to have been in Phoenician characters and to
have been buried in Dictys' tomb; brought to light when the tomb
collapsed, it was transliterated into Greek at the order of the Emperor
Nero. The letter prefacing the *De Excidio* is even more improbable, for it
purports to be from Cornelius Nepos to Sallust and explains that Nepos,
while studying in Athens, had found Dares' original manuscript and had
translated it into Latin "in the straightforward and simple style of the
Greek original,"[8] a statement of unmitigated impudence when one is
confronted with the pitiful Latin in which the *Historia* is written. The
letter concludes with the suggestion that since Dares fought in the war, he
is a more reliable historian than Homer, who lived so much later and who
had been considered insane by the Athenians because he had described
the gods battling with mortals—assertions that were to be repeated over
and over by everyone writing on Troy during the Middle Ages.

The extant Dictys actually reads like the soldier's journal it is supposed
to be. It begins with an account of the arrival in Crete of the heirs of
Atreus, including Agamemnon and Menelaus, the abduction of Helen by
Alexander (Paris) during Menelaus' absence, the negotiations to get Helen

back, and the mustering of the Greek troops, all of which Dictys says is based on the report of Ulysses; he then goes on to describe the events of the war, the fall of Troy, and the return of the Greeks as these things were observed by him. Dares' *Historia,* while covering twice as much material as the *Ephemeris,* is only one-fourth as long and is little better than an outline. It begins with the expedition of the Argonauts who were refused permission to land in Troy by Laomedon and who, after the acquisition of the Golden Fleece, returned to Troy and destroyed the city, carrying off Laomedon's sister in the process and thus motivating the abduction of Helen. Dares then covers the events of the war and the capture of Troy, and ends with the sacrifice of Polyxena, the return of Helen, and the departure from Troy of Helenus, accompanied by Cassandra, Andromache, and Hecuba.

These two works became the sources for such later treatments of the Trojan material as the *De Bello Trojano* of Joseph of Exeter, written about 1188, and the *Troilus* of Albert de Stade, in 1294 (both of which are in Latin verse), and for Benoit's *Roman de Troie,* written sometime around 1160.[9] Benoit, who cites Dictys and Dares as his sources, combined the two accounts, beginning with Dares' and continuing with Dictys' for the events following the fall of Troy. The result is a typical medieval romance in which the numerous battle scenes are enlivened by descriptions of bright banners, silken pavilions, and burnished armor, and are set off by the four love stories of Jason and Medea, Paris and Helen, Troilus and Briseida, and Achilles and Polyxena, which are treated with charm, insight into human behavior, and dramatic effectiveness. It is Benoit, of course, who gave the medieval Troy story its final shape, making a more or less coherent tale out of the Dares and Dictys material and weaving in elements not only from classical sources like the *Metamorphoses* but also from all the romances and fairy tales he had ever read or heard, so that Medea aids Jason with a magic preparation to ward off the flames, as in Ovid, as well as with a magic ring and a talisman in the form of a silver image, while Hector's horse, Galatea, is said to have been given to him by a fairy who had loved him in vain (an obvious Celtic motif), and the courtyard of Priam's palace contains a magically constructed golden tree. The names Benoit invents for Priam's bastards typify his synthesizing ability; some sound vaguely classical, some Biblical, some Breton, and some, purely fanciful, like "Né d'Amours."[10] An occasion for description, whether of a spring morning, a knight's arms, a lady's gown, a city, a castle, or a tomb, calls forth word pictures as brightly colored and formalized and as lavish of gold and precious materials as the illuminations in medieval manuscripts. In other words, with a happy disregard for the supposed historicity of his sources, Benoit incorporates into his story anything he thinks will surprise or delight his audience—an audience that wanted to hear of love and swordplay and magic and villainy described in terms familiar to them but touched with the glamour of the past. His supreme achievement, of course, is the creation of the story of the love of Troilus and Briseida, their separation, and her final acceptance of Diomedes. Since the story is his own, he is not bound by the fact that his audience would know the outcome, as is the case with the three other love stories, and he develops it with a richness of characterization and wealth of dramatic detail that are truly poetic and were, in fact, to inspire later poets like Boccaccio and Chaucer.

It is one of the ironies of literary history that no sooner was Benoit's *Roman* in circulation than it became subject to attempts to deromanticize it. Toward the middle of the thirteenth century there was a prose redaction of it in French[11] which begins with a lengthy discussion of Greece and Magna Graecia and proceeds with a considerably abridged summary of the poem. With Guido's *Historia* we come full circle; Guido writes in Latin prose, as had Dares and Dictys, and while he keeps most of Benoit's romantic inventions, he abridges the descriptions and adds embellishments of his own that he conceives to be appropriate to an historical treatment of the story.

As a work of medieval Latin prose (although admittedly in a style more pretentious than elegant), as a source for several works of considerable literary merit, and as an anthology of what the Middle Ages considered the basic materials of the Troy legend, the *Historia* has a modest but assured place as a work of literature. But actually, because of its form and early reputation, it also deserves some consideration, if not as a work of history, at least as an example of the medieval concept of historiography. This contention is borne out by the fact that, unlike that other medieval work of pseudohistory, Geoffrey of Monmouth's *History of the Kings of Britain,* Guido's *Historia* was immediately accepted as history, probably because Guido's acknowledged sources were not some mysterious Welsh book, but the works of Dares and Dictys, whose authenticity was never doubted, spurious as we now know them to be. Of course, Benoit had also cited Dictys and Dares, but he wrote in French verse; Guido, like

Geoffrey, wrote in Latin prose, and since, in addition, he cited the undisputed authorities on the Trojan War, he was considered an historian, even by Chaucer and Lydgate, who knew both the *Roman* and the *Historia.*

That the *Historia* exemplifies medieval notions of historiography is shown by Guido's attitude toward and treatment of his sources. The basic source is, of course, Benoit's *Roman de Troie.* To us it seems ridiculous that a chivalric romance could be regarded as the documentation for a serious history, and we tend to regard Guido as at worst a plagiarist and at best the perpetrator of a literary hoax. But let us look at it from Guido's point of view. For him, as for anyone else in the Middle Ages, the personages and events of the Troy legend were real—as real as the Biblical heroes David and Samson, as real as Alexander the Great and Charlemagne. If for us Otto of Freising is the most notable of the medieval historians because of his recording of contemporary events, we should not forget that *The Two Cities* is a history of the world from the Creation to Otto's own day, and in the first part puts together in one paragraph such events as the death of Joshua and the invention of the Greek alphabet by Cadmus and of the lyre and the art of medicine by Apollo. The next paragraph deals with the Trojan War and cites Homer, Pindar, and Virgil as the authorities.[12] The fact that these authorities were poets does not invalidate the historicity of their materials; after all, there were poetical works treating such recent historical figures as Charlemagne. No one has ever claimed that *The Divine Comedy* was anything but a work of poetry; it might be observed, however, that for Dante, Ulysses was probably as historical a figure as Manfred, and that both were fit subjects for poetical treatment. This view explains Guido's criticism of the poets in his prologue; he never questions the fact that they were dealing with real historical materials, but his objection is that they tampered with the text and gave history the appearance of fiction. This is to say that to the medieval mind, the materials of poetry and history are the same; it is the treatment that differentiates the two.

If this is true, what are the characteristics of the "historical" mode as distinguished from the "poetic"? If the *Historia* is compared to the *Roman,* it is immediately obvious that Guido has a very clear notion of how history should be written. To cause the story of Troy to be taken as history he had only to write it down in Latin prose, in a dignified style adorned by rhetorical devices, to embellish it with moral and philosophical

commentary and displays of erudition, to take into account any other
versions of the material known to him and to cite his authorities by name
or by the formula "some—or others—say," and, above all, to comment
critically on whatever is "fabulous," that is, anything that implies a belief
in pagan gods. This last requirement is, of course, typical of the early
Christian historians, like St. Augustine, and is usually accompanied by a
firm belief in witchcraft and demonology.

And so throughout the *Historia* we find Guido "historicizing" his
material—that is, bringing out what he thinks of as its latent historicity—in
the various ways just mentioned. His attempts at a high style usually fail,
as in his long catalogue of the beauties of Helen of Troy and his set
pieces on the seasons, which sound as if they had been lifted from a
handbook of rhetoric; but because they fail, we can see what he is trying
to do. He is better, or at least more interesting, in his learned digressions
on the nature of eclipses and the origins of idolatry, in which he cites
such authorities as Isidore of Seville, Ptolemy, and Bede. To raise the
moral tone of his narrative, he castigates Priam's foolish pride in reopen-
ing the hostilities with Greece and Helen's immodesty in going to the
temple to see Paris; and while musing over the triviality of the occasion
which led to the two destructions of Troy, he comments on the fact that
as a result of the second one, Europe was colonized by the Trojan
refugees, but concludes, "the human mind is uncertain whether the cause
of such a great betrayal was finally the cause of subsequent good."
Finally, he maintains an unfailingly severe attitude toward pagan religious
beliefs, dismissing as fiction the notions that the gods took part in the
war and that Helen was the daughter of Jupiter, and he explains that the
fire-breathing bulls and the dragon which protected the Golden Fleece
were of magical, not divine, origin, and that the message of the Delphic
oracle was produced by a demon inhabiting the statue of Apollo.

Guido did not, of course, invent these touchstones by which the
historical mode could be recognized; he had merely to be familiar with
history as it was written both in his day and for generations before. Otto
of Freising is again useful here as an example of a "real" historian whose
technique is just like Guido's. This is not to suggest that *The Two Cities*
was one of Guido's sources, though it may have been, but simply to indicate that there was a solid tradition of writing history in this particular
mode. In the passage on the Trojan War, Otto, while citing Virgil as the
authority for the traditional view of Aeneas as a brave man, also observes

that he is "according to others a betrayer of his country and a necromancer, inasmuch as he even sacrificed his own wife to his gods."[13] He discusses the founding of France and the city of "Troy" by the Trojan leader Franco, but later says that doubt is cast on this tradition by the story that the French Troy was founded by Ulysses. He begins his comments on Ulysses with the remark that "such great disasters pursued the victors that in connection with so pitiful a revolution of fortune there is room for doubt as to which side succumbed to an evil fate,"[14] and he ends by explaining that such transformations as those of Ulysses' companions into swine and Diomedes' into birds were not real, but were delusions caused by demons. It is interesting that there are more or less exact counterparts of all this in Guido, but the point is not so much the similarity of the materials used as the similarity of the conception of what constitutes historical fact, and it is this conception that accounts for the willingness of Guido's audience to accept his history as authentic.

While it is easy to see why Guido regarded his material as historical and hence worthy of the treatment he gives it, it is a bit more difficult to see how he conceived of his role in the writing of his history. After all, he did know that what he was working with was a romance in French and not the Greek histories of Dares and Dictys which he cites as his sources, nor even the Latin translation of these by Cornelius which he mentions, and the usual modern opinion is that in claiming to have translated Dares and Dictys and in never mentioning Benoit, he was committing deliberate fraud. However, in view of the universal acceptance of Guido's preposterous work as history, not to mention the acceptance of Dares and Dictys, it is just as likely that Guido himself was as much deceived as deceiving. Probably he accepted at face value Benoit's citations of Dares and Dictys, thought that the *Roman de Troie* was simply a romance-ified version of the histories of Dares and Dictys, and believed that everything in the *Roman* had been in the histories.[15] He could, therefore, have seen his role as that of removing what was actually history from the mode of poetry and restoring it to the mode of history, and in not mentioning Benoit he was following the well-attested medieval custom of suppressing the immediate source while citing the most ancient one. Furthermore, it is possible that he did not actually claim to have translated Dares and Dictys; the supposition that he did is based upon one passage in the prologue that is obscured by what appears to be an incomplete sentence, and two passages in the epilogue, of which the first is so absurdly contradictory that it has been rejected as an example of scribal blunder-ing,[16] and the second is demonstrably untrue. But let us take a look at the passages in question.

In the prologue, after a somewhat turgidly written introduction dealing with the value of written records for preserving the events of the past, and the usual dismissal of the fictions of the poets, Guido states that his book will contain just what was in the two books of Dares and Dictys, which had been found in Athens and which are in complete agreement. Since the story of the manuscript found in Athens applies only to Dares, and since the accounts of Dares and Dictys do not agree, it can be assumed that Guido had no knowledge of Dictys, or no knowledge of either work. The latter is more likely, since his usual practice when bringing in other source material is to cite the author and quote or para-phrase the relevant lines. Throughout the *Historia,* however, whenever he cites Dares he never quotes him directly, and is almost always referring to something specific in Benoit.

If Guido had never seen the histories of either Dares or Dictys, his claim to have translated them would certainly be fraudulent, but it will be noted that what he actually says is that in his work will be read the things that were recorded by Dares and Dictys, because those things have been "transcribed" by him. The text has *transsumpta* from *transsumere,* which Lewis and Short gloss as "to take . . . to adopt, assume"; "tran-scribe" is from Du Cange, while Niermeyer gives "copy," and Griffin's glossary has "transform." Any one of these would be possible and would lend itself to the extended meaning "translate," were it not for the fact that a few lines earlier, Guido has used the same verb (in the 3rd pl., pret. indic.) to describe what had been done to the historical truth of the Troy story when it was treated poetically. While it is possible for a writer, and especially Guido, to use a word in different senses in different con-texts,[17] it seems unlikely that Guido, after going to such great lengths to establish the fact that his treatment of the Troy story will be historical, not poetic, would then use the same word for the writing of his work as for the writing of a poetical version, unless the word had a more neutral meaning for him than "translate" or "transform." If, however, we take *transsumere* in the sense of "transcribe" in the first instance, and if one accepts Guido's own explanation of what happens when an historical work is transcribed poetically, i.e., that it appears to be fiction, we can apply the same kind of reasoning in reverse to the second instance: if a work of fiction which embodies historical truth, like the *Roman de Troie,* for instance, or for that matter the *Metamorphoses* or the *Aeneid,* is "transcribed" historically, then it will appear to be history, will in fact *be* the history that it actually is. This may be the way Guido conceived of the *Historia*—as an historical transcription of the history embodied in a work of fiction, and he probably considered his work as a restoration rather than a forgery.

Guido goes on in the prologue to explain that Dares and Dictys had already been translated into Latin by Cornelius, the nephew of Sallust, and this goes to show that at the time he was writing the prologue, his only knowledge of Dares and Dictys came from Benoit, since it was Benoit who thought that the heading of the letter which prefaces Dares' history, "Cornelius Nepos Sallustio Crispo" [Cornelius Nepos to Sallustius Crispus] meant that the name of the author was Cornelius, the nephew of Sallust (*nepos,* "nephew"). On the other hand, Guido's description of Cornelius' work as brief and lacking in particulars seems to indicate that he had direct knowledge of Dares' history.[18] Dares is certainly brief, but the details Guido says Cornelius omits are precisely those which Dares gives and which Guido lists in his summary of Dares in the epilogue to his own work. All of this suggests that Guido did not have a copy of Dares before him when he wrote the prologue, but that he did have a brief Latin work, ostensibly based on Dares and Dictys, that he assumed was Cornelius' translation. Quite possibly this was Joseph of Exeter's *De Bello Trojano.*[19] Compared to Benoit's thirty thousand lines, Joseph's three thousand are indeed brief; he does omit the statistics, and he only alludes to the events of the Trojan War, using them as a framework upon which to drape his highly intricate and rhetorical verses. Furthermore, it was not until the seventeenth century that *De Bello Trojano* was attributed to Joseph, the author being given either as Dares or Cornelius Nepos.[20] Of course, Guido does not indicate that his Cornelius had written in verse, but he does not say his source is prose either. Finally, the fact that the *De Bello Trojano* touches upon some of the events following the fall of Troy may very well account for Guido's belief that Cornelius had translated both Dares and Dictys.

While the prologue indicates that Guido had not read any of the sources he mentions, except possibly "Cornelius," the epilogue shows such knowledge of Dares' *Historia* as to suggest that at some time during the composition of his *Historia* Guido obtained a copy of Dares, and upon

completion of his own work, checked it against his supposed source.[21]
The result threw him into a scholarly dilemma, for in so doing, he discovered that he had been citing the wrong authority, which accounts for the manifest contradictions in the opening paragraph of the epilogue. The paragraph begins with the statement that "In this place Dares brought the work at hand to an end, and so did Cornelius. The rest . . . is from . . . Dictys." But Guido then goes on to say that "It may be allowed that Dares brought his work to an end with the capture of Troy and . . . the rest . . . is from the book of Dictys." Since the first "place" is at the conclusion of the account of the returning Greeks' adventures, and there is no "rest" to follow, these statements can be reconciled only if we remember that all through the *Historia,* whenever Guido cites Dares, he means Benoit, who he assumes had translated Dares, and if we agree that "Cornelius" refers to Joseph of Exeter, whose *De Bello Trojano* covers most of the same events as the *Roman de Troie,* including those following the fall of Troy. Accordingly, in this instance Guido meant that the material covered in the *Roman de Troie* and *De Bello Trojano* ends at this point. But when he looked at the real Dares, he realized that Dares could not have been the source for everything that was in Benoit and Joseph, and so he concluded that "the rest . . . is from the book of Dictys." He clarifies this statement by telling where Dares' narrative actually did end, repeats his contention that the rest is from Dictys, and concludes somewhat lamely that if "anything is to be found added to this work . . . it is not from the truth of the work but rather from the fiction of the work." The repetitiveness and temporizing suggest that he had begun to doubt that the *Roman de Troie* was what he had thought it was—a poetical version of Dares and Dictys—and to suspect that it was, after all, a work of fiction, or at best a work contaminated with fictions that were not in the original. But his position is still that of the scholar and historian; he has read Dares and Cornelius and assumes that where these are lacking, the deficiencies were filled in by Dictys, whom he has not read, and he also allows for the possibility of his being in error with regard to Dictys.

By modern standards of scholarship, of course, Guido should have gone back and changed the wrong citations of Dares, just as he should have completed the incomplete sentences scattered through his work, but perhaps he should be forgiven on the grounds of the hasty composition for which he apologizes at the end of the epilogue. At any rate, he has made an attempt to reinterpret his material on the basis of new information, and he then sums up the points at which Dares differs from Benoit's Dictys material, adds the statistics regarding the length of the war and number of troops and ships involved, along with the list of who killed whom (with which most versions of Dares' *Historia* ended), and includes the epitaphs of Achilles and Hector which may also have been at the end of his Dares manuscript. He then concludes, "I, Guido delle Colonne, have followed the aforesaid Dictys in all things," which is not the outright lie it appears to be, but simply the historian correcting the acknowledgment of his source. Up until this point, in referring to Benoit, he had used the designation Dares because he thought that Dares and Dictys had covered the same material. Now, knowing this is not so, and knowing that his work contains an enormous amount of material not in Dares, he changes the designation of his source to what he believes is the true one—Dictys. And it should be noted that he does not say that he has translated Dictys, but that he has simply "followed" him.

It may be argued that if Guido was so convinced that in paraphrasing the *Roman de Troie* he was reproducing the histories of Dares and Dictys, he would not have made any changes in the material he found in his source, and he does make some. But if these changes are examined, it will be observed that for the most part they are consistent with his writing as an historian and that in some cases he is even exercising his critical faculty to distinguish fictions and suppress them. This is not to say that an outline of the episodes in Benoit would not be the same as an outline of Guido, but that there will be differences of detail and emphasis.

Faced with Benoit's treatment of battle scenes, Guido omits most of Benoit's colorful touches. Guido usually begins with the statement that so many days of truce have elapsed, that morning has come, and that the troops have been drawn up. In Benoit there is usually a description of arms and equipment, of hauberks refurbished, horns sounding, banners waving, helmets laced on, bright swords, and the like. Sometimes there are exotic touches such as Pavian helmets, Castilian or Arabian war-horses, and Turkish bows, but only the last of these appears in Guido. But where it is a matter of giving the essential facts, as in the account of Hector's death, Guido follows Benoit exactly.

The really elaborate descriptions in the *Roman de Troie* are those in which Benoit is making a conscious attempt to entertain his audience with strange and unusual material, as in the accounts of the rebuilding of Troy, the Chamber of Beauty, and the tomb of Hector. Guido's modifications

of these typify his notions of historical and poetical truth. He takes over
Benoit's description of the rebuilt Troy—the marble, the gold, the crystal,
the mosaic work, the covered walkways, the castle hewn from solid rock
whose tower reaches the clouds—suppressing only the mention of the
specific colors of the marbles used. But he combines Benoit's remark on
the convenience of the fountains and wells in the castle with his knowledge that the River Xanthus flowed through Troy and with what he
knows about the Roman cloacae. He concludes that since Rome had been
founded by Trojans, it must have been modeled on Troy, and thus Troy
must have had a sewer system like Rome's, and so he provides one.
Similarly he interprets Benoit's statement that all pleasures were to be
found in Troy, such as those of dice and chess, to mean that not only
were these games invented there, but so also were most of the other
civilized forms of entertainment, such as circuses, May festivals, and the
drama. He does add, however, that "some claim comedy was first devised
on the island of Sicily." Finally, by way of a rhetorical flourish, he
includes a long catalogue of the craftsmen to be found in Troy, to many
of whom he gives esoteric names like *argiroprate* and *gineciarii,* which he
has to explain for his readers.

There is good reason for Guido's accepting Benoit's descriptions of
Troy and Ilium; in his own Sicily he could have seen palaces and cathe-
drals just as rich and elaborate as anything imagined by Benoit. When,
however, he comes to the description of the Chamber of Beauty with its
four columns of onyx, jasper, amber, and jet, surmounted by figures
which dance, make music, hold a mirror of polished gold, or display some
sort of screen on which animals in the forest or ships at sea appear, he
balks. He mentions columns of onyx with gold figures on top which he
says had been made by magic, but he concludes, "Dares fully describes
them and their appearance; which seem to be empty dreams rather than
factual truths, and therefore they are omitted." It is interesting that he
can accept creatures like the fiery bulls and dragon, and even the centaur,
and talismans such as Medea gave Jason, but not these contrivances. He
also shows himself to be critical of Benoit's apparatus for preserving
Hector's body, which involves some pipes and two basins of balsam into
which Hector's feet are placed so that the balsam will permeate the whole
body, apparently by osmosis. Guido, however, evidently considers it more
sensible to have the preservative liquid flow from a vase in Hector's head
down through all the parts of his body into another vase at his feet. Here,

as so often, Guido is interpreting the facts as he found them in the light of what he considers reasonable.

It might be expected that Guido as an historian would be critical of what for us are the most unhistorical parts of his material, the love stories.[22] This is not the case, however. In fact, for him, the love affairs are just as historical as the battles, and he is at pains to treat them suitably. Gone is Benoit's amused but sympathetic treatment of the lovers' feelings and in its place we find much heavy moralizing, not only on Medea's and Helen's lack of modesty and Briseida's faithlessness, but on Jason's deceitfulness and Achilles' weakness as well. Gone, too, are Benoit's pretty but conventional descriptions of his heroines and in their place are Guido's equally conventional ones which serve to display his notions of stylistic elegance; the minutiae of Helen's beauties include her eyelashes like reins to restrain her lively glances and her teeth and gums like lilies and roses mixed, while Polyxena's tearstained cheeks are compared to ivory tablets bedewed with drops of clear bright water. He suppresses the courtly trappings with which Benoit adorns the Jason and Medea story (she addresses him as "vassaus" and he calls her "dame," and she sends for him by means of a delightful old woman, a prototype of the Vekke of the *Roman de la Rose,* who advises Medea that it would be "plus gent" if she were to be in bed when Jason comes). He also suppresses the ambiguities of Criseyde's character and the careful counterpointing by which Troilus' and Diomedes' fortunes in war are ironically reversed by their fortunes in love,[23] since for Guido the outcome of the affair is an historical fact which should not be obscured by dramatic tensions.

In the treatment of the Paris and Helen story, however, he is much fuller than Benoit. In Benoit, the lovers hear of one another, meet in the temple, exchange words and glances, and when they part, twenty lines later, Helen knows "Qu'il la vendreit ancor veeir." Guido, realizing the historical importance of this affair—the events that have led up to it, the disastrous consequences it was to have—develops the scene in the temple in much greater detail, a good deal of which was probably suggested by the Paris and Helen Epistles in the *Heroides* and is thus "historical" for him. That is to say he would consider that although the Epistles are poetic in form they deal with historical personages who undoubtedly behaved in just this way. The catalogue of Helen's beauties represents Paris' interior monologue as he looks at her and seethes with desire, while

Helen reciprocates with a gaze equally intense, since Guido says that she does not take her eyes off Paris even to watch the ceremony. They both wonder how to approach one another, and finally Paris makes a signal, which she returns. She then encourages him to come near with a nod of her head, and from that they proceed to a whispered conversation in which they make their loves known to each other. There is more action in this than in Benoit, but there is also an emphasis on furtiveness and the hasty satisfaction of a selfish love which conveys the moral judgment of history upon an illicit affair. It is probably also the reflection of the judgment of history which causes Guido to make Achilles' character blacker than it was in Benoit, to shorten the long speeches of self-analysis by which Benoit tried to suggest the tragedy of a love such as Achilles', and to content himself with commenting that men in love always make rash promises which they cannot fulfill.

Many of Guido's changes and additions to the story as he found it in Benoit can be explained by his attempts to rationalize pagan mythology or elevate the style, but there are also the changes that result from his feeling that as an historian he should take into account whatever other sources of information about the Trojan world are known to him, and this raises the question as to just what these other sources were. Joseph of Exeter's *De Bello Trojano* is a likely one, since Guido probably thought that it was "Cornelius'" translation of Dares and Dictys. This possibility is strengthened by the fact that *De Bello Trojano* has several details in common with the *Historia,* such as the nakedness of the goddesses and the nature of their gifts in the Judgment of Paris, the story of Castor and Pollux being translated to the stars and worshipped as gods, and the digression on the origins of idolatry in connection with the Greek mission to the Delphic oracle.[24] The *Prose Roman* is another possible subsidiary source since it too contains a digression on idolatry, and the disquisition on Magna Graecia with which this work begins may have inspired Guido's.[25]

While these common details may indicate familiarity with the works in question, they do not rule out the possibility that Guido knew of other works dealing with ancient history and that these were his sources, rather than the obvious ones now known to us that do not account for every instance in which Guido differs from Benoit or for the instances in which he differs from these other sources. In any case it is likely that, just as in the larger scheme of his work Guido reworked Benoit's materials in his own way, so he also worked over the details brought in from other places.

Joseph and the author of the *Prose Roman* are comparatively brief on the origins of idolatry, but Guido gives the subject a full-scale treatment, with appropriate references to and citations from Isidore of Seville, Petrus Comestor, the legend of St. Brendan, and the Bible, discussing not only idolatry but demons and the presence of Satan in the world as well. In his discussion of Magna Graecia, because he wants to assure his readers that Sicily is of Trojan, not Greek origin, he takes the opposite position from the author of the *Prose Roman* and asserts that classical Greece is not the same as Magna Graecia, although he later indicates that he knows that Sicily had been a Greek colony. He does not state specifically that he knew that there were still Greek-speaking people in Sicily, as the *Prose Roman* declares, but the words *gineciarii* and *argiroprate,* and possibly *pantalarge,* in the catalogue of craftsmen are of Greek derivation. He does not bother to deny the *Prose Roman's* assertion that Peleus' city was "Penelope," which is now called Naples, and instead rejects the similar notion that the city of "Thetis" in Abruzzi is proof that Magna Graecia is the same as Greece, and backs up his view with Ovid's story of the Myrmidons and a reference to the legend of St. Matthew's mission to Thessaly.

It is Guido's ability to give apposite quotations and to bring in material that illuminates the subject at hand which entitles him to be considered, even by us, as a scholar, and of course, in his own day, this display of erudition confirmed his claim to be writing history. The authors he cites were standard medieval authorities, and while they do not make up a five-foot shelf, they do indicate the range of the education attainable by a thirteenth-century layman. If not all of the seven liberal arts are reflected in his work, it is probably because his university degree was in law; certainly his style gives ample evidence of his having studied rhetoric, he parades his knowledge of astronomy on the slightest pretext, and he shows himself to be fairly familiar with works of classical literature ("grammar") suitable to his text. He even makes appropriate use of his legal education by citing what was probably a gloss on a title from the Justinian code in which Aeneas is referred to.

The literary works he mentions are, naturally, the works of Homer, Virgil, and Ovid. If the first is anything more than a name to him, it is as the author translated in the *Ilias Latina,* a possibility suggested by his two diatribes against Homer for considering Achilles to be the greatest of the Greek heroes, which may indicate that he knew the story of the *Iliad.*

But with Virgil and Ovid, we are on more solid ground. Not only does he quote directly from them, but he occasionally echoes their phrasing.[26] The one work of Virgil he seems to know is the *Aeneid,* and perhaps just the first part of it, since his quotations are only from the first four books. He admires the beautiful style and knows that the poem is about Aeneas going from Troy to Tuscany, and that Virgil died before he had finished it. However, in supporting his notion that the magic ring given by Medea to Jason contained an agate, he quotes from Book I, "Graditur fido comitatus Achates," which in Guido's context means that Aeneas was advancing accompanied by his trusty agate—an amulet, not a friend. Granted that this line is so interpreted in contemporary lapidaries, still one would think that he would remember Aeneas' trusty friend Achates when he is able to remember his wife Creusa. He does not indicate any special regard for Ovid's style, but he seems to have had a reluctant admiration for him as a teller of delightful tales. He quotes the story of Callisto and Arcas from *Metamorphoses* II and the Epistle of Oenone from *Heroides* V, and he fills out Benoit's story of Jason and Medea with details from *Heroides* XII and *Metamorphoses* VII, and the latter is also his source for the legendary origin of the Myrmidons, but he almost always reminds his readers that what he is recording is "fiction" when it deals with pagan myths; in fact, he apparently brings in the story of Callisto and Arcas just to show the absurdity of pagan beliefs in contrast with the correct information as given by Isidore of Seville, whom, however, he does not mention at this point and whose commentary he misinterprets.

Isidore of Seville's *Etymologiae seu Origines* was for Guido the most respected authority on almost everything, including astronomy, geology, and geography, and he frequently makes use of it in his learned digressions,[27] often in combination with other sources. He wrongly attributes the information about emeralds to Isidore, and though much of what he says about the origins of idolatry is from the *Etymologiae,* Isidore is mentioned only in connection with the facts about Delphi ("Delphos") and the etymology of the name Leviathan. It may be that, if Guido's knowledge of Isidore was secondhand, he did not realize that the commentary on the pagan gods and paganism was also from him. Similarly, he cites Isidore with regard to the Diomedian birds, but not in connection with the colonizing of Europe by the Trojans, which is also to be found in the *Etymologiae.* The point is not so much whether or not Guido cited his sources correctly but rather that he incorporated into the *Historia* the

kind of information his readers regarded as erudite, even recondite. The
same thing is true of Guido's references to Ptolemy, Dionysius the
Areopagite, and Bede. He cites Ptolemy as his authority for the explanation of how eclipses occur, although he is actually paraphrasing a passage
on eclipses from the *Sphere*, a treatise by the early thirteenth-century
astronomer Iohannes de Sacrobosco,[28] and he ends his disquisition with
the famous anecdote about Dionysius' remark at the time of the Crucifixion that is also cited by Sacrobosco. On Guido's behalf, it should be
stated that the *Sphere* was often attributed to Ptolemy,[29] and that Guido
mentions the sun standing still for Joshua referred to by Dionysius but
not in the *Sphere*. In citing Bede, however, in the digression on idolatry,
Guido is definitely citing at secondhand, since at that point he is paraphrasing the *Historia Scholastica* of Petrus Comestor, which he mentions
here, but not when he makes use of it in a passage on the Flight into
Egypt. It will be noted, of course, that given a chance, Guido always cites
the oldest authority he knows of, even when he has not read that
authority himself but only found it mentioned in an intermediate source,
and that this practice is typical of all medieval writers.

In fact, Guido delle Colonne is very much a man of his time. If the
Historia was not written by the Judge Guido delle Colonne whom Dante
mentions in the *De Vulgari Eloquentia* as a distinguished member of the
Sicilian school of poets[30] and whose signature appears on legal documents
between 1243 and 1280,[31] it should have been. The poets of the Sicilian
school were greatly influenced by French and Provençal poetry, and the
writer of the *Historia* obviously knew at least one French poem. The
Sicilian school had its origin at the court of Frederick II, and many of its
members, like Guido, had had legal training and held government posts.[32]
Furthermore, Frederick is one of two contemporaries mentioned by
Guido, though he refers to him as the founder of a town rather than as a
patron of the arts. Frederick's court was a center not only for the arts
but for all kinds of intellectual activity[33] whose range, however, far
exceeds the amount of learning revealed in the *Historia*. Nevertheless,
Guido's interest in astronomy may stem from his being associated with a
court at which Michael Scot held the position of Court Philosopher.[34]
Finally, the rhetoric of Guido's prose is consistent with the imagery
typical of the Sicilian school of poetry as exemplified in the six poems
attributed to Guido that survive.

One of these poems, "Amor che longiamente," was twice quoted by

Dante,[35] appears in many anthologies of thirteenth-century Italian
poetry, and was translated into English by Rossetti.[36] Like most of the
others of its school, it celebrates not the beauty of the lady but the pain
of the lover,[37] and is similar in tone and language to Benoit's treatment
of Achilles' love for Polyxena. The images are those which were to become the rule in this kind of poem. The lover addresses the god of love
who, he says, is driving him on, shaking the reins and never slackening.
Love is a "dolze pena," the lover is sure he is going to die, and he
implores the lady to temper her pride with pity. The lover claims that he
loves in secret and complains "quanto è dura pena al cor dolente / estar
tacente." The last stanza is the most characteristic, and its first line voices
a sentiment which is dramatized in Guido's treatment of the Achilles
story. "Amor fa disvïare li più saggi," says the poet, and the historian
comments on Achilles being deluded "by the ill-advised passion of love
which deprives even wise men of their senses."

Guido the poet may also have been a member of the circle of poets
which surrounded Manfred,[38] but the only definite facts we have about
him are the signatures mentioned earlier and what he tells us in his
epilogue, and it is not certain that these data refer to the same person.[39]
There was a tradition that Guido the historian joined the retinue of
Edward I of England, who had visited Sicily on his return from the Holy
Land, and that he accompanied the king to France and England,
staying in England from 1273 to 1276. It was also said that he wrote a
Chronicon Magnum and a *Historia de Regibus et Rebus Angliae* while in
England, although no trace of these writings remains,[40] and there is no
indication of the English journey in the *Historia,* unless it be the reference
to the founding of Britain by a Trojan named Brutus.

A man whose name was associated with the poetry produced at the
court of Frederick II and who was already a judge in 1242[41] would have
been in his sixties or seventies by the time the *Historia* was completed—
old by medieval standards—and the epilogue does indeed sound as if it
had been written by a very old man. He speaks of having begun the work
at the urging of the Archbishop of Salerno, but of giving it up after the
Archbishop's death, when only the first book had been completed. Conventional though the phrasing is, it conveys a sense of loss and loneliness,
even of not being appreciated by the younger generation. And when he
speaks of taking up the work again, nearly fifteen years later, it is to
apologize for the fact that since he finished it in three months, he has not

beautified the style or embellished it with enough digressions, being afraid to spend any more time for fear something should happen to him. This certainly gives the impression of a man who feels he has not much time to live, and this impression is borne out by the fact that there are no learned digressions after Book XIII and very few flights of rhetoric, except for the description of Polyxena in Book XXIII.

The concluding lines of the epilogue present a rather appealing picture of the author who, despite the loss of the friend who had inspired the work, nevertheless labored to complete it so that the truth should be known, and again we get an indication of his concept of historical truth. In admitting his admiration for the styles of Homer, Virgil, and Ovid, he describes their sources as "stories" [*fabulas*] of the ancients and "fables" [*apologos*]. If Guido is not simply using *apologus* as a synonym for *fabula*, he is probably making the distinction between the true and the false he had made in his prologue, since a *fabula* is an improbable story and an *apologus* is the kind of fable Aesop wrote.[42] In other words, Guido probably means to suggest that although the poets wrote improbable stories, such as those dealing with the pagan gods and goddesses, they also wrote tales which conveyed moral truths about human behavior. He does not explain in so many words why he feels that the truth about the fall of Troy should be known, why, as he put it in the prologue, deeds of the past should not be obliterated by time, but throughout the *Historia* he has indicated that history and historical truth deal not only with the glorious deeds of the past, but also with instances of human weakness, folly, and pride. Although his view of European history commits him to the Trojan side, still he shows himself as critical of Priam's overconfidence in his country's ability to combat Greece and Hector's excessive courtesy in granting the truce asked for by Ajax Telamonius as he is of the black deeds of Achilles and the wiles of Ulysses. Benoit had not glossed over the treachery of Aeneas and Antenor or their falling out with one another, and neither does Guido. In fact, Guido's skepticism as to the ultimate benefit to mankind of the Trojan War may very well stem from his knowing that the European states had been founded by the Trojans and from his being able to look around and see those very states afflicted with the same kind of delusions and dissensions as had beset the Trojan kingdom.

One must remember that Guido's lifetime saw Pier della Vigna, whom he may very well have known, accused of treachery and committing suicide in prison; Manfred deserted by his troops and dying in battle; and Conradin, the rightful heir to the Sicilian kingdom, executed by Charles of Anjou, whose tyrannous rule was not ended until the uprising known as the War of the Sicilian Vespers. With events like these in his own background, those of the Trojan War undoubtedly had a special immediacy for Guido that explains his very real desire to present them not in the guise of exciting stories, but as sober history that would hold them up for the serious consideration of later generations. It is this kind of historical truth—the truth of a record of human behavior—that even we can grant to the *Historia,* and that we should admire Guido for attempting to convey.

NOTES

1. Guido delle Colonne, *Historia Destructionis Troiae,* ed. Nathaniel Edward Griffin (Cambridge: The Mediaeval Academy of America, 1936).

2. Benoit de Sainte-Maure, *Le Roman de Troie,* ed. Léopold Constans, Société des Anciens Textes Français, 6 vols. (Paris: Firmin-Didot et Cie., 1904-1912). There is an earlier edition of the poem in Aristide Joly, *Benoit de Sainte-More et le Roman de Troie ou les Métamorphoses d'Homère et L'Épopée Gréco-Latine au Moyen-Age,* 2 vols. (Paris: F. Vieweg, 1870-1871). This edition had appeared earlier in *Mémoires de la Société des Antiquiquaires de Normandie* (Paris: Deroche, 1869), pp. 51-900, but references are usually made to the later edition, as will be done here. Citations from the text of the *Roman* will be from Constans' edition and references to Constans' introduction will be cited as "Constans, VI."

Many later scholars have given the credit for the discovery that it was Guido who followed Benoit to Hermann Dunger, *Die Sage vom troyanischen Kriege in den Bearbeitungen des Mittelalters und ihre antiken Quellen* (Leipzig, 1869); see, for example, Egidio Gorra, *Testi Inediti di Storia Trojana* (Turin: C. Trevirio, 1887), p. 108, and Waller B. Wigginton, "The Nature and Significance of the Medieval Troy Story: A Study of Guido delle Colonne's *Historia Destructionis Troiae"* (Ph.D. diss.,

Rutgers University, 1964), p. v., n. 1. It is apparent, however, that Joly
had independently reached the same conclusion and at the same time; see
Joly, p. 453, n. 1.

As will be seen below, Guido did not follow his source slavishly, and
his embellishments and digressions have often been noted, most commentators being highly critical of his changes; see, for instance, Joly, pp. 473-
484 and Gorra, pp. 119-137. Recently, however, Raffaele Chiàntera in
Guido delle Colonne (Naples: Le Monnier, 1955) has argued that Guido's
changes are evidence of his inventiveness and originality, while Wigginton
shows convincingly and in minute detail how Guido reworked his materials not only in the style of medieval history but in such a way as to
incorporate details and themes from other medieval treatments of the
Troy story, particularly those of Joseph of Exeter and Albert de Stade, as
well as reflections of contemporary history as documented by historians
like Bartolomeo de Neocastro.

3. Olga Golubeva, "The Saltykov-Shchedrin Library, Leningrad," *The
Book Collector* (Summer, 1955):102 and 107.

4. Much of the above is to be found in Griffin, pp. xv and xvii; Joly,
pp. 484-520; and Gorra, pp. 150-51. See also Arthur M. Young; *Troy and
Her Legend* (Pittsburgh: University of Pittsburgh Press, 1948), pp. 51
and 64.

5. Joly, pp. 151-72; Gorra, pp. 1-18; Young, pp. 51 and 64.

6. *Dictis Cretensis Ephemeridos Belli Troiani Libri,* ed. Werner Eisenhut (Leipzig: Teubner, 1958); *Daretis Phrygii De Excidio Troiae Historia,*
ed. Ferdinand Meister (Leipzig: Teubner, 1873).

7. Introduction to R. M. Frazer, Jr., trans., *The Trojan War: The
Chronicles of Dictys of Crete and Dares the Phrygian* (Bloomington:
Indiana University Press [1966]), pp. 9-11.

8. Frazer, p. 133.

9. Joly, pp. 857-65; Young, p. 63.

10. Constans, VI:245.

11. L. Constans and E. Faral, eds., *Le Roman de Troie en Prose*
(Paris: E. Champion, 1922). See also Constans, VI:264-318.

12. Otto, Bishop of Freising, *The Two Cities,* trans. Charles
Christopher Mierow (New York: Columbia University Press, 1928), pp.
142-43.

13. Ibid., p. 143.

14. Ibid., p. 145.

15. Both Joly, pp. 447-55, and Gorra, p. 147, suggested this as a possibility, but both refer to Guido as a plagiarist.

16. Constans, VI:324-325.

17. A case in point is Guido's use of the phrase "presens ystoria." Constans, who believed that Benoit had used a more extended version of Dares than the one now extant, and who felt that Guido had guessed that such a text must have existed, thought that Guido employed this phrase to mean Benoit's source, whatever it was (Constans, VI:327, note 1). This is a possibility, and the phrase would then have to be translated as "the history before me" (Lewis and Short, s.v. *praesens*), instead of "the present history," i.e., the history Guido was writing. Many of the instances of the phrase would make sense in context in either translation; some of them, however, especially those with a verb in the future tense, have to refer to Guido's own work, as in the prologue when he says that what was contained in the books of Dares and Dictys will be read in the "presentem libellum" [the present little book]. On the other hand, in the epilogue, when he says that at this point Dares brought the "presenti operi" [work before me] to an end, he is referring to Benoit.

18. Constans, VI:322-23.

19. This idea and the arguments supporting it are to be found in Wigginton, pp. 82-86.

De Bello Trojano has recently been translated: Joseph of Exeter, *The Iliad of Dares Phrygius*. trans. Gildas Roberts (Cape Town: A. A. Balkema, 1970). This translation is based on the edition of Geoffrey B. Ridde-hough, "The Text of Joseph of Exeter's Bellum Troianum" (Ph.D. diss., Harvard University, 1950). The published edition currently available is found in *Dictys Cretensis et Dares Phrygius De Bello Trojano . . . Accedunt Josephi Iscani De Bello Trojano Libri Sex* (London: A. J. Valpy, 1825), Vol. II.

20. Elmer Bagby Atwood, "English Versions of the *Historia Trojana*" (Ph.D. diss., University of Virginia, 1932), p. 33. See also Roberts, pp. ix and xii, and the article referred to by Roberts: Robert Kilburn Root, "Chaucer's Dares," *Modern Philology*, XV(1917)1-22.

21. Atwood, pp. 26-30. See also Constans, VI:324. Chiàntera, how-ever, maintains that Guido made use of both Dictys and Dares. For example, Chiàntera cites instances from the catalogue of men and ships in Guido's conclusion in which the number of ships given by Guido is the same as that in Dares but different from Benoit's. He also gives several

examples from the catalogue in Book IX in which Guido's spellings are closer to Dares' than to Benoit's. However, Constans uses this same catalogue to show Guido's dependence on Benoit by reason of the number of names which look more French than Latin. See Chiàntera, pp. 223-26 and Constans, VI:320.

Chiàntera also finds details in Dictys which are not in Benoit but do appear in Guido; again, several examples consist of the numbers of the ships in the catalogue in Book IX. The evidence is far from conclusive, however, especially in the case of the other instances cited: the possibility that the description of Diomedes killing the centaur is derived from Dictys' description of Diomedes killing Pandarus, which Joly (pp. 157-58 and 229) had argued was an example of Benoit's inventiveness; the lamentation of Achilles over the body of Patroclus; the death of Penthesilea; and the slaying of Ulysses by Telegonus; see Chiàntera, pp. 229-38.

22. For an analysis of Benoit's handling of the love stories, see Joly, pp. 273-303. See also R. M. Lumiansky, "Structural Unity in Benoit's *Roman de Troyes*," *Romania* LXXIX (1958): 410-24.

23. See Joly, p. 482, and R. M. Lumiansky, "The Story of Troilus and Briseida According to Benoit and Guido," *Speculum* XXIX (1956): 727-53.

24. Wigginton, pp. 86-90.

25. As noted also by Wigginton, pp. 67-79; Wigginton, in addition, finds many verbal echoes which support the argument.

26. Gorra, pp. 127-32, comments on the extended quotations but not verbal echoes.

27. Gorra, pp. 133-37.

28. Wigginton, p. 181.

29. Ibid.

30. Gorra, p. 101; Chiàntera, pp. 30-32.

31. Chiàntera, p. 244.

32. Ernst Kantorowicz, *Frederick the Second,* trans. E. O. Lorimer (New York: Ungar, [1957]), pp. 323-33.

33. Ibid., pp. 334-59; Chiàntera, p. 31.

34. Kantorowicz, pp. 339-41; Chiàntera, p. 31.

35. Gorra, p. 101.

36. Dante Gabriel Rossetti, ed., *Dante and His Circle, With the Italian Poets Preceding Him* (London: Ellis and White, 1874), pp. 392-94. The Italian text cited here is from Gianfranco Contini, ed., *Poeti del Duecento,*

2 vols. (Milan: Riccardo Ricciardi, 1960), I:104-106. The editor doubts that Guido the poet was also Guido the historian (p. 96). Chiàntera, pp. 99-105, edits the poem from a different manuscript and comments in detail on the language.

37. Kantorowicz, p. 334. See also Chiàntera, pp. 99-105.
38. Chiàntera, p. 245.
39. Gorra, pp. 105-107.
40. Joly, p. 471; Gorra, p. 103; Chiàntera, pp. 19-20.
41. Chiàntera, p. 244.
42. Lewis and Short, s.v. *apologus, fabula.*

Here begins the prologue of the History of the Destruction of Troy, composed by Judge Guido delle Colonne of Messina.

Although every day past events are obliterated by more recent ones, still certain past events happened a long time ago which are so worthy of memory on account of their enduring greatness that age does not succeed in destroying them by imperceptible corrosion, nor
5 do the previous cycles of time gone by end in dull silence. In their case, uninterrupted records flourish on account of the greatness of the events, as long as the tale of what is past is handed down to posterity. Writings of the ancients, faithful preservers of tradition, depict the past as if it were the present, and, by the attentive readings
10 of books, endow valiant heroes with the courageous spirit they are imagined to have had, just as if they were alive—heroes whom the extensive age of the world long ago swallowed up by death. It is fitting, therefore, that the fall of the city of Troy should not be blotted out by a long duration of time. To keep it alive in the minds
15 of succeeding generations, by means of continuous records, the pen of many writers described it in a trustworthy account. Certain persons, indeed, have already transcribed the truth of this very history, dealing with it lightly as poets do, in fanciful inventions by means of certain fictions, so that what they wrote seemed to their
20 audiences to have recorded not the true things, but the fictitious ones instead. Among them Homer, of greatest authority among the Greeks in his day, turned the pure and simple truth of his story into deceiving paths, inventing many things which did not happen and altering those which did happen. For he maintained that the gods the
25 ancient pagans worshipped fought against the Trojans and were vanquished with them just like mortal men. Afterward poets, having followed his error carefully, undertook to write many misleading things in their books, with the result that they caused it to be known that Homer was not the only author of falsehoods. Ovid of Sulmo,

1

30   with his fertile pen, wove both of these together in his many books.
     He added many inventions to what had been invented and did not
     omit the truth mixed in with them. Even Virgil, in his work the
     Aeneid, although for the most part he related in the light of truth the
     deeds of the Trojans when he touched upon them, was nevertheless in
35   some things unwilling to depart from the fictions of Homer. However,
     so that the true accounts of the reliable writers of this history may
     endure for all future time hereafter among western peoples, chiefly
     for the use of those who read Latin, so that they may know how to
     separate the true from the false among the things which were written
40   of the said history in Latin books, those things which [were related]
     by Dictys the Greek and Dares the Phrygian, who were at the time of
     the Trojan War continually present in their armies and were the most
     trustworthy reporters of those things which they saw, will be read in
     the present little book, having been transcribed by me, Judge Guido
45   delle Colonne of Messina, just as it was found written with an
     agreement as of one voice in their two books in Athens. Although a
     certain Roman by the name of Cornelius, nephew of the great Sallust,
     took the trouble to translate these books into Latin, still, since he
     tried to be extremely brief, he improperly omitted, through extreme
50   brevity, the particulars of this history which would be more attractive
     to the minds of his hearers. In the contents of this little book,
     therefore, will be found written everything that took place according
     to the complete history, both in general and in particular; that is,
     what was the origin of the enmities and of the cause for offense
55   which aroused Greece against the Phrygians. (Magna Graecia, that is,
     Italy, should not be understood in the designation Greece, as some
     have wished, saying that Magna Graecia, that is Italy, which today we
     call Romania, came against the Trojans, although in fact, when Greece
     came to attack the Trojans, it was small, and indeed, all alone, with,
60   however, a few allies joined to it, as the course of this history will
     plainly show in what will be read below.) Therefore it will be
     recounted hereafter in this book what kings and what dukes of
     Greece with their armed force, and with how many ships, joined the
     aforesaid army, what heraldic devices they used, what kings and what
65   dukes came to the defense of the city of Troy, how long the victory
     was delayed, how often and in what year the fighting arose, who fell
     in battle and by whose blow, about all of which things Cornelius for

the most part says nothing. All that remains, therefore, is to approach
the material of the narrative. Here ends the prologue.

*Here begins the first book, about Peleus, king of Thessaly,
inducing Jason to set off to get the Golden Fleece.*

Among the provinces of the aforesaid Romania, in the kingdom of
Thessaly, whose inhabitants are called Myrmidons and which today
we commonly call by the name of Salonika, reigned at that time a
certain just and noble king, Peleus by name, with his wife who was
5 named Thetis. From their marriage was born that very strong, very
bold, very valiant man named Achilles. Those who wished to say that
Magna Graecia, that is Italy, came to overthrow the Trojans, say these
Myrmidons were Abruzzans, a certain people who, it is evident, live
established within the confines of the kingdom of Sicily. For this
10 reason that province is called Abruzzi, and they assert that the city of
Thetis which is located in the same province has taken its name from
the aforesaid Thetis. But those who make this claim are believed to
be in error, since the inhabitants of Thessaly are given the name
Myrmidons, and when Achilles had succeeded to the throne after the
15 death of his father, King Peleus, he accomplished with them many
wonderful deeds in battle in the Trojan War. Likewise Ovid mentions
them, giving a legendary account of their origin. For he said in
Book VII of the *Metamorphoses* that these Myrmidons were ants
transformed into men by prayers directed to the gods by a king of
20 Thessaly, at the time when the whole populace of the kingdom of
Thessaly had sickened and finally died of a deadly plague, and only
the king was left. He was near the roots of a certain tree in a certain
grove when he noticed in the same place the scurrying lines of
innumerable ants, and he prayed humbly that they be made into
25 men. And in the legend of blessed Matthew the Apostle it is clearly
shown that the Myrmidons were inhabitants of Thessaly, where the
same apostle sojourned for some time.
The history describes this King Peleus as having a brother named
Aeson, related to him by both parents, and older than he. This man,
30 when he was burdened by the long decline of his life, could scarcely
govern himself. For that reason he renounced the control of the

kingdom of Thessaly to one who was much less broken by a long old
age than he, and yielded the helm of state to Peleus, his brother. We
read that Aeson lived a long time after the reign of this Peleus, so that,
35 failing on account of his great old age, his eyes dimmed and the vigor
of his body dwindled away in old age. The same Ovid, in that same
book, the *Metamorphoses,* says he was afterward renewed to the
flower of his youth and his youthful vigor, so that a young man was
made from an aged shadow by the healing remedy and magic power
40 of Medea, about which Medea an account is to be found a little
further on. A son of this Aeson survived him, a man named Jason,
who was brave and strong and young, extremely handsome, modest,
generous, affable, tractable, dutiful, and splendidly endowed with all
beauty of character. Him the princes and nobles of Thessaly, him the
45 commoners embraced with a feeling of tender affection on account of
his superior virtues, reverencing him no less than King Peleus himself.
And yet this same Jason was no less obedient to the king his uncle
than he would have been to his father if he had been ruling, nor was
he troublesome to him, but was in all things a loyal subject, despite
50 the fact that Peleus had obtained possession of the scepter of
Thessaly. Peleus did not respond to him in the same way, although,
granted, he showed by external signs that Jason was dear to him.
Nevertheless he raged inwardly and was in turmoil lest Jason despoil
him of the kingdom of Thessaly on account of his courage and the
55 great affection Peleus' own people had for him. Therefore for a long
time he preserved within himself the rage in his mind, which he made
a shrewd attempt to conceal by means of an exhausting effort to be
patient, lest being made known by some act of his it should come
out into the open. And so he searched his heart and imagined ways
60 and means by which he might be able to destroy Jason without taint
of shame.

    Finally in those days a tattling rumor was noised about in the ears
of the multitude in many places of the world concerning a marvelous
thing; namely, that on a certain island called Colchis, beyond the
65 farthest boundaries of the Trojan kingdom toward the eastern coast,
was kept a ram whose fleece was gold, as the report and rumor
asserted. Moreover on this island was said to reign a certain king
named Aeëtes, a man powerful and rich but advanced in years. The
story says the ram with the golden fleece was guarded by the

70 miraculous favor and protection of the god Mars, since certain bulls
which spewed forth scorching flames from their mouths were assigned
to guard it. If anyone wished to have this ram with the golden fleece
he had of necessity to enter into battle with these bulls, and if he
gained the victory from them, he had to subject these same con-
75 quered bulls to the yoke and compel them to plow the land where
they were. Furthermore, when the bulls had been conquered and
forced to plow, it was also necessary to attack a dragon bristling with
scales and breathing fiery flames, and having joined in combat with
him, to destroy him, and having destroyed him, to pluck out the
80 teeth from his jaws, and having plucked them out, to sow them in
the aforesaid land plowed by the bulls. A marvelous crop sprouted
from the seed of this field. For from the teeth which had been sown,
armed soldiers immediately sprang forth, and joining in fraternal
combat among themselves on that very spot, they slew one another
85 by reciprocal wounds. Through these perilous hazards, therefore, and
by no other way, could the aforesaid Golden Fleece be had, and King
Aeëtes caused all who wished to undertake the aforesaid contest to
be given free access. Although the story speaks thus about the ram
with the golden fleece, those asserting the truth about it gave
90 evidence in another way. For they said King Aeëtes possessed a great
mass of treasure, and had entrusted what he possessed to the guardianship mentioned before through devices of enchantments and
established magical practices. Many valiant men wished to seek this
mass of treasure, because of worldly rapaciousness and the greed of
95 avarice which is the mother of all evils, but because they were
attacked and injured by enchantments, they attained not the profit
of the treasure but ultimately the loss of their lives.

When, therefore, the report of the Golden Fleece reached King
Peleus as he was looking for such a hazardous undertaking, he
100 immediately gave his most careful attention to it, considering well
that he could not more easily give Jason over to his destruction by a
safer way and without a spot on his reputation. He therefore
conceived a plan whereby he would urge Jason, with his youthful
confidence in his valor and courage, to undertake voluntarily the
105 quest for the Golden Fleece. He decided, therefore, to proclaim a
solemn assembly in the widely acclaimed dominion of Thessaly, and
because no small number of barons and knights came together there,

this assembly lasted three days. On the third day, King Peleus, having
called Jason to him, addressed him thus in the presence of the said
110   nobles: "Dear nephew, I glory in the rule of so noble a kingdom as
Thessaly, but I think myself much more glorious on account of the
extreme valor and ability of such a famous nephew, since neighboring
provinces recognize the greatness of your courage by evidence of the
fact itself, and this true reputation by continued retelling proclaims
115   you in distant places. For you bring honor and glory to the
Thessalian kingdom, and even more so to me, since while you are
safe, the kingdom of Thessaly is feared by all, and while you are
alive, no one dares be hostile to it. Furthermore, the glory of your
courage would place me with the greatest men, if by your own
120   powers, you could bring within the walls of my kingdom the Golden
Fleece which is held confined within the power of King Aeëtes, which
I do not doubt might easily be done by you, if you boldly determine
to perform the task and do not neglect to follow the precepts of my
discourse. If you should decide to accomplish these things, everything
125   in the way of provisions necessary to accomplish the aforesaid deeds
will be prepared with the greatest splendor, and you will lead with
you a band of many men chosen from among the best in the
kingdom. Agree therefore to my words and you will render yourself
glorious by carrying out these commands of mine so that thenceforth
130   you will appear to be even more in my favor, and you will rejoice in
being exalted to even greater heights by the report of your valor. Nor
will your successful effort lack a reward of great benefit to you. For
by true promises and not feigned, I assure you that I shall establish
you as future heir in the kingdom of Thessaly after my death, and
135   during my life, you will be lord and master of the kingdom itself in
no less degree than I am."

When all these things which King Peleus spoke in the presence of
so many onlookers had been understood by Jason, he was filled with
great joy and excitement and, not paying attention to the insidious
140   designs of the king, and not noticing his deceitful subterfuges, he was
convinced that what the king had said proceeded from the recesses of
a clear conscience for the greater increase of his honor instead of for
injury to his person. Trusting, therefore, in his strength and daring,
and not considering it impossible for him to do what the king
145   requested with such apparent eagerness, he joyfully showed himself

favorably disposed toward the injunctions of the king, and promised with all devotion that he would without fail carry out what had been proposed. Peleus, therefore, rejoicing at the gratifying reply of his nephew, brought to a conclusion the assembly he had called, seeking
150 to gain his own ends behind the aforesaid promises, by which he anticipated that he would mock Fortune. Considering, therefore, that Jason would not be able to go to Colchis, an island surrounded by the sea, except with ships suited for sustaining the perils of the sea, he ordered to be called to him from the kingdom of Thessaly a
155 certain artisan named Argus, who was esteemed for his great skill in working with wood. This man, at the command of the king, built from a great amount of timber a ship of amazing size which was called the *Argo* from its builder's own name. Certain people want to claim that this was the first ship which ever attempted to go to
160 distant places by being rigged with sails, and on that account scholars called any large ship which is said to have crossed the sea by means of raised sails an "Argo."

And so when the aforesaid ship was ready, and all the things which Jason required for sailing had been put into it, many nobles of
165 Thessaly, outstanding for their great valor, got aboard it with this same Jason. Among them was that incomparably strong and brave man called Hercules, born, as the poets write, of Jupiter and Alcmena, the wife of Amphitryon. This is that Hercules about whose incredible deeds the tale is spread throughout many parts of the
170 world. He by his might slew an infinite number of giants in his day and crushed the very strong Antaeus, holding him up in the air in his arms and rendering him lifeless in an unbearable embrace. He, if it is worthy of belief, boldly approached the gates of Hell, and with violent hand dragged away from them their guardian, the dog
175 Tricerberus. He overcame him with such a great blow that he was completely soaked in the froth of his venom, which was spewed out in vomit and infected many parts of the world with deadly poisons. But because a long narration from the poets about his deeds would distract the attention of the audience, because of the pro-
180 longed suspense, let it suffice that these facts about him have been touched on, since the real truth of his victorious deeds is so marvelously spread through the world that even down to the present day the Pillars of Hercules at Gades testify to what degree he

appeared as a victor. It is reported that Alexander the Great of Mace-
185   donia, son of Philip of Macedon who was himself a scion of the family
of the kings of Thessaly, which is also called Macedonia, reached
these Pillars by subjugating the world to himself by main force.
Beyond these Pillars there is no habitable place, because there is a
great sea, that is, the ocean, which at this very place rushes in
190   through the narrow channel right into the heart of our land and
forms for us the Mediterranean Sea, over which we can sail to the
inland regions of the world, as we see. Although it receives the inflow
at this very place, the outflow is shut off by the shores of Syria,
where the city of Acre especially welcomes our sailors. Our sailors
195   today call this narrow place from which the Mediterranean Sea first
flows away the Strait of Seville or Sebta, and that place in which the
aforesaid Pillars of Hercules are located is called in the Saracen
language Safi, a place which it is impossible to go beyond.

Having thus obtained from King Peleus permission to sail, Jason
200   plowed the strange seas with Hercules and his companions. The new
ship, since a favorable wind filled its sails and a breeze blew on it,
very quickly left the known regions of Thessaly and more quickly, in
its extremely swift course, burst upon the unknown regions of the
sea. And so while for many days and nights they were sailing under
205   the leadership of the Thessalian Philoctetes, and were noting carefully the course of the stars which are to be seen appearing near the
Pole Star, that is, of the Big and Little Bears which never set,
together with the constellation the Dragon nearby, according to the
accounts of the poets, since that star which sailors call the North
210   Star poets say is the last star placed in the tail of the Little Bear, and
the sailors themselves name Big Bear the Greek, and say that the
Dragon is the master. . . . About these Bears, that is, the Big and
Little, Ovid in Book II of the *Metamorphoses* says, writing fictitiously,
that Callisto and Arcas, her son, were changed into these bears. These
215   stars are also called the septentrional stars, since there are seven near
the Pole. About these stars Juno said:

You see . . . new constellations fresh set, to outrage me, in the place
of honour in highest heaven, where the last and shortest circle
encompasses the utmost pole. . . . But . . . if the insult to your
foster-child moves you, debar these bears from your green pools . . .

For Philoctetes knew the course and motion of the stars, if indeed in
these things anyone may be compared to him who was greatly skilled
in navigation. And thus, blown upon by a favorable breeze, he sailed
220   for a long time, in a direct course, until the new ship touched at the
Phrygian coasts, that is, those belonging to the Trojan kingdom, in
the port which was then called Simois by the inhabitants.

*Here begins the second book, about Jason and Hercules
and the Greeks reaching the shores of Troy, and about King
Laomedon dismissing them from those places.*

As soon as they reached shore, the Greeks, weakened by the
weariness of sea travel, with eager hearts exerted themselves to land
in order to rest. As they landed, they heard fresh water from the
springs and determined to linger for some days in order to refresh
5   themselves better, not so that they might plan to offer injury to the
inhabitants nor seek to harm them in any degree by wicked
depredations. The envious course of the fates, however, which always
troubles the repose of mortal men, for no cause drew causes for
enmity and offense out from unexpected hiding places. On account
10   of these things, a far-reaching calamity of such disastrous effect
plagued the whole world, so that so many kings and princes suffered
death in battle, and so great a city as Troy was reduced to ashes, and
so many women were deprived of their husbands, and so many girls
lost their parents and were at last led away under the yoke of
15   servitude. For although Greece gained the victory amidst such great
distresses, still for a long time the damage done by the death of its
people and the slaughter of its best men destroyed the reward of
victory. Even if these many woes were pleasing to the gods, still, the
original cause of these things, as trifling as unimportant, rightly
20   troubles human hearts; that is, that a punishment of such severity
had to be inflicted for such a trivial fault, unless perhaps it might be
said in justification that the amount of evil which took place was the
basis for good to come, since so much good has proceeded from these
evils connected with the fall of Troy. Though Troy itself was
25   completely destroyed, it rose again, and its destruction was the reason
that the city of Rome, which is the chief of cities, came into

existence, being built and extended by the Trojan exiles, by Aeneas,
that is, and Ascanius his son, called Julius. Afterward certain other
provinces received from among the Trojans an enduring settlement.
30   Such is England, which we read was settled by the Trojan, Brutus,
which is why it is called Britain. Likewise such is France, which after
the fall of Troy is said to have been settled by King Francus, a
companion of Aeneas, who founded near the Rhine a great city
which, as well as the whole province, he called France, from his own
35   name. The city of the Venetians was settled by the Trojan Antenor.
We read that Sicily also did not lack their colonizing; it is said to
have been settled first by King Sicanus, who arrived in Sicily from
Troy, which is why it was called Sicania. Later, having departed from
Sicily, leaving in Sicily his brother Siculus, which is why it was later
40   named Sicily, he went into Tuscany, which he filled with a colony of
many people. We read that the above mentioned Aeneas founded
many cities along the sea coast in the kingdom of Sicily. Such is the
great city of Naples, and Gaeta, land of an ungovernable people. Even
Diomedes, who by himself accomplished so many marvelous deeds in
45   the Trojan War, when Troy was destroyed, settled in Calabria,
although he was Greek in origin, at least until he could be received in
his own kingdom. Ovid writes that Circe, daughter of the sun,
transformed his companions into birds which were brought by
Diomedes into Calabria. Isidore of Seville says that many birds were
50   produced from the race of these which are called Diomedian and
which had the ability to know how to distinguish a Latin man from
a Greek. For this reason they cherish the Greek inhabitants of
Calabria and flee the Latin, if there are any.
      But the human mind is uncertain whether the cause of such a
55   great betrayal was finally the cause of subsequent good. Nevertheless,
the story says later on that while Jason and Hercules and their
followers were resting in the port of Simois, the report about them
reached Laomedon, king of the Trojans, that a certain people
unknown to the Trojans, that is, the Greeks, had entered the Phrygian
60   territories in a strange ship, perhaps to spy out secrets in the little
Trojan kingdom, or, more probably, to lay waste the country of
Troy. For in those days Troy was not as large as it was afterward
when it was rebuilt, and in it ruled then the aforesaid king,
Laomedon by name, who, having adopted an accursed plan (if only

65 he never had!), determined to send his ambassador to Jason with a
large retinue. When this man came to Jason he explained his mission
in these words: "King Laomedon, ruler of this kingdom, wonders
greatly at your arrival and at the fact that, without obtaining his
permission, you have entered his kingdom, in which he intends to
70 maintain the peace. He commands you most urgently to leave his
country immediately so that tomorrow he may be assured that you
have departed from all parts of his country. But if he learns that you
are contemptuous of his commands, you may be very sure that he
will order his men to avenge your offense by destroying your
75 property and ultimately slaughtering your people." After Jason had
heard the whole message, he was inwardly torn by anger and vexation
of heart, but before he replied to the words spoken to him by the
ambassador, he turned to his own men and spoke thus to them:
"King Laomedon, the ruler of this kingdom, has offered us an
80 amazingly disgraceful insult, since he has ordered that we be ejected
from his kingdom without any cause of offense. And yet, if any
kingly nobility had animated him, he should have ordered us to be
honored. For if a similar occasion had brought him to Greece, he
would have found that the Greeks would have offered him not
85 disgrace but honor. Since, however, disgrace rather than honor pleases
him, let us also please him and depart from the boundaries of his
kingdom, since it could happen and may easily be that he will pay
very dearly for his despicable plan." Then, without pause, he said to
the messenger: "Friend, we have listened attentively to the words of
90 your message, and we have received, as is fitting, the gifts which your
king, according to the custom of noblemen, has sent us. We swear by
our gods in the truth of God that we have not entered the country of
your king by design in order that we might inflict an injury on
anyone by offering violence in the manner of pirates, but since we
95 intend to go on very soon to farther regions, necessity forced us to
turn aside into this country. Say therefore to your king that we shall
depart from his country; let him know for certain that he will receive
a fitting reward, if not from us, perhaps from others, who will have
heard of this insult offered us today." Hercules, discontented at the
100 words of Jason to the king's messenger, retorted with these words:
"Friend, whoever you are, be sure to report to your king that we will
depart completely from our position in his country tomorrow at the

latest; but this day will not have been past three years, tell him, when
he, if he lives, will see us cast our anchors again on his shore, whether
105   he wants us or not, and then he will not have any freedom at all to
give us permission to leave, since a dispute such as this present one
has begun the quarrel, so that, rather than being able to hope for a
victory from it, he will be bowed down by the weight of ignominious
disgrace." The messenger of the king answered him and said: "It is
110   quite shameful for a nobleman, and especially a valiant man, to shoot
the arrows of threats, nor did the king commission me, whom he
sent, to press a quarrel upon you. I have said to you what I was
ordered to; if it pleases you to act wisely, I give you good advice so
that it may not be unpleasant to leave this country before you run
115   into more unpleasantnesses, since it is not easy to destroy people who
are able to protect themselves by sound advice." Afterward, having
sought leave from the Greeks, he returned to his king. Jason and
Hercules, without prolonging their stay, called Philoctetes and ordered
the anchors hauled from the sea and everything collected which they
120   had brought on shore in order to rest. For they were aware that if
they had wished to attack the Phrygians, they would not have been
equal to them in the encounter, nor stronger in men nor resources.
They embarked on the *Argo,* and, having raised the sails, with the
guidance of the gods they left the Phrygian shores. Then, plowing
125   through the sea, blown upon by favorable winds, they arrived safely
at the island of Colchis before too many days had passed, and
joyfully entered the port they had longed for.

There was at that time on the island of Colchis a certain city
named Jaconites, which had been established as the capital of the
130   kingdom on account of its great size, an extremely beautiful city,
surrounded by walls and towers, embellished with many skillfully
constructed palaces, filled with a large populace, and distinguished by
being the home of many noblemen. In this city, King Aeëtes lived
regally with a large retinue, since not far from the city were many
135   green groves suitable for hunting because there was a large supply of
wild game grazing on the wooded hills. Around this city extended a
broad plain, adorned with ponds and groves, while innumerable
springs bubbled forth on it and many rivers, gliding along in
continuous streams, watered this plain with little brooks. For this
140   reason, the supply of birds for hunting was abundant in it, and the

chirping of many birds sounded incessantly throughout the place with
sweet melody.

Jason and Hercules, with their companions, regally and fittingly
clad, took their way to this city by the direct route. While they were
145 hastening in the long line along the broad avenues of the city itself,
displaying measured steps in admirable arrangement, the crowd
marvelled at their being adorned with so much kingly magnificence,
and in the flower of youth and beauty, so modest in their bearing,
and seeming to excel in appearance as well as behavior. Therefore
150 with eager hearts the crowds asked who they were, where they were
from, and what was the reason for their arrival. There was no one
who would explain the reason for their arrival to those who were
inquiring until they reached the gates of the royal palace. But as soon
as the arrival of the Greeks had been made known to King Aeëtes, he,
155 not unmindful of the graciousness of his innate nobility, rose from
the royal throne and went out to meet them with a large retinue. He
embraced them warmly, receiving them with smiling face and joyful
expression; he smiled in sign of greeting and in his first gentle words
promised them peace and friendship. They afterward mounted the
160 marble stairs to the upper rooms together and entered the halls of the
palace, which were decorated with various pictures and gleaming with
the marvelous splendor of gold leaf. After they had been given the
opportunity to remain, Jason, filled with great feeling, spoke in a
modest manner and explained to King Aeëtes the reason for his
165 arrival, and humbly asked to attempt the appointed trial for the
Golden Fleece, according to the laws which had been imposed. The
king, kindly complying with his request, did not deny that he would
fulfill the wishes of Jason.

When the food had been prepared in great abundance, they set up
170 the tables, putting many gold cups on them. Just before it was time
to eat, the king, desirous of showing the Greeks all the courtesy of
his noble nature, sent for his daughter to come and graciously be
present at the feast with the newly arrived guests, whom the king
himself was receiving with great pleasure. For the daughter of King
175 Aeëtes, named Medea, was an extremely beautiful maiden, the only
daughter of her father and his sole heir in the kingdom. She, although
she had already reached marriageable age and was indeed ripe for
marriage, had nevertheless from her childhood given herself up eagerly

to the study of the liberal arts, so completely drinking in the Helicon
180 of science with eagerness of heart that no man or woman could be
found in those days who was more learned than she. But the
knowledge of that jewel by reason of which she was the more
distinguished was the art of magic, which, through powers and
necromantic means of incantations, turned light into dark, suddenly
185 raised up winds and storms, lightning and hail, and fearful earthquakes. She forced the course of rivers gliding through lower places
to pour into higher parts and overflow. She also made trees, despoiled
of their branches by the onslaughts of winter, bloom even in the
season of storms, making the young grow old and recalling the aged
190 to the glory of youth. The pagans of antiquity were willing to believe
that she could very often force the great planets, that is, the sun and
moon, to go into eclipse against the order of nature. For according to
the truth of astrology, in which she is reported to have been most
learned, the sun, running continually in the ecliptic course, does not
195 have to suffer eclipse, unless it were to be in conjunction with the
moon, [the moon] itself in conjunction being in the tail or head
(which are certain intersections of certain orbits in the sky), as well
as with some other one of the planets. For then the moon, opposing
itself between our sight and the sun, prevents us from seeing the
200 body of the sun as we are accustomed to, according to what Ptolemy
the Egyptian, who was very learned, asserts about this. Nevertheless,
she is said to have made this happen by force of her enchantments,
when the sun was not in conjunction with the moon (as we ordinarily
say, "when the moon revolves itself") but when it was in its
205 opposition, being removed from it by the seven successive signs (when
we then ordinarily call the moon "a fifteener"). But that storytelling
Ovid of Sulmo, writing fictitiously about Medea, daughter of King
Aeëtes, thus proposed it should be believed of her (which it is not
fitting that Catholics faithful to Christ should believe, except to the
210 extent that it was told as a story by Ovid). For the high and eternal
God, Who in His Wisdom, that is, in the Son, created all things,
placed the heavenly bodies of the planets according to His own law,
and placing them, He imposed on them for all eternity an injunction
that they will not disregard. For this reason we read that an eclipse
215 of the sun never took place contrary to the laws of nature except
when the Incarnate Son of God Himself humbly gave Himself up to

suffering for us. When He gave up His spirit on the tree of the cross,
the sun was eclipsed although the moon was not then in conjunction
with it. Then the veil of the temple was rent, there were terrible
220 earthquakes, and many bodies of the saints arose. Hence it was that
in those days Dionysius the Areopagite, the most eminent natural
philosopher, who lived in Athens and was very active in the schools,
although he was tainted by the error of the pagans, seeing that the
sun was eclipsed during the passion of Christ, said in stupefaction,
225 "Either the God of nature suffers or the mechanism of the world is
dissolved." This is the true and eternal God, Who has power to
destroy every element of nature and to force each of them to
transgress against the law of nature, Who by the single prayer of a
faithful one ordered the earthly course of the sun against its natural
230 law to be fixed and stand still at Sabaoth. However, all this about
Medea is therefore set forth according to the legends, although the
present history does not omit the fact that this material about her
was legendary, since it is not to be denied that she was extremely
skillful in astrology and witchcraft.
235   Medea, however, having heard the command of her father, although
she was an extremely beautiful maiden, tried, as is the custom of
women, to add beauty to beauty, that is, through beautiful ornaments. For this reason, she came to the tables of the dinner guests
decked out with precious ornaments and royal attire, elegant in her
240 entire bearing, not with a familiarity to put one off. Her father
ordered her to sit next to Jason. Oh, unfortunate and infatuated
generosity, what do you owe to politeness in the hazard of your
reputation and the loss of your honor for courtesy? Is it wise to
trust to feminine constancy or the female sex, which has never been
245 able, through all the ages, to remain constant? Her mind always
remains in motion and is especially changeable in girlhood, before
the woman, being of marriageable age, is joined to her husband. For
we know the heart of woman always seeks a husband, just as matter
always seeks form. Oh, would that matter, passing once into form,
250 could be said to be content with the form it has received. But just as
it is known that matter proceeds from form to form, so the dissolute
desire of women proceeds from man to man, so that it may be
believed without limit, since it is of an unfathomable depth, unless by
chance the taint of shame by a praiseworthy abstinence should

255   restrict it within the limits of modesty. Why, therefore, O King
       Aeëtes, were you so bold as to place a tender young woman side by
       side in intimacy with the foreign hero? If with trembling heart you
       had considered the frailty of the sex, you would not later have
       lamented that the only heir of your kingdom was carried away to a
260   foreign realm in a disgraceful flight by sea, at such a great cost that
       you were deprived both at once and at the same time of your
       daughter and of an unheard of amount of treasure. What did the
       protection of Mars avail you against the tricks and snares of a
       woman? For indeed, you will perhaps say that since you could in no
265   way avoid what was to be, you ordered your daughter to entertain
       Jason at the feast, and you placed Jason next to your child at the
       celebration of the banquet. And here the history accordingly presents
       what actually happened to you, omitting neither the proper nor the
       improper events.
270   Medea, therefore, was between her father and Jason, and although
       she was covered with blushes, still she could not control the glances
       of her eyes; in fact, when she could, she turned their glance with
       sweet looks toward Jason, so that by gazing with eager imagination
       at his face and at the features of his face, his blond hair, and his
275   body and the limbs of his body, she suddenly burned with desire for
       him, and conceived in her heart a blind passion for him. She did not
       care to eat the delicious banquet nor taste the cups of sweet drinks.
       For the sweet face of Jason which she bore locked in her heart was
       food and drink to her then, and in her love for him her heart was
280   completely filled with desire. When, therefore, it was observed by
       those around her that she had not tasted her food, they did not think
       that this was happening to her because of love but only perhaps by
       reason of shyness. Medea, however, stirred by a desire of great fervor,
       tried to conceal the sin which she was thinking of, so that not only
285   would it not be observed by those by whom it perhaps might be
       perceived, but so that she also might produce in her own mind
       arguments for plausible excuses by which she might be able to turn
       by excuses what might possibly be a wrong in a young girl into a
       right action. And for this reason it was that she softly forced these
290   words between her ivory teeth: "Oh, I wish this foreigner, who is as
       handsome as he is noble, might be joined to me in marriage," so that
       she might allow herself to believe that it was because of innocent

affection that she was longing for what was not devoid of sin and
guilt. For it is always the custom of women, that when they yearn
295 for some man with immodest desire, they veil their excuses under
some sort of modesty.

When, therefore, the feast was at an end, Medea, with the
permission of her father, retired into the inmost recesses of her
apartments, and Jason and Hercules, by order of the king, were
300 lodged in another apartment of the palace. Medea, however,
remaining alone secluded in her own room, in distress because of the
ardor of the love she had conceived, was tormented by great anguish;
and worn out by much sighing, she considered with deep concern
how she could put an end to the flames of passion by satisfying her
305 desire. When she had overcome the weakness of maidenly modesty,
she gave in to boldness, since love and shame were at war within her.
Love urged that she be bold, but shame forbade it because of the
dishonor. Thus, for a whole week, tormented by the twofold conflict,
she lamented the loss of her labor in silence.

310 It happened, however, by Fortune, who brings about a speedy end
to sufferings, that, as a result of her favorable reception to the
prayers of Medea, it came to pass that on a certain day, about the
middle of the day, while King Aeëtes in a group of his privy
councilors was considering many things with Jason and Hercules in
315 his great hall, he sent for his daughter Medea to come to him. When
she appeared, regally clad, to spare her blushes she sat next to her
father, as he ordered. Her father gave her permission in soothing
terms to enter into pleasant talk, as is the custom of maidens, with
Jason and Hercules. She was somewhat embarrassed, and rising from
320 beside her father, chose to sit next to Jason. Jason, when he saw
Medea had sat next to him, was happy, and since there was a little
space left on the seat, he moved a bit away from Hercules and placed
himself closer to the side of Medea. King Aeëtes, however, and the
rest of those in attendance, spent the day in courteous conversation,
325 and Hercules, in the presence of those in attendance, talked over
many things in a long discourse. Thus there was nothing between
Jason and Medea which by its intervention might be a hindrance, if
there was anything to be said to one another. Medea, then, having
seized a suitable opportunity of speaking to Jason as if in the
330 freedom of solitude, when she saw the rest of the company were

entertaining themselves and were conversing among themselves about
various other things, laid aside the burden of timid shyness and
modesty, and in their first conversation spoke thus to Jason: "Dear
Jason, may your noble nature not esteem it immodest or ascribe it to
335 the immorality of feminine looseness, if by chance I presume to talk
with you as if I were without reputation, and with an immodest
intent in the words, strive to call myself to your notice. Indeed, it is
fitting that counsel of safety be given by a noble to a noble stranger
who has much on his mind. For a noble is supposed to be helpful to
340 another noble out of a certain mutual courtesy. And I know that you
are noble and that, led by youthful daring, you have sought this
kingdom to obtain the Golden Fleece, and you know that in this
quest you will risk obvious danger and expose your life to the peril
of certain death. And so I have pity on your noble nature and your
345 youthful ardor, and I desire to supply you with a safe plan and
beneficial assistance by which you may without harm be rescued
from such dangers and succeed in going back in safety to the longed-
for gods of your country by means of favorable protection. You
would easily recognize that these things were to your advantage, if
350 with understanding heart you were to accept my advice and to give
careful attention to carrying it out." With his face inclined toward
her and with folded arms, Jason replied thus in a low voice to the
words which she spoke: "Ah, most noble lady, I offer you humble
thanks from my most devoted heart, because by a noble speech you
355 show yourself to have pity on my efforts. For this reason I submit
myself wholly to your kind intention, because gifts are much more
pleasing which are not sought for and are not offered on account of
previous favors and kindnesses." Medea replied to him: "Dear Jason,
do you know how many hazards have been devised against the
360 seeking of the Golden Fleece, or is it perhaps that rumor, ignorant of
the truth, has not clearly revealed their true cause to you? For
indeed, scarcely any mortal man has the ability to obtain it since it is
under divine guardianship, and it is not in man to do more than the
irresistible power of the gods is able to. For how shall he have
365 escaped unharmed from the bulls spitting flaming fire who has been
encouraged by a chance occasion to attack them, spurred on by
overconfidence, when, as he rushes against them, he is suddenly
turned into ashes and perishes, smothered in smoky cinders? If with

youthful confidence you have taken it upon yourself to attempt this
370 with so light a heart, you will have been misled by great folly, since
death alone would be the reward of such a course of action. Therefore, Jason, if you seek to act wisely, withdraw your foot from such
an unpropitious threshold, and do not approach the fatal thresholds
which are at last to take away the light of your life." Jason, however,
375 as if impatient at Medea's words, and distressed lest she pour forth
any more words like these, cut off her speech, and when he had
interrupted its course, objected thus: "Ah, most noble lady, do you
think you can alarm me by the terror of your speech, so that,
stunned by severe shocks, I shall desist from this undertaking? If this
380 were allowed, how could I gain any glory? Even during my life I
should languish under the lively scorn of everyone, and, stripped of
all honor and praise, I should be perpetually despised on account of
the completeness of my disgrace. And so my intention is fixed to give
myself up to death, if death is the reward of such a course of action.
385 For it ought to be a quality of a foresighted man, from the time
when he announces positively his intention for a certain undertaking,
to prefer death to life rather than shamefully withdraw from the
undertaking." Medea replied to him: "Well, Jason, what is certain
about this plan of yours is that you desire to prefer death to life, in
390 obvious contempt of such imminent danger. In fact, I pity your
foolhardiness and am moved to the depths of compassion at your
presuming so rashly. Hence, because of this kind disposition toward
you, I propose to place the means of saving you before respect for
my father, and to spare neither my reputation nor safety. You will
395 obtain the favor of this help from me if you frankly pledge yourself
to my counsels and do not practice deceits in carrying out what I
shall ask." Jason said to her: "Most noble lady, what you decide I
should do, I promise I shall carry it out without fail, and I call upon
the gods as witnesses." Medea replied to him: "If you will join me to
400 you as your wife, Jason, if you will take me from my father's
kingdom, carrying me off to your country, if you will be faithful
and do not desert me while I am alive, I shall certainly bring it about
and arrange it so that you will eventually fulfill your desire by
obtaining the Golden Fleece, when the dreadful dangers which
405 threaten have been removed. For I am the only one among mortals
who can elude the power of Mars and powerfully frustrate his designs

through the opposing power of my craft." Jason replied to her: "Oh, how great and inestimable are these things that you, noble damsel, promise you will give me. It is easy to see that being endowed with
410 special beauty, you shine forth among other brides of great worth, just like the red rose which in springtime surpasses in the signs of their glory the other flowers which nature produces spontaneously in fertile fields. And in addition, you will free me from the injuries of such great evils in the quest for the Golden Fleece! Yet I know that
415 the reward of such an object is not mine by right. He who would refuse so precious a gift offered by favorable fortune can deservedly be said to be wholly moved by the greatest madness and folly. Thus, noblest of women, I humbly give myself to you, both as a man and a promised husband, and I promise I shall do all that you ask, by free
420 choice and with unblemished faith." Medea was truly happy at the words of this proposal, and thus spoke again in reply to his offer: "Dear Jason, I long with all my heart to be made certain and completely sure of your promises, and so that you may make my mind firmer with regard to a safer security in these things, I ask that
425 whatever you have said be confirmed by you with your oath. Since at present there is no suitable place for it, I think it should be deferred until earth is covered by the darkness of night, which furnishes an opportunity to those who wish to do secret deeds, and protects many from the knowledge of men. And thus, when the night
430 furnishes these advantages to us, as soon as I have sent for you through a message from my chamberlain, you will come safely to my chamber, in which you will reassure me about the promises by swearing before the gods. When you have assured me in this manner, you will then possess me as yours, and then you will be fully
435 instructed by me concerning the course of your actions and their final execution." Jason immediately concluded thus with a short speech of this brief import: "Most noble lady, let it be done as you say for you and for me." When they had both ceased further talk, and when Medea had taken leave of Hercules and had also said
440 farewell to her royal father, she withdrew to her own room with many companions around her.

*Here begins the third book, which concerns Medea's
instructions to Jason about the contest for the Golden Fleece,
and the measures to be taken to do battle with the bulls
and the dragon.*

The sun had already passed the middle of the day and was already,
with the reins of his horses slack, approaching the regions of his
setting, when Medea, remaining alone in her apartment, turned over
in her mind the many things she had said to Jason and what his
5 answers had been. While she examined carefully the things they had
concluded with one another, she was overwhelmed by increasing joy,
but her joy was dimmed by a mixture of yearning as the hour she
longed for, on account of her great desire, approached slowly. For
this reason, while she palpitated with breathless yearning, since she
10 was made impatient by ardor, she measured the course of the sun
with earnest looks. She was tormented by such great eagerness for
the setting of the sun that she was completely convinced that the
rest of the day, which was still just between light and shadows, was
as long as two days. At last, as it drew on toward evening, the sun's
15 descent beneath the horizon brought on the complete darkness of
night, while the shadow of earth interposed itself between the faces
of men and the sun. Therefore, as the twilight of that night grew
deeper, the agitated heart of Medea was in a turmoil of varying
emotions, and she, bent on watching the least movement of the sun
20 until it should set, watched with even greater anxiety and yearned
for nightfall with the concomitant rising of the moon, since on that
night it was to rise at about the first hour of sleep. And so when
those living in the palace had finished what was keeping them awake,
each one would seek the quiet of sleep, and by then the freedom she
25 desired to carry out her wishes would be completely at her disposal.
Yet oh, how few things come quickly enough to the yearning heart!
By what agonizing anxieties was Medea then tormented, when she
heard her father's servants spending the long night awake, and the
setting signs by no means urged sleep upon those who were awake!
30 For a long time, then, as if she were impatient at waiting, she moved
restlessly around her room from place to place. Now she rose to look

out the door to see if by chance the people who were awake had
begun to consider sleep, now she opened the casements of the
window to see through them how much of the course of that night
35 had passed away. She was vexed by troubles like these for a long
time, until the crowing of cocks, the herald of sleep, grew loud on
every side, at whose warning those who were awake instantly sought
the repose of sleep. Then, when the whole household of the king had
gone to bed, and when silence was everywhere merged with the quiet
40 of night, Medea, not a little excited, cautiously sent an old woman,
who was her servant and very astute, to Jason. Jason, as he perceived
her, rose at once from his bed, and in company with the old woman,
walking with soft steps through the dark palace, arrived at the
apartment of Medea. Since Medea was standing at its entrance, Jason
45 with affectionate words made a short speech of greeting in the
doorway. When a similar response was returned him by Medea, he
willingly passed through the doors.

Then the old woman went away immediately, and when Jason and
Medea had been left alone in the room, and the doors of the apart-
50 ment had been made secure by Medea, Jason, as Medea suggested, sat
down on a couch spread with marvelous splendor. After she had
opened her treasure chest, Medea brought forth from it a certain
golden image consecrated in the name of the highest Jupiter, as was
the custom of the pagans, and when she had shown it to Jason in the
55 great light of blazing wax tapers, by which the whole chamber was
illuminated with the greatest splendor, she spoke to him, saying these
words: "I am asking you, Jason, to swear faithfully an oath on this
image of highest Jupiter that when by my free will I shall place
myself completely at your disposal, and am about to fulfill all the
60 things I promised you, you, with the purity of inviolate faith, will
swear that you will cherish me forever, from the hour that you
receive me as your wife, according to the power of human and divine
law, and that at no time of your life you will dare to desert me by
any kind of evil plot." At this, Jason, offering himself with devout
65 expression and touching the image physically with his hand, swore to
observe and carry out every single thing that Medea had just said.

But oh, the deceiving falsity of the man! Say, Jason, what more
could Medea ever have done for you, who, when she had set aside all
honorable consideration of decency, gave up her body and soul

70 together to you, because of a quite mistaken confidence in your
     promise alone, not considering the signs of her rank nor heeding the
     greatness of her royal dignity? For love of you she deprived herself
     of her hereditary scepter and shamelessly left her old father, after
     having robbed him of a mass of his treasure, and leaving her ancestral
75 home, because of you chose exile, preferring foreign provinces to the
     sweetness of her native land. Did she not preserve you unharmed
     from the annihilation of death, and draw you away from the stain of
     perpetual scorn? For even if you had escaped uninjured from the
     dangerous adventure, would you not, on account of the pressure of
80 shame, have lacked the boldness to return to Thessaly without having
     obtained the Golden Fleece? She, however, cut herself off from
     herself and her family, and returned you to you and yours. What lack
     of shame made you dare to mock the bond of your oath so that you,
     defiled by the disgrace of ingratitude, might deceive a credulous
85 young girl? When you had taken her away from her ancestral hearth
     and had put aside fear of the gods, whom you chose to scorn by
     foreswearing, you were not afraid to betray the confidence of the
     woman from whom it is certain you received such great benefits. The
     story says, nevertheless, that at the last you shamelessly deceived
90 Medea. But your deception, as the course of this same story does not
     omit, produced this shame, namely, that in the punishment of your
     perjury and in aversion for your broken faith, since the gods were
     powerful, you are said to have finished your life in the misfortune of
     disgrace. (More about this is not reported at present because it has
95 no bearing on the material of the present treatise.) But you, Medea,
     who are said to have been adorned with the splendor of so many
     accomplishments, say, what did knowing about the laws of the stars
     avail, through which it is said the future can be foretold? If
     foreknowledge of the future lives in them, why did you provide for
100 yourself such a terrible and wicked future? Perhaps you will say that
     because you were carried away by great love, you omitted through
     negligence to search thoroughly among the laws of the stars for the
     future costs of your evil. It is certain the judgments of astronomy
     are based upon uncertainty, of which the manifest example is most
105 powerfully and plainly seen in you, who were in no way able to see
     into the future through astronomy. For these are those uncertain
     things which, being easy to believe, certainly deceive and confuse by

means of evident error and falsity. In these things no effect of the
future is to be discovered, unless perhaps it is touched upon by
110   chance, since it is of God alone, in whose hand is the knowledge of
times and the moments of times.

      Need I say more? When Medea had received from Jason his
perjured oath, they both went to the bed, which was decked with
incredible loveliness, and after they had cast aside their clothes and
115   both appeared naked, Jason opened the gates of virginity in Medea.
And so, when they had passed the whole night in the delights of
voluptuous pleasure, although Medea enjoyed the satisfaction of her
wishes through the manly embraces and longed for acts of love by
Jason, still the spark of lust did not die down in her; on the con-
120   trary, when the acts were finished, she conceived a more intense
passion than she had before the thing was done. This is that
sensation, seducing miserable lovers by such great enjoyment, which
the more it is received by them, the more it is desired, and which the
sated appetite is not able to hate, since the desires of the heart and
125   greed for pleasure nurture continually a desire for it, while its sweet
longing rages. Already the morning star had begun to shine with the
approaching dawn of that night, when Jason addressed Medea with
these words: "It is the hour, sweet lady, that we should rise from bed
lest suddenly the light of day should catch us unaware. I do not
130   know, dearest, whether you have arranged anything for me to do
concerning my task. If, then, anything has been appointed by you, I
implore you fervently to open to me the doors of your secret
counsels so that, instructed by you, I may carry them out. For all
speed is like a delay to me concerning those means by which I may
135   take you from this island where you are and bring you to my country
where I have power." Medea thus replied to him: "Dear friend, dearer
to me than myself, I have already made a complete plan concerning
your affair, which has now become my own, a plan refined in the
crucible of careful selection and fully realized by me. Let us then rise
140   from bed so that the means for doing these things may be more
easily available to you and me concerning all these things which seem
to you to be necessary." When they were both out of bed and had
put on their clothes again with great haste, Medea, opening her chests
of treasures, took out many things from them, which she gave to
145   Jason to be used in the following order. First she gave him a certain

silver image which she said was constructed by means of binding
spells and by virtue of great craft, and which was very potent against
spells already cast, that is, annulling those which had already been
made and warding off their injuries by an eventual repulsion of them.
150 Then she instructed Jason to take care to carry it about on his
person. For he would be able to prevail over any spells whatever,
when the power of the injurious spells had been annulled. Second she
gave him the remedy of a certain sweet-smelling ointment, and told
him to anoint himself with it, assuring him that it had the power to
155 overcome flames completely, to extinguish fire, and to turn that
which had the power of combustion into harmless smoke. Then she
gave him a certain ring in which there was set a stone of such great
virtue that it would attack any poison and turn aside its noxious
force, and by its virtue it would preserve anyone who had perhaps
160 been infected by taking a maddening poison, just as if he had taken
something harmless. There was also in this same stone another very
great virtue, so that if anyone carried this stone held tight in his
hand, with the result that the stone itself stuck to the skin of the
person carrying it, he would immediately become invisible, with the
165 result that while he was carrying it in his hand, the means of seeing
him would appear to no one. Learned men call this stone the agate,
and it was first found on the island of Sicily. And Virgil wrote that
Aeneas did this when he first arrived invisibly on the shores of
Carthage, about which he speaks thus: "He stepped forth accom-
170 panied by his faithful agate." Afterward Medea showed Jason a
certain inscription which was clearly written and very easily understood, and warned him very solemnly that as soon as he reached the
Golden Fleece, when the foregoing hindrances had been removed, he
should not suddenly rush upon it, but kneeling to the gods absorbed
175 in prayer, he should read that writing at least three times, with the
effect that, since the reading had the form of sacrifice, he would,
through it, deserve to have the favor of the gods. Last and finally she
gave him a vial filled with a miraculous liquid, and she instructed him
that as soon as he came to the bulls, he should fill their mouths with
180 the liquid and moisten them with repeated sprinklings. For she
asserted that in this liquid there was such power that as soon as the
mouths of the bulls had been filled with it, they would be forced
closed, just as if stuck together with some sticky glue, so that it

185 would be not only difficult but even impossible for them to open
their mouths. Thus Medea diligently instructed Jason about these
things one at a time in order, by which procedures or means he
would be able to arrive at the glory of the longed-for victory. Medea
then put an end at last to her instructions and teachings, and when
she had given Jason permission to leave, before the arrival of the
190 menacing light of day, Jason took himself back with furtive steps to
the room which had been set aside for him.

When the dawn had risen with rosy splendor and the golden sun
had illuminated the peaks of the mountains with a faint light, Jason
rose from his pretended rest, and in a troop, namely of Hercules and
195 his men, went to the throne of King Aeëtes, on which the king had
already placed himself, with a circle of many attendants standing
around. When the king saw him, he received him with a smiling face,
and, showing signs of respect, asked him the reason for his coming.
Jason thus addressed him: "My lord, since any delay would be
200 henceforth extremely tedious to me, I request, if it pleases you, that
I might undertake with your willing permission the warlike adventure
of the Golden Fleece." The king replied: "Jason, my friend, I am
afraid that the rash boldness of your youth leads you to seek those
things which will hasten your death, and will produce infamous talk
205 about me concerning your risking disaster. I therefore advise you
urgently to wish to return safe to your country rather than to subject
yourself to so many evils through which you will be lost." Jason
replied to him: "Most noble king, my daring is not without thought
and planning. Without doubt you will be innocent in the sight of all
210 if—may it not happen!—anything sinister should befall me from that
which I voluntarily undertake." The king replied to him: "Jason, my
friend, reluctantly I allow you to carry out your desires. May the
gods grant that you will be preserved unharmed from such a great
peril." Thus Jason, obtaining the wished-for permission from the king,
215 girded himself for the journey.

There was next to the island of Colchis a certain small island,
separated from it by a small strait, where the aforesaid Golden Fleece
was guarded by the hazards already described, to which it was usual
to make the short crossing by rowing in a little boat. Jason, then,
220 coming to the neighboring shore, entered the boat after he had put
his protecting armor into it, and by means of oars placed in it,

crossed the strait from that place to the previously mentioned small island, alone and burning with hope for victory. As soon as he had touched land there, he immediately sprang forth from the boat, and,
225 taking from it his weapons and the things Medea had presented him for his safety, he immediately put on his armor, and with confident steps proceeded toward the ram with the golden fleece. Medea, shaken by sighs from her trembling heart, went into the upper regions of the palace, and directing herself toward the more lofty places, watched
230 from the highest tower, from which she carefully observed the crossing of her beloved, and even more carefully, his landing on the island. When she saw that he had taken his weapons, and was painstakingly, as she thought, prepared for the journey, she burst forth in floods of tears, by which the signs of love are indicated. Not
235 being strong enough to restrain herself from sobbing and speaking, she broke into speech in these faint words, with a slight sound and with tears flowing copiously: "Oh, dear Jason, with what anxiety am I troubled for you, with how many griefs am I tormented inwardly and outwardly, while I fear that you, being overcome by terror, will
240 completely forget my advice and will neglect the necessary instructions for your safety given to you by me! If you do this, it is not without reason that I fear not what might happen to you and to me, but rather that greatest evil, which is that I shall be forever separated from your embraces. However, I beg the gods humbly that my eyes
245 may see you actually brought back unharmed, and that I may be made completely happy by the favorable results of your deeds."

In the meantime, however, Jason took his way at a cautious pace toward the guardians of the ram. After he came to the place of Mars, he saw at once that the bulls sent forth flames so scorching and so
250 diffused in the air that the whole sky nearby was reddened by the glowing heat of the fire. Indeed the intensity of the heat and flame filled the whole place, so that because of his excessive fear of the heat, Jason could see no clear way of getting at those bulls. However, being reminded of the beneficial advice of his beloved, he anointed
255 his face, neck, hands, and all the parts of his body he could with the ointment given him by Medea. He also guarded against the flames with the image prescribed by her, which was hanging from his neck, and when he had read over the inscription as many times as we have already said it was to be read, he dared to approach the bulls

260 themselves and determined to enter battle with them. And then, since
     they spewed forth their flames at Jason incessantly, his shield was
     consumed by the flames, and his lance, devoured by the crackling
     fire, went up in clouds of smoke. Indeed, Jason would have ended his
     life in the midst of fire had he not, with repeated doses, poured the
265 liquid given him into the mouths of the bulls, and by this dosing, the
     mouths of the smoke-breathing bulls were chained as if by iron bars
     and were indivisibly bound together as if with a fastening of sticky
     glue. Then and there the emitting of flames ceased, and then and
     there the deadly fiery vomit of the bulls was swallowed up. When the
270 flames had vanished and the air was restored to the fall of its natural
     moisture, Jason grew stronger, and filled with great boldness,
     stretched out his powerful hands toward the horns of the stupefied
     bulls. By means of the horns he had seized, he tried to lead the bulls
     around here and there so he might feel if they would struggle against
275 him recalcitrantly, or if, made docile to his command, they would
     obey him meekly. They, just as if they were dispirited, were obedient
     to his will and did not attempt to arise in the stubborn rebellion of
     resistance. For this reason, Jason, with the task made safe, placed on
     their shoulders the yoke and [attached] the plow which had been
280 joined to the yoke by fastening, and hitched them, and compelled
     those bulls to plow by pricking them with a goad, and they did not
     struggle against the command of the plowman. Thus, when the soil
     had been turned, the wide field was dug up into many little hollows,
     with many furrows running both ways forming these hollows. Leaving
285 the bulls in the plowed field, Jason speedily and boldly advanced
     toward the dragon. After the dragon had seen him coming, with
     much hissing in the sounds of its dreadful voice, it made the
     resounding air echo in similar sounds, and emitting smoky flames in
     frequent puffs, it colored the neighboring air with hot and glowing
290 redness, and while it flashed its tongue in and out in quick succession,
     it poured forth deadly venom in rainlike sprinklings. The intrepid
     Jason, however, turning himself immediately to the prescribed
     teaching of Medea, held the ring with the green stone which he had
     received from Medea up to the eyes of the dragon. Stupefied by its
295 light, the dragon ceased to spit forth flames, and writhing its head
     and neck around here and there as if it were dispirited, tried to avoid
     the blazing light of the stone because it was stupefied. As Isidore

writes, this stone, which we commonly call the emerald, is found in India. The virtue of this stone without doubt is that when it is held
300 toward the eyes of any poisonous animal, whether a serpent or an animal like it, or that which is commonly called a toad in Sicily, if it is held unwaveringly toward its face with some staff or rod, the poisonous animal will not be able to endure for more than an hour that it be not removed from its sight, and will already have been
305 killed. The stone itself does not come off free from damage, since, when the poisonous animal toward which it was held is dead, it will be shattered completely into little pieces. When this dragon was fatally stunned by the green ray, the undaunted Jason immediately attacked it with his naked sword and piled blows on frequent blows,
310 which clashed harmlessly on the hard scales of the dragon. The unwearied Jason, like a heavy hammer on an anvil, did not on account of this cease from the blows, and fought for such a long time with renewed blows that the dragon, not strong enough to endure the frequent and hard force of them, stretched out along the field and
315 breathed its last in a deadly exhalation which infected the surrounding atmosphere with deadly poison. After Jason saw it was dead, he recalled the directions of Medea to his own memory; he swiftly approached and severed the head from the neck with his death-dealing blade. When he had plucked the teeth from its jaws, he planted them
320 evenly in the furrows made a while ago in the field plowed by the bulls. At once, strange soldiers were born from this seed, and as soon as the soldiers were produced from such a crop, they sought arms at once and then rushed upon each other and fought among themselves, inflicting deadly wounds. A fierce and confused battle was waged
325 among the earthborn brothers, since they did not rush to war in distinct battle lines and did not attack one another in troops; instead, with violent looks, each struggled to slay the other, although there would be no one at the end who would appear as victor, and although they fell, slain by one another with many reciprocal
330 wounds. Thus, when the works of craft had been completely wiped out by the opposing enchantments of magic art, and the dragon had been given over to death, and the brothers born from the seed of its teeth had died, and those bulls had been made as if half dead, Jason, snatched from the risk of danger from them, examined in his mind
335 with scrupulous care those things which were done, and then he

considered earnestly whatever remained to be done in the completion
of the tasks. When he perceived that everything has already been done,
he boldly and gaily directed himself with unhurried steps toward the
ram with the golden fleece. He found in it no boldness or rebellion,
340 and when he had seized it by the horns, he slaughtered it and
despoiled it of its golden covering, giving thanks to the gods from
whom he had attained the Golden Fleece with glory and victory, and
without the loss of his life.

Thus, Jason, enriched with the golden plunder, hastened joyfully
345 to the shore of the island, entered the boat, and, by use of the oars,
went to the larger island. On its shore, Hercules and his companions
were waiting for him very eagerly. They received him with great
gladness when he landed and humbly gave thanks to the gods for his
preservation, since they had thought never to have had him back
350 unharmed. Jason, however, went with his men to the palace of King
Aeëtes. And when Jason reached him, King Aeëtes received him with
feigned pleasure. For he was envious of such a victory and grieved to
be despoiled of such riches. Aeëtes ordered him to sit next to him
because he wished the crowd to see the spectacle of the Golden
355 Fleece. The crowd wondered at the appearance of that fleece, but
what they admired even more about the great victory of Jason was
how he had been able to overthrow what had been ordained by the
god Mars.

Medea, overjoyed by the favorable outcome, finally approached to
360 see Jason. Although, if she could have, she would have given him the
pleasant reward of many kisses in the sight of all these people, yet at
the command of the king she sat next to Jason as if full of shyness.
Medea told him in secret words in a soft tone of voice that he might
approach her safely in the coming seclusion of night. Jason answered
365 in a humble and low voice that he would do this very eagerly. Therefore, when the shadows of night had completely covered the whole
earth, Jason arrived at the chamber of Medea; he entered the bed at
her invitation and when they were both settled in bed as they wished,
after much enjoyment and pleasure they at length, with one accord,
370 began talking to each other about their departure together and about
the preparation of many things for the departure. Thus at the
persuasion of Medea, Jason lingered in Colchis the space of one
month. At last, having seized the opportunity of the moment, Jason

and his companions departed secretly from that island with Medea,
375 without seeking permission from King Aeëtes.

Yet, O Medea, you are said to have wished very much for the
breath of favorable winds so that you might leave your country and
flee parental control, and cross the sea intrepidly, not perceiving that
you risked bitter misfortune. You are said to have arrived in Thessaly
380 where, on account of Thessalian Jason you are described as having
finished your life with an obscure death, despised by the Thessalian
citizens, after many detestable adventures. Jason, however, was
exposed to great suffering on account of the vengeance of the gods
before he died, and his demise, since it was, so to speak, damned by
385 the gods, was concluded by a damnable death. Say, what did it profit
you that Jason incurred such monstrous losses; say, what did it profit
you that the harsh revenge and reprisal of the gods afterward pursued
him? Indeed it is commonly said that it is useless to apply the
remedies of medicinal herbs to the nostrils of a dead animal. Unless
390 perchance it pleases the gods not to demand satisfaction for an
offense except so that mortals may realize that the gods do not wish
serious faults to pass by in the sight of living men without retribution
and punishment.

Need I say more? Jason with Hercules and the others of their
395 companions landed safe and happy with Medea in the port of
Thessaly. King Peleus, inwardly dismayed at the safety of Jason,
nevertheless hid the anguish of his heart and received them all with a
smiling face, and he freely, albeit unwillingly, did not refuse to give
Jason command over his kingdom, according to the promise he had
400 already made.

Jason, not indeed unmindful of the blame incurred by King
Laomedon, cared little that he had the great and glorious victory of
the Golden Fleece, and even put off ungratefully whatever he ought
to have done according to his promise with regard to Medea, and not
405 content with the command of the kingdom of Thessaly, roused his
troubled heart to revenge and reprisal against King Laomedon. For
this reason, when he had taken much counsel with Hercules concerning these things, Hercules took on the burden, so to speak, of the
whole business. So it was that Jason and Hercules explained to King
410 Peleus and the other Greek kings that the affront to their feelings
inflicted by the Trojan king was common not only to them but also

to the princes of Greece. In the same way they asked them to dare
to undertake the vengeance for this affront, so that, in the carrying
out of this great business, they might donate whatever help and aid
415 they could. The kings and dukes of Greece did not, therefore, refuse
the promise of help, and they all unanimously approved seeking
vengeance for the acts committed by that king.

*Here begins the fourth book, about the first destruction of
Troy by Jason and Hercules.*

Hercules, however, who, as it has been said, had taken on the entire
burden of this enterprise, wishing to be a faithful servant and a careful agent in the business, speeded up his rapid journey toward Sparta
without stopping to rest. Sparta was one of the provinces among
5 those belonging to Romania, which had been made a kingdom. Two
brother kings were ruling in it, who were called, according to their
proper designations, the one Castor and the other Pollux. It is stated
dogmatically by the poets that these brothers were the sons of
Jupiter, borne to him by Danaë, loveliest of women, who, they allege,
10 also bore Helen, who is thus the sister of these kings. In connection
with the birth of this Helen, the poets fictitiously claim that Jupiter
lay with the aforesaid Danaë in the likeness of an egg. For this reason
someone stated "Jupiter said, 'I exult because Tyndaris came from
an egg,' " calling the same Helen, Tyndaris, from a certain place which
15 was called Tyndaris. Some say this place is in Sicily, on the northern
coast, opposite the Aeolian Islands, not very far from the city of
Messina. The said poets have stated Theseus carried this Helen to this
place when he stole her from her own country while she was as yet
blooming in the freshness of youth. For this reason Ovid, in the
20 Epistle of Canace, thus reproaches Paris: "The Tyndarid by an enemy,"
and so forth, and he adds afterward, "Is it to be thought she was
rendered back a maid, by a young man and eager?" and so forth.
Hercules thus approached these brother kings, Castor and Pollux,
earnestly entreating them and advising them not to delay advancing
25 mightily with him in a mighty force in retaliation for the insults of
the Trojan king. These kings, in extremely affectionate words and
with an unfeigned good will, agreed to the foregoing arrangements of

Hercules. When Hercules had taken a pleasant leave of the two
brother kings, he hastened to Salamis. For Salamis was a province
30 which had been made a kingdom from the possessions of Greece
itself, or the parts of Romania, in which King Telamon was then
reigning, a man of especially great valor and boldness in war. When
Hercules reached him, he was received with great pleasure by him.
Hercules then urged him with words of entreaty to condescend to
35 come to overthrow King Laomedon with him and with the other
Greek kings who had promised to attack Troy with him. King
Telamon, agreeing to the words of Hercules, promised to come to
Troy with him and the other dukes that very moment. Hercules,
leaving him, went back to Peleus, whom he urged with prayers and
40 encouraged to advise whichever of the greatest men of his kingdom
he could to attack Troy with the already mentioned kings and himself.
As soon as Hercules had easily enough obtained aid from him, he left
him and turned in haste toward Pylos. Pylos was one of those
provinces within the boundaries of Greece itself; over it Duke Nestor
45 held effective sway. When Hercules had explained to him the reason
for his arrival, Nestor agreed that he would certainly be delighted to
go with him in the troop of his soldiers. Duke Nestor had then for a
long time been joined by the affectionate love of intimate friendship
to Hercules, and he for this reason the more graciously and easily
50 agreed to his words. Leaving him, Hercules again came to Peleus, who
had already prepared himself for the journey with twenty ships laden
with soldiers, and the aforesaid kings had then come together into
the port of Thessaly so that they might from thence together set sail
safely, the gods willing.
55   It was the time when the aging sun in its oblique circle of the
zodiac had already entered into the sign of Aries, in which the equal
length of nights and days is celebrated in the equinox of spring; when
the weather begins to entice eager mortals into the pleasant air; when
the ice has melted, and the breezes ripple the flowing streams; when
60 the springs gush forth in fragile bubbles; when moistures exhaled
from the bosom of the earth are raised up to the tops of the trees
and branches, for which reason the seeds sprout, the crops grow, and
the meadows bloom, embellished with flowers of various colors; when
the trees on every side are decked with renewed leaves; when earth is
65 adorned with grass, and the birds sing and twitter in music of sweet

harmony. Then almost the middle of the month of April had passed
when the sea, made calm after its fierce heaving had subsided, had
already calmed the waves. Then the aforesaid kings, Jason and
Hercules, left port with their ships, cut through the seas with sails
70 spread to the gusts of the spring wind, and sailed nights and days
together until they arrived at the wished-for shores of the Trojan
kingdom. They entered a port called by its proper designation Sigeum.
When they had touched at the aforesaid port, the sun, encroached
upon by the neighboring shadow of night, was already inclining
75 toward evening. After they had cast the firm anchors into the depths
of the sea, the ships rested, strongly fastened by them, and the sailors
in the ships made arrangements concerning future procedures in the
safest way they could. Then when the shadows of night were
dispersed over the circle of the earth in the first coming of that night,
80 the moon with a little light rose from its place of origin, and when it
had risen in its course above the face of the earth, it made a false day
in the middle of the night with its counterfeit glow. Hence it was
that, encouraged by the glow of its light, the Greeks descended to
earth in fitting order, which was indeed easy for them, since they
85 found the Trojan coasts without a guard, because the Trojan king was
not expecting the attack of any enemy. And so they led their horses
from the ships, placed their arms on land, constructed tents and
raised them, and established watches and necessary guards on all sides.
   Before the sun had shed true day upon the earth, King Peleus
90 ordered the other kings, as well as Jason and Hercules and the other
officers of the army, to come to his tent. When they had come and
had taken their places, King Peleus, after he had held up his hand for
silence, spoke to them in these words and made a speech: "O men,
distinguished for so much valor, the whole earth knows the force of
95 your courage, demonstrated in all parts of the world. It is nowhere
heard or said that you have not gained the triumph of victory over
whomever you attacked with force. King Laomedon's unjust offenses
have indeed given us just cause to penetrate the boundaries of his
country. Since it has pleased the gods to have had us land for the
100 purpose of defeating the king, it is necessary that we apply our
attention to three things principally. The first thing is that we should
take every precaution for the defense of our persons against our
enemies, so that we may attain every possible safeguard against them.

The second is that we should manfully gather forces for the purpose
105 of injuring these enemies of ours and destroying them. The third is
that we are to strive with all our strength to achieve victory over our
enemies. From this last, two fortunate things will proceed for us in
the end, the gods being favorable; that is, we will attain clear and full
satisfaction for the wrongs done and also the rewards of the countless
110 riches which we expect when we have conquered these enemies. For
it is known to everyone that the whole city of Troy abounds in
countless riches, and if, by the favor of fortune, we will be able to
bring it to subjection through the palm of victory, I do not think our
ships will be large enough for the troops and their burdens. It remains
115 then, concerning the rest, that we consider every single thing by
which we may arrive quickly and safely at the accomplishment of our
wishes—may the holy gods favorably grant this and offer their aid."

After King Peleus had brought his speech to an end, Hercules was
first among the others in speaking, and, anticipating the responses of
120 the others, thus replied to the speech of the king: "You are to be
praised, O king, and the remarks which have been put forth by you
to our common hearing are also to be praised. If it is praiseworthy to
devise praiseworthy plans concerning our present task, it is still more
praiseworthy to put what has been devised into effect with urgency.
125 Accordingly, with regard to a safe plan which will be better for our
safety and our obtaining a victory over our enemies, it seems a good
idea to me that all our men and our whole people should be divided
into two equal parts immediately, before the day comes, which will
betray our coming with its light. In one of these parts will be King
130 Telamon with all his people, and also you yourself, Lord King, with
all yours, and also Jason and I, with our companies joined to us, so
that we may at once, under the silence of night, advance toward the
outskirts of the city of Troy, with its copses, groves, and adjacent
vineyards. There, secretly in our hiding places, we will wait for the
135 light of day, at which time, when notice of our arrival has been given
King Laomedon, he will arrange to attack our ships with his army,
not knowing that we are hidden around the walls of his city. Now,
when he has advanced to the ships with his soldiers, so that the
barriers of his powerful defense lie open to us, let three battle lines
140 be formed from the rest of our people. Let Nestor command the first
of them in a troop of his men, King Castor the second, and King

Pollux the third, and let them hold out manfully against King
Laomedon in this place on the shore where we are now. We who will
be in secret hiding places, as I have already said, will advance to the
145 city and thus, since Laomedon and his army will have been placed
between our forces, he will the more easily pay the penalty. For I do
not believe that the attaining of our desires and wishes can be done
more quickly by safer means."

The advice of Hercules satisfied everyone in attendance, and all
150 approved unanimously what was ordered for carrying it out. King
Telamon, King Peleus, Jason, and Hercules, in a troop of their men,
soon mounted their horses, and, supported by a band of armed men
ready for war, they disposed themselves, under the silence of night, in
silent ambushes by means of hiding places around the walls of the
155 city of Troy, while the rest of them remained on the shore, so that
they might spring to arms as an effective obstacle to King Laomedon
when he came. When the rays of the sun illuminated the earth, and
morning had been made by the coming dawn which erased the
shadows of night from the face of the earth, the ears of King
160 Laomedon were filled with the tumultuous tale of the arrival of the
Greeks. On account of this thing, he ordered all his soldiers, and
other citizens who in the flower of youth did not fear to turn to war
and arms, to seize their arms. When the phalanxes of armed men had
been formed by the king himself, he came and arranged the many
165 companies into battle formation. Without anticipating the wiles of the
enemies and the ambushes near the city, he hastened to the shore
with the whole task force of his men. Then the Greeks who were
waiting on the shore, seeing the army of armed men converging upon
them in a great attack, boldly prepared for battle, since they were
170 not confused by surprise.

Duke Nestor first advanced, taking himself and his men to the
pitched battle. When the bitter fighting had begun on both sides, one
side rushed eagerly against the other, and the other side joined the
fray in a dreadful attack. The crashing noise from the breaking of
175 spears was very great. Shields were pierced and helmets were torn off,
and a great clanging from repeated blows of swords sounded in the
air; knights fell, some wounded, others dead. The slaughter was very
great on all sides. The earth was reddened and stained with blood. At
length the Trojan multitude prevailed, when Duke Nestor, alone with

180 his single company, sustained the loss of the contest. King Castor,
that valiant man, at once entered the battle with a multitude of
armed men and manfully attacked the Trojans. At his entrance, the
battle was renewed. The clamor was very great; the Trojans fell,
because they were not strong enough to sustain the new attack. But
185 King Laomedon, like a roaring lion, rushed up swiftly; he did many
deeds of valor in his own person and killed some, wounded some, and
cut some to pieces, and he strove with all eagerness to attack the
Greeks and defend his men. The Trojans, careless of their lives,
rushing in impetuously to defeat the Greeks, pursued the Greeks with
190 deadly wounds. They exposed many of them to death, and while
they were trying recklessly to kill others, some of them fell in speedy
death. Then King Pollux, since he had observed the fluctuations of
the battle, and had seen from afar that the Trojans were prevailing
over his Greeks, furiously entered the battle with a column of his
195 men and rushed savagely upon the Trojans, and he killed many and
threw others wounded from their horses. King Laomedon, retreating
a little from the battle because he saw his men were fighting half-
heartedly, and because many of his men had fallen in battle, feared
the misfortune of a greater loss to himself, and therefore, because of
200 their threats and prayers, caused all of his men to retreat a little, and,
as it were, reduced to a single unit all those who had been brought
together. Meanwhile, indeed, Duke Nestor had fixed his gaze upon
King Laomedon, and he realized he was the king and prince of the
Trojans. Therefore when he had put aside all other concerns, he
205 turned his horse toward this king, and, in a swift charge, hurled
himself impetuously against this same king. But since King Laomedon
sensed that he was rushing at him, he intrepidly turned the reins of
his horse toward Nestor, and, both urging on their horses with spurs,
they both came rushing together. King Laomedon, however, broke
210 the shaft of the spear which he was carrying in his hand against
Nestor, and Nestor would indubitably have been mortally wounded
by the blow of this spear if he had not preserved himself from harm
by the protection of his trusty armor. Nestor did not thrust at
Laomedon with his spear in the same way. Instead, throwing it
215 manfully against the king himself, he cleft his shield in two parts. The
king, severely wounded by this blow, fell from his horse and landed
prostrate on the ground. Then King Laomedon, neither dazed by the

fall nor frightened by the wound, immediately raised himself from
the ground, and, with his unsheathed sword, boldly and aggressively
220 went for Nestor on foot. A certain young knight named Cedar, who
had just that very year been made a new knight, as a faithful subject
to his lord felt shame for his lord when he saw King Laomedon
battling on foot in such great peril, and urged his horse in a charge
against Nestor. When he thrust at Nestor aggressively with his lance,
225 he struck him on the chest, and by attacking him manfully, he threw
him down from his horse right at the feet of his king. The king,
indeed, when he saw Nestor before him prostrate on the ground,
attacked him with an attack of great force, and assailed his helmet
with repeated blows with his bare sword. He broke the crown of the
230 helmet and shattered the nosepiece completely and wounded him
badly in the face. Nestor had actually fallen, cut down by
Laomedon's right hand, while, weak from wounds and with a
fountain of his blood flowing uninterruptedly, he was powerless to
protect himself; but a multitude of Greeks ran to his assistance and
235 attacked King Laomedon. Although many of the Greeks then fell
dead, still while they were resisting, Nestor, as soon as he had been
pulled from under the feet of the horses and removed from
Laomedon's hands, mounted his horse. King Castor, however, while
he was fighting in the midst of the struggling men, saw Nestor thrown
240 from his horse by Cedar. Desiring to take vengeance on him, with
slackened reins he made his way furiously toward him. Before Castor
could reach Cedar in his charge, a certain Trojan named Seguridan,
closely connected to the same Cedar by the ties of consanguinity,
thrust himself completely between the two, and when he had made
245 an attack on Castor, Seguridan broke his lance against him without
any harm to Castor. Then, indeed, King Castor attacked this same
Seguridan bravely with his spear and pierced his side with a mortal
wound.

Cedar, however, when he saw Seguridan, his first cousin, wounded,
250 was filled with fury and hurled himself against Castor, hoping to
avenge him with his naked sword. He attacked him forcefully, and
by violence wrested his shield away from him. For this reason, when
he had removed the visor of Castor's helmet, he struck him in the
face with deadly intent, so that, attacking him forcefully, he threw
255 him from his horse. He violently snatched Castor's horse away from

him and gave it to his squire to keep, and, launching insulting words
at Castor, he reproached him for wounding his first cousin. Castor,
however, while he was on foot and the Trojans were exerting themselves to intercept him, defended himself against the Trojans with
260 considerable boldness. Since, however, he was waging war alone
among so many, he was powerless to resist, and would have been
captured by the enemy if King Pollux had not raced to his aid with
the greatest speed, accompanied by seven hundred valiant Greek
knights. With his knights he made an attack against those who were
265 trying to surround King Castor, broke the line by fighting with great
courage, freed his brother, and gave him someone else's horse. Pollux,
roused to flaming rage, hurled himself with all his strength against a
certain Trojan named Elyacus whom he first found before him. Now
this was that Elyacus, the son of the king of Carthage, King
270 Laomedon's nephew, the eldest son of his sister. While Pollux was
pursuing him in a fierce attack, he wounded him mortally so that he
fell down dead from that wound, in the sight of King Laomedon.
Then King Laomedon burst into floods of tears, miserably bewailing
the fall of his nephew. In pain and deep anguish, he called together
275 his whole army, which he urged by doleful tears to make a powerful
attack in reprisal for the death of his nephew. Then, when he had
sounded a blast on his horn, about seven thousand knights advanced
to the king at the sound of the horn. When they had made the attack
against the Greeks, they valiantly assaulted them, killed, wounded,
280 and slew them cruelly at the point of the sword so that they turned
disgracefully in flight. The Trojans pursued them all the way to their
ships on the shore.

Then King Laomedon might have been granted victory and the end
of the war, but a certain Trojan named Dotes, mortally wounded,
285 hardly able to move, came to the king from the city of Troy. In
doleful words and with anguished sobs he revealed to him the fall of
his city, asserting that his city of Troy had been cut off by his
enemies. When King Laomedon heard this, he heaved anxious sighs
from the depths of his heart, and, calling his people toward him by
290 the sound of his horn and abandoning the already conquered Greeks
on the shore, he hastened his steps toward the city. King Laomedon
had then not yet advanced far in the troop of his armed men when,
looking from a distance, he saw a great part of his enemies had

marched out of the city and were hastening toward him in armed
295   phalanxes. Likewise he saw behind him that the Greeks, whom he had
already more or less conquered on the shore, were hastening against
him with renewed spirit and the greatest haste. He was bewildered
and did not know what to do between these two forces, since he
perceived he was in the midst of his enemies and hemmed in on all
300   sides. Need I say more? A very bitter battle was begun between the
two, and the unequal contest between them raged hotly, for the
Greeks exceeded the Trojans by a greater number. The Trojans fell
and were slaughtered by numerous blows of swords. That valiant
man, Hercules, as brave as he was bold, arrived without delay, and he,
305   sitting on his bold steed, pressing on with death-dealing wounds,
broke the line and the phalanxes and dispersed the adversaries. On
account of his might, the enemy, since they were unable to resist him
or withstand his strength, opened the way for him through the
troops, since on all sides they died before him and fell down dead.
310   Finally he turned himself in a furious attack against King Laomedon,
who presented himself to him fearlessly. Hercules cut off Laomedon's
advance violently and killed him as he stopped him, and when he had
cut off his head, he hurled it with violent rage into the midst of his
own men. After the Trojans had seen this, they wept for themselves
315   because they were deprived of their king's guidance, and they had no
hope of returning to their city, nor did they expect with any hope to
be able to flee for the sake of defense to any other place. Then
bodies of Trojans fell here and there, and the conquered Trojans left
the field, striving for the protection of flight. If there were any of
320   them whom the protection of a long flight could save, they were able
perhaps to flee the hands of the Greeks, though the rest succumbed
in the mortal combat, and through the blows of swords, the mortal
combat came to an end.
        Then the Greek victors with their victorious arms entered the city
325   they had longed for and found it only half full of women, children,
and old men, fleeing in fear of death to the temples of the gods.
Many of those women, miserably bewildered, fled here and there,
carrying their children in their trembling arms. Frightened girls,
wandering here and there, did not know where to go for their safety
330   after they had left their homes, full of countless treasure, which all
the conquering Greeks were seizing, despoiling, and plundering. The

Greeks were doing this with the greatest ease, since they were at their leisure to plunder for the space of one whole month. Finally, indeed, when they had pulled down the high walls of the city itself, they
335 destroyed the lofty palace and indiscriminately delivered the towering buildings to calamitous ruin. They destroyed everything completely, and when they had looted all the temples of the city in the manner of pirates, and delivered to the cruelest death whomever they found fleeing from them, old men and children indiscriminately, and when
340 they had delivered the buildings of the temples to ruin, they led away the young and beautiful girls they found as captive brides and conducted them to their ships, leading them into perpetual servitude.

As they rushed into the palace of King Laomedon before they had destroyed it completely, on the very threshold of the donjon they
345 found Hesione, a young woman of marvelous beauty, the daughter of the said king—would that she had never been found or born! Hercules gave her to King Telamon as the reward of victory, for the reason that the same King Telamon was the first to enter that city as victor. But, oh, the marvelous ingratitude of the victor if the palm of victory
350 joined Hesione to you! Noble gratitude ought to have joined her to you, so that you would have joined to you in the union of the marriage torch such a very noble maiden of such beauty, who was lovely of face and formed with all beauty of character, and you would not have wrongly dishonored her on account of the shameful
355 passion of lust when you made her your concubine, she who did not deserve this and who could hardly have been given to you in lawful marriage. For from this Hesione proceeded the whole substance of the raging madness from which afterward the greatest causes of war proceeded, after they had been nourished for a long time, and from
360 which irreparable losses followed. When the city of Troy had been completely destroyed, as has just been said, the Greeks, with all the goods they had taken from it, got aboard their ships. They left the Trojan shore and committed themselves to the open sea, with sails spread for easy rowing, and returned safe and victorious to Greece.
365 Thus all Greece exulted with exceeding joy at the victory of these Greeks and at the acquisition of so many goods, and since they were grateful for all these things, they rendered up sacrifices and offerings to appease the gods. Greece, completely filled with the spoils of the Trojans, was made rich. Now that the victors had been enriched,

370 those who were then in that time their heirs were wealthy for a long
     time afterward because of the unfailing riches from that source.

*Here begins the fifth book, about the building of the great
Troy founded by King Priam.*

Since the city of Troy was completely destroyed and demolished, and
Laomedon the king was miserably killed, and so many knights and
noble citizens were delivered over to death, and so many women and
girls were led away under the yoke of servitude, and the noble
5 Hesione, the daughter of that king, was made a harlot subject to the
lust of Telamon, farseeing men should therefore earnestly consider
that such are the unforeseen results of actions in this world. For this
reason it is necessary that men refrain from trivial and even slight
offenses. For slight injuries quite frequently tend to be like fire,
10 whose little spark, nourished with hidden sustenance, suddenly bursts
out from under the ashes into very great, searing flames. Kings and
princes should also learn not to oppose foreigners who come to their
kingdom and are not motivated by any evil intent to look into the
secrets of their kingdoms. For the envious course of the fates, the
15 enemy of happiness, always prevents the highest things from remaining on the heights for very long, and in order to bring the condition
of men more easily to ruin, it attacks the mighty, through unper-
ceived and obscure snares, and leads them to misfortune, taking its
cause from trivial and unthought-of matters, so that by using
20 foresight and with the aid of caution they are not able to protect
themselves. And so, when the first Troy was destroyed by the fates
acting under this pretext, such was the very unfortunate end of the
very noble King Laomedon. But oh, would that his end had been the
end and final incursion of such great disaster, seeing that, because of
25 so slight a provocation as was King Laomedon's denying the briefest
hospitality on the desolate shore of his country to the Greeks, who
were sailing to another place, he brought upon himself the penalty of
death in retaliation for such a crime (if it can be called a crime);
besides, the foremost people of his kingdom were given over to death
30 and his own daughter was carried away into foreign regions under the
disgrace of base harlotry! But that envious dispenser of men's fates

can cause tares to grow from the slightest sliver of a root. While she
begins her approach secretly and stealthily, later a huge amount of
evil follows, until a most wretched conclusion follows, and her final
35 departure is rounded off by perpetual losses. Hence it is that our
times do not fail to record faithfully what a great mass of evils
followed the preceding evils, until that most noble and marvelous
great Troy which was founded later, after the overthrow of the first
Troy, was soon completely overthrown, and so many kings, so many
40 princes, and so many thousands of men were swallowed up by death
in battle, all because the capture of Hesione, who was still alive,
remained in living memory. Our pen is directed to telling the things
that happened to her and to them, one at a time and in their order.

King Laomedon had a certain son, borne to him by the queen, his
45 wife. His name was Priam, a man of great valor and distinguished on
account of his very wise counsel. At the time of his father's death, he
was not present in Troy, since for many days just past he had been
on a military expedition in remote territories, engaging in battle with
certain of his own and his father's enemies. At the time when the
50 Greeks were attacking Troy, he had, in a long siege, confined a castle
which had rebelled against him, and, prolonging that siege in the hope
of victory, he passed the time with his wife and children, waiting
anxiously for the capture of this castle. He had as wife a very noble
lady named Hecuba, who had borne him five sons and three
55 daughters. The first of his sons was called Hector, a knight of
unheard-of valor, aggressive and courageous, whose many virtuous
deeds are honored in continued remembrance and will, not without
cause, be recounted for a long time, The second son was named Paris,
also called Alexander, the most handsome of all young men, skilled
60 above all others in the mastery of bow and arrows. The third was
named Deiphobus, a valiant man, distinguished by the great intelligence of his counsels. The fourth was named Helenus, a man of great
knowledge, for he was learned in the teachings of all sciences. The
fifth and last was named Troilus, a young man as courageous as
65 possible in war, about whose valor there are many tales which the
present history does not omit later on. The first of the daughters was
named Creusa. She is supposed to have been the wife of Aeneas.
Anchises had this Aeneas by Venus, and the present history will
relate many things about him, and Virgil wrote about him after the

70 fall of great Troy in his work the *Aeneid*. The second was named
    Cassandra, who, although she excelled in womanly virtue, excelled
    more in liberal arts, being familiar with them and having knowledge
    of the future. And the third and last was named Polyxena, a girl of
    amazing beauty and immense charm. In addition King Priam had
75 thirty natural sons, borne to him by several different women. These
    men were distinguished by the rank of knighthood and were very
    brave warriors. They are: Odinal, Antonius, Exdron, Deluris,
    Sinsilenus, Quintilienus. Modenius, Cassibilans, Dinadaron, Dorascarus,
    Pythagorus, Cicinalor, Eliastras, Menelaus, Isidorus, Carras,
80 Celidomas, Emargoras, Madian, Sardus, Margariton, Achilles, Fanuel,
    Brunus, Mathan, Almadian, Dulces, Godelaus, Duglas, and Cador de
    Insulis.
        And so while King Priam with his wife and all his children was
    occupying himself with the war and the siege of this castle, the
85 dreadful rumor reached him that his father, Laomedon, had been
    killed by the Greeks, Troy surrounded and completely destroyed, the
    nobles killed, and his sister Hesione led away into exile and servitude.
    Priam was stunned at the report of such rumors and was torn by
    excessive grief, and leading a life of tears and continuous weeping,
90 poured forth and heaped up in mourning anguished laments with
    words of grief; on the spot he dissolved his whole army, put an end
    to the war, left the camp of the besieged castle, and hastened with
    rapid steps toward Troy. When he saw it completely overthrown and
    levelled to the ground, he wept as he regarded his own irreparable
95 loss and that of his people, and he continued his mourning for three
    days. But at last when the storms of flowing tears had subsided, and
    the peace of satisfaction had, so to speak, been restored to his bitter
    heart, and when he had put aside groans and laments, after consider-
    ing the plan for a long time, it suited him to rebuild conquered Troy.
100 He ordered that it be built of such size and strength that it would
    fear no hostile attacks and it would truly be able to maintain a
    stubborn defense against an attack of its enemies. Hence it was that
    when he had procured laborers from all sides, experts in the arts of
    building, carvers of marble, workers in stone, and very skilled
105 architects of all kinds, he ordered them to raise up blocks of marble
    which were amazingly differentiated in diverse ways by their ingrained
    colors. When they had removed the debris and cleared the ruins from

the place where the first Troy had been located, in the name of the
god Neptune he built a city of amazing length and breadth, which he
110 insisted should be called by the same name, Troy.

Moreover, it took three days to go the length of this second Troy,
and the width the same. Neither before nor after its foundation is it
read that there had been built a city of such size, of such beauty, or
of a similar appearance. For its foundations were established in the
115 depths of the earth, made with deep excavation and ample width.
From the surface of the earth up to top of the city, the ramparts
were built up in an amazing arrangement of walls two hundred cubits
high on all sides. The surface was inlaid with marble stones of many
different colors, so that they pleased the sight of those gazing at
120 them. On the crown of these encircling walls, there were towers, one
not far distant from the next, which rose high above and overhung
the walls. Entrance to and exit from this city was provided for by
six gates, the first of which was called the Dardanian, the second the
Thymbraean, the third the Ilian, the fourth the Scaean, the fifth the
125 Trojan, the sixth the Antenorean. Each of these gates was fortified by
strong towers along the sides and adorned with carvings of marble
images on all sides. Each of these permitted peaceful entrance to
friends wishing to enter and threatened the fierce and bold attacks of
proud resistance to any enemies. The outer side of these walls was
130 also protected along the circumference by a deep trench with hidden
pitfalls, and a broad plain widened the distance between the trench
and those walls.

Within the city itself, countless palaces were built, and in it,
countless homes for citizens were formed by means of handsome
135 buildings which adorned that city along the extent of its many
avenues. They assert it as a fact that no house, no lodging in the city
of Troy, was constructed whose topmost part was not raised at least
sixty cubits in height above the ground, and all reinforced with
marble stones marvelously carved with images of beasts and men. Its
140 avenues extended in a long and straight line, in the midst of which
the brisk and invigorating air of dawn poured forth sweet and varied
breezes. Along the sides of these avenues, because there had been
erected countless vaulted arches on marble columns, a free passage
which had been made under the shelter of these arches was available
145 every day to pedestrians, so that as they walked they were not vexed

by the raging winds nor unwished-for drenchings from storms of rain
from the sky.

Along these avenues were located the special places of business, in
which workers, set apart in fixed locations, toiled in their daily labors
150 and trades. Here the architects dwelt, here painters, here makers of
statues, here workers in marble, here litter bearers stood, here dealers
in hounds, here carters, here joiners, here mule traders, here gilders of
plaster who painted statues and images in gold, here silversmiths,
here glaziers who made cups of glass, here workers in bronze, here
155 metalworkers who made metal bells, here designers who made seals,
here workmen who sewed shirts and breeches, here spindlemakers
who draw out spindles for women from iron on the anvil, here sellers
of measuring rods, here surveyors, here potters, here goldsmiths, here
workers with lead, here makers of windowpanes, here tanners, here
160 fullers, here wagonmakers, here carpenters, those, namely, who fitted
revolving wheels on carts, here burnishers of armor, here harness-
makers or rather *pantalargae* who place work of gilded bronze on
the reins, here trumpetmakers, here armorers, here *ginaeciarii* who
are called weavers, here geometers who divide the acres of farm land
165 by number, here dyers who dye linen and wool garments in many
colors, here bakers, here peddlers, here chandlers, here chapmen
whom we commonly call merchants, here *argyropratae*, that is,
sellers of money, and here are many others who ply petty trades for
money.

170   Through the middle of this city ran a river called Xanthus, which,
by dividing the city into two equal parts, in its unfailing course
offered many conveniences to the inhabitants of that city. For since
countless mills had been constructed on the bank, these mills in daily
use turned coarse-ground grain into fine flour for the sustenance of
175 the inhabitants. In addition, this river, flowing through hidden
channels on account of the requisite abundant supply of water,
purified the city by prearranged floods, by means of skillfully made
canals and underground sluices, and by these baths the accumulated
impurities were cleaned away. The Tiber at Rome was arranged like
180 this river, and as it burst forth in the midst of Rome, it divided into
two parts the city of Rome which was made in the likeness of Troy
by the Trojan Aeneas.

Then Priam ordered that people of all the neighboring kingdoms,

scattered throughout other cities and places, be gathered together to
185 inhabit the city of Troy. By this multitude the city was made
extremely populous, dignified by many nobles and on all sides filled
to capacity by the varied colonization of many commoners. They
established various kinds of various diversions in this city by means
of various inventions in it. In it the engrossing pleasures of chess were
190 first invented; there the games of dice which lead suddenly to
quarrels on account of the unexpected losses and momentary profits
of the little cubes. There they say tragedy and comedy were first
instituted, although some claim comedy was first devised on the
island of Sicily. There, it may be read, were devised circus games and
195 the May festivals, which took place customarily at the beginning of
the month of May, that is, at the beginning of spring, when the trees
were putting forth many shoots and the flowers were in the first
bloom of youth. There many other kinds of games were invented,
which usually soothe the souls of men and bring the delights of
200 pleasure before the faces of men, to gladden the minds of the
onlookers.

But King Priam, however, for the location of his dwelling and a
site for his own mansion ordered the great and famous Ilium, as his
great palace was called, to be constructed in a higher place of the
205 city out of the towering native rock in the city. And the master
fortress of great security which was hewn by force from this native
rock was glorious Ilium. From its foundation to the highest point
which roofed it over in the shape of a sphere, its height reached a
summit five hundred feet above the tops of the towers not far from
210 it on the ramparts, which were themselves far higher than that same
height. On account of their enormous height, the summits of its
towers were concealed by a cloak of clouds streaming by continually,
and from their very lofty summits the complete extent of adjacent
regions in the whole province, and even distant spots, could be
215 conveniently observed. The outer surface of this Ilium's walls, which
presented itself to the view of those gazing upon it, did not glitter
because some shining whitewash had perhaps been plastered over it,
but because it was completely veneered with slabs of marble,
decorated with a variety of colors, and carved with diverse figures
220 which gladdened the sight of those gazing. Not thus did heavy marble
work decorate its windows, since the largest part of them was

constructed of panes of shining crystal. Thus [were] the piers of
these windows, thus the capitals and bases. In the inner part of the
aforesaid palace, among other structures marvelously vaulted, King
225 Priam established a certain hall which was extremely long and
correspondingly broad, the outer surface of which was sheathed in
marble slabs; its vaulted ceiling was paneled with wood of cedar and
ebony, and diversified materials divided its floor of mosaic work into
different colors. The throne of the king was set up at the end of this
230 hall, where the royal table was located, stretched out in its great
length, completely constructed of delicate inlays of ivory and ebony.
On each side of the tables the long row of benches offered
comfortable seats to the dinner guests. At the other end of this hall
there was an altar of amazing artistry, covered with jewels and gold,
235 and raised in the name of highest Jupiter, to which easy ascent was
made by twenty steps shining with the decoration of mosaic work. At
the summit of this altar, accordingly, gleamed a golden image of the
god Jupiter which had been placed there; it was fifteen cubits in
length and was entirely made of fine gold of inestimable value, which
240 was beautified by the appearance of various jewels, and enriched by
pearls placed here and there in various designs. The trust of King
Priam in this god Jupiter was supreme and unshakable, since he
considered the throne of his kingdom would flourish in long
prosperity by this means and that the power of his scepter would
245 endure to time immemorial.

But after King Priam, according to the intention of his mind, had
brought the city of Troy to the proposed conclusion, he surveyed
everything with deep emotion, and considering in his active mind that
the city he had founded was flourishing with great strength and
250 power of endurance, that he was supported on all sides by such a
powerful people, was strong in a great number of valiant men, and
had great riches in abundance, with firm resolve he turned his restless
thoughts back to the serious injuries which had been offered him a
while ago by the Greeks. He became impatient with inactivity, and
255 earnestly enjoined his solemn assembly to convene in that city.
Hector was then in the regions of Pannonia, which was subject to
Trojan rule, where he was attending to his father's government. When
all his citizens and all his sons, except Hector, had assembled in
court, together with others allied to him, this king, sitting in state

260 upon the royal throne, with the whole populace hanging on his
words, addressed them thus, as soon as it was quiet, saying: "O men,
faithful and dear to me, companions of my injuries because you have
shared this evil; in fact, you also know by experience how the Greeks,
spurred on by an earlier pretext, as trivial as it was absurd, attacked
265 our country with stubborn pride, and, in great harshness and cruelty,
took my parents from me and yours from you. They carried away my
sister Hesione, the daughter of a very noble race, under a cloud of
great ignominy, and they hold her in the vile yoke of servitude,
dishonored by usage as a concubine. They force your sisters,
270 daughters, and wives, whom they have carried away from their
ancestral homes, to serve them in servitude with the most menial
tasks. Our former city of Troy, peacefully possessed for a long time
by my ancestors, they wickedly took from them and gave it over to
extermination and ruin. When they had completely ruined your
275 homes and the dwellings of your ancestors, they exposed the riches
stored up by my ancestors to looting, and they divided your property
and goods as spoils. It would then be an application of justice that,
with the favor of the gods who always oppose the proud, there
should be by the common agreement of all of you a common revenge
280 for so many evils. For you know we have a city which is large and
safe and fortified with many defenses. You know we are supported
by fighting men of great boldness. You know we are very strong in
military power, rich in many kinds of equipment for war, and that
we are copiously supplied with great wealth and are rich in many
285 things to eat. We can command the great assistance of powerful men,
and the great approval of our allies is near at hand. The time appears
to be favorable for us to turn hands and arms against our enemies
and adversaries for our revenge and to strive manfully for their
destruction. Because, however, the outcome of wars is always
290 uncertain, and the fates of those who fight are doubtful, it would
seem to be safer to refrain from the conflicts of battles if such a
serious wrong, such an ignominious and shameful injury, did not burn
in my heart. Should I be able rationally to refrain from extraordinary
grief of heart, knowing that my sister Hesione, cast forth into exile,
295 is detained by a stranger, not in the union of the marriage bond, but
instead is tortured by the constant defilement of disgraceful adultery?
At the least it would be suitable, in the early stages of our dealings

with them, to make it plain to these Greeks by our threats and
injunctions that if they are willing to restore my sister Hesione to me,
300 no complaint will be directed against them by us in the future; but
concerning the rest, we shall be forced reluctantly to conceal in
silence the injuries done us in order to divert the envious course of
the fates from our perpetual security and peace." Satisfied with these
words, King Priam brought his speech to an end.
305   Then all those in attendance together unanimously approved the
wise counsel of the king. For this reason Priam, as soon as he had
perceived the approbation of his faithful followers, chose Antenor as
his messenger and legate for the carrying out of this business, for
Antenor was a man of great intelligence, diligent, and most adept in
310 legal knowledge. The king exhorted him by prayers and commands to
offer willingly to undertake the task of this mission and the carrying
out of such an affair, and to be faithful in its execution. Antenor
consequently showed himself faithful to the commands of the king
and faithfully offered no delays to the carrying out of the aforesaid
315 negotiations.
     When the ship was ready and the several things accomplished for
sailing, Antenor at once anxiously entered the ship, and with the
mast whistling because the sails were spread to the gusts of favorable
winds, he sailed so long and so many days and nights that he touched
320 safely at Menusius, a city in the regions of Thessaly, where by chance
King Peleus was staying. When Antenor had first been honorably
received by him, King Peleus inquired of him the reason for his
coming. Antenor replied to him with these words: "I am sent to you
by King Priam. For King Priam demands these things from you by
325 me his messenger. He certainly does not consider that the serious
injuries which you unworthily offered him have disappeared from the
records of your memory, when without the reason of a serious
offense you attacked the kingdom of his father, whom you wickedly
delivered to death, completely destroying his land. Furthermore, after
330 annihilating his subjects, you led away into servitude and exile those
miserable ones whom the fates wished to live. Besides, you
villainously carried off his sister Hesione, a royal maiden (would that
she had been married!). For he who detains her disgracefully violates
her, and she is defiled by being treated as a concubine. Therefore, so
335 that the madness of war may cease henceforth and future quarrels

may not result, quarrels which ought to be detested among good and
serious men, King Priam asks and advises you, since you are a king of
great prudence, that you, if it pleases you, be willing to bring it
about that his sister, at least, be ordered restored to him, seeing that
340 all other losses and injuries have been overlooked by him." After
King Peleus had heard all these things he suddenly kindled his wrath,
and without restraining the onslaught of his anger, he scoffed at
Priam with haughty words, blaming him for weakness of mind, and
he ordered the departure of Antenor with threatening insults,
345 asserting that if he prolonged his stay in his land for even a minute,
he would have him miserably killed.

When Antenor had heard this from King Peleus, without seeking
leave he hastily entered the ship, and, departing from the port,
committed himself to the deep ocean. He sailed the unknown seas a
350 like number of days and nights and arrived safely at Salamis. King
Telamon was then present in the city of Salamis, and, disembarking
from the ship, Antenor went to talk with him. When King Telamon
saw him he did not receive him with a friendly expression, since he
nurtured a continual enmity against the Trojans because he had taken
355 Hesione. Finally he demanded from Antenor the reason for his
coming. Stating that he was an ambassador of King Priam, Antenor
explained to him the details of his mission in these words: "King
Priam, lord of the Trojan kingdom, asks respectfully that Your
Highness restore to him his sister Hesione, whom you are subjecting
360 to most unfitting servitude in your hall, since it does not contribute
much to your reputation to violate the daughter and sister of a king
in a shameful alliance, when she should have been honored with an
offer from one equal or even superior to you in rank. Still he will not
be troubled concerning these things which were done to him by you
365 in detestable fashion if Your Grace will provide for the restoring of
her, and King Priam could perhaps still dispose of her in a proper
marriage." When these words of Antenor were ended, and when
Telamon had fully comprehended them, Telamon burst out in sudden
and severe anger, and, uttering these words with a mocking expression,
370 thus offered this objection as an answer: "Friend, whoever you are,
I am stirred with great wonder at the lack of seriousness of your king,
since I am not joined to him nor he to me by any signs of friendship,
and for that reason it is not my desire to hear his entreaties. For

your king knows that to avenge a certain crime, certain other Greek
375 nobles and I, with an army, attacked King Laomedon, the perpetrator
of the crime, and that I, shedding not a little of my blood, was the
first to enter the Trojan city by force of arms. On account of this,
and by the assent of the whole army, Hesione was handed over to me
as the reward of victory, to do with her as I wished. I think this was
380 no trifling gift, since she is endowed with extreme beauty,
distinguished by much learning, and lovely in the possession of praiseworthy virtues. It is not for me to give back as a trifle something that
precious, obtained at that much peril to my life. Therefore tell your
king he will not be able to obtain Hesione unless at the point of a
385 slaughtering sword. Furthermore, I think you showed yourself a great
fool when you volunteered to assume the burden of such a mission,
since you should have known that in doing so you were subjecting
yourself to obvious peril and to the power of those who persecute
you and those like you with hateful insults. Depart then quickly from
390 this land. If you do not do this instantly, I would have you know
that you will without doubt be risking your life."

When Antenor heard this he hastened instantly to the ship, and
entering it, immediately gave himself to the guidance of the winds,
and by a pleasant voyage reached Achaia, where the kings Castor and
395 Pollux, who were described above, were staying together. Antenor,
disembarking from the ship, approached them, and when he had
explained to them the nature of the mission given him by Priam
concerning the restoration of his sister and the injuries inflicted by
them without cause, concerning the loss of his parents and the fall of
400 his city, and concerning the pillaging of his possessions, Castor replied
thus with angry speech to the aforesaid explanation of Antenor:
"Friend, whoever you are, we do not believe nor do we think we
affronted Priam undeservedly, since King Laomedon, his father, had
furnished the cause of his woes, who being, so to speak, incautious
405 and attacking unadvisedly, first rashly offered an affront to certain
great men of our land. We therefore seek enmity rather than peace,
since we have taken on the spirit of hostility against him and his
people, as much on account of previous events as on account of the
consequences of those previous things. I do not believe that he had
410 much love for you, he who urged you to the handling of this
business, since you have shown that your life is not very dear to you

because you have presumed to approach our territories on such an
errand. So let no delay keep you in this land, because if you do not
leave quickly, you will realize that you are putting your life in
415 danger."

Antenor, however, when he had heard these words, left these kings
without seeking leave and hastened to the ship. When the anchor had
been raised from the sea, this ship with Antenor got under full sail at
once, and sailing in a direct course toward Pylos, reached it safely.
420 There Duke Nestor was staying, accompanied by many of his nobles.
Antenor, disembarking from the ship, went to him, claiming he was
the ambassador of King Priam, and explained to him, as he had to
Castor and Pollux, the nature of his mission, in all details. Nestor,
however, when he understood the words of Antenor, was provoked to
425 anger, and changing color from the fury of his rage, looked askance
at Antenor with severe aspect and replied to him, speaking these
words vehemently: "Vile slave, whence came that audacity and
presumption that brought you to presume to poison my ears with the
uttering of such a speech? Assuredly, if my noble nature did not
430 restrain me, I would order your tongue to be plucked out of your
throat, because it is used in such speeches and for dishonor to your
king. I should cause your limbs to be dismembered by having you
dragged along the ground by horses. Therefore, depart from my sight
speedily. If you do not do so at once, what I have mentioned will
435 really happen to you."

But Antenor, stunned with horror at such a speech and fearing the
tyrannous savagery of this Nestor, left him directly. He reached his
ship and with spread sails quickly went from this coast of pirates. As
he was cutting the deep seas on his return, the hateful fury of a
440 storm covered the sky with a dark fog, and the rains poured down
with gusts of contrary winds in amazing peals of thunder and dreadful
flashes of lightning. The waves, stirred up by the winds, rose in high
mountains. Now the ship, diverted into the yawning troughs of the
seas, sought the dangerous depths, now raised on the surges of the
445 waves through the flood it sought the mountainous peaks of the
tempest. The evident peril to their life weighed upon the sailors in
the ship and they poured out various prayers to the gods for deliverance from the danger. Thus when this ship had been subjected to
these obvious perils for three days, on the fourth day the distress of

450 the storm ceased, and the rage of the wind was softened and ceased.
      The seas were calm, the waves were still, and the sailors, now
      snatched from a watery death, took comfort, so that by sailing in a
      straight course they later reached port on the Trojan shores. When
      they had disembarked on the land they had longed for, before any-
455 thing else they went quickly to the temples of the gods where as
      suppliants they fulfilled their vows to the gods, so that, after offering
      victims to the gods, and after pouring a sacrificial libation, according
      to custom, Antenor approached the great palace of King Priam safe
      and unharmed, in a group of many people who were overjoyed at his
460 return.
          When King Priam was seated with a group of his most important
      followers and also with many others in attendance, together with his
      sons who were mentioned before, Antenor reported and related in
      order what had happened to him in Greece. For he told the harsh
465 answer made to him by Peleus, the threatening insults given him by
      Telamon, the despicable answers of Castor and Pollux, and the severe
      and violent fears produced in him by Nestor. After King Priam had
      heard all these things, he was very disturbed and was tormented with
      immoderate grief, because he had learned that his ambassador had
470 been so despicably received in Greece, and he almost despaired for
      the recovery of his sister.

*Here begins the sixth book, concerning the advice offered by
Paris as he was about to set out for Greece.*

      After the mission of Antenor had made King Priam certain of the
      hatred of the Greeks, which the Greeks were cherishing with lasting
      fervor against him and his people after so many long years, and also
      that the hearts of the Greeks could not be softened to restore his
5   sister Hesione, he burned more ardently in his whole being to begin
      what he had resolved, and he longed wholeheartedly and with vital
      concern to send his people against Greece in a great naval expedition
      as an affront to the Greeks. But, say, King Priam, what unhappy
      quirk of fate incited your peaceful heart to such unfortunate
10   boldness, so that you were not able in the least to restrain the
      impulses of your heart by mature counsels (although, granted, these

impulses are not in the control of man), so that while it was possible,
you might have withstood evil counsels, and while it was possible,
you would have known how to conceal your past losses, which
15 perhaps through the course of so many years could have been
destroyed by forgetting? Did you, indeed, pay no attention to what
is usually talked of by everyone, and what is said to have happened
to many men who, while they were trying to avenge their dishonor,
were overwhelmed, as the evils increased, by the addition of greater
20 dishonor? It would have been safer to cling to what is likewise
commonly said: "Let him who is well off be in no hurry to change;"
for he who is sitting on level ground does not have a place to fall
from. But you wished to submit yourself to the fickle fates, with the
result that you will give to future generations much material to be
25 reported concerning your unfortunate overthrow and the final defeat
of your people, and concerning the second ruin and destruction of
your city—most enjoyable tales, in a way, since hearing of the adverse
fortunes of other men is pleasing and delightful. But the present
sequence of the historical account reveals what happened afterward to
30 you and yours.

King Priam, when he had called together all the principal people of
Troy and gathered them together in one place in the palace of Ilium,
thus addressed them: "See, just as Antenor went forth according to
your advice, sent to Greece to recover my sister from the Greeks, so
35 that the hatred which we bear among them might be ended, and
inducements to wars in the future might be avoided; he has now
returned, as you know, and it is known to you what dire and hateful
answers he received from them, because in their considerations they
are not ashamed of the very heavy damages and the very serious
40 injuries they have inflicted upon us. And oh, that they, led by
repentance, might acknowledge at least by a word what evil they have
done! But rising up in greater pride and arrogance, they threaten us
with more serious things. May it not happen, then, that what they
threaten may befall us through evil fortune. May it also not happen
45 that they escape the penalty they deserve for so many acts committed
violently by them without cause, a penalty that should be inflicted
on them by us, with the favor of the gods. For we believe that we
are more powerful in men than they, and that we have a protected
and safe city, which is certainly secure from the wiles of all enemies,

50 even if a greater number of men should be arrayed against us. For we
    are strong in the possession of many very valiant knights and foot
    soldiers, who are skilled in the rigors of fighting; we have in abun-
    dance a full supply of food which will not fail in all future demands;
    we luxuriate in extraordinary wealth; and we seem to lack nothing
55 for carrying on the hostilities of offense or for reserves for defense.
    It seems pleasing to me, then, if it seems acceptable to you, that we
    exert our forces in some way, at least, against these Greeks, our
    lawless enemies, and that at least in the early stages of the assault we
    send our people over with fierce attacks against their lands and
60 territories. Let our people rush upon their lands and their men
    suddenly, while they are ignorant of our wiles, and bring upon them
    the greatest damage and slaughter before they are able to raise a
    trained army for their defense. For this is the chance for everyone of
    us to commit his person and property to fortune for the restoration
65 of our losses and for vengeance for our grievous injury. It should not
    terrify us that these Greeks obtained victory against us and our
    predecessors. For it is known that the conqueror is many times
    overcome by the conquered."
        And so, since all those in attendance agreed wholeheartedly with
70 the words and advice of the king, they offered themselves with all
    their goods and people. On account of this, King Priam revealed his
    pleasure in the things offered in common with such willing hearts and
    in the boldness of intense zeal and blazing courage. Thus the king,
    immeasurably pleased with their offerings, granted each one permis-
75 sion to leave with affectionate words, and the king himself remained
    in the palace with all his sons, both legitimate and natural, since they
    were all with him then. For at that time Hector was present among
    them since he had already returned from the regions of Pannonia at
    the command of this king his father. As soon as it was quiet the king
80 addressed them all in these words. But before he burst forth with
    these words, tears streamed down his face, and he poured forth his
    words in this fashion, amidst sobs and tears: "Do you not turn over
    in your mind the death of your grandparents and the servile condition
    of Hesione, who is treated as a concubine while you are alive and in
85 great strength? It will be meet and right for you to rise and strive
    with all your might to avenge such shame, and if not for the
    vengeance of your grandparents, at least for the satisfaction of my

wish, because on account of this I am constantly pained by great
anguish and countless woes, and since I have brought you up from
90   your tender years, you should be the sharers of my woes by natural
and good reason." Turning toward Hector he said to him: "You
especially, my dearest son Hector, firstborn among all your brothers,
who surpass the rest of your brothers in superiority of arms and
deeds of courage, you ought to embrace these my counsels and you
95   should boldly assume the execution of my precepts. Accordingly, you
are to be the sole leader and chief in this undertaking, and all your
brothers and all those subject to our rule are to obey you strictly
because you know how to subdue the proud by your mighty power
and influence and to force the obstinate to bend by the boldness of
100 your spirit. For from this day forth I remove myself completely from
what will take place concerning the present business, and I place the
responsibility completely on your stronger shoulders, because you are
strong in your youthful hardiness for waging war and winning in
active warfare, which my weak nature does not let me do, since I am
105 already declining toward old age."

And when King Priam had ended his speech, Hector replied to the
words of his father with an expression of modesty and an utterance
of honorable words: "My dearest Lord King, would it not be
inhuman in men and at variance with human nature for those who
110 have suffered not to seek revenge for injuries received? And if we,
who flourish in such great nobility that the slightest injury against us
is very shameful (since the quality of the persons injured increases
and decreases the quality of the injury), if we seek vengeance for the
injuries inflicted upon us, we are not debased from human nature,
115 since we see that even irrational animals are possessed by this desire.
Accordingly, there is no one among your sons, dear father, who is
more strongly obliged to seek vengeance for the death of our grand-
parents than I, who am the first of your sons in order of birth and
should be likewise first in the vehemence of reprisal. Therefore more
120 than the rest I desire with all eagerness to seek vengeance for them,
so that those who cruelly shed the blood of my ancestors and subjects may die by my right hand, even though drenched in my blood.
Nevertheless, wise King, I beg to recall one thing to your memory,
namely, that you consider, as a prudent and sagacious king, not only
125 the first beginnings of this war, but also the things which follow in

the middle and the result which will take place in the end. For it is
not wise or admirable to fail to examine a plan thoroughly and with
particular care, to be concerned with the beginnings of an affair and
not attend to its end. For what good does it do anyone to do well by
130   accident at the outset of an affair which will come to be finished by
a disastrous conclusion? It is therefore more admirable to refrain from
these beginnings which have uncertain results and which tend more
to misfortune than fortune. That beginning can be called fortunate
the end of which has been fortunate. I have blurted out these words,
135   here, wise king, with such boldness of speech, so that eagerness for
revenge may not unadvisedly carry away the spirit of your desire in
an affair the outcome of which is uncertain, whether it will turn out
either prosperously or adversely. You know, dearest father, that all of
Africa and Europe is today controlled by Greece, and you know also
140   what a large number of soldiers support the Greeks, with what valor
they fight, what great riches they possess, and with what strength
their dominion flourishes. The power of Asia today is not equal to
the power of so many men, since, although many men live in Asia,
still they have not been made ready enough for war through training
145   in fighting. It is therefore more certain than doubtful for us that if
we take arms against those more powerful than we, without a unified
plan, we shall with great difficulty, or never, be able to attain the
desired result. Therefore, to what end should we seek to disturb our
condition by severe hardships, our condition which today is eased by
150   such peace and shines with such happiness? Why should we leave a
pleasant repose to come miserably to the sacrifice of our persons?
Surely Hesione is not to be redeemed at such a high cost that (let it
not happen!) the exchange will be made of, perhaps, the best of our
men—perhaps all of them—for her. It is not improper, then, to close
155   one's eyes to the fate of Hesione, since she has already for so many
years been used to her wrongs, and death can tear her away from
living air in a short time, with the result that a basis for peace would
be provided for us all. Dear father, do not in your opinion think that
I advance this thought from fear of fighting or from weakness of
160   heart, but I fear the malign occurrences of fortune and I fear that the
authority of your rule will falter under the deceiving quirks of
fortune. Let us be permitted, while it is still possible to hold back, to
abstain from this action, since there is a warrantable and sound reason

165 for objecting to beginnings which, though they may be attractive at
the outset, may—if we are forced to continue in the chosen course of
action—terminate in grief and loss."

The wise and valiant Hector was silent after these words. But Paris,
who had heard the words of Hector attentively, rising at once to his
feet poured forth these words: "Here, O King, dearest father, which
170 of us can plausibly have fears about a favorable conclusion resulting
if we take up hostile weapons against our enemies? Are we not as
valiant, as powerful, as wealthy, and established in as strong a city?
Who can plausibly believe that we, established thus happily and safely
in our homes, can be overthrown? Therefore, dearest lord, let what
175 you have said be carried out boldly, namely, that our ships be sent to
lay waste Greece, which has afflicted our people with enormous
injuries and plundered them with irreparable losses. In addition, order
me, if it is your pleasure, dearest father, to set out with these ships,
because, in truth, I am sure the gods wish me to be able to defeat
180 Greece decisively and to plunder it extensively, and also to seize some
very noble woman from the aristocracy of Greece and bring her
captive to the Trojan kingdom, so that she may easily be exchanged
as the ransom for your sister Hesione. But if you must inquire how I
know this, I will present to your understanding a sure sign concerning
185 it, a sign which I have surely received from the gods themselves. For
not many days have elapsed since I was living in Minor India at your
command, when the summer sun was at its solstice, and when the sun
was running its course near the beginning of Cancer. One day it
suited me to go to the groves of Venus to hunt, in a troop of many
190 hunters. When I entered the groves at dawn, after I had with many
hardships searched them diligently for something to hunt, I was able
to find no game which pleased me. The sun was already standing at
the meridian and was not far from sinking toward evening when
finally, as fortune provided, a deer appeared, wandering in the lonely
195 places of these groves, and I in my eagerness thought to overtake it
by pursuit. For this reason, I left my companions, who could not
follow me in the speed of the chase, and when I was at a great
distance from them, I arrived alone in the dark shadow in the
loneliest part of these groves, which is called Ida, where the deer
200 vanished from my sight, perhaps because of the leafy trees of these
groves or because of the great swiftness of its flight. Then, being

tired, and assuredly my horse was also, I ceased from pursuing the
deer farther, because my horse was drenched with sweat and, pouring
forth showers of rain, as it were, suddenly shed profuse drops, one
205 after the other. Need I say more? I wearily dismounted from the
horse and tied him carefully by the reins of his bridle to the branch
of a tree near me; then I stretched out on the ground where the
green grass grew luxuriantly (the shadiness of the trees prevented
dryness), and when I had put down the bow and quiver I was
210 carrying, I arranged them into a makeshift cushion for me to lie on.
Without delay, drowsy slumber overwhelmed me, seizing me with
such rapid heaviness that it seemed to me that I was asleep in no
time at all. While I was so heavily drugged with sleep, I saw in my
dream a miraculous vision—that a god, namely Mercury, was leading
215 three goddesses with him, namely Venus, Pallas, and Juno. As soon as
he had approached me, with the aforesaid goddesses a little distant
from him, he said to me: 'Hear me, O Paris. Behold, I have brought
these three goddesses to you because a quarrel has arisen among
them, concerning which they have decided to submit themselves to
220 your judgment alone, so that this dispute among them may be broken
off by your decision. For while they were enjoying themselves at a
solemn feast once, a certain wonderful apple of precious material,
beautifully engraved, was thrown among them, which contained an
inscription on it in Greek letters that it was to be given to the most
225 beautiful of them. Since, therefore, each contends that she surpasses
the other in beauty, and from that thinks that she deserved the
reward of the apple, they submit themselves to your decision in this,
and each of them promises you through me a reward for your
judgment, to be paid without fail by her whom you consider to be in
230 first place for beauty and for the receiving of the apple. For if you
decide to prefer Juno, she will make you the greatest among the
other eminent men in the world; if Pallas, you will attain all human
knowledge as a reward; if Venus, you will carry away from Greece a
very noble woman, more beautiful than Venus herself.' I, however,
235 when I had heard of these promises and gifts from Mercury, replied
to him that I would not give the truth in this judgment unless they
all presented themselves naked to my sight, so that by my observation
I might be able to consider the individual qualities of their bodies for
a true judgment. Mercury immediately told me, 'Let it be done as

240   you say.' When the aforesaid three goddesses had put aside their
clothes, and when each of them in turn had presented herself naked
to my sight, it seemed to me, by following the judgment of truth,
that Venus in her beauty clearly excelled those other two, and
accordingly I decided that she was mistress of the apple. Venus then,
245   rejoicing at this victory of the apple, without fail confirmed in a
gentle voice the promise made me by Mercury. As they left me, I was
immediately released from sleep and from the dream. Do you think,
dear father, the promises of the gods could be esteemed vain? Indeed,
I think it is utterly certain that if you sent me against Greece, I
250   would undoubtedly bring back the woman with me, according to the
divine promises. Send me therefore, gracious father, because sending
me will assuredly fill your heart with delight." And with these words
Paris made an end to his remarks.

When the aforesaid reply of this Paris was ended, Deiphobus, the
255   third son of the king, arose, and when silence had been accorded his
speech, he was unable to keep back the plan that he had thought of,
and he explained it in these words: "Dearest King, if in every affair
which is to be undertaken one would wish to examine carefully with
particular deliberation the individual events which could take place in
260   the future, there would never be anyone who would boldly submit
himself to the burden of any undertaking. For if farmers always
thought with careful deliberation how many seeds are carried off by
the thievery of birds, perhaps they would never put the seeds in the
furrows. Therefore, dearest father, let the ships be made ready for
265   the advance upon Greece, since the plan of Paris cannot possibly be
opposed. For if it happens that he takes some noble woman away
from Greece, it may easily turn out that by exchanging her we can
recover Hesione, on whose account our whole maligned race and
nation are defiled by the foulness of hateful epithets."

270   Then Helenus, the fourth son of the king in order of birth, rose
from his own seat after Deiphobus had ended his speech, and revealed
the direction of his thought in these words: "Magnanimous King, for
God's sake, do not let a blind passion for revenge prevent your
wishes. You know that, by the favor of the gods and with your
275   consent I have been instructed and made completely erudite in
knowledge of future events, with the result that your diligent study
of past events has long recognized that no prophecies have ever

proceeded from my mouth which did not attain pure truth. Therefore, do not let Paris presume to attack Greece. For let your mind hold it
280 as certain that if Paris goes to Greece to make an attack against any land, this your noble city will be completely overturned by the Greeks and your citizens and all of us descended from your loins will be killed. Refrain, therefore, from these things whose end is grief and the bitterness of death, lest from this undertaking you yourself should
285 be cut to pieces, and Hecuba, your dearest wife, be destroyed, and all your people be cut down by the cruel sword, since all these things will actually happen in the future if Paris presumes to go to Greece with an army." And having said these things in sorrow, he took his seat again.
290   At these words of the wise Helenus the spirit of the king faltered, and he was not a little bewildered and filled with hesitation. On account of this, complete and utter silence fell among those in attendance, and there was no one among them who would presume to utter a sound in speech. Then that Troilus, the youngest, last born
295 of the king's sons, when he saw the others were silent because they were greatly disturbed, broke the silence and poured forth these words: "O noble and very spirited men, why are you disturbed about many things at the voice of one pusillanimous priest? Is it not suitable for priests to fear war and avoid aggression, since weakness
300 alone makes them love pleasure and grow fat in the sole enjoyment of abundant food and drink? For what wise man can maintain for certain that the ignorant minds of men could foretell the future acts of the gods? For it is not wise to believe this, since it proceeds only from a stupid weakness of mind. Then let Helenus, if he is shaken by
305 fear, proceed to honor the gods in the temple, and let him allow others who are led forward by the stigma of disgrace to demand the required revenge in conflict of arms. Why, glorious King, are you disturbed at his words, which are as useless as they are foolish? Order the ships to set sail and the army to prepare for the military expedi-
310 tion, since it is not to be borne that the Greeks offered us such a great dishonor without retaliation and vengeance."
    With these words Troilus was silent. The rest of those in atten-dance praised his spirit and his speech, and all approved of his advice, so that the council was dissolved by the command of the king, and
315 the aforesaid sons of the king, together with the king himself, went

to take their places at the dinner tables which had been made ready. Afterward King Priam, when he had attended the feast, sat on his throne, and, because he was excited about his plans and was yearning so vehemently with his whole being for their execution, he called his sons

320 Paris and Deiphobus to him. He expressly ordered them to go quickly to the province of Pannonia to bring back with them valiant knights who would go with them in the ships to Greece. On the very same day King Priam summoned Paris and Deiphobus to the journey; they departed immediately, as soon as they had taken leave of the king.

325 Then on the following day, King Priam called all the citizens of the city of Troy together for a general assembly, and when they had come together, he addressed these words to them: "O loyal and beloved citizens, you know very well by how many hateful injuries and countless losses we have been provoked through the overbearing

330 acts of the Greeks, and it is not a secret that you have suffered injury, since we have become a legend, even to foreigners. The virtual servitude of my sister Hesione does not permit my desires to be appeased, since in memory of her I am constrained by grief which continued reports do not allow to be abolished by any means. For you know I

335 sent the experienced Antenor to Greece for her recovery, and since he was not heard by the Greeks, the substance of my grief is doubled. But because wounds, which do not feel the benefit of medicine, must be cured by iron, I have proposed that Paris set off for Greece together with an armed band and a navy, with a full complement of

340 knights, so that he might powerfully attack our enemies and inflict what losses he can. Perhaps he will bring to our city some noble woman whom he has carried off from them by force, through whom, the gods being willing, I shall be able to gain the exchange of my sister. Because I have decided not to carry this out without the

345 approval of your council, I decided to bring this to the notice of the people, so that if it seems to you to be sound, it will be adhered to more firmly at the very outset. For although all these things affect me closely enough, they will also affect all of you together. What affects everyone, according to the sayings of the wise, should be

350 approved by everyone."

When the speech of the king was ended, while silence was widespread everywhere, one of the knights in attendance arose. His name was Panthus, the son of one Euphorbus, a great philosopher, about

whom Ovid has reported that the soul of the great Pythagorus passed
355   over into him. He arose and uttered these words: "O most noble
King, since I have been completely inflamed with the zeal of faith
toward Your Majesty, may Your Majesty receive kindly those things
which I do not fail to recall to your memory since they are offered
with loyal intention. For Your Highness knows that I had Euphorbus
360   for a father, who possessed the breath of life for more than one
hundred and eighty years, and who had complete foreknowledge of
future events because he was imbued with the knowledge of all
philosophy. He said many times to me, and affirmed it as certain,
that if your son Paris should go to Greece in order to lead a wife
365   away from the Argives in the manner of a pirate, that this your noble
city of great Troy would be reduced to ashes by the Greeks, and you
and all your people would be cruelly and vilely killed. For this reason,
most wise king, let Your Majesty not fear to agree with my words,
since it is not safe to scorn words of wise men, especially in affairs
370   the restriction of which will not harm your dignity, and the pursuit
of which could be the cause—let it not happen!—of your perpetual
ruin. Why do you seek to lay snares for your peace of mind and to
submit your tranquility to chances which have in them all kinds of
dangers? Therefore you should refrain if it pleases you, so that you
375   may happily spend your happy days without pain or distress, and so
that your son Paris will not reach the boundaries of Greece or at
least that someone else be directed to Greece."
At the words of Panthus proposing such things, the murmur was
very great among those attending, as they violently attacked both the
380   arguments of Panthus and his father's prophecies. Oh, would that
they had agreed with them, for perhaps those outrages which
followed afterward would never have taken place! But because the
inevitable fates establish future calamities, it pleased everyone that
Paris should go to Greece with the navy. And so the assembly ended,
385   and everyone left. After it had come to the attention of Cassandra,
the daughter of the king, that the council was definitely resolved that
Paris should go to Greece, she burst into loud wailing, as if she were
mad, and, shouting in a loud voice, she broke out in these words:
"Ah, most noble city of Troy, why do such frightful and severe fates
390   drag you down, so that in a short time you will be overthrown
because of very hazardous undertakings, and the lofty tops of your

turrets will be destroyed and given to sudden ruin? Ah, unfortunate
King Priam, what crime will it be said you committed to cause you
to bewail the death and perpetual servitude of yourself and your
395 men? And you, Queen Hecuba, with what contamination of wicked-
ness are you surrounded, that you will see all your offspring succumb
to cruel death? Why do you not prevent Paris from going to Greece,
since he will be the cause of such great ruin?" When she had ended
her clamor, she rose and went to the king her father, and, with
400 showers of tears, mournfully warned her father to desist from the
undertaking, in the manner of one who by the frequent warnings of
her knowledge foresaw future events, and having foreseen them,
divulged them in mournful tones. But the opposition of Fortune, who
had already in her course given voluntary impulses and unfortunate
405 inspirations, hastened toward the end by ordaining the rapid progress
of events thereafter. If the arguments of Hector, the warnings of
Cassandra, the exhortations of Helenus, and the objections of Panthus
had been heard and believed, you would have lasted and endured to all
eternity, O noble and lofty Troy! But after the inexorable Fates decree
410 that misfortunes and evils shall happen, they represent the opposite and
contrary in the minds of men and recommend them as favorable.

*Here begins the seventh book, about Paris going to Greece
and about the abduction of Helen.*

The sun had already completed its course between the Hyades and
the Pleiades, and since it was in the sign of Taurus, the month of
May was adorning the fields of the country with various flowers, and
the trees, growing green with new leaves, were giving promise of fruits
5 to come by the profusion of their blossoms. It was at this time that
Paris and Deiphobus, coming back from the regions of Pannonia,
brought with them three thousand knights who were of great repute
on account of their great valor in the practice of arms. When twenty-
three large ships had been prepared and loaded with an abundance of
10 all things necessary, King Priam ordered and enjoined Antenor and
Aeneas, who were mentioned above, and in addition Polydamas, the
son of Antenor, to prepare to go along with Paris to Greece with the
fleet. When they had agreed faithfully to do this, King Priam also

called together into one place everyone who had been deputed by
15 him to set out in the aforesaid fleet, and addressed them thus, saying
these words: "It is not necessary henceforth to repeat many speeches
to you concerning the business you have undertaken, since the urgent
reason which vexes my heart is fully known to you, which is why I
have ordered you to set out for Greece. Although that ought to be a
20 very strong reason, that is, to seek vengeance for the insults offered
to you and me, still the overwhelming reason is rather that I may
then recover my sister, who is being cheapened in great dishonor and
painful misfortune. You should rise up with boldness to obtain her,
since we appear justly to take arms against her captors in order to
25 recover her. For you also know that the Danäi have offended both
you and us unjustly, and that we justly take arms against unjust
offenses, since he who seeks to avenge himself after provocation may,
according to justice, be forgiven. I advise you, therefore, to give
manfully whatever service you can to recover my sister. For now the
30 time is favorable for your worth to be advertised to your enemies and
for the valor which is strong in you to appear openly. Accordingly if
the chance should offer itself for obtaining our wishes, the gods
approving, know that I am ready to proceed upon your request to
supply you liberally with great assistance, so that all the Danäi may
35 be terrified by our might and forced to bewail their heavy losses on
account of the strong force of our courage. Respecting the execution
of this kind of business, you will have Paris as first in command and
leader, with Deiphobus second to Paris, in council with the wise
Antenor and Aeneas, who are to set out with you in the present
40 business."
    At the end of the discourse, the whole army boarded the ships,
and after Paris and Deiphobus had taken leave of the king in tears,
they entered the ships. The lines were cast off, the anchors weighed,
the sails raised, and the ships struck out upon the deep, upon the
45 deep sea, in the name of the gods Jupiter and Venus. Since the ships
sailed well, by a pleasant voyage they touched at the widely scattered
Cyclades, islands belonging to Romania. While they were trying to
pass through these, so to speak, unknown islands by rowing sturdily,
and were navigating through them by sticking closely to the shores
50 bordering on Greece, chance threw a certain ship in their way. In this
ship was sailing a certain king of one of the greater kingdoms of

Greece. His name was Menelaus, and at this time he was going with
his ship to the city of Pylos because he had been summoned by Duke
Nestor. Menelaus was the brother of King Agamemnon, and had
55 Helen as his wife. Helen was esteemed in those days for marvelous
beauty. She was the sister of Kings Castor and Pollux who were then
staying together in Cunestar, a city belonging to their kingdom, and
who had brought with them their niece Hermione, the daughter of
the Helen mentioned above. But while the Trojans were regarding this
60 ship, they saw it turn from their path on an oblique tack, and so the
Greeks could not recognize the Trojans, nor the Trojans the Greeks.
For this reason the Trojan ships, blown by favorable winds, entered
upon a safe course and came to a certain island named Cythera,
which was under the jurisdiction of the Greeks, which today sailors
65 call the island of Citrius. When the Trojan ships had touched at this
island of Cythera, the Trojans eagerly entered its port. After they had
cast the anchors into the depths of the sea, tied the ships with stout
ropes, and placed them in safe locations, they went safely ashore in
their boats.
70   There was, however, on this island of Cythera a temple to Venus
which had been built in ancient times. It was of wonderful beauty
and full of great riches, since the inhabitants of the adjacent provinces
possessed and exhibited by pagan rites the greatest faith in Venus,
who was then principally worshipped there. In very great reverence
75 they observed her annual festival, since at that place they often
received answers from the goddess herself concerning what they had
sought from her. Then in those days the principal festival of this
Venus was being celebrated, and on account of it, countless men and
women from neighboring regions had taken themselves with great joy
80 to that island to offer their prayers in that temple. After Paris learned
of this, he went to the temple fittingly decked and in a troop of
many followers, and appeared in that temple with innocent expression, and in the presence of the people then in attendance, with
devout prayers poured forth his offerings according to Dardanian
85 custom, with immense prodigality in great amounts of gold and silver.
Paris was graced with great beauty, exceeding all his followers and
the others in good looks. As soon as those in attendance in the
temple saw him, they wondered greatly at his beauty and at the regal
pomp with which he made his splendid appearance. For this reason

90   all those in attendance longed fervently to become acquainted with
       him and to know who were his companions, where they had come
       from, and especially, who was Paris. And in the end, the matter was
       not concealed by the Trojans from those who wished to know. For
       they told them he was Paris, son of the king of Troy, and that he
95   had come to Greece with a great troop of his nobles at the command
       of his father in order to seek again from the kings of Greece a certain
       sister of his father, whose name was Hesione, whom the aforesaid
       kings had given to King Telamon, when, during the reign of King
       Laomedon, they had destroyed the city of Troy. Various things were
100   said among them about what they heard.
       But a tattling rumor, which acquired great force as it went along,
       was spread about the neighboring regions concerning the beauty of
       Paris as he entered the temple, and reached the ears of Helen by
       many reports. After Helen had learned of this, the eager appetite of
105   changing desire, which is wont to seize the hearts of women with
       sudden lightness, excited Helen's heart with an ill-advised passion, so
       that she wished to go to the ceremonies of this festival in order to
       see the festive celebrations and to look at the leader of the Phrygian
       nation. But oh, how often these kinds of spectacles have led many
110   very shameless women to shameless ruin by the observation and sight
       of games and pastimes, when young men come and practice their
       charms and with sudden rapacity seduce the captivated hearts of
       women from the follies of the celebration to the peril of their honor.
       Since young men have an easy opportunity to see young girls and
115   others urged very strongly toward worldly trifling, now by their eyes,
       now by soft speeches of flattery, now by touches of the hand, now
       by the encouragement of signs, they ensnare the hearts of women
       who are themselves easily moved by secret sophistries and the
       pleading of charming lies. May he perish who first brought it about
120   that young women and young men they do not know dance together,
       which is a manifest cause of many disgraceful acts. Furthermore, on
       account of these dances, many girls who were chaste till that time
       fall outrageously to the treacherous attacks of men, from which
       scandals often arise and the deaths of many follow. Therefore,
125   although it is right to go in groups to the temples of the gods and to
       attend their festivals, still it is evidently and clearly wrong when it
       tends to the corruption of hearts which, moved at the sound of

instruments and diverse songs and melodies, ruin themselves.
But you, Helen, loveliest of women, what spirit seized you so
130 that in the absence of your husband you left your palace on
such a frivolous account, and went through its gates to look at
an unknown man, when you could easily have restrained the
rein of the bridle so that you would have preserved your
modest abstinence within the palace of your kingdom? Oh,
135 how many women the coming and going and readiness to run
about to common places bring to ruin! Oh, how pleasing to
women should be the walls of their homes, how pleasing the
limits and restraints of their honor! For an unrigged ship would
never know shipwreck if it stayed continually in port and did
140 not sail to foreign parts. You, Helen, wished to leave your
palace and visit Cythera so that, under the pretext of fulfilling
your vows, you might see the foreign man, and under the
pretext of what is lawful, turn to what is unlawful. For the
sight of this man was the venom by which you infected all
145 Greece with the result that so many Danäi finally died and so
many Phrygians were poisoned with severe pangs. Need I say
more? In order to accomplish the desire she had already
conceived, Helen called together certain members of her household and bade them prepare the things necessary—horses and
150 retainers—because she wanted to go to the temple of Venus at
Cythera, where the solemn feast of Venus was being celebrated
and where Helen wished to fulfill certain vows. For Cythera was
not far from the kingdom of Menelaus, since it was, so to
speak, opposite it, and was separated from its shores by a little
155 strait. Without delay, the horses and retainers were prepared,
and Helen, in royal attire and with her retainers, mounted her
horse and arrived at the shore. She sailed in a short journey to
the island of Cythera where she was received with great honor,
as much by the inhabitants as by the others, as if she were the
160 queen of this island. At last she went to the temple of Venus
to fulfill her vows, and there she presented her offerings of
many and valuable gifts to the goddess Venus.

When it was made known to Paris that the queen, that is,
Helen, the wife of King Menelaus, had come with marvelous
165 splendor to the temple of Venus in a great retinue of her

people, Paris, elegantly adorned, went to the temple. For by a
previous report, he had already heard long ago that Helen, the sister
of Kings Castor and Pollux, was esteemed for her incredible loveliness.
As soon as he saw her he coveted her, and while being easily kindled
170 from the torches of Venus in the temple of Venus, he seethed with
intense desire. Fixing his gaze attentively upon Helen, he observed her
closely, noticing that every part of her was imbued with great beauty.
For he admired her thick golden hair which shone with radiant
splendor and which a parting of snowy whiteness divided into equal
175 portions in the midst of the hair, and whose waves were controlled as
if by the law of a fixed treaty by narrow gold bands winding serpent-
like here and there. It fell over her milky forehead, and the snowy
plane extended toward her gleaming temples where the cloud of
golden hair rose above the brightness shining forth. No unpleasant
180 roughness wrinkled the level plane of her forehead. He admired also
the twin eyebrows at the lowest part of her shining forehead; they
were golden and so formed that they were becomingly raised and
showed themselves like two arches, with the result that they were not
blackened in a great cloud of dreadfully dark hair, but, shaped with
185 proper balance, adorned with greater brightness the twin circum-
ferences of the eyes. He also admired the eyes representing the beams
of two stars, whose orbs, as if they were formed by a skillful setting
of jewels, were not greatly restrained in their lively motion by modest
glances and promised steadfast constancy of heart. The reins of the
190 eyelashes also restrained them on account of the proper length of the
lashes. He also admired the marvelously beautiful regularity of her
nose which, dividing her cheeks into two equal parts did not slope
with great length toward the base, nor, diminished by excessive
shortness, cause the position of the upper lip to be unsuitably high.
195 Thus, since it was not swollen with too much thickness, it did not
spread out in great width, while the nostrils were joined without
much space intervening, and they did not display themselves with the
sight of a great opening. He also admired the great beauty and
brightness of her complexion, which was suffused with milky white-
200 ness, while roses mixed with roses decked her cheeks, since with no
change of time did the rosy color in them seem to languish with
faded power. Since the snowy color of the lines between cheeks and
lips was thus intermingled, the lips seemed to form again a rosy dawn

arising, which did not appear to refuse sweet kisses on account of
205 their great thinness, but pouting becomingly with their firm swelling
caused those who saw them to desire kisses with eager passion. He
admired her ivory teeth which were very small and even, no one
bigger than another, and the rosy gums which embraced them in a
straight line and seemed truly to represent lilies mixed with roses.
210 A chin completed the total outline of her round face; it was cleft in
the middle by a little hollow, round in shape, while the slight double
swelling under the hollow of the chin seemed to pour forth crystal-
line brightness. He also marveled that the little column of her neck
presented a snowy brightness, which, being formed of delicate flesh,
215 was whitened to an extravagantly milky whiteness by the radiance of
snowy splendor, while a necklace composed of several strands defined
her radiant throat. He also admired how her even shoulder blades, by
a gentle descent to her flat back, with a depression between them,
joined each side gracefully and pleasantly. He admired her arms,
220 which were of a proper length to induce the sweetest embraces, while
her hands were plump and a little rounded, and the slender tips of
her fingers, which were proportionately long, revealed ivory nails.
These arms, hands, and fingers shone with the milky-white brilliance
of clear radiance. He admired the even expanse of her broad bosom,
225 on whose surface two breasts like two apples, rising lightly as air,
culminated in twin nipples. Finally, observing her figure was of even
proportions, he considered and conceived the hidden parts to be of
more superior beauty, until truly he considered and clearly comprehended that in the formation of her person, nature had not gone
230 astray at all in anything.

With the greatest eagerness Paris placed himself close to Helen,
without disregarding the limits of modesty, and while he was fixing
his gaze upon her eyes, Helen returned his glance as he watched with
the answering reply of her glances. For the appearance of Paris
235 pleased Helen more than what the commendations of him which had
circulated had predicted, since she herself was the judge and witness
of his appearance, maintaining in her heart that she had never seen a
man of similar handsomeness nor one so suitable for her to love. Did
Helen therefore bend her glance toward the pleasures of the festival
240 which were taking place in the temple, or did she turn her head
toward the conversation of the foreigners? Because she was completely

consumed by a desire to look at Paris, she was completely weighed
down by anxiety, and she did not turn her eyes away to watch anything else. When Paris saw her caressing him with her eyes, he rejoiced
245   that his eyebeams were mingled with Helen's eyebeams. Thus through
reciprocal and pleasing glances they revealed to each other that they
agreed together in the violence of their mutual love, and while both
wondered inwardly how each would reveal the secret of his intentions
to the other, Paris dared to deliver the first indications of his desire
250   by exchanging signs instead of words. Helen, violently shaken by a
similar passion, felt Paris' desire and repaid it with a similar sign. She
also advised him by a nod that in the commotion of the revelers, he
might move closer to her. At which Paris, putting aside all pretext of
bashfulness, approached Helen's place, and what he had expressed
255   furtively by signs, he made known in a voice which was nevertheless
furtive and low. Thus while the others were occupying themselves
with what was joyfully taking place in the temple, and were not
heeding the wiles of those lovers, each advised the other what they
eagerly desired in their hearts, with voices dissolved in sighs, and
260   agreed between themselves with brief speech concerning whatever
should be done for their wishes. When this was done and Paris had
humbly taken leave of Helen, he left the temple with his retinue and
Helen followed him as he left with sweet glances as long as she could
see him.
265   As Paris went forth he was happy, though disturbed by love. He
arrived at the ships where he immediately had all the chiefs of his
army summoned to him, and when they were gathered in one place,
he spoke to them thus with spirited words: "O most courageous men,
it is known to all of you for what reason it has pleased our king,
270   Priam, to send us over to Greece. For it was his whole intention to
have his sister, Hesione, back again through our effort. If getting her
seems impossible to you, we should at least devote our effort to
injuring the Greeks in whatever way we can. For see, the recovery of
Hesione has been made impossible to us, since we know she is held
275   by King Telamon, a man who is indeed very strong and who is so
intoxicated with her love that he will not agree to restore her to us
without the violent conflict of war. We are not powerful enough to
be able to surpass this King Telamon in strength. We do not have
enough power to subjugate any Greek city, since the number of

280 Danäan people in these parts is so great. It remains, then, that we
should not set aside ungratefully that excellent gift which, as I think,
the gods have offered us in this place. For we see on this island, to
which our fates have drawn us, with the approval of the gods, that
the temple of Venus is filled with the chief citizens of Greece and the
285 best women from the adjacent provinces, whom the festival of Venus
has persuaded to come. Among others is the queen of this kingdom,
that is, the wife of King Menelaus. Furthermore, the temple is rich
with great wealth. If we attack it and those who are staying in it, if
we are able to lead them away captives, we will have the profit of
290 very great and very rich booty, booty not only from the persons
captured, but also from the goods, since there are many gold vessels
in the temple, there is a great amount of silver, and it is bursting with
a great abundance of golden tapestries. Why should we seek elsewhere
what rather offers itself to be accepted by us? I say that, if it
295 appears praiseworthy to you, when the shadows of night come, we
shall all rise secretly in arms and attack the temple in order to
plunder it, and we shall lead off to the ships the men and also the
women who are in it as our captives, and especially Helen, because if
we are able to take her away as a captive to Troy, by her capture
300 will result the certain hope that by exchanging her King Priam may
easily recover his sister. Therefore let each one of you see what we
should do about this before the opportunity for doing what we plan
is taken away from us."
        Finally, when he had finished his discourse, many of those in
305 attendance did not approve of doing it, but on the other hand, many
did approve. However, afterward, when they long considered the plan,
it was settled among them that, with the coming of night when the
moon had darkened the rays of its light, they would attack the
temple in an armed band and expose everything they could to
310 looting. It happened that when night revealed the stars, and the moon
was about to set, the Trojans seized their arms in the silence of night,
and when they were armed, they left the ships safely guarded by
armed men and entered the temple suddenly. They attacked the
people they found in it who were free from the suspicion of hostility,
315 and seized them, unarmed, at the point of the sword and led them
captive to the ships. They plundered their goods, despoiled the
temple, and looted everything. Paris captured Queen Helen and all

her companions with his own hand; he found no resistance or objection in her, since she was animated by consent rather than dissent.

320 Paris led her with all her followers to the ships, and when he had sent
her on board under safe guard, he returned to the looting. A very
great uproar from the protests of the captives was breaking the
silence of the night, and especially from those who preferred to die
rather than to be captured. Consequently the uproar from the great

325 tumult assailed the ears of the inhabitants who resided in a fortified
castle on a higher place above the temple. When they had been
roused by the shouts of the dying and of the others who had tried to
recover themselves by the aid of flight to the castle, they rose
dumbfounded from their beds, seized weapons and, descending in

330 arms from the castle by a rapid march, attacked the Trojans. For
there was in this castle a band of many bold youths, who fell upon
the Trojans just as if they had been trained in the mastery of arms,
and assailed them with fierce resistance, thinking to be able to kill
them and recover the captured people. It was a very great struggle,

335 from which there proceeded great carnage. But at last the Trojans,
who outnumbered them by much more than four times over because
of their troops of many armed men, attacked them and forced them
to flee, and pursued them at the point of the sword up to the base
of the hill of the castle. An end was made to the battle, and since the

340 Trojans had won the victory, they returned joyfully to the ships,
leaving nothing valuable in the temple, from which they had obtained
much booty and countless riches.

They accordingly boarded the ships which were filled with the
aforesaid riches and a multitude of captives, and when they had

345 raised the sails to the gusts of the winds, they were given a pleasant
voyage, with the result that, voyaging with favorable rowing for some
days, on the seventh day they reached the shores of the Trojan
kingdom and gaily entered the port of a fortified town, about six
miles distant from Troy, which was called Tenedos by the inhabitants.

350 When they had dropped anchor and tied the ships securely with
ropes, they joyfully descended to earth, on which they were received
with as great honor by the citizens of the town as by their own
people. After Paris had landed there, he sent his messenger to King
Priam, who immediately after he had reached the king reported to

355 him that Paris was unharmed and had arrived safely at Tenedos with

his men, and he recited in order the individual deeds Paris had done, just as if he had been present at the aforesaid deeds. King Priam exulted with great joy at the telling of these things, and when all the other events had been disclosed to the nobles of Troy, and to all the
360 commoners, they all prepared a solemn feast.

While Paris was at Tenedos, just as happy as when he had arrived there, Queen Helen was among the other mournful captives, and, as was apparent to those who were present, she was tormented with great anguish, while her face and bosom were wet with continual
365 mournful tears, and in a sobbing voice she bewailed the king her husband, the kings her brothers, her daughter, her native land, and her sons, and in distress and with frequent lamentations she would not touch food or drink. Since Paris regarded this as painful and grievous, he went to console Helen with humble and devoted words.
370 Because Helen was exhibiting profound grief and Paris could not bring her spirit back to consolation or comfort, he burst out against Helen in these words, as if he were moved by rage: "What is this, lady, that you are every day shaken by such grief and will not be quieted? Who is it who can long hear such grievous sounds with
375 patience, since you spend both days and nights in tears and laments? Do you think this will not hurt you or will not offer harm to your person? Surely you should have been satisfied by so many tears; if you had drunk as much water as the tears you are said to have shed, the water would overflow from your full breast. Therefore, lady, if
380 you please, make an end of your tears and henceforth be calmed and consoled, since in the kingdom of my father no want can trouble you, nor even those captives, whom you may command to live in plenty. For you will be honored according to your rank as a noble, surrounded by all delights, and respected for your very exalted
385 position, and your companions in captivity, whom you may command to be freed from their chains, may live safely in my father's kingdom, just as comfortably as in their own homes." At these words Helen, wiping away her tears, thus replied to Paris: "I know, lord, that I must of necessity follow your wishes, whether I want to or not, since
390 a woman, and especially one held in captivity, is not able to prevail over masculine force. Accordingly, if anything good is offered to me, a captive, and to the other captives with me by anyone, he who offers such things can hope for reward from the gods, since human

nature prompts one to sympathize with the afflicted, and the com-
395   passion of human beings pleases the gods." Paris replied to her:
"O noblest of ladies, whatever you demand shall be done without
fail." As soon as he had taken her by the hand, although she interposed a little resistance, he raised her from her seat and led her with
him to a place where many things were set forth with the greatest
400   magnificence, and where it would be possible for them to confer
secretly between themselves about all the details. Paris at once spoke
to her thus: "Do you think, lady, that if the gods and the Fates have
brought you away from your people and have wished you to come
to my country, such an exchange would be detrimental to you, so
405   that you would not have greater riches and more precious delights?
Or do you think the Trojan province does not exceed Achaia in
wealth, and that the latter only is wealthy in all precious things? Do
you think, O queen, that I wish to besmirch your dignity by a
licentious love? Indeed you will have greater wealth in abundance
410   and you will lead a life with more worthy pleasures, and as a companion in marriage you will have me whom you should not deem
unworthy since I am of equal or higher rank than your husband.
I propose to join you to me as a cherished wife and to live with you
forever in the sacred bonds of matrimony, nor should you think it
415   dreadful that you are exchanging the weak kingdom in which you
lived until now for greater kingdoms, since many kingdoms in Asia
are subject to the Trojan kingdom, and they will obey you with all
loyalty and submission. Nor should the loss of the husband you have
left cause you remorse, since he is not of as high rank as I nor my
420   peer in enterprise, nor at all equal to me in fervent passion. For all
my affections are kindled from the flames of your love, and you
should certainly expect more honor from him who cherishes you
more. Therefore, henceforth cease to grieve any more, and moderate
your tears and murmurs of complaint, and in these requests I ask that
425   you will hear and grant my humble entreaties." She responded: "Who
can refrain from tears who is as anguished as I with the pangs of such
great grief? I should have preferred the gods to have appointed
otherwise concerning my fortunes. Since it cannot be otherwise, I
unwillingly grant your entreaties, since there is no power within me
430   to resist your will." Then she immediately burst into sudden tears
and sobs which Paris again strove to calm with speeches. When she at

last had ceased crying, Paris sought leave of her in a low voice. And
with the coming of evening, Paris took pains to serve her no less with
caresses than with rich food in abundance.

435   With the passing of the silence of night and the coming of daylight, Paris took Helen, clad in royal garments given her by King
Priam, and caused her to mount a marvelously handsome horse,
decked with golden reins and with a golden saddle, with all other
captives mounted on horses in a great company, according to their
440   rank, and he ordered them to advance in a great train of knights.
Finally Paris, himself, and Deiphobus, Antenor, Aeneas, and also
Polydamas, and many other nobles mounted on spirited horses,
accompanied Queen Helen with the greatest splendor and honor.
When they had left Tenedos they proceeded to Troy at a slow pace,
445   and as they came near that city, King Priam in a retinue of many
nobles came out to meet them, and after he had greeted them and
received them with a happy face, he went to Helen, welcoming her
with deep affection and a joyous expression, and he humbly pledged
himself to her in gentle words. As they arrived at the gate of the city,
450   where a huge multitude of people poured forth, attending the
celebrations and great dances with all kinds of music, King Priam
dismounted first from his horse, and on foot conducted Queen Helen
by the golden bridle of her horse, and led her into his lofty palace.
Need I say more? Great were the pleasures which were enjoyed by
455   the entire Trojan city. Great were the feasts which took place on
account of the arrival of Paris and his men who had returned with
him unharmed. At daybreak on the following day, with the gracious
consent of King Priam, Paris took Helen to be his wife in the temple
of Pallas. On account of this, all Troy piled feasts upon feasts, added
460   celebrations to celebrations, and for eight successive days spent the
time in continuous games and excitement.

     After it had come to the notice of Cassandra, daughter of King
Priam, that Paris had united Helen to himself in marriage, she burst
out in a terrible voice, with complaints and wailing, exclaiming loudly
465   and saying: "Why, unfortunate Trojans, do you rejoice concerning the
nuptials of Paris, from which there will be so many future woes for
you, and because of which you will lament your deaths and those of
your sons, whom you will see cut down in the sight of their fathers,
and bereaved wives will see the cruel deaths of their husbands? Ah,

470 lofty Troy, which is about to be overturned in dreadful ruins, how
wickedly you will perish and be destroyed! Ah, miserable mothers,
with how much grief will you lock up the confines of your hearts
when you see the entrails of your offspring torn out and their limbs
torn asunder limb from limb! Ah, miserable Hecuba, whence will you
475 produce so many tears at the death of your sons, whom the bloody
swords of the wicked will slash and kill? Ah, blind people, ignorant
of awful death, why do you not tear Helen with violent hand from
that unlawful husband, and why do you not hasten to restore her to
her lawful husband before the fierce blade hastens and the sharp
480 sword boils in your blood? Do you think Paris' theft can be passed
over without serious punishment and bitter revenge, through which
your final destruction will come about? Ah, unhappy Helen, a terrible
seductress indeed, how many griefs you will produce for us! Therefore, miserable citizens, drive away this wicked destruction from your
485 homes, and while it is possible, shun death for life." Since the
aforesaid Cassandra was pouring forth these and other harsher words
with continuous complaints, and in her distress would not by any
means cease her warnings to King Priam, King Priam ordered her
seized and secured with iron fetters in prison. It is said this Cassandra
490 was detained there for many days, and if her laments and complaints
had penetrated the Trojan hearts more effectively, Troy perhaps
would not in the least have bewailed its eternal misfortunes, which
even to the present time mournfully soothe the ears of men and are
at no future time to be destroyed by the silence of oblivion.

*Here begins the eighth book, about how the Greeks, who had
received a report of Helen's abduction, began to plan what
they would do about it.*

While things were proceeding propitiously in the city of Troy
(actually unpropitiously on account of the hidden snares), and when
the Trojans had not yet reached the island of Tenedos, a tattling
rumor, flying about by means of confused narrations, came to the
5 ears of King Menelaus, to his great stupefaction. He had not yet left
Pylos nor the company of Duke Nestor. After the particular events
had been revealed to him, that is, the plundering of the temple on

the island of Cythera, which was subject to his kingdom, the death of
his people wickedly slaughtered there by the Trojans, the capture of
10   the women and others who had been led away to Troy, and finally,
the abduction of his Helen, whom he cherished more than himself
with a very tender affection, he was distressed by the pangs of great
grief. He fell flat on the ground, his spirits failed, and he could not
speak. But after a long time he recovered his powers, and in great
15   physical pain from grief, he bewailed the defeat of his people, the
abduction of the captives, and the absence of his Helen, who had
been carried away under the stain of such great reproach. He bewailed
her beauty which was to be dishonored by foreign hands. He bewailed
those pleasures which he did not think she would have in a nation of
20   barbarians. There was no end to his laments and tears. At last, when
this was known to Nestor, Nestor came to Menelaus, whom he had
made his close and dear friend, and joined in his tears, and with
soothing speeches and kind words tried to console his grief. While
Nestor could not put an end to his tears and weeping by any counsels,
25   Menelaus quickly prepared to return to his kingdom. Nestor did not
desert him but accompanied him, in tears, with a band of many
knights.

After he had reached his kingdom, he sent by a faithful messenger
for his brother, King Agamemnon, to come to him, and likewise
30   Kings Castor and Pollux. When they had heard his message, all three
kings reached him by a rapid journey. Agamemnon, however, when
he saw that his brother Menelaus was tormented by such grief,
addressed him with these words of consolation: "Why, brother, are
you weighed down by such grief? Although a just cause for grieving
35   disturbs you, still it is not the act of a prudent man to display by
outward indication the disturbance of his heart. For grief revealed
outwardly in adversity provokes friends to greater grief, and engenders
greater joys in enemies. Pretend, therefore, to show happiness,
although grief abounds, and pretend not to care about these things
40   concerning which a reasonable anxiety should pain you. Neither
honor nor vengeance is to be obtained by painful anxiety or rivers of
tears. Revenge is therefore to be sought with the sword, not by
murmurs of complaint. For the character of a wise man appears when,
having considered the adversity of hostile fortunes, he knows how to
45   endure the trials and does not let his spirit sink beneath the

oppressive weight of evils. Arouse, therefore, the spirit of your valor
against these evils, so that when righteous grief provokes you, you
will take on the inflexible spirit of vengeance, and so that the severe
wrongs done to you and to us will not pass by without punishment,
50   which is not to be sought in tears but in retaliating with great
courage. For you know that we have great forces, and in the manage-
ment of this revenge we have many allies, since in this the whole
empire of Greeks will arise, and, advised by us, not a single king will
refuse to take arms against the Trojans. In a very strong force and
55   with a great fleet, we shall all go to Troy, and if it happens that we
pitch our tents on its shore, it will be difficult, in fact impossible, for
the Trojans to dislodge us from the shore. Before that happens, their
nobles will be delivered to death and their commoners into harsh
servitude, when the Trojan city will be in our power and completely
60   overthrown, and that Paris, the doer of so many evils, if he happens
to be captured, will pay the bitterest penalties and be hanged on the
gallows like a vile thief. Therefore all sadness and grieving must cease
and we shall send our messages to all the kings of Greece, and to the
dukes, counts, officers, and nobles, so that they will powerfully assist
65   us in avenging the cause of this dishonor to us."
    When Agamemnon had made an end of his words and speeches,
Menelaus meekly agreed and thus speedily sent forth letters among all
the princes of Greece. Among the others who came at once were
these noble men: the valiant Achilles and Patroclus and the very bold
70   Diomedes. As soon as the matter of the whole undertaking had been
explained to them, all agreed unanimously to be gathered into a very
great army and in a great fleet, so that they might go in strength to
Troy to recover Helen and to obtain vengeance for the lawless
offense. However, for the execution of this undertaking they decided
75   first of all to choose someone as prince and leader, whom the whole
army would obey, and under whose kingly leadership this army would
be soundly directed. By the common consent of all those present,
King Agamemnon, a man of great valor, esteemed by all on account
of the intelligence of his counsels, was chosen as their commander
80   and leader.
    When all had pledged full power to him, the said brothers Castor
and Pollux, thinking the Trojans had not yet arrived in Phrygia, set
out upon the sea with certain of their ships to see if perhaps they

could recover Helen before she happened to reach Troy. Certain
85   people say, however, that the said brothers did not by any means
await the summons of Menelaus, but, as soon as the report of the
abduction of Helen reached them, set out upon the sea with a great
fleet. Whatever happened in this respect, when these brothers had set
sail with the intention of pursuing the Trojans, they had not had even
90   two days of good sailing when suddenly the sky, obscured by clouds,
became dark on all sides, and when the clouds burst, the clamorous
thunder roared, swollen with flickering lightning flashing in inter-
mittent light, and the minds of the sailors were stirred by fear. Then
the clouds quickly poured down watery showers in rain, and as the
95   tempestuous rage of the winds increased, the sea heaved, swollen into
huge waves. Its surface was made very dark by the thickness of the
atmosphere, and tossing peaks of waves arose, stirred up by the
hostile clouds and spewing forth flecks of foam here and there, from
which the black sea, as if it were boiling, was made white. Imme-
100 diately, the masts broke, the sails split, the lines snapped, the yards
fell, and all the rigging of the ships was lost. The ships were dispersed
by the great fury of the winds and separated one from another.
However, the ship in which the brothers were sailing together, with
its rudder broken by the force of the opposing tempest, and its masts
105 grinding together with a great clamor, and its proper course forsaken,
was borne through the sea in an uncertain journey by the adverse
waves, now here, now there, since, on account of the great damage,
it drove through the sea, sometimes straight ahead and sometimes off
to the side, until, swallowed in the troughs of the sea, with its keel
110 ripped open and the decks torn asunder, it plunged between the
waves, seen by no one. It is thought, more or less truly, that the
aforesaid two brothers and the rest of the sailors in it perished there
by drowning. In the same way the other ships following it, seized by
a similar storm, perished in different parts of the sea. However, while
115 the death of these brothers was unknown to people, and there was
no one who could show for certain what was the cause of their death,
certain ones wished to believe that, as a divine reward they were
made gods and immortal, translated into the sky, as the ancient
pagans would have it. Hence it is that poets say that they, when they
120 were taken up into the sky, formed the sign in the circle of the
zodiac which even until the present day is called Gemini, because it

was made from these twin brothers, although ancient philosophers
have said the sign of Gemini is so called because the sun, passing
through the zodiac, stays in it two days more than in the other signs.
125 Whatever is said, the two aforesaid brothers brought about the
unfortunate result of their death instead of the recovery of their
sister Helen.

Dares the Phrygian wished in this place to describe the form and
appearance of several of the Greeks and Trojans, and, although he did
130 not mention all, at least he described the most famous. For he asserts
in the book which he made, written in Greek, that he saw them all
with his own eyes. For very often during truces made between the
armies he went to the Greek tents, and he observed the nature of
each of the chief people, gazing at them so that he would know how
135 to describe their characteristics in his work. For he said first of all
that Helen was famous for excessive loveliness, whose size and
appearance we have presented clearly enough above, with this
addition, that he said that between her two eyebrows she had a
certain small and delicate scar which became her in marvelous fashion.
140 King Agamemnon, a man of great height, but gentle, gleamed with
milky whiteness. For he was strong and powerful, and his limbs were
formed in accordance to his strength. He was fond of exertion while
impatient of quiet, intelligent, daring, with great eloquence and charm
in speaking. Menelaus, his brother, did not attain such height, but in
145 his form preserved a mean of proper stature between tallness and the
limits of shortness. He was valiant in arms and very spirited in his
appetite for fighting. Achilles truly was adorned with marvelous
beauty with wavy golden hair, large grey eyes, and a loving glance; he
had a broad chest and shoulders, large arms, thick loins, and was of
150 an adequate height. He was distinguished on account of his great
courage. None of the Greeks then was stronger than he; he was eager
to fight, generous in giving, and lavish in spending. Tantalus, indeed,
was big of body, very brave, with flashing eyes, his fair skin suffused
with red, truthful, humble, avoiding quarrels but very eager in a just
155 fight. Ajax Oileus was thick of body, with broad shoulders, thick
arms, very tall, and always clad in rich garments. He was truly very
faint-hearted, and glib in talking. Ajax Telamonius was adorned with
great beauty, and although he had black hair, it was curly. He
delighted in singing, had a pleasant voice, and was the author of a

160 great number of songs and melodies. He was a man of great valor,
very fierce, who did not choose to make a display of his courage.
Ulysses, indeed, surpassed all the other Greeks in handsomeness; he
was valiant but full of shrewdness and wiliness, a very great teller of
lies, who could pour forth merry and pleasant words which were
165 chosen with such eloquence that he had no equal in the composition
of speeches. Diomedes had attained great height and had a broad
chest and sturdy shoulders; he was ferocious in appearance, deceiving
in promises, valiant in arms, avid for victory, and feared by many,
since he was very quick to do injury. He was extremely impatient
170 with those serving him, and he was very annoying to the servants. He
was quite licentious and endured great pains on account of the
passion of love. Duke Nestor was tall in stature, with large limbs and
thick arms, most eloquent in speaking, intelligent and practical and
always distinguished for trustworthy advice, easily irritated, and, once
175 provoked to anger, could not be restrained by any moderation,
although it would last only a short time. No friend could equal him
in the great sincerity of his loyalty. Protesilaus was handsome and
graced by proper height; he was very valiant and no one was swifter
than he, and he was very spirited in arms. Neoptolemus was tall in
180 stature, with black hair, large but round eyes, wide chest, broad
shoulders, joined eyebrows, and he stuttered in talking. But he was
learned in laws and of great skill in pleading. Palamedes, the son of
King Nauplius, was very handsome in appearance, tall and slim, but
of moderate height, spirited in battle, affable, tractable, urbane, and
185 most lavish of gifts. Polidarius was quite stout and swollen with such
fatness that he could hardly manage himself or stand erect, very
spirited, but exceedingly stubborn and obstinate. He did not know
how to be happy, and was always careworn from too much worrying.
Machaon truly was formed in even proportions, for he was not too
190 tall nor diminished by excessive shortness. Still he was haughty, very
spirited, with a high forehead on account of baldness, and he never
slept in the daytime. Briseida, the daughter of Calchas, was graced
with great loveliness, neither tall nor short nor too thin, endowed
with milky whiteness, with rosy cheeks, blond hair, and joined eye-
195 brows; this juncture, which was filled with hair, showed as a slight
flaw. She was famous for great eloquence in talking; she was pliable
because of great compassion. She attracted many lovers by her charm,

and loved many, although she did not preserve constancy of heart
toward her lovers. Besides these and other nobles, Dares writes that
200   the king of Persia came to aid the Greeks in a great band of knights,
whose appearance and form he does not omit among the others. For
he writes that he was of great stature, that he had a very fat face
with freckled skin, and a beard and hair as red as fire.

Dares also describes with his pen those who were in Troy. For he
205   writes that King Priam was tall in stature, slender and attractive, that
he had a low voice, that he was a man of great energy, and that he
was very fond of food in the morning. He was an intrepid man,
without fear, and detested the flattery of men. He was in every way
truthful in what he said; he loved justice. He loved to hear musical
210   sounds and songs of love. There was no other king who cherished his
comrades in arms with greater honor, or who enriched them with an
abundance of greater gifts. Of the sons of this King Priam, there was
none who was distinguished by as great spirit as Hector, the firstborn.
It was he who in his time surpassed all others in courage. He was a
215   little hesitant in speaking. He had very tough limbs, able to sustain a
great amount of exertion. His form was large. Troy did not produce
another man of such vigor or so magnanimous. He had a great head
of hair. No offensive or improper word ever left his mouth. The
exertion of battle was never tedious to him. He was never wearied by
220   the toil of fighting. We read that there was no one in any kingdom
who was loved so much by his subjects. Deiphobus, the second son
of King Priam, and the next, Helenus, his brother, were of one shape
and just alike in appearance so that there was no discrepancy between
them. One could hardly be distinguished from the other, if anyone
225   looked at them suddenly. Their own appearance was just like that of
their father, King Priam. The only dissimilarity that marked the three
was that King Priam was advanced in age and these two were
flourishing in the glory of youth. One of the two, that is, Deiphobus,
was esteemed for great valor in arms; and the other, that is, Helenus,
230   was very learned in the disciplines of the liberal arts. Troilus, although
he was large of body, was even larger of heart; he was very bold but
he had moderation in his boldness. He endeared himself to young
girls, since he was pleased to maintain a certain reserve toward them.
In strength and valor for fighting he was another Hector, or second
235   to him. Moreover, in the whole kingdom of Troy, no young man was

celebrated for such great strength and such great daring. Paris was
charming on account of his great beauty, with blond hair, so that his
whole head looked like shining gold. He was surpassingly skillful in
mastery of the bow and in the skill of hunting, and he was fearless in
240 the activity of arms and a knight who was unyielding in battles.
Aeneas was thick of chest, small of body, and wonderfully prudent
in deeds and temperate in words. He was famous for great eloquence,
full enough of sound advice, wonderfully wise, and acquainted with
much learning. He had a pleasant face with great expressiveness, since
245 his eyes were lively and shone with great beauty. There was no one
among the Trojan nobility who possessed so much property, well
supplied with castles and rich in manors. Antenor was tall and slim,
full of talk but intelligent. He was a man of greatest enterprise, very
cautious, the beloved favorite of King Priam, and when the occasion
250 presented itself, he mocked his companions with great wit. Nevertheless he was absolutely mature in all seriousness. Polydamas, the son of
this same Antenor, a handsome young man, was noted for great valor,
was of praiseworthy character, with a tall and slender body like his
father's, but a little darker in complexion. He was very brave and
255 strong and extremely powerful in arms; although he was rapidly
aroused to anger, he was curbed by great moderation. King Memnon
was handsome in appearance but large, with wide shoulders, thick
arms, a sturdy chest, and wavy, golden hair. The orbs of his eyes
were a brilliant black in color. He was a knight of great valor, who
260 performed very courageously and laudably in the Trojan War. Queen
Hecuba was tall of stature, inclining toward the masculine rather than
the feminine kind in appearance. She was a marvelously sagacious
woman, noble, learned in many subjects, very devout, very modest,
and loving works of charity. Andromache, the wife of Hector, was
265 graced with great loveliness, with a long waist, and gleamed with
milky whiteness. She had eyes which sparkled with great brilliance,
round cheeks, rosy lips, and golden hair. She was the most virtuous
of women, temperate in all her acts. Cassandra was of proper height,
very fair, with a freckled face, lively eyes, seeking maidenhood and
270 fleeing, so to speak, any wifely activity. She knew how to predict
many things about the future, since she was rigorously and clearly
instructed in the knowledge of the stars and other liberal arts.
Polyxena, the daughter of King Priam, was a very delicate maiden,

graced by great loveliness. She was indeed the very ray of beauty, for
275 nature had formed her with great care, and nature had erred in
nothing, except that she had made her mortal. It would be useless
effort to explain her appearance in particular details since she
surpassed, so to speak, the beauty of all other women. Therefore it is
understood that all parts of her had beauty in abundance and that
280 she was distinguished for virtue so that she held all kinds of vanity
detestable.

Of these only did Dares the Phrygian wish to describe the forms
and appearance, of the Greeks as well as the Trojans, since in both
armies there were many conspicuous for great courage, whose names
285 and courage while fighting here and there will be narrated individually
and in order. It remains, therefore, that our truthful pen be sharpened
in order to reveal the course of this history in its continuous acts one
after the other in succession.

*Here begins the ninth book, about the number of ships the
Greeks took to Troy.*

It was the time when winter had already shed its frost, and its cold
was dispelled on account of the season, and the ice was already
melted when, since the snow had melted, various streams were already
swelling in their various courses through the hollows of the valleys,
5   and sluggish winter, which lacks heat and fire, was finally fleeing on
account of the imminent approach of spring. The sun was running in
the last stages of Pisces, while the last and final days of the month of
February were approaching, and the month of March which was to
follow was already near. At this time the whole Greek army, well
10   supplied with a large fleet, had assembled in the port of the city of
Athens. Let the readers of the present history know, therefore, that
never, from the creation of the world, had so many ships come
together, filled with so many knights nor with a company of so many
warriors, as what they will read about, revealed by a descriptive
15   account. You must know that Agamemnon, king and leader of the
army of the Danäi, brought with him from his city, that is, Mycenae,
one hundred ships loaded with warrior knights; Menelaus, also, the
husband of Helen and brother of this Agamemnon, brought sixty

ships full of knights from his kingdom which is called Sparta. From
20 the kingdom of Boeotia, Archelaus and Prothenor, kings and lords of
it, commanded fifty ships. Duke Ascalaphus and Count Helimus
commanded thirty ships from the province of Cythomenia.
Epistrophus and King Tedius brought fifty ships along with a great
company of knights from the kingdom of Forcis. Ajax Telamonius
25 brought fifty ships from his kingdom and from his noble city,
Salamis. In his retinue were many dukes and counts, and they are:
Duke Teucer, Duke Amphiacus, Count Dorion, and Count Theseus.
Old Duke Nestor arrived from Pylos with fifty ships. King Thoas
brought fifty ships from his kingdom of Tholia. King Deximais
30 brought with him fifty ships from his kingdom. Ajax Oileus brought
thirty-six ships from his kingdom, which is called Demenium.
Polibetes and Amphimachus, lords of the province of Calydon,
brought thirty ships. From the kingdom of Thrace that most eloquent
King Ulysses brought fifty ships. Duke Melius brought ten ships from
35 his city which is called Pigris. Prothotacus and Protesilaus, dukes of
the province which is commonly called Phylaca, brought ships to the
number of fifty. From the kingdom of Triconicus, King Machaon and
King Polidus, brothers, sons of the former King Colephis, brought
twenty-two ships. From his noble city which is called Phthia, Achilles
40 brought fifty ships. King Thelephalus brought twenty-two ships from
his island kingdom which is called Rhodes. Eurypylus brought fifty
ships from his kingdom, which is called Ortomenia. Duke Antiphus
and Duke Amphimacus, lords of a certain wild province which is
called Hesida, brought eleven ships. King Polipetes, from his kingdom
45 which is called Richa, and Duke Losius, his mother's sister's son, had
sixty ships brought. The valiant Diomedes, with Thelenus and
Euryalus in his company, brought eighty ships from his land of Argos.
Poliphebus offered seven ships from his kingdom, which was not yet
distinguished by great fame. King Fineus, from his kingdom, which he
50 held from the Greeks, brought eleven ships. King Protheylus, from
his kingdom which is called Demenesa, brought fifty ships. King
Capenor brought the same number from his province of Capadia.
Treorius, from his kingdom which is called Beisa, brought twenty-two
ships with him.
55   The whole number of the aforesaid kings and dukes was sixty-
nine. The ships of the Greeks totaled one thousand two hundred and

twenty-two, not counting Palamedes, son of King Nauplius, who came
last with his ships, as reported later below. Homer in his time said
there were one thousand one hundred and eighty-six, but perhaps
60   from weariness he did not describe the whole number.

*Here begins the tenth book, about the Greeks sending to
Delphos to obtain an answer from it as to what they were
to do concerning their course of action.*

After the aforesaid kings, dukes, and princes of Greece had assembled
in the port of Athens with their ships, it happened that Agamemnon,
that very valiant man, who as leader and prince was diligently maintaining vigilant care of the whole Greek army, began to consider
5   carefully how he might afterward successfully approach the undertaking. Accordingly he ordered the Greek kings, dukes, and princes to
come to him in a certain field outside the walls of that city, where
seats had been made ready. When all had come before him there, and
were seated in order, and silence had been ordered by Agamemnon
10   by a motion of his hand, Agamemnon himself poured forth these
words to them: "O noble men, who have united in this company in
your strength and courage, you clearly perceive and see how great is
the power of your forces, and how great a multitude of men is in the
band of warriors you have brought together. Whoever saw in past ages
15   so many kings, dukes, and princes collected in one place and agreeing
in purpose? So many young men outstanding in arms and warfare
joined together to wage war courageously against the enemy? Is he
not led by obvious madness and overwhelmed by the spirit of blindness who would dare to rebel against us and to provoke our troops to
20   battle? To be sure, of all of us who are gathered into this army, I
know one hundred who are so powerful that truly one of them alone
would suffice to carry out and bring to a happy conclusion that
which we are all together yearning for. For no one of us is in any
doubt as to what dishonor disturbs us at present, or what injuries
25   offered us and ours have recently provoked us to take arms justly
against the Trojans and to begin cruel conflicts against them. However, both reasonable necessity requires, and righteous grief impels us
to this, namely, that we may arise in complete unanimity to pursue

our vengeance with ardent hearts so that at the very beginning we
30 may place a bit in the mouths of those who slander us and wipe out
our shame in such a way that the Trojans will not thereafter leap to
commit similar things. Concerning the excesses committed against us,
if they are not troubled by the punishments you owe them, they will
not fear to proceed afterward (may it not be so!) to worse things.
35 For our ancestors were not accustomed to let anything dishonorable
go by in silence which could be shamefully ascribed to them by
publishing the reproaches of slanderers, nor should we, therefore, in
the same way, close our eyes to what we and ours could be shamefully accused of by our successors, especially since so many of us
40 agree in one desire and purpose, and we are assembled in such an
array of power. For who is there today who could measure our
powers? Actually there is no one to be seen who would dare boldly
to arise to attack us, except the foolish people of Troy who, led by
blind and obstinate counsel, hurl themselves to attack us on account
45 of ill-advised and foolish plans. Does not the greatest part of the
world know how certain of our people attacked King Laomedon, the
father of this Priam, with weapons of war, and killed him and a
countless number of his people, overthrowing completely the city of
Troy, then held by that same King Laomedon? Are there not among
50 us here in Greece today many of them who, after they had been
carried away by our men according to the violent law of spoils,
bewail their perpetual servitude in our provinces? To be sure it is
neither impossible nor improbable for a thousand more powerful men
to do what was done by four or five men less powerful than they.
55 Indeed I know that they know that we have united against them, and
therefore, they have begged the approval of many allies and have
sought for great support so that they may ably oppose us and boldly
defend themselves against us. For this reason it seems agreeable to
me, if it is granted graciously by you, that before we have weighed
60 anchor and left this port in safety, we send our special devout
messengers to the island of Delphos to the god Apollo so that they
may receive from the god himself and from other gods of ours a
response concerning what is fitting and allowable for us to do hereafter in these matters which we are, with their approval, about to
65 undertake."
    And thus King Agamemnon made an end to his speech. When he

had said these things, and when all the aforesaid kings, dukes, and
princes had heard the discourse of King Agamemnon, they praised it,
and thus all approved unanimously that it be done as he had decreed.
70 For this reason, they all agreed with one voice to choose Achilles and
Patroclus for the execution of this task, so that they might go to the
island of Delphos and humbly seek an answer from the god Apollo,
for the common good, which in a special way concerned them and all
the others in common. Without delay, the aforesaid Achilles and
75 Patroclus entered the harbor by safe rowing, in order to carry out
faithfully the aforesaid business, and with the favor of the gods, they
had a pleasant voyage and arrived safely, by the swiftest course, at
the island of Delphos.

The aforesaid island of Delphos was surrounded by the sea on all
80 sides, and it is certainly believed that this was the island of Delos,
which [name] was applied to it perhaps by a fault of writers. This
island is situated in the middle of the islands of the Cyclades, that is,
located in the Sea of Hellespont. For this reason it is one of the most
important of these islands in the midst of the Cyclades. On that
85 island, as Isidore relates, Latona gave birth to Apollo and Diana, and
so Apollo was worshipped on it in a temple built in a miraculous
structure of walls. It is called Delos because when the flood receded,
it was first illuminated by the rays of the sun before all other lands,
and the moon was first seen there. For it is called Delos, that is to
90 say, "manifestation," for *delos* in Greek means "manifest" in Latin.
Because the sun and moon were first seen from this island, the pagans
claimed that this island was the land of the sun and moon, and that
for that reason they were born on it, since the sun is called Apollo
and the moon, Diana. This same island is also called Ortygia, because
95 quail were first born there, which the Greeks call *ortygiae*. The
pagans said that this Apollo was a god. They said he was the sun,
Titan himself, that is to say, one of the Titans who did not attack
Jupiter, and that the same was Phoebus, or Ephoebus, that is,
"youth," because the sun is born daily. Likewise the same Apollo was
100 called Pythias from the python serpent killed by him. From this, certain women skilled in predicting the future were called pythonesses,
since the same Apollo prophesied to them at their request. It is
written about this pythoness in the Old Testament, in the First Book
of Kings, that at the prayer of King Saul, she made Samuel stir when

105 he had been dead a long time. In this temple there was a very great
image all made of gold in honor of this god Apollo. Although it was
made of gold, and in truth was deaf and dumb, still, the pagans,
according to their error, embracing idolatry (which chiefly prevailed
among them because they lacked the true worship of the true God,
110 who in His Wisdom, that is, in the Son of God, Our Lord Jesus
Christ, created all things of nothing), clung to the worship of deaf
and dumb gods, who assuredly had been mortal men, believing and
considering that those who had no power were gods. But the answers
which were given by them were given not by them but by those who
115 walked about in their images, who were surely unclean spirits, so that
through their answers men were kept in the perpetual blindness of
error.

However, how idolatry came into being and had its evil beginning,
and how answers were given by unclean spirits, since we now have
120 the opportunity, we have taken care to describe briefly in this place,
and how the aforesaid idolatry was ended, when through the glorious
coming of Our Lord Jesus Christ, all the idolatry in the world ceased
on all sides and vanished completely on account of its exhausted
vigor. For it is certain in the writings of the Church, according to the
125 truth of the Holy Gospel, in which the light of pure truth is present,
that when King Herod was deceived by the Magi and sought to kill
the Child, that is, Our Lord Jesus Christ, Savior of the World, an
angel appeared in a dream to Joseph and told him that he should lead
the Mother and Son into Egypt. When the Child arrived there with
130 His Mother, all the idols in Egypt fell down together, and there was
not one idol to be found in Egypt which was not torn to pieces.
Isaiah says about this: "the Lord will ascend upon a swift cloud, and
will enter into Egypt, and the idols of Egypt shall be moved," in
order to show that through the coming of Our Lord Jesus Christ, the
135 Savior, all idolatry was completely overthrown and had to cease. This
is why the Jews say Ishmael fashioned the first image from clay, but
the pagans say dogmatically that Prometheus made the first image
from clay, and that from him developed the art of making images and
statues. They are called pagans because they were always without the
140 Law, and were always thus, so that they are stated to have been born
serving idols from the first. The origin of idolatry is said, indeed, to
have proceeded first from Belus, king of Assyria. For this Belus was

the father of King Ninus, and when he was taken by death, he was
given a sumptuous tomb by his son Ninus. Ninus, his son, in his
145 memory, ordered an image constructed of gold which was amazingly
like his father, so that for his comfort and in memory of his father
he could imagine by the sight of the image that he was seeing his
father. Accordingly, King Ninus worshipped this image as if it were a
god and ordered it to be worshipped by his people, and he handed it
150 down to be believed by all Assyrians that he was deified in Heaven.
And so, after not much time had gone by, an unclean spirit entered
into this idol of King Belus and gave answers to those who sought
them. This is why this idol was called Belus among the Assyrians.
Some say Bel, some Beel, some Baal, some Beelphegor, some
155 Belzabuch, some Beelzebub. From the example of this idol, the
pagans proceeded to the worship of idols, imagining that dead men
were gods and adoring them as gods. This is why they said the first
god was Saturn. This Saturn was the king of Crete, his name being
taken from that planet which is called Saturn. When he was dead he
160 was said to be a god, having neither father nor mother. It was said
about him in legend that since he was extremely wise in magical
practices, he foresaw that he would produce a son, whom his wife
was then bearing, who would cast him from his kingdom and force
him to be miserably exiled. This is why he ordered his wife to give
165 him the son she was carrying so that he could devour him. But when
the son was born, she hid him and showed his father a certain little
stone, saying that she had borne this little stone and nothing else.
The father swallowed it on the spot. It is said that he fathered three
sons and one daughter, that is, Jupiter, Neptune, and Pluto, and the
170 daughter, Juno. The pagans said that these are all gods. Then Jupiter
or Jove acquired the name of the planet Jupiter, and the pagans
worshipped him by the name of the highest god. Next they claimed
that Mars was the highest god of war. Next the sun, which they
called Apollo, who was worshipped chiefly in the island of Delos, as
175 was said. Next Venus, named after the planet Venus. Next Mercury,
named after the planet Mercury, who they wished to assert is the son
of that Jupiter. Next Luna, who was also called Diana, the daughter
of Latona, as was told above. Thus throughout the different nations
of men the pagans worshipped different idols. So it is they wor-
180 shipped Isis in Egypt, Jupiter in Crete, Juba among the Moors,

Faunus in Latium, Quirinus in Rome, Minerva in Athens, Venus at
Paphos, Vulcan at Lemnos, Bacchus at Naxos, and Apollo at Delos or
Delphos, as was said. They also established many names of other
idols, in doing which each expressed his own feelings. But now it is
185   established, according to the tradition of the most sacred Roman
Church, that as soon as the Creator of the world created angels in the
empyrean heavens, He made that angel who was preferred before all
the others, about whom the prophet said: "The cedars in paradise
were not higher than he, the fir trees did not equal his top, neither
190   were the plane trees to be compared with him for branches: no
[precious] tree in paradise was like him in his beauty." Therefore
God made him beautiful and gave him command over all the other
angels. He was puffed up by great pride when he said, "I will place
my seat in the north, and I will be like the Most High," and he
195   immediately fell from eternal bliss with his legions, and the Devil and
devils were made. Hence the name *devil*, that is, "flowing down." On
account of this it is said, "How have you fallen, morning star, from
the midst of glowing jewels?" Lucifer fell, who had fed on delights
in Paradise, and wounded by Death, he descended into Hell. From
200   this, Christ in His Holy Gospel said, "I saw Satan like lightning falling
from Heaven." He was the Leviathan. Because this material is not
known to many, we have decided to describe it in a short account in
this place. For Isidore writes in his *Etymologies* that the Hebrews call
him Behemoth in the Hebrew tongue, which means in the Latin
205   language "a brute beast." For he is an evil spirit, full of uncleanness
and impurity, and accordingly, when he was first cast out, God
changed him into a brute beast, that is, into a crooked serpent, and
since he was of huge size, he was called a dragon. About this, David
declared: "This great and spacious sea, etc."; then he added, "This
210   dragon which thou hast formed to deceive them." He is also called
Leviathan, according to Isidore, a water serpent. For this reason it is
read in the *Apographia* of Saint Brendan that while he was voyaging
through the ocean, this saint saw that this beast was of amazing
length and huge size, and that he was cast down in the depths of the
215   sea and confined there at the command of God until the Day of
Judgment. On that account he is said to be crooked and in the sea,
because in the churning sea of this world, the Devil is engaged with
deviousness in capturing the souls of the miserable. This is that

Leviathan who was made a serpent and who from the beginning of
220 his banishment envied the honor of our first parents; he dared to
enter the Paradise of pleasure, and walking erect, just like a man,
influenced our first parents by concealed temptations and by lies, so
that, by boldly transgressing the command of God, they deserved to
be cast out from the glory of Paradise just as he deserved to be cast
225 out from the glory of Heaven for his sin. Granted that which is read
at the beginning of Genesis, according to Mosaic tradition, where it is
said: "Now the serpent was more subtle than any of the beasts which
God had made. And he said to the woman: 'Why hath God commanded you . . .'" and so on; still, according to the tradition of the
230 Sacred Scriptures of the universal Catholic Church, it is believed, as
Bede writes, that the Devil then chose from a certain race of serpents
a certain serpent which had a girl's face and moved its tongue for
speaking what it did not understand. In the same way, the Devil
speaks here daily through fanatics and those who, being possessed, do
235 not understand; that is, through men whose bodies are possessed by
demons, as it is written concerning this in the *Historia Scholastica*
near the beginning, where the author is pursuing the history and
exegesis of the Book of Genesis. Hence, whatever is known to us
Catholics through these Sacred Scriptures, it is certain that that
240 Leviathan, that is, the Prince of Devils, cast down from the height of
heaven, either by making himself bodily into a serpent, or by entering in his own person into a serpentine animal, with his cunning
temptations cast our miserable parents and their descendants into
perpetual ruin. This is sufficient talk about idolatry and about
245 knowledge of Leviathan.

Now to pursue the plan as we intend, let us turn our pen to the
narration of the present history. Demons, therefore, entered into deaf
and dumb idols which the pagans then worshipped, and it was they
who produced the answers being sought for. From this David says:
250 "For all the gods of the nations are demons, but the Lord made the
heavens." Through the wiles of this demonic deception the god
Apollo revealed his answers to the petitioners on the island of Delos.

After Achilles and Patroclus, the Greek messengers, had reached
this island, they took the proper hour for entering the temple, at the
255 advice of the priests in the temple who served the god who was
worshipped in it, and they entered this temple humbly with devout

heart. When they had made their offerings with a lavish amount of
large donations, and as the messengers of the Greeks were seeking to
have an answer from him concerning the affairs of the Greeks, this
260 Apollo replied to them thus in a low voice: "Achilles, Achilles, go
back to the Greeks by whom you were sent, and tell them they will
assuredly go in safety to Troy and carry on many battles there, but
they will be victors without fail in the tenth year, and will completely
ruin the city of Troy, and will deliver King Priam, his wife, their
265 children, and all their nobility to death, and will only permit those
to live whom the will of the Greeks chooses." When Achilles had
understood this, he was made very happy by it, and as he remained
there in the temple, a marvelous coincidence took place. For a certain
Trojan priest named Calchas, the son of Thestor, a man of great
270 knowledge and experience, had entered the temple at the command
of Priam, as his messenger, in order to elicit likewise an answer from
the god Apollo as to what would truly happen to the Trojans in the
war with the Greeks. After he had made his offerings in many ways
to this god, the god responded: "Calchas, Calchas, beware of return-
275 ing to your country, but go at once in safety to the Greek fleet,
which is now at this island with Achilles, since through it you may
quickly join the Greek army, never to be separated from the Greeks.
For, by the will of the gods, it is to be that the Greeks will obtain
the victory against the Trojans. You and your counsel and learning
280 will be very necessary to these Greeks until they obtain the aforesaid
victory." When Calchas, by asking, had learned that it was Achilles
who was in the temple, he hurried to him at once, and as they met
one another on the spot, they received each other in the bond of
friendship and disclosed to each other the truth concerning all the
285 aforesaid. For this reason Achilles, with a joyful expression, took care
to honor the aforesaid priest Calchas by many rewards.

When they had raised the anchors from the sea and had sent
themselves with their ships over the deep, they arrived safe and sound
at Athens. When they had disembarked from the ships, Achilles
290 presented the priest Calchas to King Agamemnon and all the other
kings, dukes, and princes of Greece. After Achilles had reported the
answer of the gods concerning their future victory against the Trojans,
and how this same Calchas, the messenger of King Priam, had
obtained a contrary response, and about Calchas' being ordered not

295 to return to Troy but to stay with the Greeks during the upheavals of
     battle, all the Greeks were happy, and celebrated the festal day with
     great rejoicing. They welcomed this priest Calchas into their confidence
     and received him with sincere affection, promising him to fulfill his
     wishes willingly in all things. Thus this festal day was brought happily to
300 an end.

*Here begins the eleventh book, about the Greek army leaving
Athens.*

     The Greeks, when favorable answers had been set forth by the gods,
     had already fulfilled the days of celebration. On the following day,
     after the celebration had ended, Calchas, that Trojan priest, in the
     train of Achilles and Patroclus, went when it was morning to the tent
  5 of King Agamemnon, where already many of the kings, dukes, and
     princes of Greece had assembled before who were waiting in the
     presence of King Agamemnon. When Achilles, Patroclus, and Calchas
     had greeted Agamemnon and the others and had disclosed the oracle,
     and when those assembled had obtained the proper report and reply
 10 from them, they disposed themselves among the others in convenient
     places. As soon as Calchas had obtained silence, he spoke these words
     in the public assembly of the aforesaid nobles: "O most noble kings,
     dukes, and princes, who are brought together in order in the present
     audience, was it not your chief intention to take arms against the
 15 Trojans, your declared enemies, who by a great outrage committed by
     them have aroused your courageous forces against them? Why there-
     fore do you delay in what you have begun, since it is always harmful
     to delay when ready? Do you believe or think that King Priam does
     not have his spies among you secretly, who by their agents send word
 20 to him about every detail of your slothfulness? For to act thus is
     nothing other than to agree to allow him a period of freedom so that
     he may acquire the army he has sought, and may every day collect
     allies, when already so much time has passed since you should have
     invaded his kingdom in a powerful force. Have not many months of
 25 the present summer gone by, in which a favorable time for sailing
     presents itself to you, when the seas are completely calm and caress
     those who wish to sail, and the sweet breezes breathing and sighing
     on the level surface of the sea lure those wishing to sail by the sweet,

calm weather? Why does not your heart burn to burst upon the seas
30 in the burning heat of summer, so that when you have obtained a
sweet breeze for sailing, you will reach the shores of your enemies by
easy rowing, and the report concerning your careful preparation will
terrify their ears so that they will not rejoice at your overscrupulous
inactivity, through which your desires are so much suppressed? Do
35 you believe the promises of the gods to you are trifles, when they
could be changed to the contrary on account of the vice of ingratitude? Break off your delays, therefore, weigh anchor, and raise the
sails on high so that you may hasten quickly in your journey against
your enemies, the gods willing, and speedily and happily attain the
40 promises of the gods." Thus Calchas made an end of his speech and
was silent.
　　Accordingly, when these words of Calchas had been understood by
everyone, while they were all together approving them, Agamemnon
immediately ordered the whole army to move at the sound of the
45 trumpet and to embark upon the ships immediately, in order to
depart at a favorable time from the port of Athens. Without delay, at
the sound of the trumpet, they all embarked upon the ships, undid
the knots of the ropes which were firmly fastening the ships, and,
when the anchors were raised from the sea and loaded on the ships,
50 they raised the sails, and as the breath of the winds touched them
and spread them, they committed themselves to the deep ocean. In
sailing over the sea they had not yet removed themselves the distance
of two miles from the regions of Athens when suddenly the bright
sky, which was smiling upon the sailors, was obscured by dark clouds,
55 producing an artificial night. For this reason the sky roared in the
complaints of frequent thunder, and frequent flashes from its rapid
lightning converted the artificial night into day, and heavy rains
poured down, drained from the clouds, Because of all these things,
the rough winds raised the swollen seas in mountainous waves. For
60 this reason the greatest fear and trembling seized the sailors, as they
saw they were in danger of death. But that Trojan priest Calchas,
after he had done his exorcizing, since he was very skilled in it, said
he perceived the cause of the great disaster. For he said the goddess
Diana was aroused by great wrath, "because there was no sacrifice
65 made to her concerning your departure from the port of Athens by
those wishing to set forth." He therefore persuaded King Agamemnon

to turn all his ships instantly with slack sails toward the forest of
Aulis, where in the temple in which the aforesaid Diana was worshipped, Agamemnon himself might offer a sacrifice to this goddess
70 with his own hand. "For after Diana has been pacified she will make
the storm disappear and suitable weather for sailing will present itself
to you."

Without delay, according to the counsel of the aforesaid Calchas,
at Agamemnon's command all the ships with sails changed and
75 rudders adjusted to them arrived safely at the forest of Aulis, which
was not far from them. King Agamemnon quickly landed and went to
the temple of Diana. With faithful heart he dedicated to her in
sacrifice certain offerings with his own hands. Accordingly, the storm
at sea disappeared and the sky everywhere cleared and removed its
80 garments and put aside its clouds. The seas became quiet, and those
wishing to sail were charmed by its pleasant surface. From this
occurrence, certain wise men who toil in the fine points of astronomy
claim that Diana, who is herself the moon, is the mistress of journeys
and roads. They decree she is propitious in her orbit, although she
85 may be strengthened in the tenth or eleventh house by the favorable
aspects of other lucky planets. Astronomers make use of this reasoning even to the present day.

When the storm at sea had been calmed after the sacrifice offered
by Agamemnon to Diana, the whole Greek army, ordered by the
90 sound of the trumpet, at once boarded the ships. After a pleasant
voyage, they arrived with safety in Trojan territories and successfully
entered the port of a certain fortified town, where, when the ships
had been safely received, since the harbor was large enough for them,
the Greeks consigned their ships to protected moorings. Dares the
95 Phrygian, however, in his book omits the name of this fortified town
and port, perhaps because the Greek army stayed in it such a few
days. It is thought, however, as it is found in other books, that it was
called Sarranabo by the inhabitants. The inhabitants and occupants of
this outpost came to the shore in an armed band by a hurried march,
100 thinking to prevent the Greeks from landing, uniting against them
with foolish and ill-advised plans. Because of this they foolishly
attacked the Greeks, who had already landed, wearied and tired from
the sea, and started a foolish war with them. A countless number of
Greek warriors landed and exacted from them the punishment for

105 their foolishness. For they pursued them at the point of the sword,
and since they could not withstand the Greeks on account of the
latter's great number, they delivered themselves to the aid of flight.
On account of this they hastily strove for the turrets of the castle,
scattering before the face of the Greeks. The Greeks, then, pursuing
110 those miserable men who were hardly able to save themselves by
precipitous flight, freed the captives by death, and delivered to death
each of them they caught. With violence they scaled the castle, which
they found with gates open to receive the fleeing inhabitants, and
entered it and cruelly attacked the miserable people they found there,
115 who were already exhausted because of failing strength. They
slaughtered them with the sword, seized the castle, and looted it.
When they finished the looting, they cast down the walls and all the
fortifications of this castle into sudden ruin. Without delay, when
they had borne off all they found and overthrown everything in ruin,
120 the victorious Greeks went back to their ships and boarded them.
They immediately set out on the sea and came in a direct course to
the port of Tenedos. Arriving there safely, they cast the anchors of
their ships overboard, lowered the sails, and gaily entered the port.
    Now there was at the aforesaid Tenedos a certain castle con-
125 structed with great strength, manned by many of the inhabitants from
all around, rich with great wealth, since that place was delightful
because of all the pleasures of land and sea. It was about six miles
from Troy, as was told above. The occupants of this castle, fearing
that they would be destroyed, immediately rushed to arms, fortified
130 the castle with fierce men and arms, and planned to oppose the
Greeks strongly by a bold defense. The Greeks, however, when they
had conveniently tied their ships together in the port and had put
them at safe moorings, landed in arms in a huge body of fighting men
and violently delivered everything they found to rapacious looting,
135 and carried out severe attacks against those who were bending all
their efforts in hostile endeavors against them. The fighting grew
cruelly heated between them and the Trojans of this castle, and a
fierce combat raged between them. Because of this, many Trojans
fell, slain by swords, but more of the Greeks. The Greeks, because of
140 their defeat and vengeance, showed themselves panting more eagerly
for death and more courageously for wounds. Many of the Greeks
died in the midst of all this, and also very many Trojans. At last the

Trojans could not withstand the countless number of Greeks and
committed themselves to the protection of flight, and there was no
145 other choice for those who were allowed to flee than to arrive at the
high walls of Troy by escaping through flight. Indeed, those who did
not benefit by flight were slain by the sword and lost their lives
cruelly by bitter death. Thus when all the outer wall of this castle
had been surrounded by the Greeks, they attacked the aforesaid
150 castle, assailing it with great force. The Trojans, in their battle lines
on the top of the walls, opposed the Greeks with a fierce and terrible
defense. Now they struck them down by hurling stones, now they
pierced them with quivering lances, now they harried them with sharp
javelins, and now they gave them deadly wounds and delivered them
155 at last to death by frequent sallies of arrows from the ballistae. The
Greeks lined up different kinds of machines and set up various
battering rams in various places, and raised as many military scaling
ladders as possible, and then fiercely assailed the Trojans in a deadly
attack. In this attack, many of the Greeks were hurled from the
160 ladders, and, spinning as they fell, reached the ground and with
broken necks, breathed their last. Indeed the Greeks were dying
everywhere. At last the Trojans, wearied by the great effort, defended
themselves with a weakened and debilitated resistance. At which the
Greeks, with an irresistible force of fighters concertedly pressing
165 forward against the Trojans, gained the castle by means of ladders,
some through the windows, others through the cleared tops of the
walls, and raised their banners along the walls. Then in reprisal for
their men killed by their opponents, they slaughtered as many as
they found, either by the sword or by the fall. They spared no one
170 and, with no respect for age, killed all whom they had cut down with
the sword. When no Trojan remained alive among them, the Greeks
examined all the hiding places in the castle, seizing with greedy
looting whatever they found that was useful, carrying it off, and
when all places were completely emptied by the removal of things,
175 they at last decided to destroy this castle. After its lofty walls were
laid flat and everything was broken in ruins, and the walls had
crumbled and fallen to the surface of the ground, lofty Tenedos was
razed to the ground as much by the violence of the battering as by
the devouring flames of the fires which were set. After they had
180 destroyed and seized everything, the victorious Greeks returned to
their ships with their great booty.

*Here begins the twelfth book, about the Greeks sending
to Priam for restitution for Helen and for the damage done
by Paris.*

The Greeks had obtained complete victory over these two castles and
their garrisons, and while they were leading a more relaxed life at the
port of Tenedos and its plain, King Agamemnon was giving careful
attention to the business of his command. He ordered all the Greeks
5   who had succeeded in taking loot from the supplies and spoils of the
Trojans in the two castles to come to him and to bring in all of the
aforesaid loot they had taken. At once, when they had heard the
bidding of their leader, they all observed obedience and quickly came
before him with all the things captured by them, and brought with
10 them all the aforesaid captured booty into the presence of this King
Agamemnon. When equal portions had been made for distribution by
this king, he distributed them to each, according to the merits and
qualities of those who had not sought to avoid death or wounds in
obtaining victory over these two castles. When he had finished the
15 aforesaid equal portions among the fierce warriors, as has been said,
this king ordered all the kings, dukes, and princes of the Greeks to be
summoned by the voice of a herald to come on the following day at
sunrise, with all the other leaders of their army, to this plain, where
this king intended to hold a general assembly.
20   On the following day when it was morning, all the kings, dukes,
and princes of the Greeks, and the officers of their army, assembled
gaily enough on this plain, and, when they were settled in their
proper places, Agamemnon, the aforesaid king, with his right hand
and by verbal order, demanded complete silence, and thus burst into
25 speech among them with these remarks: "Dear kings, dukes, and
princes, and all officers in the circle of the present gathering, we have
assembled for a necessary reason. It is enough that through all distant
parts of the world the strength of our army is recognized, since the
world publishes the greatness of our strength everywhere. Neverthe-
30 less, any power which lacks pride and does not know the fault of
stubborn self-love is pleasing and acceptable to the gods. For it is
known to all how many evils come from the exaltation of pride, and
the gods themselves oppose the proud with wonderful resistance. For

the proud do not have friends and they collect enemies everywhere.
35 If anyone becomes a friend to a proud man, it is necessary that he be
an enemy to many. Let us therefore curse the fault of pride as much
as we can in all our dealings, and especially in this present, so that
our deeds may shine forth by the sole aim of righteousness and
justice, and no one may attribute the fault of pride to us. For you
40 know that we have come here with the great part of our army to
obtain vengeance for the injuries offered us by King Priam, and we
have invaded the boundaries of his kingdom with a powerful force,
and we have already inflicted such great damages and losses upon him
that if the Trojans were hostile to us before, they have now been
45 made more relentless. For we know they are forearmed with a great
army, and they obviously know we are near them, and if they could,
they would immediately take cruel revenge for the injuries recently
done to them. For they have a strong city strongly walled all around,
and also we believe their strength against us has doubled, because
50 whoever defends himself in his own home among his acquaintances
and friends or in his own territory is said to prevail by means of
great advantage. Does not the crow who is quiet in his nest, although
he may be weaker in strength, carry on savage struggles against the
falcon before he is seized by him, and does not the latter often
55 retreat wounded? Obviously I do not pour forth these words among
you so that we may doubt that we can overthrow the Trojans and
destroy their city, however strong it may be, and swallow up all the
Trojans in final ruin, but because we will deserve to be commended
with great praise if in all things we are about to do in this under-
60 taking, we exert ourselves with the guidance of discretion, and avoid
pride. For ill-advised heedlessness usually plunges many into the abyss
of death, and to begin an undertaking, which has not been thoroughly
thought out with much examination and advice, leads at once to
ill-considered acts through the impulse of pride. We know besides that
65 Priam was the king who not long ago sent us special messengers to
ask us to restore his sister Hesione to him. But we, swollen with great
exaltation of pride, refused by shortsighted answers to hear their
request, which if it had been heard by us, the heavy losses at Cythera
would not have been thus wickedly inflicted upon us, and Queen
70 Helen, who is esteemed among the best women in Greece on account
of her virtue and that of her people, would not have been abducted

from the magnificent residence in her country. We who seek her
restoration and revenge for the wrongs done to us would not go to
such effort and expense at such a great distance from the homes in
75 our country, completely ignorant as to whether the future would be
propitious or the opposite. In accordance with your pleasure and by
sound advice, if it seems acceptable that we should avoid adding
efforts to efforts, and that we might deserve to be back home in the
glory of our honor, let us send our special messengers to this King
80 Priam, so that he may voluntarily restore the abducted Helen to us
and make satisfaction to us for those things which Paris did to us. If
King Priam acts wisely and causes this to be accepted, our return to
our country will be honorable, and by rights we ought not to demand
any more from the Trojans. If, indeed, he causes it to be refused, two
85 praiseworthy acts will fight for our rights, that is, justice and our
exonerated army. When what has happened has been published by us
to all parts of the world, the madness of the Trojans will be rebuked
by those who hear of it and our course commended everywhere,
since it is exonerated from all fault of pride. If afterward we inflict
90 the severest punishments on the Trojans in our revenge, by killing
them everywhere at the point of the sword, and by completely
destroying their land, and leading their wives away into continual
disgrace and perpetual servitude, there will be no one who will be
able with reason to rebuke us for this. Therefore, if it pleases you,
95 let it be considered whether to carry this out in action, according to
the advice of my speech."

When he had said these things, there were many of those in attendance who said the previous remarks were not to be followed, and
others who approved arranging that it be done as the king had
100 commanded. When they were finally unanimously agreed upon this,
they elected Diomedes and Ulysses as their messengers. These two
immediately prepared for the journey, and when the sun was already
standing in the middle of the sky, they arrived at the walls of the
city of Troy, and entering it, went to the grand palace of King Priam,
105 where, when they had dismounted from their horses, they climbed
the marble stairs. When they had reached the entry of the spacious
court, they marveled at the buildings of this palace, buttressed with
work of such marvelous skill, but they marveled even more when
they saw in the middle of the court itself a certain tree made by

110   magic arts and constructed with clever ingenuity. While its trunk was
      of gold, slimmer than a lance and twelve cubits in height, at the top
      of its trunk the tree itself, of an amazing breadth, poured itself out in
      branches which sheltered the whole court by their length and profu-
      sion. In fact, the branches were made partly of gold and partly of
115   silver, as were the leaves and blossoms, while the fruits gleamed,
      formed of a great diversity of jewels.
          The dukes, contented with their long inspection, mounted, in a
      train of many people, to the gates of the vaulted halls, and when
      they arrived where King Priam was sitting in a great company of his
120   nobles, they did not honor the king with any speech of greeting. But
      they sat down opposite him, and Ulysses thus addressed him: "King
      Priam, if at first we do not seek you out with words of greeting to
      you, do not wonder, since we consider you as a deadly enemy, and
      an enemy ought not to ask for the greeting of his enemy. King
125   Agamemnon, whose ambassadors to you we are, sends you word by
      us that you should let Queen Helen be restored to her king, since you
      carried her violently away from the boundaries of her kingdom, and
      that you should endeavor immediately to make reparations on the
      Greeks' terms for the heavy losses inflicted on them by your son
130   Paris. If you do this, you will enjoy the safety of sound advice. If,
      however, you by chance scorn to fulfill this, consider how many evils
      will finally befall you and yours. For you will succumb to an
      unfortunate death, all your people will perish by a cruel death, and
      your noble city will be in ruins, brought to nothing."
135   When King Priam had understood Ulysses' words, without waiting
      for any deliberation or advice, he responded thus to Ulysses: "I am
      moved with great wonder at what you have said, since you require
      such things from me as would hardly be suitable from a conquered
      king and enemy placed in exile. For I do not think your Greeks
140   surpass me by such great strength that I should be compelled to do
      what you say. They seek satisfaction for themselves from me when
      they are the reason—although perhaps there was another reason—for
      their unworthily killing my father, brothers, and those related to
      them, completely destroying my city, delivering my subjects to death
145   and exile, and abducting my sister Hesione—might she ever be treated
      as royalty! But she is disgraced by the vile condition of harlotry
      while they seek to urge me to satisfy them! I, however, wished

nonetheless to pass my life in silence regarding such great evils, and
not to be eager for the clash of battles, and so I sent my ambassador
150 Antenor so that they would at least condescend to restore my sister
Hesione, with nothing else requested concerning the wrongs which
had been committed. How much dishonor, how many threats they
inflicted upon my ambassador is obvious enough to you and to me.
This is not the proper occasion, therefore, for me to hear the words
155 of your embassy; certainly I should rather die disgracefully first.
Accordingly, let King Agamemnon be certain above all that I shall
never seek peace with the Greeks, who have afflicted me with so
many griefs. Were it not that the office of ambassador defends you,
I should also have you, who have used such words to me, killed with
160 the vilest death. Therefore go back to your people, because while I
see you I will not be able to refrain from seething with great rage."
    At which Diomedes, immediately bursting into laughter, said thus:
"O King, if you are not without anger simply at the sight of us, you
will not be without anger for the whole period of your life, since the
165 Greeks are close to you in a very great army. This is not the time for
delaying further, but rather you will see us and them always in arms
before your city, attacking you and yours. If you are irritated with
great grief by us, alone and unarmed, how much more will you suffer
when you see more than one hundred thousand Greeks in arms
170 against you, against whom no defense will save you, but rather you
will feel the unfortunate annihilation of your cruel death? Before
such evils happen to you, you can utter in freedom and safety words
which are, in effect, idle."
    Then many of those in attendance were incensed at Diomedes'
175 words and wished to fall upon him and do him serious injuries, even
surging toward him with bared swords. But King Priam, rising from
his throne, shouted loudly at them not to dare to do him any injury,
since it was not wise to reply to a fool according to his foolishness.
"Let it be fitting for the fool to show his foolishness, and for the
180 wise man in his wisdom to tolerate the errors of fools. Just as a fool
is free to utter foolish words, so it is praiseworthy for a wise man to
hear what is said and to smile at what he hears. The foolishness of a
speaker is recognized by his foolish words. I would prefer first to
suffer in person rather than expose to injury any ambassador who is
185 in my court. For anyone can easily reproach himself for a small and

mean deviation. Sit down, therefore, everyone, and let no one of you presume henceforth to offer any more dishonorable words."

Thus when they had ceased, Aeneas, who was then sitting next to King Priam, with no one else in between, was unable to moderate his
190 words, and spoke thus: "O Lord King, it is not right that a fool should be answered according to his foolishness. It is right that he who utters foolish things receive discipline in accordance with his foolishness. I could say so much and such dishonorable things in your presence that by right you would be able to order me killed. If he
195 were not in your presence, it would not be improper that he, who has already spoken so ridiculously, should die, since he does not shrink to wound Your Majesty boldly with such fierce and bitter words, and disgracefully presumes to disturb you by these words. I advise him therefore to leave this place unless he wishes to exchange
200 his presumptuous foolishness for wisdom."

Diomedes, not a bit taken aback, replied thus to the words of Aeneas: "O you, whoever you are, I know well by your speech that you are no upright judge but a shrewd speaker in rebuttal. I wish very much that I might be able to find you in some suitable place in
205 which I might render you the appropriate thanks you deserve for the words you have spoken in this pleasing speech. I see well how happy is that king who keeps you in his councils, you who know so well how to counsel your king so that your king may be the doer of wrongs and thus easily prone to dishonor."

210 Ulysses, however, prudently interrupted Diomedes' words and advised him to utter no more words. And then Ulysses spoke thus to King Priam: "O King, we have understood completely everything you have said. Hereafter we shall depart from you and report faithfully to King Agamemnon all the things which were said by you." Thus at
215 once they both went down from the palace, mounted their horses, and at a speedy pace reached their army. As soon as they had dismounted from their horses, they together entered the tent of King Agamemnon, where the leaders of the army were staying with Agamemnon. When they had reported to them all that had been said
220 by King Priam, the Greeks were greatly amazed at the answer of Priam, and they began many kinds of plans as to how to proceed against the Trojans in these things, about which we shall report below one at a time and in order. Truly, however, before we advance to the

course of the narrative, some things are to be said about Aeneas.

225   He was that Aeneas, the offspring and son of Venus and Anchises, who after the fall of the Trojan city fled by sea with the Trojan survivors, and by sailing through the Tyrrhenian Sea with certain of his ships, after many adventures was made prince of the city of Rome and of the Roman Republic. From his race proceeded in great felicity

230   that great and glorious Caesar Augustus. It is also about him that the Emperor Justinian makes glorious mention in his book of laws, that is, in the *Liber Authenticarum,* in the rubric that the name of the emperor is to be placed on legal documents. He says there that if the rest of the emperors after the great Caesar Augustus are called

235   Caesars, with much more reason should all the emperors from the earliest times be called Aeneases after Aeneas, who first governed the Roman Republic imperially, as if with the imperial scepter. The continued fortunes and successes and, in addition, the many exploits of this Aeneas were, for the most part, described by Virgil, while he

240   lived, in his work the *Aeneid,* although he was cut short by death and was not able to finish his work completely.

Here begins the thirteenth book, about the Greeks sending Achilles and Telephus to obtain provisions for the Greek army.

As these things were going on, as was related above, King Agamemnon, by a public proclamation, ordered all the kings, dukes, and princes to come to a general council on the plain of Tenedos. Immediately after they had arrived at this place, Agamemnon tersely

5   explained the gist of his plan in these words: "Among other things which are very necessary for our army to do, the most urgent is that we take care and solicitude that our army, while it is engaged in the wars, has an abundance of provisions, for without a great supply of provisions, our army will hardly be able to advance. For this reason,

10   if it seems acceptable to you, we shall send our messengers, valiant and loyal men, to Messa, without delay, in order to keep having continuous supplies, since Messa is esteemed for its very great fertility. These messengers are to decide on the provisions in such a way and arrange things so to our advantage that they will manage to

15 have our army abundantly supplied with the provisions, continuously
and without fail, in ever increasing amounts." When Agamemnon had
finished his speech, all in attendance approved his plan, and at once
the valiant Achilles and Telephus, a son of the late Hercules, were
unanimously chosen for the execution of this undertaking, so that
20 they would go to Messa in a great company of warrior knights in
order to carry out these things.

In this province reigned a king named Teuthras, who had held his
kingdom in peace for a long time, since a troop of many knights and
an aggressive band of young fighting men lived in it. Many have
25 wished to say that this was Sicily, which was always overflowing with
an abundance of many provisions, and was called Messa from the city
Messina in it, which is located at the entrance of this island on part
of the coast of the kingdom, and possesses an amazingly safe harbor,
in which the ships of a large number of fleets are protected in safe
30 moorings at all times. Certain people have wished to say that the
aforesaid city of Messina is so called because the crops produced and
gathered in the territories of adjacent places are brought to it because
of the port—crops which are afterward conveyed abroad by sailors to
different parts of the world for the sake of profit. Others, however,
35 say this city was designated Messa, from the title of a certain king
named Messanus, who, while he was reigning in the island, wished
this city to be called by his name. But Dares the Phrygian tells
nothing about this in his work, but simply has Achilles and Telephus
come to Messa in order to seek provisions. Since perhaps it was other
40 than the island of Sicily, it could have been closer to Greece than the
island of Sicily, which is quite far from it, although it has been
recorded that Sicily was subject to the rule of the Greeks.

Achilles and Telephus reached this province of Messa with a troop
of three thousand valiant knights in a large fleet. When their ships
45 had touched the shore of this country and they had landed, King
Teuthras, with many knights and many fully-manned troops of foot
soldiers, came to the shore where Achilles and Telephus had landed
with their company. They immediately rushed to arms since they
rightly suspected that the king and his men were coming against them
50 because he did not by any means wish to allow them to be in his
land, and with dauntless courage they presented themselves in battle
against the attackers. Need I say more? The battle raged very fiercely

on both sides; here and there corpses fell, cut down by the sword.
Many of the Greeks fell, but many more of their enemies. Although
55   the Greeks were distinguished by great courage, still they were hardly
able to resist their adversaries, who were three times as many. Truly,
all the Greeks would have perished wretchedly had it not been for
Achilles' marvelous feats of arms. When he had studied the quantity
and qualities of the fighters with great care, he saw and recognized
60   King Teuthras in the thick of the fighting, inflicting amazing losses
against his enemies. For this reason Achilles hurled himself impetuously into the conflict, broke the line and scattered it, and killed all who
placed themselves in his sight and who did not open way for his
passage. Like a roaring lion he reached King Teuthras, attacked him
65   with bare blade, harassed him with frequent blows, pierced him with
wounds, forcefully tore loose the fastenings of his helmet, and seizing
the king, he hurled him violently to the ground. In his rage he had
raised his sword and was about to kill him. But Telephus, who was
fighting second to Achilles, as he perceived Achilles wished thus
70   cruelly to kill King Teuthras, and with his raised right hand wished to
cut off his head, thrust between them and received the descending
blow on his shield, and in a gentle voice humbly begged Achilles that
in his kindness he give up the final death blow, since King Teuthras
was mortally wounded, almost dead, and vanquished, who with his
75   clasped hands offered himself to him as conquered. Achilles, answering Telephus, immediately said: "What reason moves you to practice
such gracious kindness toward our declared enemy, who, trusting only
in arms, first provoked us by such a cruel pursuit? It is right that he
fall into the trap which he prepared." Telephus replied: "Lord, this
80   king was once associated with my father in great friendship, and once,
when I came by chance to his land, he showed many honors to me
and showered his favor and useful assistance upon me in the greatest
quantity. On account of which I should loathe the loss of his life and
hate his death." Achilles said to him, "Here, take him; and do what-
85   ever you like with him."

   After Teuthras had been snatched from Achilles' hands and rescued
from instant death, the battle came to an end. The troops departed;
the victorious Greeks returned to their ships. King Teuthras was taken
back to his palace half-dead. At his entreaties, proffered with great
90   protestations of submission, Achilles and Telephus entered with him

and were received in his palace as guests with great honor and an
abundance of rich gifts. Not many days after, King Teuthras, worn
out by the deadly wounds inflicted by Achilles, had been brought to
the point of death by their weakening effect, and seeing the rapid
95   approach of the final hours of his life, he ordered Achilles and
Telephus to come to him. When they had come to him and found
him lying on the royal couch, King Teuthras spoke to them thus:
"Glorious dukes, may you long enjoy prosperity. I speak to you
especially, Telephus, my dearest friend, because already I am arriving
100   at the end of my life and am no more able to avoid the destruction
of death. Therefore, since the fates have not wished to offer me a
legitimate heir of my own family, do not let my present kingdom
remain as property without an heir, for I obtained it with great effort
and with too much effort maintained it unchanged until now. How-
105   ever I would undoubtedly have lost what I had already obtained,
unless that valiant man, who excelled all other valiant men on
account of his courage, the most victorious Hercules, your father, had
not rushed swiftly to my aid at my prayers while my kingdom was
already occupied by a large number of my enemies and I had no
110   hope of regaining entrance. He alone, solely by his mighty courage,
routed all my enemies in a hard-fought war after killing many of
them, with the result that his kingdom was then and afterward
delivered from all hostile attack, and he gave it to me free and in
peace and quiet. Hence it is that I have held the seaport of this
115   kingdom not by my merits or my mighty courage, but only through
the affection and courage of your kind father." (From this point,
those who think that the province of Messa was Sicily corroborate
their opinion with great firmness, asserting that Hercules came to
Sicily. Hence it is said that in one part of Sicily, in the barbarians'
120   part, Hercules set up his pillars in order to be remembered. This is
called today the Place of the Pillars, and the land once lying within it
was called Herculea, although some would wish to call it Heracleia,
by corrupting the name of Hercules. But these things are not certain.
In that land, formerly cultivated by the barbarians and given over
125   completely to ruin, there survive today certain pillars which are
commonly called the Pillars of Hercules, and there Frederick II,
prince of the Roman Republic and king of Sicily, once had some land
piled up, thinking that this place would be good to live in on account

of the situation, although it was located right on the sea and lacked
130 any safe harbor. This land, however, filled with people on account of
the good qualities of the location, is up to the present day called
Terra Nova.) King Teuthras, however, delaying his final end, although
he had interrupted his speech, continued to Telephus in these words:
"Since, therefore, my son Telephus, that man your most victorious
135 father obtained this kingdom for himself by means of his own
courage (and I did not consider it restored to me by him but rather
given in trust by him), and, since the fates did not wish to give it to
him alive, the fates have granted it to you with reason, as a right to
be held by you in his place, whose son and heir you are. For this
140 reason, with the intention of making a bequest in this my present
will, I name you my heir, both to this kingdom and to my other
goods, so that you may govern it and possess the scepter and crown
of this kingdom. However, you will take care to give me royal honors
in a royal burial, and to celebrate my funeral in regal fashion." When
145 he had spoken and written these things, King Teuthras forthwith
finished his life as death came upon him. After he died, Telephus,
saddened by his death, together with nobles of his kingdom, gave his
body an honorable burial. His tomb was constructed from very
precious marble, in which Telephus ordered the body to be laid. On
150 the face of this tomb he ordered this epitaph to be carved:

King Teuthras lies here, whom Achilles annihilated in death; he gave the
scepter of his kingdom to Telephus to keep.

When this was done, all the nobles of the kingdom, and all the
populace throughout their cities, performed the oath of fealty and
homage to Telephus, now newly made king, who had for a long time
been designated by the title of duke in his own right through his
155 father, and they accepted him as lord and king. Afterward this King
Telephus, with the intention of ruling, took over the government of
his kingdom. Achilles, however, loaded the ships with all the supplies
and provisions and other necessities intended for carrying on life, and
ordered King Telephus, who wished to proceed with him to the Greek
160 army and actually return, to stay and remain in this kingdom in
which he had been made king, although he was reluctant, advising
him and adding commands to the advice that he should exercise
vigilance and incessant care about the uninterrupted flow of

provisions and other things to eat to the Greek army. Telephus
165 offered to carry out the aforesaid things with all loyal devotion and
affection. Then Achilles left Telephus and sought the deep sea with
his ships, and by sailing in a direct course, arrived safe and sound at
Tenedos, where the Greek army was then staying. He disembarked in
a train of many men and went to the tent of King Agamemnon,
170 where the kings, dukes, princes, and the officers of the army had
speedily gathered. They received Achilles with great happiness and
embraced him warmly with the greatest rejoicing, and with friendly
kisses they showed their affection to this man whom they held more
dear than the rest, and more powerful in all things. When he had
175 reported all the things which were done in the province of Messa,
both about Telephus being made king and about the ships being
loaded with provisions because of this, and also about the unfailing
amount of provisions promised by Telephus for the times to come,
with the result that the Greek army would never hereafter have to
180 fear any lack of provisions, all were very happy with increasing joy,
and on all sides they praised with good reason Achilles' glorious
course of action. When he had ended his words, Achilles went back
to his tent, where he was received with great joy and high spirits by
his Myrmidons, who offered him many favors and gifts.
185   Since, then, Dares Phrygius digressed in this place in telling this
matter, and decided to tell what kings, and how many, and what
dukes and princes came to the defense of Troy, before he said anything about the next actions of the Greeks, successively and in order,
it is fitting that, just as above we described the kings and dukes and
190 others who came with the Greek army, in this place we make
mention of them, if not of all, at least of the important ones. For it
should be known that although Dares Phrygius says nothing about
their kingdoms, three kings came with more than three thousand
armed knights, that is, King Pandarus, King Thabor, and King
195 Andastrus. Likewise from a certain province which is called Colophon,
which is said to be an island of great beauty and which has many
rich cities, there came four kings in a train of five thousand knights.
The first of them was called King Caras, the second King Imasius, the
third brave Nestor, and the fourth King Amphimacus. From the
200 kingdom of Lycia with three thousand knights came King Glaucon
with his very brave son Sarpedon, who was bound to King Priam by

the bonds of friendship. From the kingdom of Lycaonia came King
Euphemus with one thousand knights tried in battle. From the
kingdom which is called Larissa came two kings with fifteen hundred
205 knights, that is, the great Hupon and King Eupedus. From the kingdom which is called Thabaria came King Remus with three thousand
knights, and in his company there were seven counts and four dukes
who were loyal to Remus by feudal oath. They all carried arms the
color of glass-green or yellow, without any design, and in the lines of
210 battle King Remus and his men could be easily recognized, although
there were others who bore these same arms. From the kingdom
which is called Thrace (that is, that Thrace which is located in the
east) came King Pilex and Duke Alchamus, leading with them eleven
hundred knights. From the kingdom of Pannonia came King
215 Pretemessus and a first cousin of his, Duke Stupex, with as many as
one thousand knights, although his whole kingdom consisted of
gloomy mountains, groves, and dark woods. Towns were rare in it,
and there were almost no fields. It is said that many satyrs and two-
horned fauns flourished in it abundantly, and also that there were
220 many marvelous sights in it. In this land are many different kinds of
birds and wild animals, and its company of knights was more skilled
than the rest in the use of lances and bows and arrows. From the
province of Boeotia came three dukes with twelve hundred knights;
that is, Duke Ausimus, Duke Fortinus, and Duke Sanius. From the
225 Bithynian kingdom, which lies far to the east, full of all kinds of
spices, came two brother kings, that is, King Boetes and King
Epystrus, with a thousand knights. From the kingdom of Paphlagonia,
which is so close to the regions of the rising sun that the kingdom is
almost impossible to see on account of its great remoteness, came
230 that very rich man, that is, King Philimenis, who was rich because of
the gold and jewels which are frequently found in the rivers Tigris
and Euphrates, on whose banks this kingdom of Paphlagonia is
located. With him came two thousand knights who had shields which
were not constructed of wooden material but from tanned leather,
235 shining, however, with much gold, and ornamented with various
jewels. This King Philimenis was of very great stature, no less than
the stature of a giant. From the kingdom of Ethiopia came King
Perseus, and in his train the valiant King Memnon, with knights,
dukes, and counts who were his subjects. Also in their train, and with

240   three thousand knights, came Sigamon, the brother of King Memnon
mentioned above. From the kingdom of Thereus came King Theseus
and his son Archilogus, with one thousand knights, since King
Theseus was joined to King Priam by the strict ties of blood relationship. From the island which is called Agresta came two kings whose
245   names are not given, and with them, twelve hundred knights. From
the kingdom of Delissenia, which is beyond the kingdom of the
Amazons, came a certain old king, very distinguished for great
intelligence, whose name was King Epistropus; he was learned in the
seven liberal arts. He brought with him one thousand knights and an
250   archer who was marvelous to see, since one half, above the waist, was
man, and below the waist he was a horse, and that half which was
human was all covered with hairy skin, just like the skin of a horse.
He had flaming eyes, just like red fire, and was skilled with the bow.
His appearance was terrible, and he inflicted many terrible deeds upon
255   the Greeks as he fought, and gave them as many injuries as possible,
while he slew many Greeks with deadly wounds. Now the knights
who came with these kings, besides the knights of King Priam and the
king of Minor India, were in number thirty-two thousand. For we
read that never since the creation of this world were so many knights
260   and so many young men ready for war collected into one place when
the flower of all the knighthood of the world had come together in
one place, as much on the Trojan side as on the Greek. Let the
readers of the present history consider for how trivial a cause and
how feeble a reason the death of so many men took place. Surely
265   causes of offense should be abhorred to the extent that they are
undertaken for a feeble reason.

*Here begins the fourteenth book, about the Greeks leaving
the island of Tenedos and going over to besiege the city of
Troy.*

The Greeks had not yet left Tenedos when that glorious Palamedes,
son of King Nauplius, with thirty ships loaded with knights, arrived
there. The Greeks were greatly pleased at his arrival, although they
made many charges against him concerning his delay and why he had
5   not come more quickly and hastily to Athens. He excused his absence

reasonably by saying that he had been detained by a grave illness. This Palamedes, however, was regarded with great honor among the Greeks, since he was first or second among the Greek nobles, capable of fighting courageously, intelligent in all counsel, especially of war,

10 very wealthy, and well provided with knights. The Greeks accordingly asked him to make one of their council. Palamedes graciously agreed to their request.

The Greeks, and especially their officers, met in one place for many days and nights, so that they might examine the definite plans

15 by which they could easily and conveniently come to besiege Troy. They prepared at first to carry out this business under the shadows of night. But they were moved by fear concerning the departure of the ships from that place where they were and their arrival on the coast of the city of Troy, lest the darkness of night and especially

20 having no real knowledge of the places could offer a hazard to the ships and sailors, with the result that they abandoned this proposal, and having considered anew many plans, they now approved the plan suggested by Diomedes alone, when he spoke these words among the Greek councilors: "Listen, all kings and princes who are now present

25 and can turn to my words, and pay attention to what they mean. We should be dismayed and overwhelmed by the shame of dishonor that already a year and more has elapsed since we came to this land, and we have not been able to summon up the courage to leave it so that we could go to or see Troy. What have we accomplished in the

30 interim? Truly nothing other than that we have given our enemies the ability—we have sharpened their wit and understanding—to discover something against us, so that they may be able more easily and forcefully to lead us to ruin. For see, we have learned as a certainty that ever since we came here and did not depart, the Trojans have

35 added greatly to their troops, and have prepared the defense of their city with new walls, ditches, and pits with ingenious palisades. They have had an easy opportunity of doing all this, and of procuring the causes and occasion for their victory, since they have already conceived and certainly maintain that we do not have the boldness to

40 proceed. The longer we defer this business, the greater losses and dishonor we shall obtain for ourselves. For I think that, if we had once been able to kindle such hatred that, in the direct route and by continuous rowing, we had arrived at the shores of Troy very

suddenly, that the landing would have been easier for us, since the
45 Trojans would have been unsuspecting when we descended upon
them, and now it is necessary to attack them forewarned and forearmed. I advise, therefore, if it pleases you, that, when the ships are
ready, we at once prepare for the journey at dawn, and, as soon as
we have made warlike preparations, that we go by a rapid course to
50 the shores of Troy and land with mighty courage for fighting, and
with all speed establish against this city the siege we have desired. For
we should realize that, according to the will of the Trojans, this will
never be done by us, except through the hazards of war and through
the great concentration of our forces placed everywhere. Let us
55 therefore break off our delays, having put aside all deliberation, and
let us place behind us whatever could be said in opposition (whatever
our fate may be, prosperous or otherwise) since truly it is necessary
that it be done thus, and we cannot conveniently arrive at the
accomplishment of our aims in any other way."
60 Everyone was thoroughly pleased by the advice given by Diomedes.
For this reason, on the following day at sunrise, with great caution,
they weighed anchor, left the port, and proceeded out upon the
broad sea, where, when they had taken counsel thoroughly as to
which ships should go first and which should follow afterward, they
65 committed themselves to the deep ocean. They appointed one
hundred ships to go ahead at first, with sails extended, with standards
and banners of war flying, with fortified platforms also erected in
them, and defended by a great mass of armor. After them they
caused another one hundred ships to follow. Then the rest of them
70 followed over the ocean and, proceeding in order, sailed in a direct
course toward Troy. It was not long before those sailing in them saw
the coast near Troy and the outposts beyond the city, and soon they
saw Troy itself. So it was they approached the shores of Troy by
turning the direction of the rudder, and busied themselves in landing.
75 The Trojans, however, saw these ships approaching their coast and
shores in such a great number, and suddenly sprang to arms. In armor
they mounted their armed horses, and without awaiting the permission of king or duke, hastened to the shore at an inordinate speed.
The Greeks, seeing such a large troop of armed knights coming to the
80 defense of their shores, wondered at their great number. They were
moved by an even greater wonder when they saw the Trojans bear

themselves so valiantly and skillfully under their protective armor.
There was not one among them so daring or so bold or so brave that
he did not feel his heart waver and tremble at the sight of the multi-
85 tude of Trojans.

Because the Greeks were not able to land in any other way except
by the blows of naked swords and the conflict of deadly warfare,
they all seized their arms with greatly renewed boldness. Accordingly,
Protesilaus, king of the Phylacians, who was in the first line of the
90 approaching ships, since he was first among the first one hundred
ships, tried courageously and with great boldness to reach land safely.
Many of these ships, driven by the great rage of the winds, with
ᵔxtended sails, came to land. Many of them were thus dashed to
pieces so that many of the sailors on them lost their lives in the sea.
95 Those of them who were able to reach land alive were slain by the
Trojans with great suffering, beaten down by many savage blows. The
air resounded with the blows of the fighters, clouds of arrows in a
continuous stream darkened the sky, and the water near the shore
was red with the blood of the slain, and by their deaths it was clearly
100 perceived how costly the landing of the Greeks was. It has never been
recorded that any army ever landed in hostile territory in such great
adversity and in such great peril. After these hundred ships, the
second hundred following them arrived in this place. They did not,
however, strike as suddenly as the first, but when they had very
105 properly lowered the sails, they tried to reach land, guided by caution.
For this reason, those sailing in them were now eager to land. They
were courageously met by the Trojans in an armed band and were
prevented from access to the land. The Greeks who were in these
ships made ready a countless number of ballistae, and by frequent
110 flights of arrows kept the Trojans away from the shore. Many fell in
death from these deadly flights. When the Trojans retreated a little
from fear of the ballistae, the Greeks sprang from the ships and
arrived on land, and endeavored to succor the sailors in the first ships,
if there were any. Then they began a terrible and deadly battle with
115 the Trojans. Here King Protesilaus, who had already landed, performed miracles against the enemy because of his personal valor.
Accordingly he slew a countless number of Trojans with his sword
and offered his Greeks amazing support and assistance. If it had not
been for him alone, all the Greeks who reached land and landed

120 would have undoubtedly incurred the final deliverance of death. What
     did his bold defense profit Protesilaus, since perhaps seven thousand
     Greeks were waging war against one hundred thousand Trojans?
     Accordingly they engaged in mortal combat. When the Greeks saw
     they could not be aided by flight to the ships, since it would not be
125 safe to board the ships, and they did not consider that it would be
     advantageous to commit themselves to the waves and yawning depths
     of the sea, they chose to lose their lives on land rather than to be
     swallowed up in the obscure depths of the waves. Accordingly they
     carried on the battle with what spirit they could. However many of
130 them fell, cut down by the sword, and the thirsty sands drank
     streams of blood from those who fell by the sword, and the Trojans,
     on account of their number, raged cruelly against them. The Greeks
     defended themselves with great difficulty and with great loss of men,
     until they were forced to retreat to the edge of the shore. All would
135 have perished suddenly by bitter death had not Archelaus and
     Prothenor just then reached land with their ships. They disembarked
     from the ships with great courage for fighting, whether their enemies
     wished them to or not, and in a great army of warriors aided their
     countrymen and also rushed at the enemy and defended themselves
140 with great vehemence. The battle was renewed with the rest, who
     with regained courage showed themselves more fierce in battle; they
     waged war bitterly, and without doubt fought with great peril to
     themselves. Then Duke Nestor arrived and reached land with his ships,
     and with their hearts thirsting to aid their countrymen, he and his
145 men landed safely and suddenly joined in the battle. Lances were
     broken, many flying arrows whistled through the air, swords clashed,
     the dead fell, and the air was filled with the confused shouts of those
     falling to destruction. Archelaus and Prothenor, valiant men, slew
     many of the Trojans. Then King Ascalus and King Alacus reached
150 shore with their ships and landed with their fighting men. They
     hurled themselves boldly into the battle and attacked the Trojans
     manfully, so relentlessly and so bitterly that they forced them to
     retreat. The countless number of the Trojans who had not yet arrived
     at the battle directed themselves impetuously toward the Greeks, and
155 since the battle was stirred up to greater fury, the Greeks were forced
     to retreat, and because they could no longer resist any further, they
     came to the edge of the shore in their retreat. Then King Ulysses

reached land with his ship; he disembarked and came to the battle
with a great troop of fighting men. A very fierce battle ensued. The
160 Greeks renewed their strength at Ulysses' arrival, and, making an
attack against the Trojans, assaulted them courageously. Ulysses, however, like a roaring lion in the thick of the fray, distinguished by his
arms and by the lance which he bore in his hand, killed many of the
Trojans; now he wounded some, now he cast others off their horses.
165 When Philimenis, king of Paphlagonia, saw him fighting with such
valor and wreaking great havoc among the Trojans, he rushed on
horseback against Ulysses and hurled him from his horse, and Ulysses
had of necessity to fight on foot. But Philimenis brandished against
Ulysses the spear which he carried in his hand, and struck him a blow
170 so heavily and so severely that he split his shield and reached the
plates of his shining hauberk. After it had been severed and opened
by the blow, Ulysses was not able to withstand the blow and fell
flat on the ground. He was not, however, stunned by the great force
of the blow, and arose quickly. He brandished against Philimenis the
175 lance he was carrying in his hand, and with the great strength of his
arms struck a deadly blow over the top of his shield at the throat of
Philimenis. Since his weapons were shattered and his hauberk was
split, the sharp piercing lance of the attacking Ulysses severed the
jugular veins of his throat. By reason of this, Philimenis, mortally
180 wounded, fell half-dead from his horse. Because the Trojans thought
he was dead, they snatched him from the hands of the Greeks by
fighting very valiantly, and when they had placed him on his shield
as if he were lifeless, they carried him back to Troy. The Trojans
were thrown into great disorder at the supposed death of Philimenis,
185 and if it had not been for the unexpected reversal which took place
then, because Philimenis had been wounded, the entire Greek army
which had disembarked and were fighting on the land would have
been conquered without fail and would have lamented a final loss of
their lives. But at this point, Thoas, king of Tholia, with his ships,
190 King Agamemnon, the commander of the entire army, with his, King
Menelaus with his, and the noble Ajax Telamonius with his, reached
shore, suddenly landed, and engaged in combat with the Trojans as
the Trojans were exerting themselves in the very bitter battle with
the other Greeks who had landed a little before. They brought all
195 their horses out of the ships, and when they had mounted them, they

joined in the battle with great courage for fighting. As they made an
attack against the Trojans, they broke their lances, and in the clash
they threw countless Trojans from their horses, some dead and some
mortally wounded. When the fighting was renewed, many of the
200   Trojans died. Then Protesilaus, king of the Phylacians, wearied by
much exertion, since he had endured so much fatigue of battle that
day, retired a little from the fighting, and, so that he might catch his
breath, went to the edge of the shore where the fighting had first
begun. There he perceived that almost all his men had died in the
205   fighting, and he shed many tears in secret for their deaths, and, much
moved by this, recovered his angry mood and took himself again to
the fighting, hoping to achieve the vengeance for the death of his
men by the destruction of many Trojans. He removed his horses and
those of his other men from his ships which had finally escaped the
210   fury of the winds, and mounted his horse in all his strength, desiring
to avenge the death of his men. Accordingly, in his fury he killed
many Trojans with his naked sword, threw many from their horses,
and wounded many of them. Then King Perseus of Ethiopia came
from the city of Troy with a great company of knights and entered
215   the fight with furious resolve, and at the arrival of the Ethiopians, the
battle was more furiously resumed. The Trojans took such courage at
their arrival that, just as if they were renewed in strength, they
impetuously scattered the Greeks, afflicted them with severe wounds,
overpowered them, and when they were overpowered by violence,
220   forced them to retreat to the shore. There the Greeks would surely
have been completely conquered, had not the valiant Palamedes
reached land with his ships. When they had brought the horses from
the ships, he at once mounted his horse in the desire to fight and to
bring assistance, and, rushing with his knights into battle, he began a
225   mortal combat. At his arrival the Greeks attacked with renewed
boldness, and this Palamedes, in his raging desire to slaughter Trojans,
turned toward Sigamon, the brother of King Memnon and nephew of
King Perseus, who was then accomplishing marvelous things on his
own in the activity of arms. With the courage to fight, Palamedes
230   attacked Sigamon, and when he had struck him with his keen lance
through the midst of his ribs, he disemboweled him and threw him
dead from his horse. After he had abandoned him, he turned to the
thickest part of the Trojan line, scattered the troops, and killed

countless Trojans, who feared him as they did death and gave way
235 before him in his encounters. The noise of the destruction and
slaughter was very great. The Trojans were not able to withstand the
onslaught of Palamedes and were forced to retreat a long distance
across the land. The Trojans were now forced to turn their backs and
save themselves by flight. Then that very valiant knight, the very
240 brave Hector, as if aroused by the noise of the shouting, emerged
from the city of Troy with a band of many men and entered the
combat. He was flaming with kindled rage and gleaming in flashing
arms and with a sharp lance; he carried a shield made of gleaming
gold, adorned with the sign of three lions. He assaulted the Greeks
245 powerfully, and as he cut the line right through the middle, he went
with undeniable courage for fighting to meet King Protesilaus, who
had not ceased to slay Trojans at the point of his sword. Hector
attacked Protesilaus with bare blade, since he had long before
shattered his lance against the Greeks, and raising his arm in his
250 mighty strength, he struck Protesilaus so that he slit him from the
top of his head to his navel, his armor not protecting him. Thus that
noble and valiant King Protesilaus fell dead, and Hector, abandoning
him, rushed upon others, and it is a fact that those whom he reached
with the point of his sword ended their days. He had not moved
255 about among the troops very much and yet he had cut off so many
by death that the rest, terrified by fear, avoided him as they would
the destruction of death. As one asked the other who it was in the
midst of the affliction and destruction, indirectly they knew it was
he, that is Hector, bravest of all. The Greeks fled before his face,
260 unable to stand his deadly blows, and thus while he persisted the
Greeks failed. But he left the battle when he was wearied. The Greeks
regained the field and their strength—which had happened eight or
ten times that day. The sun was already declining toward evening
when Hector, somewhat wearied by his efforts in arms, entered the
265 city, leaving behind the rest who were carrying on the very savage
combat. The Trojans were courageously persisting against the Greeks,
and the Greeks, already almost overcome, were preparing to flee,
when that very brave Achilles reached land with his ships and his
Myrmidons. He landed and entered the fight with all his men, and
270 rushed savagely against the Trojans. The Greeks revived at Achilles'
approach because more than three thousand warriors came in his

company. A very great fight was begun; great was the carnage and
very great the slaughter; the bodies of the dead fell everywhere, and
more of them were Trojans. For the brave Achilles pursued them at
275 the point of the sword; he killed a countless number, overthrew them,
and wounded them with much bloodshed. Now all the other ships
reached land, now all the warriors in them landed and entered the
conflict. Since the Trojans were not able to withstand their might, on
account of the great number, and Achilles was slaughtering them,
280 they were compelled to flee, and they strove to recover themselves by
means of flight to Troy. There a great clamor burst forth, and
anguished screams resounded on account of the fate of the dying and
the suffering of the wounded. There Achilles, drenched in the blood
of the slain, left behind him on all sides a countless number of
285 corpses, and he added many from those fleeing. Then the fleeing
Trojans reached the gates of their city and in great tumult endeavored
to enter them. The slaughter was very great. There Trojans who could
not enter because they had been cut off by their pursuers lay dying
on the threshold, and sons cut down in the sight of their fathers
290 breathed their last. Great and incalculable carnage took place in the
entrance, and it would have been even greater had not the courageous
Troilus, Paris, and Deiphobus, with many knights, come to the aid of
those who wished to enter. The carnage ceased at their approach, and
as the shadow of night overtook them, the battle was broken off. The
295 Trojans accordingly secured the stout gates of their city with bolts,
and Achilles returned to the shore with the Greeks in great glory.
     Then King Agamemnon, when he had reconnoitered for a suitable
place, commanded the tents to be put up in it and advised everyone
to situate himself comfortably. When all of the officers had raised
300 their tents and pavilions, they all situated themselves at as convenient
posts as they could, and those who did not have tents constructed
new huts and prepared new lodgings and shelters for quarters. They
set up convenient stables as best they could for their horses, and
when they had brought all the necessary things from the ships, they
305 tied those ships firmly with stout ropes and moored them securely by
the weight of many anchors heaved into the sea, and that night, at
the decision of Agamemnon, they made the siege permanent with
great ease, when with many fires and blazing torches they scorned
the shadows of night. And it appeared to the army that the artificial

310 glow was no less than if the brightness of day were shining. For their
safety they set up many stakes, one following upon the other, just as
many in those close to them as in those placed at greater distances.
The Trojans offered them no hindrance that night, since their gates
were closed and no one came out of them that night. And truly, after
315 the siege was established as well as was possible that night, the
watchful Agamemnon, whom rest and sleep could not possess,
ordered guards and sentries on all sides who, with the sound of pipes
and with the greatest amount of weapons, would protect the whole
army from unseen ambushes, and on account of their vigils, the rest
320 could lie down in confidence and safety. For the remaining portion
of the night, those who were wearied with sailing the seas and who
had been hard pressed in battle stretched themselves out to take the
repose of sleep without putting aside their arms, until the coming of
day revealed the clear dawn. This, then, was the first battle between
325 the Trojans and the Greeks, when the Greeks landed.

*Here begins the fifteenth book, about the second battle, now
that the siege had been established.*

The shadows of that night were removed when they were put to flight
in the morning by the rising dawn, and the sun lit up the surface of
the earth with its rays. When it was daylight, that valiant and
aggressive man, Hector, the leader and commander of the Trojan
5 army, who was very troubled concerning his command, ordered all
his warriors to arm and to come to a certain level field which was
situated in the middle of the city of Troy, where the temple to the
goddess Diana had been constructed. After they had been disposed
according to shrewd military tactics into troops and phalanxes, and
10 after he had established battalions from them sufficient for that day's
battle, he commanded one of the gates of the city of Troy, which
was called the Dardanian, to be opened. When he had called two of
his kinsmen to him, that is, Glaucon, son of the king of Lycia, and
Cicinalor, his own natural brother, he granted the command of the
15 first battalion and delegated it to them. He placed one thousand
fighting knights in that first battalion, assuredly brave men and
experienced in combat, as many from the kingdom of Lycia as from

Troy. When they had been dismissed by Hector in the name of the
gods, they went out the Dardanian gate under a banner of victory
20 and approached the Greek army with cautious and slow steps. Then
to this aforesaid first battalion the aforesaid Hector added another
thousand skilled knights, whom he entrusted to the leadership of
Theseus, king of Thrace, and Archilogus his son, men who were not
without great valor, and he graciously dismissed them in the name of
25 the gods so that they might readily join the first battalion. Then he
set up a second battalion, to which he deputed three thousand of the
bravest and fiercest knights, which he committed to the leadership of
the aggressive king of Phrygia, King Xantipus, and King Alcanus, men
of great courage. At the command of Hector and beneath a victorious
30 banner, they went through the aforesaid city gate and proceeded
cautiously toward the Greek army. Moreover, Hector himself gave the
leadership of the third battalion, which was made up of three
thousand knights, to the aggressive Troilus, and advising him with an
affectionate speech, he uttered these words: "My dearest brother, the
35 greatest joy of my heart, the unbounded boldness of your heart
makes me fear greatly that you will behave thoughtlessly and rashly
in battle. I ask you to preserve yourself with all care, and steer away
from great foolhardiness, so that you will not give yourself over
completely and carelessly to your courage, but will manage the
40 fighting so wisely that our enemies, who are trying to cause us as
much misfortune as possible, will not rejoice at your heedlessness. Go
then happily in the name of the gods, who favor us, and return
victorious and unharmed to your city, just as I wish." Troilus replied
to him: "Dearest lord, with the gods on our side, you have no need
45 to fear anything and I shall never turn away from your commands,
dearest brother and lord." When he had said these things, he went
joyfully out the gate of the city, with the aforesaid three thousand
knights with banners showing their coats of arms. On his shield, the
field was all azure with three gold lions depicted on it, and he
50 advanced boldly toward the Greek army. Hector next arranged the
fourth battalion in which he placed three thousand seven hundred
knights, whom he placed under the leadership of the king of Larissa,
who was called Hupon. For this Hupon was large, a very strong man,
extremely warlike, and very fond of fighting, to such a degree that in
55 the whole army of the Trojans no one was considered stronger than

he, except Hector. In his company was that eloquent man, the very
valiant Ardeleus, from the aforesaid kingdom of Larissa. They were
eager to go toward the Greek army, and when they had obtained
Hector's permission, they went out through the same gate of the city.
60 Hector also made Dinadaron, his natural brother of whom he was
very fond, leader of this fourth battalion, along with this king of
Larissa, on account of his valor. The fifth battalion Hector formed
under the leadership of the king of Cisonia, with his people from
Cisonia. Now, these Cisonians were very strong and so extremely tall
65 of stature that they were thought to be like giants. The arms of this
king were green or yellow without any device. Hector made
Polydamas, his brother, leader of this battalion, and as soon as
Polydamas had obtained Hector's permission, he hastened toward the
enemy with his company. The sixth battalion, of men from Poenia,
70 Hector established under the leadership of their king, Pretemesses,
and their duke, Serepes, who were especially valiant men. But these
people advanced to war without armor, and did not bear hauberks,
helmets, or shields. These people, however, were skilled with the bow
and long arrows, which were covered with feathers down to the
75 notched end, while the tips of their heads were crowned with points
made of sharp iron applied to them, with which these men, riding
swift and strong horses, could inflict deadly wounds on their enemies.
Hector also put Deiphobus, his own legitimate brother, in charge of
this battalion, and he, when he had obtained leave of Hector, went
80 boldly with his company toward the enemy. Hector added an incalculable number of armed knights to this battalion, and especially
those who were said to be from the kingdom called Agresta, under
the leadership of Esdras and Phylon. This King Phylon had a
marvelous chariot, all made of pure ivory, while its wheels were of
85 ebony, covered over with pure gold. Its body was covered over with
jewels and precious stones and joined with gold and silver. This
chariot had just enough room for two brave and bold knights. Hector,
however, placed his brother Pythagoras over these two kings, that is,
Esdras and King Phylon, and he quickly went with them against the
90 enemy when he had obtained leave from Hector. Hector then, persisting manfully in the preparation of his plan, assigned the glorious
Aeneas, about whom we have often remarked above, to the seventh
battalion. To his company Hector allotted all the soldiers and knights

of the district of Cunius, who were ruled by a certain noble com-
95   mander named Eufremius. They all, when they had obtained leave of
Hector, left the city, and with proper speed joined the other
battalions mentioned before. Hector established that the eighth
battalion would consist of Xerxes, king of Persia, and his people, to
which he assigned Paris, his brother, and warned him that, although
100   he would reach the other battalions quickly, he was still not to enter
the fighting, unless he himself were there, since he intended to follow
him quickly with the next battalion. Paris answered that he would
obey his orders very faithfully, and when he had thus taken affectionate leave of him, he gaily departed from the gate of Troy in the
105   company of men assigned to him. Hector decided to place the ninth
battalion under his own leadership, forming it from the most noble
and most courageous knights born in the city of Troy, and in it he
took ten of his natural brothers, whom he knew were very spirited
and very expert in fighting, and he arranged that there should be five
110   thousand fierce knights in it, who would go out to battle with him in
his company.
      Hector himself, armed at all points with the necessary trusty
weapons, mounted his horse, which was named Galatea, about whose
size, boldness, beauty, and other marvelous virtues Dares has written.
115   When Hector was mounted, and armed as he was, he went to speak
with King Priam, his father, to whom he said these words: "Dearest
father, you will have with you fifteen hundred knights whom I have
assigned to your company. With them, and all the foot soldiers of
this city, you will be near the Greek palisades, that is, those which
120   are farthest from the other palisades. Be careful that no one dares to
go beyond those palisades, except when I so order, so that, when
necessity forces us, we shall have you in a safe refuge of security, and
also as reserve and defense. For I shall have certain messengers with
me who will go and come from me to you, and will continuously
125   report and report again the stage of the battle and what it is right for
you to do, according to the progress of the fighting. You and your
company will be a watchful and cautious guard, so that by no
trickery, wiles, or fraud may our enemies invade our city while we are
fighting, cut it off, and plunder it, and you will always be a bulwark
130   against them, injuring them fatally, and you will be in support of our
command and a reserve for our safety." King Priam replied to him:

"Dearest son, let everything be as you have arranged. For after the help of the gods, I have no hope or trust in anything except in the might of your courage and in the wise guidance of your cautious
135 disposition. I humbly entreat the gods that they will preserve you safe for me and will protect you from all opponents."

Hector, when he had asked leave of his father, left and joined the battalions which he himself had prepared. Hector was noble of purpose and of great courage, unconquerable in battle, a very bold
140 fighter, and the wisest prince and leader in the command of the army. He bore the same heraldic device on his shield as was painted on his armor; it was a field all gold or yellow and in the middle one red lion was painted. In the name of the gods he went out the gate in his company, with flags flying, and although he was the last to go, his
145 battalion came to be first, surpassing all the preceding battalions because of his courage, and he took the first place by placing himself in charge of the first battalion.

The noble women, however, who remained in the city, mounted all the walls of the city, in order to be able to watch the conflicts of
150 the battle from them. There the daughters of Priam ascended together with the noble Helen, who trembled very much in her heart because of many things, since fear and doubt produced many and various images in her.

Although Hector had thus arranged his battalions, was Agamemnon
155 at all negligent or remiss in the arrangement of his? On the contrary, he was arranging his people in twenty-six battalions. He made Patroclus the leader of the first of them, who led with him all his people, and in addition, all Achilles' people, that is, the fierce Myrmidons. For Achilles did not go to war that day, since he was
160 remaining in his tent, taking care of certain of his wounds. This Patroclus was a noble man and duke, sprung from a noble race of ancestors, distinguished in bearing and rich with great wealth. Achilles bound him to him in such a close bond of friendship that the minds of both were as one spirit, and what was for one of them was
165 completely for the other. Agamemnon assigned King Merion and King Idomeneus to the second battalion, in which he placed three thousand knights, and Menesteus, duke of Athens, with all his fierce men from Athens. The third battalion he gave to King Ascalaphus and his son Philimenis, under whom were placed all the people of Cumania, who

170   were very experienced in war. He set up the fourth battalion under
the leadership of King Archelaus and King Prothenor, and with them
the very brave Seguridan and all his people from Boeotia were
assigned to this battalion. Menelaus led the fifth battalion with his
men from Sparta who were subject to the rule of his kingdom. King
175   Epistropus and King Celidis with their people from the province of
Fodis led the sixth battalion under their leadership. Ajax Telamonius
led the seventh battalion with the people from his province of
Salamis, and in his company there were four counts, namely, Theseus,
Amphimacus, Dorius, and Polisarius. Thoas led the eighth battalion.
180   Ajax Oileus led the ninth. King Philitoas led the tenth. King
Idomeneus and King Merion led the eleventh; Duke Nestor led the
twelfth. King Henes, son of Mabens, led the thirteenth. Ulysses led
the fourteenth. Umelius led the fifteenth. In the sixteenth were the
men who were once Protesilaus'; they were thirsting to avenge the
185   death of their lord. King Polidarius and King Machaon led the
seventeenth. The king of Rhodes led the eighteenth. Eurypylus, king
of Ortomenia, led the nineteenth. Xantipus, king of the Lidians, led
the twentieth, and also King Amphimacus. King Philoctetes, lord of
Larissa, led the twenty-first. Diomedes and Stelenus led the twenty-
190   second. Eneus, king of Cyprus, led the twenty-third. King Prothailus
led the twenty-fourth. King Capenor of Capedia led the twenty-fifth.
King Agamemnon himself led the twenty-sixth and last, since he was
the commander of the whole army.
When all the battalions on both sides had been formally set up,
195   each side went out to the open plain to fight. But that very brave
Hector, who was first to be impatient of calm, spurred his horse
powerfully in a charge before all the others, striving as if enraged
against the first line of Greeks. When he perceived this, Patroclus,
who, as was said, was the leader of the first battalion of Greeks,
200   advanced swiftly, charging on his horse in a straight line against
Hector, and sought him with his sharp spear, and since he hurled it
manfully, he pierced the shield which Hector manfully opposed to it,
and reached the inner armor and broke something from it, but did
not, however, reach inside to the bare flesh. Hector, neither shaking
205   nor staggering from the violence of the blow, was kindled with very
ardent fury, and did not offer Patroclus similar payment of a blow of
the lance, but rushed upon him with naked sword and struck him

cruelly on the head with a blow of the sword, so that he divided his
head through the middle into two parts. For this reason Patroclus was
210 not able to stay on his horse, since he had arrived at the last gasp of
his life, and he fell to the ground dead in the midst of the fighters.

But Hector, when he saw that Patroclus had been hurled headlong
from his horse and was dead, inspected and regarded the arms with
which Patroclus had been armed, and was seized with the desire of
215 having them. He got down from his horse and, holding his horse by
one rein, approached Patroclus' body, thinking he would strip him of
his gleaming arms. But King Merion, with three thousand armed
knights, appeared in the defense of the corpse, and when he had
come up to the body with all his men, he engaged Hector with the
220 aforesaid great number of fighters, so that Hector would not be able
to strip those arms from the body. With angry heart he said these
words to Hector: "Rapacious and insatiable wolf, you are certainly
not going to be able to eat this food. It will be proper for you to
seek food elsewhere, because you are going to see immediately more
225 than fifty thousand fighters opposed to you, who will strive only for
the fall of your head." Then this king and the others tried valiantly
to hurl Hector to the ground by a concerted attack against him, and
were exerting themselves to snatch his horse away from him, so that
Hector, at the pressure of so many attacking him, was forced to bend
230 a knee to the ground. Raising himself upright by his mighty strength,
whether the Greeks wished or not, he ably mounted his horse, and
speeding toward King Merion, he furiously sought to attain vengeance
from him. But King Glaucon and King Theseus, with Archilogus, his
son, relieved Merion with three thousand other armed men, attacking
235 Hector valiantly. Hector slaughtered and delivered to death the first
Greek who ran at him, seeking him with his naked sword, and so
also many of the others who did not fear to attack him. The battle
raged savagely in the interim. Hector went back to Patroclus' body
again, still intending to strip it. He dismounted from his horse, not
240 caring that Idomeneus, king of Crete, with two thousand fighters, had
arrived to oppose him in the battle, and while Hector was pressing
forward to strip the body, King Merion again attacked Hector with a
great troop of knights, assaulting him so forcefully that he by no
means allowed him to arrive at his desire. On the contrary he and his
245 men struck him with many and frequent blows. When Hector found

himself on foot and maintaining a mortal combat against so many
mounted knights, he piled strength upon strength and bitterly
attacked the Greeks with his naked sword, killing as many horses as
possible, and maiming legs, arms, and feet, so that in a short hour he
250 slew fifteen of those who were trying to cut him off. Merion, meanwhile, when the body of Patroclus had been raised from the ground
before him, received it on his horse, and carrying it with him, brought
it back to the Greek tents.

The Greeks, nevertheless, were persistent, and they strove in a
255 great troop either to surround Hector or to snatch his horse from
him, so that they did not allow him any opportunity to mount his
horse. Among them was a very brave knight named Carion de Petra,
who was straining eagerly after Hector. But seeing that Hector was in
such peril, one of Hector's assistants, since had had two sturdy lances
260 pointed with sharp iron, hurled one of these lances against Carion de
Petra, who with one hundred other knights was pressing upon Hector
more than the others, with the result that Carion gasped his last,
mortally stricken by the blow. Then this same attendant hurled the
other lance against another who was likewise trying to overwhelm
265 Hector, and he, stricken by the blow in the same way, fell headlong
down to the ground dead. Next this same attendant shouted loudly
at the Trojans so that they would run quickly to Hector, who was in
such great peril. Cicinalor, one of Hector's brothers, as he heard the
voice of the man shouting, first rushed upon the Greeks in the very
270 great valor of his fighting, with the whole battalion in which he was,
and when a way had been made through the Greeks by violence, he
reached those hundred knights who were harassing Hector so bitterly.
For this reason thirty of them expired, cruelly destroyed by death.
On account of this, the Trojans, with renewed courage, regained the
275 field and forced the Greeks to retreat. At this, Hector, rejoicing not a
little, mounted his horse and charged furiously into the fray. Turning
himself unrestrainedly against the Greeks with blows of his naked
sword, since he had given up all hope of despoiling Patroclus, he
killed many of the Greeks whom he met in his charge, and as many
280 as he met before him he either killed or overthrew, mortally
wounded. All the Greeks wishing to avoid death fled from his sight
and opened a clear way for him, so that when, completely drenched
in the blood of the slain, he had passed through a great number of

battalions, there remained scarcely five on whom he could employ his
285 strength.

Then Menesteus, duke of Athens, came to the battle with three
thousand armed men, and by going with all his people to the left
side, he arrived at the Phrygian battalion in which was Troilus, who
was oppressing the Greeks amazingly, and in which were King
290 Antiphus, King Machaon, and King Alcanus, who were leading this
battalion with the same Troilus. After they had joined their battalions
together, they engaged in the mortal combat with all their might.
Then Duke Menesteus advanced powerfully with his lance toward the
fighting Troilus, attacking him so strongly that he hurled Troilus
295 willy-nilly from his horse. He landed in the midst of many fighters in
an amazingly crowded place, since he fell among the feet of countless
horses and their riders, who were fully intent on carrying on the
mortal combat in fear of death. Menesteus, truly, was extremely eager
to capture Troilus, and so that he might be able to take him captive,
300 he piled strength on strength, and he showed such eagerness and
exertion that he dragged Troilus from under the feet of the horses,
seized him, and hurried to lead him captive in a great phalanx of
soldiers. But a certain knight, named Miseres, shouted loudly to the
men of Phrygia, saying: "O brave men, why have you come to war?
305 To acquire honor or shame? Do you not see and perceive that
Troilus, son of King Priam and brother of Hector, has been captured?
Surely if you permit him to be led away, you and your heirs will be
considered defiled by the taint of perpetual shame. Turn your forces,
therefore, to his recovery, and take care to do this speedily, before
310 he is removed from your mighty power." Then King Alcanus,
burning with rage, took a certain lance and rushed swiftly against the
Greeks who were hastening to lead Troilus to captivity, and struck
one of them so manfully with it that he felled him with sudden
death. Afterward he threw himself against another and wounded him
315 mortally. Thus it happened that by the assistance of those rushing to
his aid in a great troop, Troilus was freed from the hands of those
wishing to lead him away, and with very great courage for fighting he
mounted his horse with the speedy assistance of King Xantipus, who,
with his battalion, had raced swiftly to the liberation of Troilus.
320 This King Xantipus furiously attacked Menesteus and struck him
manfully from the side, and if Menesteus had not been protected by

his trusty armor, Xantipus would have undoubtedly slain him.
Menesteus, grieving at the loss of his captive, savagely urged his men
to fight, and when the Greeks arrived to help him, he engaged in a
325   mortal combat with a great number of fighters. There was, as a result,
a great heap of the slain on both sides. Meanwhile Hector, who had
not been able to give in to weariness from the exertion of fighting, in
his rage killed many Greeks, laid them low, and wounded them. But
Menesteus, who had been overwhelmed by great grief on account of
330   him because he had lost his captive and the greater part of his men,
rushed through the line as if he were crazed. While he was rushing to
overthrow the Trojans, that Miseres, through whom he had lost his
captive, came to meet him. Menesteus recognized him by the armor
he was wearing. Hence, by manfully directing the charge of his horse
335   against him, he attacked him powerfully with his strong lance and
hurled him from his horse and cast him among the feet of the
fighters. He left him when he could harm him no more, and attacked
another whom he likewise hurled from his horse. At this point,
Hupon came up on the side of the Trojans, and in his train came
340   Eripisus with two thousand of his warriors and with all the men from
the kingdom of Larissa. King Prothenor and King Archelaus went out
against them with their people from Boeotia. A fierce battle was
waged between them. Not long afterward Polydamas, son of Antenor,
came up on the Trojan side, in a great company of warriors, and
345   when he saw so many of the Trojan battalions gathered together in
one place, he decided that the battalion with which he was coming
should be separated from the others and go toward the Greeks from
another direction. Hence it happened that when the aforesaid
battalion was going toward the Greeks from another direction, up
350   came King Remus, who had advanced from Troy with three thousand
armed knights. Menelaus immediately attacked him with all the
Spartan knights of his army. Thus King Menelaus and King Remus
were struggling together, and they each cast the other from their
horses by the force of the blows of their lances. Polydamas then
355   attacked Mereus, Helen's nephew, a duke, who was only twenty years
old and who already in the flower of his youth was considered a
valiant knight. Polydamas struck him so violently with a severe blow
of his lance that he wounded him fatally, since he broke and shattered
the armor which Mereus had trusted would protect him, so that he

360 fell from his horse and was dead when he reached the ground.

As soon as Menelaus saw he was dead, he was wracked with intense grief, for he loved him tenderly. Since he sought to avenge his death upon the Trojans, he struck King Remus with his naked sword and broke his helmet and shattered his armor; the fierce blow pene-
365 trated to the flesh of King Remus and wounded him so seriously on the head that he fell from his horse half-dead. Because his men thought he was dead, they did not take any care to help him; on the contrary, they decided to retreat from the battle and they would have put this into effect if Polydamas had not detained them against
370 their will. They afterward showed such force and diligence in recovering their king that they dragged him almost dead from under the horses' feet and conducted him, more dead than alive, to their encampment. Then King Celidis, who in those days excelled all others on account of the nature of his beauty (Dares writes about him that
375 no one could describe his appearance and that the queen of Feminea loved him with such fervent ardor of affection that she held him dearer than herself) . . . . This King Celidis strove in attacking Polydamas to cast him from his horse by a blow of his lance. Polydamas, blazing with anger on account of the great pain, met him
380 with his naked sword and struck him so severely on the head with the force of his strength that he hurled him dead from his horse. Meanwhile Hector, in assisting his men, had of necessity forced the Greeks to retreat, and placing himself between the lines, broke them, wounding many of the Greeks fatally, until he arrived at the battalion
385 in which the men of Salamis were, who were manfully fighting under the leadership of Thesalus, their king. This King Thesalus was conspicuous on account of great valor, and had wounded many Trojans fatally and had killed many of them. When King Teucer arrived from the Greek side, he attacked Hector and struck him so strongly with
390 his lance that he wounded him seriously. When Hector turned the reins of his horse toward him for vengeance, he escaped by flight and removed himself a great distance from the sight of Hector, so that his troop withdrew completely from Hector. But Hector was not able to restrain the anger of his heart, and in his fury he rushed against a
395 certain Greek commander whom he happened to meet first, and with a blow of his sword, slew him immediately and cruelly. The greater part of the Greek battalions thus surrounded Hector so that the

Greeks might kill or capture him. While he was among them, Theseus
spoke to Hector with affectionate words, gently warning him to leave
400 the fighting lest he perish unwisely among so many, since his loss
would, so to speak, deprive the whole world of a great knight. Hector
accordingly rendered him affectionate thanks for this.

At this point, while the very savage battle was raging, and the
Trojans were persisting against the Greeks, and Polydamas was
405 fighting courageously against them at a little distance from Hector,
Menelaus and Telamonius attacked Polydamas. Telamonius, who
assailed him first, threw him from his horse by striking him mightily
with his lance, and with their combined strength, Menelaus and
Telamonius captured Polydamas, who was on foot in the fighting with
410 a broken sword, and when the straps of his helmet had been broken
by them, his head was unprotected. They hastened to send the captive back to the Greeks. But Hector, who was not far from them,
looked in his direction and saw Polydamas surrounded by many
Greeks, and from the sound of those who were shouting soon heard
415 that he was down and taken and was being led away captive. At once
Hector rushed angrily against those who were surrounding Polydamas
and killed many of them, wounding them mortally and hurling them
down. So it was that a way was necessarily opened to him and he
wounded fatally all who attacked him until he reached those who
420 were intending to take Polydamas captive, and rushed against them so
furiously that he killed thirty of them, and the others leading
Polydamas away took flight, and thus Polydamas was freed by the
amazing strength of Hector.

Then King Epistropus, King Menelaus, and King Telamonius, with
425 their battalions, all came together in one place and pressed against the
Trojans so mightily that by their vehemence they put them to flight,
and they were compelled, so to speak, by necessity, to leave the field,
despite the fact that Hector was there among them. He was performing miracles, though he was unable to hold out against so many.
430 Because his horse had died under him, he was manfully defending
himself on foot so that none of the Greeks was so daring or confident that he presumed to raise a hand against him. Some of his
natural brothers saw that the Trojan army was half vanquished and,
since they did not see Hector, they assembled in one group and
435 sought him earnestly among the troops so that they reached him by

their courageous effort. They gave Telamonius a deadly wound, and
Dinadaron, one of these brothers, attacked Polixenon, a noble Greek
commander, who was riding a powerful and spirited charger, and he
struck him mightily and cast him off this charger, and seizing it by
440   the reins, offered it to Hector who was fighting on foot. Hector
mounted it at once. All Hector's natural brothers performed miracles
in feats of arms among themselves. Deiphobus came up with the
whole battalion which Hector had assigned to him; that is, with those
men from Poenia who carried bows and arrows, with which they
445   wounded many of the Greeks. Deiphobus himself seriously wounded
King Teucer in the face. Thus the Trojans who had already taken
flight regained courage and returned to the fight. For this reason the
battle was resumed more relentlessly.

      While Theseus was persisting against the Trojans, Quintilienus, one
450   of the natural sons of King Priam, and King Modernus with him,
rushed upon Theseus, seized him, and strove to kill him while he was
a captive. When Hector shouted to them not to harm him, they
released him, and at the command of Hector they allowed him to go
free. He humbly gave thanks to Hector and approached the Greeks in
455   freedom. Then King Thoas with those of Calydon came to the battle
on the Greek side, and King Philitoas came with him, and they hurled
themselves into the struggle. King Thoas, however, attacked
Cassibilans, one of King Priam's natural sons, and in the sight of his
brother Hector struck him so heavily that he fell dead from his horse.
460   Hector was extremely angered and grieved by his death, and yearned
fiercely to overthrow the Greeks. He killed many of them, now he
wounded some, now he hurled some from their horses, so that by the
power of his strength and the daring of his men, the Greeks were
compelled to flee.

465   Meanwhile Nestor arrived on the Greek side with five thousand
warriors. King Esdras and King Phylon in his chariot came to meet
him, with their men who were from Agresta, under the leadership of
Jeconias, the son of the king of that nation. They engaged in fighting
on both sides, from which there was a great heap of the slain. King
470   Phylon fought manfully and killed many Greeks. At last the Greeks
surrounded him and sped to kill him. Then Jeconias said to King
Esdras, "Do you not see that Phylon has already been captured by
the Greeks? If it pleases you, let us aid him speedily." Then the

Trojans made an attack against the Greeks, whether the Greeks wished
475 them or not, and the Trojans aided King Phylon, freeing him from
the hands of the Greeks.

Meanwhile Hector entered the fray with his natural brothers, and
also with Deiphobus and Polydamas, who, as they were accomplishing
miracles in arms with their Trojans, intended, in their courage and
480 strength, to bring the Greeks to the point at which the Greeks would
leave the field and flee in defeat from the face of the Trojans. But
Menelaus and Telamon resisted so manfully that they frustrated the
desires of the Trojans. Then Aeneas came up with his men from
Comus under the leadership of Eufrecius, their commander, and
485 Hector pressed so fiercely and strongly against the Greeks with them
and the others that the Greek warriors were forced to flee. But Ajax,
who was manfully fighting for the Greeks, as he saw his men wish to
turn in flight, was oppressed with great grief. Looking behind, he saw
many Greek battalions which had not yet entered the fray, and which
490 were speeding to the battle with outflung banners, and without doubt
all the flower of Greek knighthood was coming in those battalions.
He therefore urged the Greeks to cease fleeing and continue the fray,
since their assistance was at hand. At this the battle was resumed
more fiercely. Aeneas and Ajax came together in hate and animosity,
495 and in the strong charge of their horses, each drove against the other
so manfully and so powerfully that both fell from their horses, continuing their fight among the feet of the horses.

On the side of the Greeks King Philitoas of Calydon aided Ajax
with three thousand knights, since until then better luck in battle
500 favored the Trojans, who with courage for battle were harnassing the
Greeks so that they left the battle, escaping by flight. The two
battalions which came to war with Philitoas opposed the wishes of
the Trojans and did not allow them to prevail. Thus in the heat of
the battle, Philitoas attacked Hector and broke his lance against him.
505 Because he was courageous, Hector struck him with his lance so that
he wounded him fatally and cast him from his horse, and he fell
headlong among the feet of the horses.

Then Huners came up on the Greek side with his battalion in a
full complement of fighters, and Ulysses with his, who we learn
510 waged war in the Turkish style, and likewise King Humelinus. All
these Greek kings led ten thousand knights with them to battle. What

could the Trojans do, since on that day nearly all of their battalions had assembled in the conflict and they, worn out with great exertion, could hardly attack others and had hardly strength remaining to
515 defend themselves? Meanwhile Paris came up with the men from Persia from the right side and entered the fight, and, attacking the king of Frisia, a first cousin to Ulysses, he cut him off in his strength. The Greeks were extremely saddened at his death. Ulysses, however, seeking to avenge the death of his cousin, rushed upon Paris furiously,
520 and exerting himself against him, struck his horse so strongly with his lance that it fell dead to the ground, and as a result, so did Paris, its rider. But Troilus, who saw Ulysses persisting against Paris, rushed upon him at once, and with his naked sword struck him so powerfully on the head that since he had forcefully cracked his helmet and
525 shattered it, the plates of his hauberk thus pressed heavily into his face, so that, fixed in his face they spread gore in bloody streams over his whole face. Ulysses, however, remained unshaken on his horse, and with his naked sword wounded Troilus on the face while he was striving to attack him.
530   Then the Trojans would really have been forced to retreat if Hector and his brothers Troilus, Paris, and Deiphobus, with the other natural brothers in addition, had not manfully resisted. For all that day Hector, running here and there, had left his own battalion which he had assigned to himself from among the Trojans for carrying on
535 the war, thus leaving his own battalion without leadership. But seeing that the Greeks were prevailing against the Trojans, he returned to his own battalion and joined it. The Trojans who were assigned to the aforesaid battalion rejoiced, accordingly, that they had recovered their lord and commander. Hector spoke to them with affectionate words,
540 reminding them of the injuries done them in the past by the Greeks, and recalled to their minds what the Greeks would do to them (let it not happen!) if they were by chance victorious. He advised them accordingly and urged them to grow more powerful in war and to strive wholeheartedly for victory from now on. When everyone had
545 applauded him with faithful resolve, Hector led them to the battle against the Greeks from the right side through a certain valley. There was very great slaughter, and many Greeks died, for Hector overthrew them without end.
     Then King Thoas, who had killed Cassibilans, a son of King Priam,

550   rushed through the line and did much damage against the Trojans.
      When the natural sons of King Priam recognized him definitely, they
      all gathered together to avenge the death of their brother. They all
      attacked King Thoas together, and threw him from his horse. Since
      his sword was broken, he was not able to protect himself, and since
555   the straps of his helmet were broken and had been boldly snatched
      away from him, his head was unprotected and they all tried to cut it
      off. They could have done it easily had not the duke of Athens
      rushed savagely upon them and seriously wounded Quintilienus, who
      was pressing King Thoas severely, and hurled him from his horse.
560   Afterward, while he was persisting mightily against another man, Paris
      struck him between the ribs with an arrow from his bent bow. But
      the duke of Athens, caring nothing for this, by his power and courage
      delivered King Thoas, although wounded in many places, from their
      hands. This duke escaped free from their hands on account of the
565   help of the many who manfully aided him.
          While Hector, however, was resolutely straining for the conquest
      of the Greeks, King Humerus, from the Greek side, wounded Hector
      in the face with an arrow sent from his bent bow. Hector attacked
      him at once, and struck him heavily on the head with his bare
570   sword, so that his head was divided into two parts. For this reason,
      King Humerus fell dead and will no longer bend his bow or shoot
      arrows. Then the Greeks at the sound of a certain horn had seven
      thousand warriors gather against Hector, who with his men defended
      himself amazingly. Meanwhile Hector left the battle and hastened to
575   the king his father, advising him to aid his people. The king approached
      the battle with three thousand warriors who were fresh in their
      courage. Then the conflict was very great and the slaughter most
      extensive among the Greeks.
          Ajax and Hector met in battle, and both fell from their horses.
580   Menelaus killed a certain Trojan commander. Celidonas, however,
      killed Moles de Orep, nephew of King Thoas. Madon de Clara
      attacked King Cedius, whom he struck so terribly on the face that he
      plucked out one of his eyes. Sardellus, however, killed a certain other
      Greek commander. Margariton attacked Telamon but Telamon
585   wounded him severely. Fanuel, however, hurled King Prothenor from
      his horse. Thus the rest of the natural brothers, sons of King Priam,
      bore themselves manfully in the deadly attack against the Greeks.

Among these feats, King Duglas rushed upon Menesteus, duke of
Athens, and tried manfully to attack him with his stout lance.
590 Menesteus, although he lacked a lance, sought him with his naked
sword and struck him so powerfully on the helmet over the face
that the nosepiece broke and he wounded him on the nose. Deamor,
however, seeing his brother thus wounded on the face and nose,
rushed upon Menesteus so powerfully that he hurled him from his
595 horse. Menesteus at once arose on account of the courage of his
heart. Another of their brothers approached Menesteus, although he
was on foot, and harassed him cruelly, and thus all three brothers
cruelly pressed forward against Menesteus, and hastened with every
intention of either killing him or capturing him. Menesteus manfully
600 defended himself from the aforesaid three brothers. In truth, since
many usually prevail over one, these three brothers shattered his
armor with blows of their swords, broke his shield and cracked his
helmet, especially Thoras, the oldest brother, who was pressing on
and harassing him amazingly.
605 King Teucer, who saw Menesteus was in such peril, sped hastily to
his assistance. Hector, however, ran to meet him there, seeking to
overthrow Duke Menesteus and King Teucer by violence, and without
doubt it would have ended badly for both had not that very strong
Ajax attacked Hector with a thousand knights whom he brought with
610 him in his company. At this, the king of the Persians came up on the
Trojans' side, with five thousand knights under the leadership of Paris.
As Paris blew on a horn he hurled himself manfully against the
Greeks, as the other Trojan battalions also came up. Hence the war
kept up savagely in the interim, and the Trojans prevailed over the
615 Greeks by means of Hector's extreme courage, and compelled the
Greeks to retreat. This Hector then, as Dares writes, killed a thousand
Greek knights.
Meanwhile, as Hector was rushing among the troops in order to
fight, Merion happened into his path before a certain Greek tent.
620 Seeing Merion, Hector said to him: "Wicked traitor, behold, your
hour has now come when you will receive the proper reward for
daring boldly to take Patroclus away from me." He made an attack
upon him and threw him from his horse. Hector dismounted at once
and on foot hurled himself against him, and with unsheathed sword
625 speedily cut off his head. Then he hastened to strip him of his armor

with which he was still clad. But Menesteus, duke of Athens, who
suddenly saw this, took a lance and rushed upon Hector from the
side, and Hector did not notice his movement. Hence Menesteus
struck him heavily and wounded him. Fearing Hector's rage,
630   Menesteus at once retreated. Hector, though, feeling that he was
wounded, left the battle and prudently had his wound bandaged so
that the blood could not seep from it, and immediately took his way
back to the battle. Then he killed many Greeks on account of the
impulse of his rage. For, as the book of Dares testifies as truth, after
635   his wound he killed more than a thousand Greek knights on that day.
        Hence he brought the Greek army to such weariness and weakness
that there was no one among the Greeks who had the spirit to defend
himself, and the unlimited skill of Agamemnon was not enough so
that he could approach the battle. Hence the Trojan army, proceeding
640   in great courage against the fleeing Greeks, pursued them to their
tents. The Trojans manfully entered these tents like victors and looted
them, taking away many of the weapons and the very great supplies
of gold and silver, which they found in their chests, and, loaded
down, they carried all the equipment back to their garrison.
645   This is the day on which a permanent end might have been made
to the war, and the Trojans would then have been absolute victors.
But the fates, who arrange for future adversities to happen, destroy
everything by hidden snares, by which they complete those adversities which they have arranged for the future. Oh, how slight and weak
650   was the reason that blinded the eyes of the Trojans and especially
Hector, who was not able to avoid the destruction of his own person
nor the future ruin of all his people, since on that day the Trojans
were in such power that they could finally have killed all the Greeks
who had come against them, and freed themselves from imminent and
655   future dangers. For indeed it is not a laudable discretion in any wise
man, when he is impeded by serious and fatal danger, and fortune
smiles upon him, so that by unexpected and favorable events he is
able unexpectedly to free himself, not to receive with a grateful hand
the favorable occurrence which fortune suddenly offers him, but to
660   be ungrateful, and finally not to follow it up by taking that which in
one hour the favorable event presents to him. For if in that hour he
does not receive and accept the thing, but sends it away by delaying,
he will never afterward reach that which he could have obtained at

one point. For the fates, if the good they present is not received at
665 once by some ungrateful person, afterward refuse to give it to him, as
one who had lost it through the fault of ingratitude. Thus it happened to the unfortunate Hector that day when he could have
obtained the triumph over his enemies in great glory, while he was
rushing through the lines pursuing his enemies, who were fleeing
670 before the face of him and the other Trojans as if they were
conquered .... On the Greek side he met his first cousin, the son of
Hesione and the son of Telamon, who was called by the name of
Ajax Telamonius, and who was advancing against him in a hostile
fashion with great courage in fighting, since he was a man who was
675 very powerful on account of his strength, and was a very bold
warrior. These two who were so bold began to battle with determination, but as they were fighting each other they exchanged words,
and Hector recognized the son of his aunt and that they were related
by blood ties. Hector accordingly became very happy at that point,
680 and when he had laid down his arms, he softened toward him with
great affection and promised to please him in all things, and advised
and asked him to come to Troy to see the large family of his kinsmen. He refused, however, and not neglecting the safety of his Greeks
and his country, asked Hector, if he had such great affection for him,
685 to manage it and bring it about that the Trojans would cease to fight
further and would not pursue the fleeing Greeks further, but that
they would go back to Troy, sending the Greeks away in peace on
that day. The unfortunate Hector promised. He at once, by a blast on
the trumpet, ordered it and brought it about that all the Trojans
690 retreated and ceased fighting. The Trojans had already set fire to the
Greek ships and were already setting all the ships adrift, but at the
voice and command of their leader, they desisted completely from
everything, and greatly disturbed and disappointed, went back to the
city and entered it. This was the trivial cause for which the Trojans
695 on that day ceased from obtaining their victory which they never
afterward were able to reach, because the fates opposed.

*Here begins the sixteenth book, about the third battle, when
the siege of Troy had already been established.*

Accordingly the gates of the city were secured with locks, and at the
coming of night the bolts were fastened. A little before the rising
dawn the Trojan fighting men who were not wounded took weapons
and armed themselves with them, and waited for the light of day so
5 that they might go out to battle against the Greeks at the command
of Hector, their leader. But when it was day, the Greeks sent
messengers to Priam, asking for a truce of two months, to be confirmed by a treaty. King Priam and Hector agreed to this in a council
of the officers of their army. The Greeks, meanwhile, gave to those
10 of their dead whom they wished funeral rites and burial; they decreed
the bodies of the rest of the dead, however, should be consumed by
fire. Achilles, however, could not be consoled for the death of
Patroclus, and lamented his death for quite a long time, with sorrowful and tearful cries and in floods of tears. At last when he had built
15 Patroclus a tomb from blocks of special marble, Achilles had the
body of Patroclus buried in it with great honor and sealed it firmly
and securely. In the same way the Greek nobles, with the greatest
honor, placed the body of Protesilaus in a marble burial vault of very
precious work, as it was then the custom for the greatest nobles to be
20 buried. In the meanwhile the Trojans, while this truce lasted, had
those who were wounded in battle cared for and treated on the
advice of skilled physicians, so that at the end of the aforesaid two
months those who had been wounded were restored and healed
completely. King Priam, who could not be consoled for the death of
25 his natural son Cassibilans, because he loved him more tenderly than
fatherly feeling requires, spent quite a long time in tears and laments.
Finally he had him buried in a very precious sepulchre in the temple
of Venus.
     Cassandra, however, hearing the groans and laments, cried out in
30 raging tones, saying: "Oh, miserable Trojans, why do you endure the
loss of your families when similar things will happen to all of you in
the future? Why do you not seek peace from the Greeks, before you
all perish wickedly by the slaughtering sword, and the noble city of

Troy is given over to complete and total ruin, and before mothers
35 deprived of their children, and the children themselves, weep in
perpetual servitude? Surely Helen was not worth such a grievous and
deadly price that we should all perish to the last one by great
suffering." Since Cassandra would not make an end to such exclamations, King Priam ordered her to be seized and put out of the way
40 for quite some time, under guard and in close restraint.

Meanwhile Palamedes was complaining among the Greeks concerning the leadership of Agamemnon who had previously been chosen.
For Palamedes said Agamemnon was unworthy of the great power of
command over so many kings and dukes, and claimed that since he
45 himself was more worthy he did not wish to have Agamemnon as his
superior, because he had not elected him, and he had not been
elected by all the kings, who were more than thirty in number, but
only by three, without the knowledge of all the others. There was no
other course of action about this then.

50 Truly, when the treaty given for the truce had elapsed, Agamemnon, extremely wary in the performance of his command and excited
by the proper anxiety and solicitude, organized all his battalions with
watchful diligence as to the order and arrangement in which they
should proceed to the battle. Accordingly, he entrusted the first
55 battalion to Achilles, the second to Diomedes, the third to Menelaus,
the fourth to Menesteus, duke of Athens, and all the other following
battalions were disposed of very prudently by the same Agamemnon.
Hector also arranged his battalions very judiciously. In the first he
placed Troilus and in the rest, leaders who were men distinguished by
60 great vigor, according as it was his care and vigilance.

Hector, without delay, went in great boldness out the gate of the
city with his battalions, and by crossing the Greek palisade arrived at
the open plain with his men. Hector, of course, first hurled himself
into conflict against Achilles, whom he knew well, and since each of
65 them, that is one against the other, forced his horse to charge, and
both ran manfully against the other, each hit the other, and both fell
from their horses. Accordingly each brave man assailed the other
brave man, and both fell to the ground together. Hector rose first,
mounted his horse impetuously, left Achilles, and hurled himself
70 rapidly upon the troops. He killed the greater part of those he met,
wounded others, cast others cruelly from their horses, and in his

might and courage divided and pierced all the Greek battalions by
attacking bravely, and advanced wherever he wished, drenched in the
blood of Greeks, striking them cruelly with his naked sword. Shortly
75 after, Achilles rose, mounted his horse, and making an attack against
the Trojans, killed many of them, and by dealing wounds he rushed
about through the troops for such a long time that he came upon
Hector fighting courageously. At once each sprang at the other with
their sturdy lances, but Hector struck Achilles so mightily that,
80 although his lance broke into many fragments, Achilles could not
stay on his horse, but fell headlong from the horse and reached the
ground, while Hector determined to seize Achilles' horse. But when
many opponents attacked Hector, Achilles quickly mounted his horse,
assailed Hector with his naked sword, and struck him so powerfully
85 on the helmet over his head that Hector, necessarily wavering on
account of the strength of Achilles' arm, could hardly hold himself
firmly in the saddle. Hector, however, was incensed with great rage
on account of the pain, and rushed upon Achilles, assailing him in
great might with his naked sword, piling blow upon blow, and struck
90 Achilles on his helmet so that rivers of blood flowed down his face.
Such a deadly combat was maintained between the two, that if both
together had persisted longer in the fight, either one would have
killed the other, or both, perhaps, would have killed each other. Their
friends coming up, therefore, that is, from the battalions on both
95 sides, were hardly able to separate the two, one from the other.

Diomedes next entered the battle with a large battalion of warriors,
and from the other side, Troilus with his officers. Diomedes and
Troilus both came together to fight, and threw each other from their
horses. Diomedes rose first, mounted his horse, and struck Troilus,
100 who was standing on his feet, so violently on the helmet that he
broke the rim of his helmet. Troilus by virtue of his strength killed
Diomedes' horse, so that both were battling together on foot. The
Greeks made Diomedes mount his horse and the Trojans made Troilus
mount his, and both renewed their struggle. Diomedes prevailed by
105 greater vehemence and seized Troilus and tried to lead him captive to
his garrison. The Trojans then bitterly attacked Diomedes and, at
great peril to themselves, snatched Troilus from his hands.

Then Menelaus came up, rushing through the battalions; Paris
advanced on the side of the Trojans. They immediately began to fight

110 resolutely. Hector, panting to fight as if he were furious, killed
whomever he met. Then there came to meet him a certain new knight
named Boetes, who in his courage boldly attacked Hector. Hector
struck him so heavily on the head that he cleft him in two parts from
his crown to his navel, and he immediately expired and died. Hector,
115 however, seizing his horse, had it taken away by one of his attendants. King Archilogus, Boetes' kinsman, saw this, and while he strove
to avenge the death of his kinsman, advanced resolutely against
Hector. Hector rushed upon him, and not being prevented by his
armor, cut him in two with his sword, so that he gave up the ghost
120 and died among the fighters. Then King Prothenor, led by boldness
and daring, attacked Hector from the side and smote him so mightily
that Hector, who had not been aware of his stratagem, was hurled
from his horse. Hector arose immediately and mounted his horse,
rushed upon Prothenor, and struck the aforesaid so terribly by virtue
125 of his strength that he sliced his body in two halves.

Achilles, however, after he saw Prothenor was dead, was seriously
grieved by his death since he was related to him by blood. Archilogus
also joined with him in like grief since he was connected quite closely
to him by blood relationship. Achilles, and Archilogus along with
130 him, determined to recover the body of Prothenor, which they were
by no means able to do. For as the Trojans increased greatly in
courage, the Greeks were necessarily compelled to flee, and the
Trojans forced them to fly headlong. They pursued those who fled to
their tents, killing some and wounding others fatally. Then day was
135 already verging upon the shadows of night, and since the darkness of
night was arriving, the battle was ended.

Here begins the seventeenth book, about the fourth battle
between the Trojans and Greeks.

Accordingly when twilight came before the faces of men, and when
everywhere in the space of the sky could be seen the stars that
night, which impairs the eyes of those looking at the appearances of
the rest of things, displays openly on account of the shadows of its
5 darkness, all the kings, dukes, and princes of the Greeks assembled in
the early part of this night at the tent of King Agamemnon, where

only those many plans concerning the death of Hector and how he
should be killed were examined. They said that if Hector did not lose
his life and if he continued in the battles, the Trojans could never be
10 attacked in such a way that the Greeks would be able to attain the
victory from them. He alone was the defender of all the Trojans and
the deadly attacker of the Greeks. At last they all decided in this
council that Achilles should take upon himself the accomplishing of
the task, and he would bring it to an end not so much by means of
15 his strength as by means of his ingenious cleverness. With earnest
resolve, Achilles undertook to carry this out since he was especially
interested in this because Hector aspired greatly for the death of
Achilles, and unless Achilles looked out for himself, he could easily
perish at the hand of Hector, if fortune were unpropitious. In this
20 way the Greeks ended their council and one by one turned to their
tents for the sake of their evening rest.

When daylight came on the following day and it was morning, the
Greeks rushed to arms in troops. Hector, the bravest of all, had
already gone out the gate of the city, impatient of rest, and had
25 arrived at the field to fight with his battalion which he had formed
especially of fighters who were natives of Troy. Aeneas hastened after
him speedily, following with his battalion, then Paris, then Deiphobus,
then Troilus, then the rest with their battalions which had been
organized before by Hector. Hector advanced to the battle first before
30 all, with all the Trojan battalions in which there were, as Dares writes,
one hundred and fifty thousand warriors on the Trojan side. A mortal
combat was engaged in between both sides. Paris entered the combat
with those warriors from Persia with bows and arrows, and killed
countless Greeks and gave mortal wounds to others. Meanwhile King
35 Agamemnon entered combat, and Hector attacked him at once.
Hector hurled him from his horse seriously wounded. Achilles then
assaulted Hector and broke his helmet on his head by the force of
many blows. But Aeneas and Troilus rushed upon Achilles then in a
great crowd of warriors.
40   Then the very brave Diomedes attacked Aeneas, whom he wounded
seriously. As a reproach he said to Aeneas: "Greetings, good coun-
cilor, who gave Priam the trusty counsel concerning me in his
presence. But know now for certain that if you too often frequent
these battles and if you happen to fall into my hands, that for certain

45 you will die at my hands." Then he made a charge against him and
    threw him from his horse.
        At this Hector assaulted Achilles and oppressed him amazingly. As
    soon as he had broken his helmet he attempted to seize him, but the
    son of Tydeus who saw Achilles thus cut off rushed furiously upon
50 Hector, and with his raised sword, in the force of his arms struck him
    and wounded him seriously. Hector, however, who was by no means
    stunned by the blow or the wound, took his sword and, in a great
    fury of rage, rushed so powerfully upon Diomedes, who was still
    persisting manfully against him, that he hurled him from his horse.
55 Troilus, seeing Diomedes hurled to the ground, descended from his
    horse, and on foot turned his naked sword against Diomedes.
    Diomedes manfully defended himself against this Troilus. Achilles and
    Hector battled together.
        Meanwhile Menelaus, Ulysses, Polimites, Neoptolemus, Palamedes,
60 Stelenus, Menesteus, Duke Nestor, King Thoas, Euryalus, Philitoas,
    and Theseus came to the conflict on the Greek side. On the Trojan
    side came all the kings who had come to the Trojans' assistance, with
    a great number of their people, and in addition, all the battalions
    which Hector had arranged previously. An extraordinary battle was
65 engaged in by both sides. King Agamemnon and King Pandalus ran at
    one another at the same time and both fell from their horses. King
    Menelaus met Paris and both then recognized each other. While both
    tried to injure one another, Menelaus wounded Paris by a blow of his
    lance. But on account of the protection of his trusty armor, Paris was
70 not seriously harmed. Notwithstanding, Paris was not able to resist
    the power of the blow, and thrown from his horse, he fell to the
    ground. Overwhelmed by great shame he blushed on account of
    Helen, since Menelaus thus so dreadfully dishonored him.
        Meanwhile there was a very great struggle in fighting between King
75 Arastrus and Ulysses. Ulysses hurled him from his horse, and when he
    had seized the horse, he ordered it taken to his tent. Polimedes
    attacked old Ampon and wounded him fatally so that he breathed
    his last and died from the wound. Neoptolemus approached King
    Archilogus and both fell from their horses. Polydamas rushed upon
80 Palamedes whom he hurled wounded from his horse, and jeered at his
    weakness with vile words. King Stelenus and King Caras met to fight
    with each other. King Stelenus hurled King Caras, wounded, from his

horse. Philimenis rushed upon the duke of Athens, whom he cast
from his horse, took the horse from him and handed it over to his
85   own men. Philitoas rushed upon King Remus and both fell from their
horses. King Theseus and King Euryalus both met fighting, wounded
each other, and courageously cast each other from their horses.
    King Priam's natural sons were doing amazing deeds by means of
their valor that day, killing many of the Greeks and wounding many
90   of their kings. King Telamon approached King Sarpedon, and both
fell, seriously wounded, by the strong impulse of their sturdy lances,
so that they fell half-dead in the midst of the fighters. King Thoas
and Achilles, who were related to each other, both approached Hector
at once and attacked him with hard and frequent blows, snatched
95   Hector's helmet from his head and struck him in many places from
which there flowed many rivers of blood. But Hector, persisting
manfully against King Thoas, struck him in the face so that he sliced
off half his nose. Then Hector's natural brothers hastened quickly to
aid him; they oppressed the Greeks amazingly, captured King Thoas,
100 and gave King Telamon a deadly wound, casting him from his horse
so that he was carried half-dead back to the Greek tents, and King
Thoas was sent back to Troy in captivity by Deiphobus and Antenor.
    Menelaus intended to injure Paris greatly, but Paris, who well knew
this, shot Menelaus with an arrow smeared with deadly poison from
105 his bent bow, and wounded him so gravely that he was carried half-
dead back to his tent by his men. There Menelaus' wound was
bandaged with the help of physicians, and when the wound had been
soothed by the medication of ointments, Menelaus returned to the
battle and searched for Paris, furiously eager to be revenged on him.
110 Menelaus found Paris and attacked him with a blow of his lance,
wishing to kill him, which indeed he might have accomplished had
not Aeneas placed between them the protection of his shield. For
Paris was then unarmed, since he had voluntarily doffed his armor,
and when Menelaus realized this, he thought he could more easily
115 deliver him to death. Aeneas then, in a very great company of
knights, because Paris was not armed, accompanied him to the
garrison of the city, lest Menelaus injure him. Hector approached
Menelaus, attempting to capture him. His wish was frustrated, however, because a countless number of warriors advanced at once to his
120 aid. For this reason, when he had let him go, he attacked the Greek

troops with his men, killed them, and on account of his might and
that of his men, the Greeks were forced to flee and the Trojans
pursued the flying Greeks. But the day was verging upon sunset, the
battle was ended, and the battalions on both sides separated from
125 each other.

*Here begins the eighteenth book, about the fifth battle
between the Trojans and the Greeks.*

When the Trojans had entered the city and the gates were closed with
the required firmness, and sufficient watches were set, those who
were wearied from the battle duly gave themselves up to nightly rest.
Then when it was morning, King Priam decreed that there would be
5 no fighting that day, but sent for his privy councilors, that is, Hector,
Paris, Troilus, Deiphobus, Polydamas, Antenor, and Aeneas, to come
to him. When they had come and were standing before him, King
Priam said these words: "You know that we hold King Thoas
enclosed in our prison. Without provocation by us, he has in his
10 insane presumption come to destroy our city and kill our people
undeservedly. For this reason it seems just to me that he who wished
us to perish should perish by a cruel death through us, so that he
should either be hanged from the gallows or, by another method, be
infamously decapitated. Reveal to me, therefore, what seems to you
15 to be sane counsel about this matter."
Aeneas, however, who first answered the king's words, humbly said
to the king: "My Lord King, may it never happen to you that Your
Highness may be brought to such an outrage, since King Thoas is one
of the nobles of Greece, and is supported by important friends and
20 relatives. Since you have many who are dear to you, any one of
whom could be captured by the Greeks, the Greeks could afflict with
similar punishments this person dear to you, which perhaps you
would not wish done for all the world. And so it would be more
beneficial to preserve King Thoas safely in captivity, so that you will
25 be able to exchange him profitably for the recovery of one of your
men similarly captured in battle." Hector quite approved the advice
of Aeneas as praiseworthy. King Priam then persisted in his intention
and again addressed them: "If you decree it is to be done thus, the

Greeks will immediately think and say that we are suddenly smitten
30   by fear, because we do not dare to do justice to those who have
offended us nor be revenged, although I will agree completely with
your advice and opinion concerning this."

Thus when the council was ended, Aeneas said that he wished to
go see Helen, and for this reason he brought Troilus and Antenor
35   with him. When they had entered the Chamber of Beauty, where
Queen Hecuba was then residing with Helen in a company of many
noble women, Aeneas and Troilus comforted Helen with nothing but
many affectionate speeches. Queen Hecuba, accordingly, since she was
wise and prudent, urged them with words of quite impassioned
40   eloquence to protect their persons, the city of Troy, and King Priam.

The Greeks were then uttering subdued protests among themselves
and bemoaning their losses and the death of their men wickedly slain
by the Trojans, and they said they were engaged in a very great folly
since they would submit themselves to such heavy losses of men and
45   property when they could safely withdraw from them. On that night
the clear atmosphere was removed by a thick dark fog, and it poured
down much watery rain in a storm with many clouds, just as if it had
never poured rain or as if perhaps the gods wished to flood the earth
and repeat the deluge of Deucalion. And (which was more serious),
50   on that night the fury of the winds increased so much and so severely
that all the Greek tents were violently uprooted from their places on
the ground, which brought the Greeks great distress and trouble and
hardship. At last night was driven away, and the shadows fled,
accompanied by the aforesaid storms. The serene splendor of the
55   coming day appeared and illuminated the whole surface of the earth.
The Greeks then speedily donned their armor and hastened to
advance to the battle.

Achilles first among the Greek battalions sought the field; then
Diomedes, Agamemnon, Menelaus, and the duke of Athens. Achilles
60   first rushed impetuously upon Hupon, the king of Larissa, who was
as huge as a giant, and Achilles hit him with his lance and struck him
so that he fell dead from his horse. King Ortomenus approached
Hector, and was immediately killed by Hector. With great courage
Diomedes slaughtered King Antiphus who was fighting against him.
65   Then two kings, one of whom was called Epistrophus and the
other Cedius, entered the battle and rushed upon Hector. King

Epistrophus hurled many abusive words at Hector, whom he well
knew, and after the words made an attack and hit him manfully with
his lance, but he could not remove him from his saddle. Hector,
70 accordingly, angered at his words and deeds, approached him and
ruthlessly killed him and said to him: "Go now, if you can, and speak
out among the dead the abusive words which you monstrously
published to the living." Cedius, then, seeing that King Epistrophus,
his brother, was dead, was wracked with great grief, and in the
75 anguish of his grief he called to him at once the thousand knights
whom he had brought to the assistance of the Greeks, together with
many others, and ordered them to pursue Hector and kill him so that
he would be able to accomplish the revenge he wished for his
brother's death. Without delay, the knights with King Cedius pursued
80 Hector and found him among the troops, and rushed upon him and
cast him from his horse. While King Cedius thought to wound him
fatally with the sword in his outstretched arm, Hector, who saw the
blow coming from the outstretched arm, struck that arm so that he
divided the arm from the shoulder and sliced it off, and drawing near
85 to the king, who now fell from his horse, Hector killed him speedily.
Aeneas then killed Amphimacus as he was fighting. King Menelaus,
however, and likewise the duke of Athens, King Telamon, King
Ulysses, King Diomedes, King Archilaus, King Machaon, and King
Agamemnon, with all their battalions, entered the battle. A monstrous
90 and deadly battle was engaged in, and many on both sides fell slain.
The sun had already established the middle of the day when all the
Greeks who had assembled in one place rushed upon the Trojans, and
in the boldness of their courage oppressed the Trojans so severely
that they, driven by necessity, turned in flight. Achilles, with his
95 ability and strength, killed King Philis, who was fighting with him.
But Hector, in a raving fury at that, killed two of the Greek kings,
that is, King Alpinor and King Dorius. The Trojans, on account of
the courage of Hector, who was fighting fiercely, recovered the field,
and pressed fiercely against the Greeks.
100 King Epistropus then boldly came out from Troy with three
thousand warriors who all manfully joined in the fray, attacked the
Greeks ruthlessly and overwhelmed them, and the much more so
because this King Epistropus had brought a certain archer with him.
This archer, however, was a man above the waist, a horse below, and

105 in all parts of him, both above and below, he was covered by the hair
     natural to horses. His face, however, although it was like a human's,
     was all red, the color of fire, as if it were a glowing coal, and from
     his mouth he produced the neighing of a horse. His eyes were blazing
     in his face with the fury of fire, since they looked like two glowing
110 flames, and on account of this those looking at him were terrified by
     the greatest horror. He wore no protection of armor but entered the
     battle with a bow in his hand and a quiver full of arrows. At his
     entrance, the horses of the fighters were very terrified, and despite
     the fact that their riders urged them on with many pricks of spurs,
115 they turned and were swept away, as it were, in sudden flight. With
     great effort the warriors kept them in the battle, although these
     warriors, no less than the horses, feared the attack of the archer
     because he slaughtered many of the Greeks with his bow and arrows.
     Meanwhile Hector killed Polixenart, duke of Salamis, who was
120 pressing upon him eagerly, and this duke breathed his last and died.
     Since the archer was rushing among the troops to kill Greeks, and the
     Trojans were pressing ruthlessly upon the Greeks, they hastened of
     necessity to turn in flight toward their tents, and the Trojans pursued
     them up to their tents. There a wonderful event took place. For
125 while the archer was savagely harassing the Greeks who were fleeing
     before him, and the Trojans were pressing upon the Greeks among
     their tents, Diomedes, who was hastening in flight to the tents,
     attacked the archer before one of the pavilions, since he could in no
     way avoid him on account of the Trojans, who were manfully striving
130 to oppose him from the rear. It was extremely necessary, therefore,
     for Diomedes, unwilling and afraid, to attack the archer, for if he
     wished to retreat, since he was seriously wounded, he would fall into
     the hands of the enemy, who would by no means permit him to live.
     Accordingly, while the archer struck Diomedes with his arrows,
135 Diomedes manfully struck with his sword the creature which was
     without armor, so that it fell dead to the ground.
        Meanwhile the Greeks recovered the field and the Trojans were
     forced to retreat. Hector, in a charge of his horse, named Galatea,
     rushed upon Achilles. Achilles resisted him, and both cast each other
140 from their horses by the blows of their lances. Achilles first rapidly
     mounted his horse, and stretching out his hand, took Hector's horse
     Galatea in it, endeavoring to take him away. Hector, however, shouted

loudly in anger to his men not to allow the horse to leave. On
account of this, an infinite number of knights, intending to recover
145 the horse, manfully attacked Achilles, and a fierce battle was engaged
in on both sides. The natural brothers of Hector, fighting with great
courage, violently snatched Galatea from the hands of those detaining
him and restored him to Hector, who was afterward very happy.
While these things were going on with the destruction of many,
150 Antenor penetrated into the Greek battalions to fight, and the Greeks
rushed against Antenor in a great crowd of warriors, seized him, and
sent him in captivity to their tents. Since the day was already declining toward evening and the sun was already verging upon setting, on
that day, on account of the shadows of the coming night, the strife
155 was cut short, in spite of the fact that Polydamas, Antenor's son,
who was not present at his capture, was undertaking many things for
his recovery in the battle.

Here begins the nineteenth book, concerning the sixth battle.

As dawn rose on the following day, and the radiance of the sun was
shed all around, the battalions from both sides went out on the field
and engaged in a mortal combat which was fought all that day until
the shadows of night. Many of the Greeks were killed that day, but
5 more of the Trojans, for the Greeks had the best of it in the battle.
With the arrival of the night of that day, there was no more fighting.
On the following day the Greeks sent Diomedes and Ulysses as
ambassadors to King Priam, so that when a treaty had been agreed to
a three months' truce would be granted by King Priam. Dolon, a very
10 rich and noble knight who had been born in Troy, meeting these
ambassadors, and accompanying them, presented them to the sight of
King Priam. The ambassadors then explained frankly to King Priam
the reason for their embassy, as King Priam, with a retinue of a
countless number of his nobles, was at a table loaded with different
15 foods. King Priam replied to them, with words of great politeness,
that he would have a council immediately afterward. At once, when
he had called his councilors together, all agreed to the giving of the
aforesaid truce except Hector, who altogether disagreed about granting
the truce, claiming that the Greeks sought this truce because of

20 trickery and guile, giving as a false pretext that they wanted to bury
their dead, when, in fact, they lacked provisions and in the interim
would have an easy opportunity to acquire them; "and we in the
meanwhile are consuming our provisions which are nevertheless
necessary for us in order to maintain as many people as are closely
25 confined with us in this city." But because it was accepted by all,
Hector did not wish to go against the unanimous advice of so many.
Anyone who is wise, when he is joined in council with many men,
although all agree in one opinion, should not, if it appears otherwise
to him, decide upon silence on account of the agreement of everyone,
30 but should in fact say what appears right to him. For it has happened
and does still happen many times that the opinion of one man, even
a man of lower rank, will draw many wiser men to his opinion, seeing
that his advice is sounder, although it frequently happens that the
opinion of the many usually prevails, even if someone else furnishes
35 more profitable and better advice. Hector did not disagree with the
advice given by all, although it seemed otherwise to him, since he did
not wish to take a stand against the advice of so many judges, and so
a truce of three months was granted. This was agreeable to both the
Greek and the Trojan warriors, so that they rested from battle during
40 the time of their truce.
      While the aforesaid treaty lasted, King Thoas was freed by the
Trojans and Antenor by the Greeks, the one in exchange for the
other. Calchas, however, the priest of the Trojans who at the command of the gods had left the Trojans and attached himself to the
45 Greeks, had a daughter, distinguished for great beauty and charming
behavior, whom everyone called by the name of Briseida. Calchas
ernestly solicited King Agamemnon and the other Greek kings in
behalf of his daughter, Briseida, so that they would demand this
daughter from King Priam, if it pleased them, so that she would be
50 restored to her father. They presented this request to King Priam
with many prayers. The Trojans accused this priest Calchas of many
things, claiming that he was a most wicked traitor and accordingly
deserved death. King Priam, however, willingly released Briseida at the
petition of the Greeks during the exchange of Antenor and King
55 Thoas.
      While this treaty lasted, Hector went to the Greek camp. Achilles
was glad to see him since he had never seen him unarmed, and at

Achilles' request, Hector dismounted at his tent with a retinue of
many of his nobles. While they were talking among themselves of
60 many things, Achilles spoke these words to Hector: "Hector, Hector,
it is pleasing to me that I see you unarmed, because I have never
been able to see you without arms, but it would be more pleasing to
me if you were quickly to undergo death at my hand, as I wish. For
on account of your courage in fighting I have felt that your power
65 and strength are great, since I have experienced the shedding of my
blood as a result of a heavy blow of your sword. Although my heart
is often anguished concerning this, still it is shaken by even greater
anguish because you delivered to death my closest friend, Patroclus,
whom I loved sincerely no less than myself. You separated me from
70 him whom true love joined to me with a bond of indissoluble
affection. You may, however, consider it certain that before a year
has elapsed, the death of Patroclus will be cruelly avenged upon you.
For it is necessary that you die cruelly at my hands, and the more so
because I realize that you are yearning wholeheartedly for my death."
75 Hector replied to him in these words: "Lord Achilles, if I strive
for your death and if I hold you in hatred with my whole heart, you
should hardly be surprised, since I believe you know it cannot
proceed from justice that I should love him who pursues me with
irreconcilable hate and who dares to attack me and mine in my
80 country in the clash of such a great war. For love can never proceed
from war nor loving affection from hatred. For love has its origin in
the pleasant harmony of minds and hostility proceeds from hate,
whose mother is chiefly war. Of course I wish you to know that your
words do not frighten me; on the contrary, if I am alive two years
85 from now and my sword is strong, I certainly hope to prevail by my
mighty courage so that not only you but truly all the officers of the
Greek army who are maintaining continuous warfare against me will
succumb cruelly to bitter death at my hands. I know that you and
all the leaders of the present Greek army are deluded by the greatest
90 folly. You have, indeed, dared to take up such a burden that, borne
down by its weight, you will encounter nothing other than the
destruction of death. I am sure that you will be overcome by death
before your sword will prevail against me. But if such great presumption of strength encourages you to think you can prevail over me in
95 might, make all the Greek kings and princes agree concerning this

with sincere intentions and maintain it firmly that, when a battle has
been waged between just us two, if it happens that you vanquish me,
my parents and I will undertake to live in exile away from this kingdom and all our kingdoms forever, and will relinquish these kingdoms
100   to the rule of the Greeks. I shall make you sure of this by sufficient
precautions through a sufficient number of hostages and through
corporal oaths before the gods. If you do this you will be able to
benefit not only yourself but also the others, who by refraining from
war will maintain their safety with honor. If it happens that I con-
105   quer you, make all the Greek army leave this country and depart
from us in peace, freed from all disturbance."

Achilles, however, grew heated with rage at the words of Hector,
and almost completely drenched with the moisture of his sweat, he
offered to do battle. He boldly promised to fight, and approaching
110   Hector, offered his gage to him as a sign of confirmation. It is impossible to say with what eagerness of heart Hector received it. But
Agamemnon, when he had heard the tumult of many persons speaking of this, hastened with many Greek kings to Achilles' tent, where,
after all the Greek officers had been assembled at once, they all
115   unanimously objected, for they did not wish to confirm what
Achilles had recklessly agreed to. For it did not please them to
subject themselves to the snares of fortune so that the life and death
of so many kings and princes would hang on one knight. Likewise the
Trojans on their part expressed disagreement and refused to let it
120   take place, with the exception of King Priam, whom it pleased to
submit himself to such a chance, because he well knew the strength
and might of Hector, and it was very easy for him to boast of the
victory of such a great knight. But because he could not oppose the
opinion of so many men to whom this affair was important, he
125   followed the rest in rejecting the duel. Thus Hector, when he had
taken leave of the Greeks, went back to Troy and entered it.

Troilus, however, after he had learned of his father's intention to
go ahead and release Briseida and restore her to the Greeks, was
overwhelmed and completely wracked by great grief, and almost
130   entirely consumed by tears, anguished sighs, and laments, because he
cherished her with the great fervor of youthful love and had been led
by the excessive ardor of love into the intense longing of blazing
passion. There was no one of his dear ones who could console him.

Briseida, who seemed to cherish Troilus with no less fervor of love,
135 revealed her grief to be no less in words of lament, and was completely drenched in floods of tears. She thus sprinkled her clothes,
face, and breast with continuous showers of water distilled from the
fountain of her eyes, with the result that her clothes were so
drenched with the moisture of her tears that if anyone had squeezed
140 them and wrung them out with his hands, her clothes would have
poured forth a great amount of water from the wringing. She
scratched her tender face with her nails, and her golden hair, released
from the restraint of bands, she tore out of the milk-white skin of
her head, and while with her hard nails she furrowed her cheeks
145 tinted with ruby coloring, they seemed like torn lilies mixed with
torn roses. While she was bewailing the separation from her beloved
Troilus, she often swooned in the arms of those wishing to sustain
her, saying that she would prefer to seek death rather than to
possess life from the time when it would be necessary for her to be
150 separated from him on whose life the pleasures of her life depended.

With the coming of darkness that night, Troilus went to Briseida,
and although he was likewise in tears, he advised her to moderate her
grief. While Troilus thus yearned to console her, Briseida often fainted
in his arms. Between sweet kisses moistened by sorrowful tears, he
155 often tried to bring her back to her senses that night. With the
approaching of the hour just before day, however, Troilus departed
from Briseida in great anguish and grief, and when he had left her, he
hastened to his apartment in the palace.

But oh, Troilus, what youthful credulity forced you to be so
160 mistaken that you trusted Briseida's tears and her deceiving caresses?
It is clearly implanted in all women by nature not to have any steady
constancy; if one of their eyes weeps, the other smiles out of the
corner, and their fickleness and changeableness always lead them to
deceive men. When they show signs of greater love to men, they at
165 once at the solicitation of another suddenly change and vary their
inconstant declaration of love. If perchance no seducer appears to
them, they seek him themselves, secretly with furtive glances while
they are walking or more frequently, while they wander through
shops or while they linger in the public squares. There is truly no
170 hope so false as that which resides in women and proceeds from
them. Hence a young man can deservedly be judged foolish, and one

advanced in age even more so, if he puts his trust in the flattery of
women and entrusts himself to their false declarations.

175   Briseida, accordingly, at the command of King Priam, prepared
herself with great magnificence for the journey, and Troilus and many
other Trojan nobles accompanied her for a great part of the way.
When the Greeks arrived to welcome her, Troilus and the Trojans
went back, and the Greeks welcomed her into their company. Among
them then was Diomedes, and as Diomedes looked at her, he was
180   immediately on fire with the flames of ardent love, and desired her
with vehement longing. When he had joined Briseida and was riding
at her side, he was unable to contain the flames of his ardor and
revealed to Briseida the love of his burning heart. He tried humbly
enough to tempt her with many affectionate and flattering speeches
185   and also, to tell the truth, with grand promises. But Briseida, in her
first impulses, as is the custom of women, refused to give her consent,
but still, not wishing to deprive him of hope, she could not after his
many words refrain from speaking with gentle words to Diomedes:
"At present I neither refuse nor accept the offer of your love, since
190   my heart is not so disposed that I can reply to you in any other
way." Diomedes became quite happy at these words, since he
perceived that he was not to be completely excluded from placing his
hope in her. Accordingly, he stayed with her up to the place where
Briseida was to go, and when she had reached that point, he went
195   promptly to her as she was dismounting from her horse, and, without
anyone realizing it, slyly took away one of the gloves which Briseida
was wearing on her hand. Although she alone perceived it plainly, she
concealed the pleasing theft of the lover. Then the priest Calchas
came to meet his daughter and received her in his tent with happiness
200   in his face and in his heart. And although Diomedes was very doubtful of the love of Briseida, still love and hope attacked him with great
affliction in his heart.

When Briseida was alone with the priest her father, she accosted
him with harsh words in a flood of tears, saying to him: "How,
205   dearest father, were your senses deceived, when you, who used to be
esteemed for great wisdom, so that you who were honored and
exalted so much among the Trojans, since you were made almost
their lord and sole ruler in everything, and had such great riches in
abundance among them, and were supported by a multiplicity of

210 great possessions, are now become their betrayer and have denied
your country, whose defender you should have been in all things?
How have you now chosen to please yourself better by abjuring your
country and living in poverty and exile, and especially among the
mortal enemies of your country, who have approached thus hostilely
215 in order to attack your family and your country? Oh, with how great
a taint of shame among men are you covered, who used to be
honored so gloriously by your countrymen! The great infamy of
dishonor will never be removed from you who are so much defamed
by the lasting ignominy of disgrace. Do you think that even though
220 you are reproached among the living, that after your death you will
not also lament in hell pains worthy of the sin of such great
treachery? Accordingly it would be better for you and for us, your
family, to lead our lives in some place of solitude and loneliness, or
in trackless groves, or on some island far from people, rather than be
225 defamed and blackened by the stigma of such disgrace. Do you think
that the Greeks consider you to be loyal, who are a known traitor to
your own country? Indeed you have been deceived by the trifling
replies of Apollo, who, you say, ordered you to desert your ancestral
home and your gods in bitter hatred and to attach yourself thus
230 closely to your enemies. Obviously it was not the god Apollo, but
rather, I think, a band of infernal furies from whom you received
such a reply."
        At this Briseida, overwhelmed by many sobs and tears, made an
end to her mournful speech. Calchas replied to her with a certain
235 brevity of speech. He said to her: "Ah, darling daughter, do you
think it is safe or secure to spurn the orders of the gods and especially not to follow those in which we can be safe with honor? For I
know for certain through the promises of the infallible gods that the
present war cannot be extended for a long time and that the city of
240 Troy will be destroyed and ruined within a short time, with all its
nobles destroyed and its whole populace cut down by the edge of the
sword. For this reason, dearest daughter, it is much better for us to
be here than to perish by a hostile sword."
        Upon the arrival of Briseida, all the Greeks were pleased at the
245 very lovely face of this Briseida, since all the officers of the Greek
army had approached this pleasing vision, asking her for reports
concerning the city of Troy and the state of its citizens and also of

its king, all of which Briseida revealed to them with great eloquence
in many words. Hence all the officers received her with fatherly
250 affection, promising they would hold her dear as a daughter and
would honor her in everything. In leaving her they lavished many
gifts and presents upon her.

That day had not yet declined toward the hours of evening when
Briseida had already changed her recent intentions and the former
255 plans of her heart, and already it accorded more with her wish to be
with the Greeks than to have been with the Trojans up to this time.
Already the love for the noble Troilus began to moderate in her
heart, and in such a short time, so suddenly, and so unexpectedly,
she became inconstant and began to change in everything. According-
260 ly, what is to be said about the constancy of women, whose sex has
as its property to dissolve its plans with sudden frailty and to change
and be fickle in the shortest time? For it does not fall to a man to be
able to describe their ficklenesses and wiles, since their flighty
intentions are more wicked than it is possible to say.

Here begins the twentieth book, about the seventh battle.

Accordingly, when the three months' truce had elapsed, at the coming
of the following day, the Trojans prepared for battle, and when the
Trojan battalions had been drawn up by Hector, he went out first
with these battalions to battle, leading with him fifteen thousand
5 knights whom he had assigned to his battalion. Troilus followed
immediately after him with ten thousand other knights. Then Paris
left the city and with him were men who fought with bows and
arrows, those from Persia, to the number of three thousand, on strong
horses and well armed; then Deiphobus went out to war with three
10 thousand other warriors, then Aeneas with all the rest who were
ready to fight. All those on the Trojan side were one hundred
thousand valiant knights with great courage in fighting, as Dares
writes in his book. On the Greek side, Menelaus advanced to the
battle with seven thousand armed men. Then next Diomedes, with
15 the same number; then Achilles, with the same number; then King
Antiphus in a company of three thousand knights; then King
Agamemnon with an extremely large number. King Filis of the Greeks

first attacked the Trojans with his battalion. Hector immediately
came to meet him without hesitation, and struck him so powerfully
20 with a blow of his lance that he hurled him dead from his horse. At
the death of King Filis, the uproar was very great. A mortal combat
took place, from which great slaughter resulted. While King Xantipus
advanced on the Greek side, wishing to avenge the death of his uncle,
King Filis, he killed many Trojans. He pursued Hector and attacked
25 him. Hector, in opposition, rushed upon him angrily and wounded
him so seriously that he slid dead to the ground.
    Then the Greeks, grieving together over the death of King
Xantipus, piled force upon force and heavily oppressed the Trojans.
Hence many of them died, and Achilles, who was pressing very
30 fiercely against them, killed many of their nobles. Among them he
killed Duke Lychaon and Euforbius, men distinguished for great
courage, who had striven manfully to aid Troy when they had come
to its assistance. Hector, however, had been wounded on the face that
day; he did not know by whom. From this wound a great amount of
35 blood poured forth, and on account of this the Trojans were of
necessity forced to retreat. But Hector then raised his eyes and
directed his glance toward the walls of the city. He saw Helen, and in
addition, his wife and sisters, standing on the walls, watching the
battle on both sides.
40   Furthermore, the Greeks were already repulsing the Trojans to
such an extent that they had driven them almost to the walls of the
city of Troy. On account of this Hector was greatly embarrassed, and
so, since he was kindled with the fury of shame, he rushed upon
King Merion, the first cousin of Achilles, whom he struck heavily
45 with his naked sword on his helmet. By thrusting with accumulated
blows so that he broke the rim of his helmet, Hector made a cleft in
the helmet through which his sword reached the skin, and as he
broke the bones of his head, he gave him a fatal wound, so that King
Merion breathed his last and died.
50   When he perceived this, Achilles, after he had taken a very thick
lance, rushed upon Hector so that he damaged his hauberk though he
still did not remove him from the saddle. Hector, however,
approached Achilles with naked sword, assaulted him violently upon
his helmet, and broke the helmet, and the sword sank in so that it
55 tore the inner plates fixed on the hauberk below, and still his blows

did not injure the flesh beneath. Achilles could not withstand such
serious blows with sufficient firmness so that he swayed unsteadily on
the horse. Hector said to him then: "Achilles, Achilles, you are very
anxious to approach me, but you seek the fire with your next
60   approach, as without doubt you will approach the departure of
death." While Achilles was wishing then to respond to Hector's words
with a reciprocal reply, behold, Troilus arrived in a great crowd of
warriors. He came between Hector and Achilles and separated them
one from another, desiring nevertheless to injure Achilles fatally and
65   to put the Greeks to headlong flight, so that at that time more than
twenty Greek knights perished at the point of the sword. For this
reason the Greeks were compelled to retreat.

At this point, however, Menelaus arrived to aid the Greeks in a
company of three thousand armed knights, and they entered the
70   battle. On account of this the Greeks, in the confidence of their
strength, undertook with boldness to recover the field. But King
Odemon arrived on the Trojan side with a great battalion of his
people, rushed upon King Menelaus, hurled him from his horse, and
wounded him in the face. Troilus, therefore, and King Odemon, tried
75   to cut off Menelaus, and then captured him and attempted to lead
him captive to the city. But they were prevented by tumultuous
troops of soldiers and could not by any means get him far from the
battle.

Then the fierce Diomedes came up, supported by many people. He
80   suddenly rushed upon Troilus, hurled him from his horse, and took
his horse from him. He sent it by a special messenger to Briseida as a
gift, ordering the aforesaid messenger to announce to Briseida that
this was the horse of that beloved Troilus, and that he had cast this
Troilus from it by the fierce might of his arms, and to beseech her
85   humbly not to drive her servant, Diomedes, from her thoughts. The
messenger accordingly hastened at once to Briseida with the gift of
this horse and offered her the horse sent by Diomedes, and faithfully
told her the words which Diomedes had spoken to him. Briseida then
happily received the horse and spoke these words to the messenger:
90   "Be sure to tell your lord that I cannot hold him in hatred who loves
me with such purity of heart." Then the messenger departed from her
and hurried to his lord, while the conflict of battle was still going on
there. Diomedes, excited at the words of the messenger, rushed back
and forth among the hostile battalions.

95   As the Trojans were pressing forward against the Greeks, the
Trojans turned the Greeks in flight and pursued them at the point of
the sword to their tents. Unless Agamemnon had then aided the
Greeks in a very great company of warriors, they would have been
completely vanquished then and would have finally lost everything.
100 The battle was renewed more resolutely between them, the Greeks
regained the field, and the Trojans of necessity retreated. Polydamas
then rushed on with a huge number of warriors, aiding the Trojans
with great courage, when the Greeks in an armed band had already
violently driven them back to their trenches. When Diomedes saw
105 Polydamas rushing violently upon the Greeks, he rushed upon
Polydamas, exerting himself to injure him mortally by striking with
the force of his couched lance. But Polydamas attacked Diomedes so
courageously that he threw down and forced to the ground Diomedes
and his horse. Diomedes was seriously hurt by the blow. Polydamas
110 then caught Diomedes' horse by the reins as it rose from its fall and
gave it to Troilus who was fighting on foot, and Troilus speedily
mounted it.

    Then Troilus attacked Achilles with speed. Troilus took him on in
his courage and manfully rushed upon Achilles, so that he cast
115 Achilles from his horse and wounded him seriously. Achilles, however,
was not stunned by his headlong fall and was not troubled by the
almost deadly injury of such a blow, since he rose with the greatest
rapidity and tried to mount his horse. But the Trojans manfully
resisted him. Then Hector advanced to this place, and, as Dares
120 writes, Hector savagely slew a thousand knights who were trying to
defend Achilles. Achilles was so sorely pressed by him that, weakened
by great weariness, he had hardly the ability to defend himself. He
would undoubtedly have been captured had not Telamon and the
duke of Athens rushed up speedily, and with great effort made
125 Achilles mount his horse.

    With the arrival of dusk that night, there was no more fighting,
and the warriors on both sides, breaking off the battle, went back to
their garrisons. However, the bitter fighting went on for thirty days
continuously. On account of this many were slaughtered on both sides,
130 but more of the Greeks. Six of the natural sons of Priam were killed
during these days, and Hector was again wounded on the face. Priam
accordingly sent his messengers to Agamemnon to seek a truce of six
months, which they agreed to grant him, confirming it by a treaty.

Here begins the twenty-first book, concerning the eighth battle and the unfortunate death of the very brave Hector.

When the six months given according to the treaty had been confirmed, Hector had his wounds treated, lying at that time in the noble
Chamber of Beauty at noble Ilium, about whose marvels Dares has
written. For he said that it was completely built of twelve blocks of
5   alabaster, though it was perhaps twenty paces long. He said its pavement was made of crystal, and the walls were likewise encrusted with
different precious stones, and in the four corners were set four
columns of excessive height made from onyx. The capitals were also
of onyx, and the bases the same. On the tops of the columns were
10   placed four gold images, marvelously constructed by magical arts.
Dares fully describes them and their appearance which seem to be
empty dreams rather than factual truths, and therefore they are
omitted in this place, although the said Dares professed that they
were true. Meanwhile King Priam had his natural sons who had died
15   buried honorably among the other brothers and made each of their
individual tombs very costly.
    Diomedes was all aglow with the love of Briseida, so that he did
not know what he was doing. His mind was completely given up to
different anxieties, as is the fashion of lovers who desire mistresses
20   whom they cannot have. He had no appetite for food and drink.
While he was wasting away in continuous wakefulness, he often went
to see Briseida to comfort his grief, and begged and implored her
with many tears to give in to him. But she, who was much esteemed
for her cleverness and astuteness, took care to delay the hope of
25   Diomedes with clever wiles, so that she might afflict him more when
he was already afflicted by the burning of love, and heightened the
vehemence of his love to a greater degree of ardent love. For this
reason, on account of her shrewdness, she did not deny that she was
unwilling or willing, and she tried to place Diomedes in hope and
30   expectation.
    When the six months given according to the treaty had elapsed,
the fighting was continuous for twelve days following. During these
days many nobles were killed on both sides, since on account of the

burning heat of the hot summer at that time there was great
35 mortality among the Greeks who continued in the field. Agamemnon
accordingly requested King Priam for a cessation of hostilities by a
truce of thirty days. King Priam granted him this.

Then when the aforesaid thirty days had elapsed, each side prepared for battle. On the night before the first day of battle, after the
40 expiration of this truce, Andromache, the wife of Hector, saw in a
dream a most terrible vision of Hector—that if Hector marched out
that day to battle, he would not be able to escape being killed in that
battle. Andromache had already given Hector two sons, the first
named Laomedon and the second, Astyanax; this younger one was
45 still at the present being nursed at his mother's breast. Andromache,
therefore, since she was terrified at this vision, burst into floods of
tears and ventured that very night to reveal that vision to Hector in
bed where she was lying with him. She implored him with devoted
prayers to pay attention to the meaning of the vision and not to dare
50 to go to battle that day. Hector then, exceedingly angry at his wife's
words, rebuked her and reproached her with very bitter words,
claiming that it was not wise to believe the deceptions of dreams
which always delude dreamers. In the morning, however, when it was
daylight, Andromache summoned King Priam and Hecuba, his wife,
55 and revealed to them the prophecy of her vision, humbly beseeching
them not by any means to permit Hector to go to battle that day.

When it was morning and all the Trojan battalions were drawn up
by Hector, Troilus marched out first to the battle, then Paris, then
Aeneas, afterward Polydamas, then King Sarpedon, then King
60 Epistrophus, then King Ethoas, then King Forcius, likewise King
Philimenis, then the rest of the kings who had arrived to assist Troy.
King Priam gave all the aforesaid kings and battalions permission to
go to battle, since the Greeks had already issued forth from their
camp to battle. Furthermore, he ordered Hector expressly not to
65 mingle in the fray. Hector then was completely enflamed with rage
because of this. He therefore spoke many insults and remonstrances
to his wife, since he realized that it was through her, at her suggestions, that it was brought about that he should not go out to battle.
However, disregarding his father's orders, he asked his attendants for
70 arms. The attendants gave them to him, and he armed himself with
them. But when Andromache, his wife, saw this, she was moved by

great grief and threw herself with much crying at his feet, with her
little son whom she was carrying in her arms, and with repeated sobs
she humbly begged him to lay aside his arms. When Hector refused to
75 comply, Andromache swooned frequently at his feet, saying: "If you
refuse to have pity on me, at least have pity on your little son, lest
his mother and your sons perish by bitter death, or, wandering in
exile throughout the world in great poverty, are cast down into the
greatest shame." Queen Hecuba his mother, and Cassandra and
80 Polyxena, his sisters, and Helen also cast themselves at his feet, asking
him in tears to lay aside his arms and remain safe in his palace. But
he was not moved by their tears and prayers.

When, accordingly, he was armed, he went down from the palace
and mounted his horse, since he intended to go to the battle in all
85 haste. Andromache, who had become as if bereft of her senses from
much grief, went to King Priam, crying aloud, with torn garments,
scratched cheeks, and hair unbound and dishevelled. She had so
scratched her face with her nails, that, with the blood flowing down
on all sides, she could hardly be recognized by those who knew her.
90 And throwing herself at the king's feet in great grief, she warned him
and tearfully prayed him to hasten quickly to Hector so that he
might recall him to the palace and bring him back before he
happened to mingle in the fray. King Priam, without delaying further,
mounted his horse, pursued Hector quickly, and reached him before
95 he had gone very far away. When, with angry heart, he had seized his
reins, he warned and begged Hector in tears, and entreated him by
the divinity of the gods to return and proceed no further. Finally,
with great objection to his father's orders, Hector obeyed. He
returned unwillingly and went up into his palace, but did not, how-
100 ever, trouble to remove the armor with which he was clad.

Meanwhile a mortal combat had been engaged in. Diomedes and
Troilus both arrived at the battle and in the charges of their horses
attacked each other in earnest with grim blows of their lances, and
undoubtedly one would have slain the other if Menelaus had not
105 reached them with his battalion and interrupted the contest between
them both. Menelaus, however, rushed boldly upon King Miseres, king
of Phrygia, and cast him from his horse. The Greeks seized Miseres
and endeavored to lead him away captive, until Polydamas rushed up
speedily, for he, by his strength and the power of his battalion,

110 manfully prevented the king of Phrygia from being led away captive.
The Greeks, seeing that they could not lead him away captive,
proposed to cut off his head. But then that very brave Troilus
arrived, and he, after many of the Greeks had been killed by him,
delivered Miseres from their hands. Ajax Telamonius entered the
115 battle with three thousand warriors, rushed upon Polydamas, and
hurled him from his horse, but Troilus rushed up quickly and made
Polydamas, who had been cast down with great effort, mount his
horse.
 Then Paris entered the battle, and on the Greek side, Achilles, who
120 rushed so powerfully upon the Trojans with his men that the Greeks,
on account of the ability of Achilles, turned the Trojans in flight, and
the Trojans were compelled to flee. They hastened to withdraw to
the city. Meanwhile, Achilles tried to cut off Margariton, one of the
sons of King Priam, and although Margariton resisted manfully,
125 Achilles killed him. Then a very great uproar was made at the death
of Margariton who had been cruelly slain. Telamonius, however,
powerfully pursued the Trojans, but Paris and the rest of King Priam's
natural sons manfully defended them. They could not, however,
prevail by their might to a great enough degree to keep the Trojans
130 from being compelled to headlong flight, and they entered their city,
bringing Margariton's dead body to the city.
 When Hector heard that Margariton was dead, he was wracked by
great grief and earnestly demanded who had killed him. He was told
that it had been Achilles. Then Hector, as if filled with fury, angrily
135 strapped on his helmet, and without the knowledge of the king his
father, advanced to the battle, and at once in fury killed two great
dukes, that is, Eurypylus and Astidus. Then he manfully attacked the
Greeks, scattered them, wounded them and killed them, and the
Greeks then recognized him on account of the deadly blows of his
140 sword. They fled from his sight, and the Trojans fell upon the Greeks
and fought with them mightily. Then the Greeks seized Polydamas
and tried to lead him captive away from the battle, but Hector freed
him, and on account of his might, killed those leading him. When he
saw this, a certain very great Greek commander, named Leochides,
145 rushed upon Hector, thinking to put him to death. But Hector, all
ablaze with anger, rushed upon him, and in the fury of his anger,
Hector killed him.

Then Achilles, as he saw Hector had rapidly put to death so many Greek nobles and countless others, decided in his mind that unless he
150 rapidly put Hector to death, the Greeks would never be able to prevail against the Trojans. Therefore he earnestly examined in the recesses of his mind how he could quickly accomplish and fulfill this. While Achilles was meditating earnestly upon these things, Duke Policenes met Hector among the troops, and Hector rushed upon him
155 and killed him, in the sight of Achilles. This Policenes had come to the aid of the Greeks on account of love for Achilles, hoping also to marry one of Achilles' sisters, and had come, a very wealthy man, from upper India. Achilles rushed madly upon Hector, intending to avenge Policenes' death. But Hector brandished against Achilles a
160 certain spear whose iron point was very keen and sharp, and since he struck him in the groin, he gave him a serious wound.

Achilles left the battle wounded, but when the wound had been bound, he returned to the battle with the intention of putting Hector to death, even if it happened that he himself would afterward be put
165 to death. Hector in the meantime had rushed upon a certain Greek king, had seized him and was trying to drag him in captivity away from the troops. He had cast his shield over his back so that he might more easily snatch the king away from the troops. For this reason he displayed his unprotected chest in battle since he lacked the defense
170 of his shield. When Achilles realized that Hector did not have the protection of his shield over his chest, he took a very strong lance, which Hector did not observe, and rushed upon him and wounded him mortally in the abdomen, so that he fell dead from his horse. King Memnon, then, as he saw Hector dead, approached Achilles, cast
175 him from his horse and gave him a deadly wound, so that his Myrmidons brought him back to his tent on a shield as if he were dead. The Trojans deserted the field as if vanquished, and with no resistance from the Greeks entered their city into which they had taken the dead body of Hector.

Here begins the twenty-second book, about the tomb of
Hector and about Palamedes taking command of the Greeks.

When Hector was dead and his body had been brought into the city,
the lamentation was very great among all the citizens. For there was
not one of the citizens who would not have preferred to have his son
delivered to death in exchange for the life of Hector, if the fates or
5   the gods had decided thus advantageously with regard to their wishes.
The Trojan women, also, the maidens as well as the matrons, spent
their days mournfully in their homes, and raised their tearful voices
in plaintive exclamations, saying that henceforth they, together with
their sons and husbands, would not be able to breathe freely since,
10 lacking Hector, they lacked their constant safeguard which had made
them breathe freely. He had kept them safe from the wiles of the
enemy, when their enemies had come earnestly with wiles against
both them and their husbands, either to surround them and kill them
or to cast them and their children into perpetual servitude. Thus they
15 passed the long days, always in much weeping and pangs of grief.
All the kings and nobles who were in Troy brought the body of
Hector to the palace of King Priam, with torn garments and bared
heads, with the greatest of wailing, and put it down. After Priam saw
it, he was shaken by indescribable grief. He fainted often upon the
20 corpse of Hector. He would have often fallen upon Hector's body
every few minutes if he had not been violently dragged away from it,
and without doubt he would accordingly have departed from this life.
Likewise his grieving brothers were all wracked by grief at his death,
since they would have preferred to die rather than to live from then
25 on. What can be said, accordingly, of Queen Hecuba, his mother, of
his sisters, that is, Polyxena and Cassandra, what of Andromache, his
wife, whose weaker sex made them more susceptible to the pangs and
flowing tears of grief and to a long series of lamentations? Indeed,
since it would seem to be hardly necessary to reveal their lamenta-
30 tions by specific descriptions at this point, they are omitted as useless, since it is a fixed rule among all men that the more affectionately
they love, the greater are the pangs of grief that afflict them. It is
inborn in women by nature to reveal their griefs in loud exclamations

and to make them known with impious and grievous speeches.
35   And because the body of Hector had become a corpse, since such
is human weakness, and could not long be preserved above ground
without corruption, King Priam, in a council of many master craftsmen, minutely examined whether the body could always be in the
sight of men without a sealed tomb, so that the dead body would
40   falsely appear as if alive, without any horrible odor. For this reason
these master craftsmen, who were very clever and ingenious, at
Priam's command had the body placed in the temple of Apollo which
had been built of old near the Thymbrean Gate of the city of Troy.
The master craftsmen decreed that a certain tabernacle should be
45   constructed of suitable size next to the high altar of the temple, and
that it should be raised up on four columns molded of solid gold. On
each of these columns was placed a certain image which looked like
an angel, made from base to summit from the same material as the
columns, so that the images were on the columns, and the columns
50   had pedestals and capitals with marvelous carvings. The canopy of
this tabernacle was naturally all of gold, but its decorations were all
of precious stones of every kind and in a marvelous supply and
quantity, whose bright and shining splendor seemed to pour forth day
at night and the rays of the sun in the day. This tabernacle, however,
55   was raised above the surface of the ground and placed on some
crystal steps, and the ascent to the tabernacle was by these steps. On
high, above the peak of the canopy of this tabernacle, the aforesaid
master craftsmen fixed a certain golden statue, representing a likeness
of Hector, with his naked sword in his hand, and his glance and
60   expression were toward that place where the Greek army was staying
in its tents, so that he seemed to offer threats to the Greeks with his
naked sword. On account of the skill of their amazing mastery, they
caused the body of Hector to be seated in the middle, its weight
supported by a throne, and placed so skillfully that it sat on its
65   seat as if alive, clad in its own garments except at the bottom of its
feet. For, in an ingeniously constructed aperture in his head they
placed a vase full of pure and precious balsam, which had mixed in it
other elements which had the ability to preserve life. The liquid of
this balsam and these elements flowed first to the front of the fore-
70   head, through the inner parts, then to the eyes and nose, and in
addition, descending in a straight course through the inner parts,

reached the cheeks through which it preserved his gums and teeth, so that his whole face, with the great amount of his hair, was kept alive and preserved. Then this liquid, descending through his throat and
75 gullet, flowed to his chest, and through the inner bones of his arms reached his hands out to the ends of the fingers. And so this liquid, descending on each side, flowing copiously, preserved the flanks in such a condition that they appeared to be living flanks. By continuous instillations it spread itself to the contents of the body and through
80 them reached the legs, from which in a continuous course it arrived at the feet. In his feet there was another vase full of pure balsam. And thus through these applications, the corpse of Hector appeared falsely to be just like a living body, since it was preserved with many precautions for endurance. The aforesaid knowledgeable artists made
85 four lamps, composed of gold, which contained inextinguishable fire. Thus, when the design of this tabernacle had been completed, they placed around it an enclosure of ebony wood which could be closed sometimes and opened sometimes, so that the body of Hector, so placed, might be seen more plainly by those wishing to see how it
90 looked. King Priam afterward established a great company of priests to spend the time with unwearied care in continuous prayers to the gods and to remain in continuous guardianship of this tabernacle, and King Priam arranged that there would be all things in abundance for the sustaining of life of the aforesaid troop of priests serving the gods.
95   Agamemnon, however, during all this, with Hector dead, and Achilles, as was said, with a deadly wound, called together the kings and officers of the Greek army, and when they had come before him, he spoke to them thus, saying: "Dear kings and princes, we should with devoted heart give humble thanks to the gods who have deigned
100 to kill our relentless foe, that is Hector, by means of Achilles. For when this Hector, who cruelly slew so many of our kings, was alive, we could hope for no victory from our enemies. On account of his fierce courage he has killed from among our officers, King Protesilaus, King Patroclus, King Merion, King Cedius, King Polixenes, King
105 Prothenor, King Xantipus, King Alpinor, King Archilogus, King Dorius, King Polixenart, King Isidus, King Pollibetes, King Leochides, and many other nobles of our people. What then can the Trojans expect, since he is dead, if not their eventual destruction, and what else should we expect, if not that we will be victors over them

110 without a long delay? Because we cannot enter any battle in the
certain hope of victory without the presence of this courageous
Achilles, it would be good and profitable, if it appeared acceptable to
you, that until Achilles has recovered his strength, we should dispatch
our messengers to King Priam so that, when we have obtained a truce
115 of two months confirmed by a treaty, we might in the interval burn
the corpses of the dead, the stench of which overwhelms us, and in
the interim bring our wounded back to the advantage of health."
Thus Agamemnon made an end to his speech. All those present
unanimously approved the advice and speech of Agamemnon, and
120 they urged him to do this. Ambassadors were sent to King Priam and
they were granted the truce of two months which they had sought.
     During this truce, Palamedes complained vehemently among the
Greek kings about the command of Agamemnon. One day when the
said kings had assembled in Agamemnon's tent, and Palamedes was
125 pouring forth his usual words against King Agamemnon, Agamemnon,
answering in his discretion (for he was restrained in all things on
account of his great wisdom), spoke thus in response to the words of
Palamedes, in the common hearing of all who were then present: "My
friend, Palamedes, do you think that hitherto I have rejoiced with
130 great pleasure at the power of the rule given to me, when from the
beginning I neither asked for it nor took care to have it given me,
and when I looked for no profit on account of the preferment, but
from it have acquired constant cares and labor of mind and body in
order to lead the kings and princes under my direction to safety in all
135 things? And if it should happen that I should lose this power, it
would be more than enough for me to be under the command of
another leader, just as it is and was enough for any of the kings and
princes to be under my leadership. I think I did not make many
mistakes during my rule or by fraud or negligence do anything which
140 could impute evil to me. If your consent was not asked in choosing
me to rule, you should not wonder, since you were not present at the
business of my election and afterward you did not come to the army
before two years had elapsed, during which, if we had awaited your
consent, our army would still be located in the port of Athens. Lest
145 perchance it be thought that I am very eager for this command, and
perhaps too desirous for it, it is pleasing to me that another be
elected, for whose election I am prepared to work with the other

kings in harmony and great affection. For you cannot say, Lord
Palamedes, that our army cannot be led without your advice, since in
150 your absence and without the precepts of your counsel many acts and
deeds have been done in this army, which have turned out well
enough for all in common."

When Agamemnon had brought his speech to an end, nothing
further was arranged or discussed about this that day. Agamemnon,
155 therefore, about evening on that day, summoned the whole army by
the voice of a herald to approach at once the tent of Agamemnon on
the morning of the following day for a general assembly. It happened
that when it was morning, all the officers of the army and the rest
approached for the assembly. Agamemnon accordingly spoke to them
160 thus: "Friends and brothers, I have hitherto borne the burden of
commanding you, under whose weight I have many times toiled most
laboriously, examining thoroughly in my troubled mind all sound
means by which the officers as well as the men under my care and
rule might be led soundly. It has happened by the permission of the
165 gods, however, that under my care and guidance we have already
been brought fortunately through many fortunate events to safe
harbor. Since it is fair that everything should not depend solely on
one man, but by equal distribution should weigh upon the rest of the
group who will be equal to the imposed burden and who will not
170 sink under its weight, since it is already time to relieve me of the
burden of this command which has rested heavily upon my shoulders
for so many years, and that we elect another from our kings and
princes who, when the choice has been made, will rule us soundly
and guide by his wisdom throughout the expected vicissitudes...."
175 Agamemnon thus made an end to his speech, and it pleased all those
present to elect another for their leader since it is a natural error in men
to show joy about a new rule and to rejoice at novelty and changes.
After they had all together considered the election, they elected
Palamedes as their leader and yielded him the power to rule the whole
180 army. Thus it was that when the assembly had been adjourned, all went
back to their tents. After Achilles had learned by reports of the change
of Agamemnon and the substitution of Palamedes, he was strongly
displeased, and with angry heart asserted to those present that the
change of Agamemnon was neither necessary nor good, since the man
185 substituted was not his equal nor like him in intelligence of command,

and since changes should always be accomplished for better opportunities. But since the election had been proclaimed by so many in common, it remained firm then.

Here begins the twenty-third book, about the ninth battle and the death of the king of Persia, and how Achilles was ensnared by love of Polyxena.

And so when the two months given according to the truce had been passed through in their entirety, King Priam, desiring to avenge the death of his son with blows of his sword, personally drew up the battalions, and when they had been arranged under their leaders, he
5   decided to enter the battle in person, after he had chosen twenty thousand knights for the forward line. Thus, as Dares writes, one hundred and fifty thousand horsemen marched out to battle that day on the Trojan side. Deiphobus marched out first, then Troilus, then Paris, then King Priam, followed by Aeneas, then King Memnon, then
10 Polydamas, and they all hastened rapidly up to the Greek palisade. Palamedes had already drawn up his battalions, and he and they were coming out to oppose the Trojans. They engaged in a mortal combat, which resulted in the fall of a great number. King Priam, however, rushed upon Palamedes, threw him violently from his horse, and
15 leaving him prostrate, hurled himself furiously upon the Greeks. He killed many Greeks and wounded and overthrew many. King Priam did many things that day in his own person which were almost incredible deeds, seeing that a man so advanced in years could have fought so fiercely and so manfully.
20   Deiphobus was then pressing constantly against the Greeks, while at this point King Sarpedon was marching to battle on the Trojan side, and he rushed boldly upon Neoptolemus, the bravest of all the Greeks. But Neoptolemus, charging on his horse, met King Sarpedon, and with a stout blow of his lance cast him off his horse to the
25 ground. King Sarpedon sprang up violently from his prostrate position and as soon as he was on foot, he rushed upon Neoptolemus with his naked sword and struck him so powerfully on the thigh with his naked sword that he gave him a deadly wound. Then the king of Persia entered the battle with his battalion, and with the help of the

30 other Trojans caused King Sarpedon to mount his horse. The duke of
     Athens and Menelaus rushed violently upon him in a great crowd of
     warriors, and when they had spread out their battalions on all sides,
     they surrounded the Trojans in their midst. The Greeks then killed
     the king of Persia, and with a great number of fighting men they
35 compelled the Trojans to retreat, in whose defense King Sarpedon
     accomplished a great deal on account of his martial prowess.
        At this, however, King Priam and his natural sons, who courageous-
     ly followed him everywhere in order to aid the Trojans, strove
     furiously after the Greeks, manfully pressed against them, and over-
40 whelmed them with great slaughter. There was no one on the Trojan
     side that day so valiant that he did as much in the force of arms as
     did King Priam himself alone, whose strength was reinforced by grief
     and rage. But the Greeks, having gone into council, assembled in a
     huge multitude of knights at that place where the Trojans would have
45 to have passage back to their city, and after they had besieged this
     place, they seized it. When the Trojans were compelled in retreat to
     approach this place, they found the way across the place occupied by
     a great number of warriors, and a very grim battle was waged there.
     If it had not been for King Priam, who approached this place from
50 above in a huge multitude of warriors, countless numbers of his
     people would then have been cruelly lost. Paris, however, coming up
     from the side in a great troop of extremely fierce men, hurled himself
     upon the Greeks with them, and with bows and arrows they pursued
     the Greeks with deadly intent, wounded them, and very often
55 delivered them to death, so that the Greeks, being unable to sustain
     the deadly rain of arrows from which many had already died,
     hastened to go back in retreat to their tents. When the Trojans saw
     them going back, they did not by any means try to pursue them, but
     entered their city with slow steps. On account of this, the fighting
60 was cut short on that day, and everyone attributed the honors of war
     for that whole day to King Priam.
        But in the morning when it grew light, the Trojans sent to the
     Greeks to demand a truce. The Greeks agreed to the treaty which was
     asked for and the truce which was demanded, but the duration of
65 this truce is not found set forth in the book. During the course of
     this truce, therefore, the body of the king of Persia was mournfully
     brought into the city. The grieving was very great among the citizens

and especially with Paris, who had loved this king sincerely and with
entire affection. For this reason Paris ordered that the body of this
70 king be transported overland to the kingdom of Persia so that this
king might be buried where the kings his ancestors had customarily
been buried with regal honor, and in the presence of his two sons
who were themselves kings.

     While the truce granted by this treaty lasted, the time came for
75 the city of Troy to celebrate the anniversary of the demise of Hector.
The Trojans had decreed that at this time fifteen days of solemn
mourning would be observed, and after these days they decided that
a funeral feast should be held, as was then the custom of kings and
nobles of high birth. During this truce the Greeks entered the city in
80 safety and the Trojans went safely to the Greek camp. Then Achilles
was seized with an ill-advised desire to go to Troy and see the city
and the celebration of the festival mentioned above. He went
unarmed, therefore, to the city, and entered the temple of Apollo,
where the body of Hector had been placed, as was described above.
85 There a multitude of heroes and noble women were moaning in
anguish before the body of Hector. For the tabernacle of Hector was
open on all sides so that it was clearly exposed in plain view for anyone wishing to see it. To tell the truth, the simulated figure of Hector
was in the same condition in which it was when he was first placed
90 upon the throne. The virtue of the spices and the liquid of the balsam
still maintained the body of Hector. Queen Hecuba was present at
the feet of the body with her lovely daughter Polyxena in a retinue
of many noble women, who, with their hair dishevelled over their
breasts and shoulders, in great bitterness of heart uttered tearful
95 groans from the depths of their souls. Polyxena had not lost the
beauty of her face at all, despite the great pangs of her anguish. The
vivid color of her cheeks which colored her face with the redness of
roses was not at all faded from its vivid brightness and freshness on
account of the anguish of her grief, nor was the natural rosy color
100 removed from her lips, nor did the floods of tears flowing from her
eyes darken the splendor of her eyes. In fact, it seemed to the onlookers that the tears flowing down her cheeks seemed to have the
appearance of a tablet of new ivory, gleaming with milk-white
radiance, which someone had bedewed with drops of brilliant clear
105 water; so also her beautiful golden blond hair scattered in many

strands looked like gold, so that it almost seemed to be not hair but
rather threads of gold bound together. When Polyxena raised her
hands to tear her hair, it did not seem to be touched by human
hands but to be sprinkled profusely with milk.

110   As Achilles looked at Polyxena and contemplated her beauty, it
came into his mind that he had never seen a girl or any woman
distinguished by the appearance of such beauty. And since two
attributes existed together in her, that is, both free and noble birth
and a superior amount of beauty, and since Achilles fixed his gaze
115 upon her with a longing heart, the arrow of Cupid unexpectedly
wounded the mighty Achilles, and penetrating to the inner recesses of
his heart, it took possession of him and forced him to become
intoxicated by the great ardor of love. While he thought to please
himself by gazing at her frequently and to ease the deep desire of his
120 heart, he made himself the cause of a greater rending of his wound.
As he noted and perceived the beauty of Polyxena, he ruined his
own, for, because of the great desire of love, his appearance declined
into sudden ugliness. Need I say more? Achilles was so ensnared by
the love of Polyxena that he did not know what to do. He cast off
125 all other responsibilities and took interest only in Polyxena, as long as
he could look at her. On account of this he further extended his
injuries, and fixed the wounds of his love more deeply in his heart.
    When day had declined into evening, Queen Hecuba left the tem-
ple with her daughter Polyxena after they had ended their weeping,
130 while Achilles pursued her as long as he could with loving looks,
which were the cause and origin of his sickness. He was accordingly
bewildered and made restless by the languor of his great desire, and
he turned toward his lodging, sought his bed, and threw himself upon
it. He was overwhelmed by the many anxieties crowding in upon him,
135 and his heart was torn inwardly and he felt and perceived that his
immense love for Polyxena was the efficient cause of his languor.
Then he forced out these words in a soft whisper: "Alas for me,
because I, whom the bravest and stoutest of men could not conquer
by any means, whom not even the very brave Hector, who surpassed
140 the bravest of all, could conquer, am now overwhelmed and cast
down by the sight of one frail girl! If this is the efficient cause of my
woe, how can I hope for the healing of a wise physician, since she
alone may be physician and healing remedy for me, and she will not

be moved to imperil her right conduct by either my prayers or
145 presents of great riches or the hardiness of my strength, or my free
and noble birth? What madness has seized my heart that I love and
cherish her who should hold me in deadly hatred, since I have arrived
in her kingdom to deprive her of her parents and have already deprived her of her illustrious brother? With what effrontery shall I be
150 able to allure her to an act of compliance, who far surpasses me in
nobility and wealth and is distinguished by her surpassing beauty over
other women—all of which preserves the haughtiness of her mind? It
seems clear that all ways by which I can heal myself in safety are
closed to me." He turned to the wall and in secret dissolved com-
155 pletely in tears, so that no one could perceive his grief. At last he
dried his tears and exchanged them for frequent sighs. He was wholly
occupied with much deliberation and examined silently in his mind
ways by which he could improve his condition. He rose then from his
bed, asked his attendants for water, washed his face and removed the
160 signs of his tears.

*Here begins the twenty-fourth book, about how Achilles
was preoccupied by the love of Polyxena and did not wish
to fight.*

When night came on that day, while the treaty was still in effect,
Achilles, lying on his couch, spent the whole night sleeplessly,
considering how he might send his messenger to Hecuba in secret, to
negotiate with her. His plan was that if she wished to yield him her
5 daughter, Polyxena, to be joined in the bonds of matrimony, so that
she would grant her to him as a wife, he would manage and arrange
that the whole Greek army would depart from the siege of Troy and
return to Greece without injury to the Trojans, and that every cause
of offense would be allayed with no other conditions added. For this
10 reason, with the rising of dawn that morning, he speedily called to
him one of his men who was in his confidence and very faithful to
him. When he had revealed the secrets of his heart to him, and had
enjoined him to keep them faithfully concealed by silence, he
unhesitatingly ordered him to go to Queen Hecuba in secret, with the
15 plan of the orders given him. The man immediately carried out the

commands of his lord and prepared quickly for the journey, and coming in secret to Queen Hecuba, he faithfully revealed the mission of his lord.

Queen Hecuba, who was known for great discretion, when she had
20 understood the words of the messenger with her gentle soul, although she heaved many sighs from her heart, thus responded to the messenger: "Friend, go back to your lord, and promise him freely on my part that, as much as it is in me, I am ready to carry out his wishes in a happy frame of mind. But in order for this business to come to
25 a proper end, it is necessary for me to discover the will of King Priam, my husband, and of Paris, my son. When I am informed of their responses, see that you return on the third day to receive an answer from me as to what can be done." When he had heard the words of Hecuba, the messenger returned to Achilles. After Achilles
30 had heard the response of the messenger, he was relieved of his grief, since the hope of the words gladdened his mind, and in the confidence of this hope he rested a bit.

When Queen Hecuba had seized the opportunity of speaking to the king and Paris, she reported to them secretly the words which
35 Achilles had sent her by his messenger. After King Priam had heard them, he bowed his head for a long time and said nothing, while he considered her words from many different points of view. Finally he responded thus to Queen Hecuba: "Oh, how hard it seems to my mind to receive as a friend him who has injured me so severely by
40 hatred and great enmity so that he has removed the light of my eyes by killing Hector, on account of whose death the Greeks undertake bold deeds against me, and strive for the extermination of my people! But so that henceforth we may avoid more serious things in the future, if by chance there are any, and so that my other sons at least
45 may be preserved from harm, and so that I may rest in my old age from the exertions of battle, I give unwilling consent to your wishes, provided that he first does what he promises, lest perchance he intends to deceive us by any crafty machinations." Paris, then, when he heard the king's word, approved the king's advice and readily gave
50 his consent, because among those promises of Achilles, Helen, his wife, was not to be returned to her husband, but on the contrary should remain with Paris perpetually.

On the third day following, Achilles sent his messenger mentioned

before to Queen Hecuba. When he had approached her, Queen
55   Hecuba told him secretly that she had received a response from King
Priam her husband and Paris her son, concerning the words sent to
her by Achilles, "by which it pleases them both, and me likewise, to
fulfill the wishes of Achilles, if, however, he first definitely redeems
the pledge of his promise. It is therefore in his power to accomplish
60   his wish in this present business, but in the meanwhile, until he can
carry out this thing, let him act discreetly and cautiously." Thus,
when permission had been given to the messenger, the messenger
went back to Achilles, to whom he revealed faithfully everything
which had been said to him by Queen Hecuba.
65   Since Achilles was bound by the bonds of fervent love, when he
perceived that by no other way could he satisfy his wishes concerning Polyxena, he was plagued by many troubles and cares, while he
turned over in his anxious mind the considerable promises he had
made King Priam, which were absolutely not in his complete power.
70   For it is a usual and typical weakness in all lovers that when they are
seething with the yearning of desire, on account of their ill-advised
passion, they promise great things which are impossible for them.
Achilles thought, nevertheless, since he was confident of his worth
and reputation, that if he refused to aid the Greeks further, the
75   Greeks would agree with him concerning their withdrawal, and that
when the siege of Troy had been raised, they would return to their
own country.
     On account of this, Achilles, with the consent of Palamedes, called
all the Greek kings and princes together for a conference. When they
80   had assembled, Achilles put forth these words among them: "Kings,
dukes, and princes, my friends—all of you who with me have taken
up the burden of the present war as princes, acting all together—what
ill-advised spirit of contentiousness has spurred us on so that for
recovering the wife, that is, Lady Helen, of one man, that is, Lord
85   Menelaus, we have left our kingdoms to be torn asunder by others,
and our countries, our wives and sons, and have come to a foreign
land? For her recovery we have already recklessly paid a heavy price,
and we have exposed our persons to death and countless hardships,
since already many of our nobles and brave and stout knights have
90   been delivered to death, who might perhaps have lived till today in
safety with us. I have received many wounds from which I have lost

much blood, and it was not many days ago that I received such a
wound in killing Hector that I did not believe I could ever live after
it. Is Helen of such value that for her recovery so many nobles have
95 to die? Obviously there are in different parts of the world many
noble women from whom King Menelaus can choose not just one but
two or more for a wife, for whom it would not be necessary for all
Greece to undergo so many hardships. For it is not easy to vanquish
the Trojans thus easily, since they have a very strong city strengthened
100 by many warrior knights and foot soldiers. Since we have already
given the very brave Hector over to death, and many of their nobles,
this should abundantly suffice for us from now on, so that we may
return with glory and honor to our own country. For if we depart
without recovering Helen, this cannot seem very grievous to us, since
105 we have among us Hesione from Troy, and she is the sister of King
Priam, whom Helen cannot surpass in noble rank."

Thus Achilles made an end to his speech. But King Thoas, and
Menesteus, duke of Athens, opposed Achilles with a great flood of
disapproving words. Likewise the majority of the kings and princes
110 reproached Achilles' advice and did not wish to agree to Achilles'
advice. For this reason, Achilles was moved by great wrath and
ordered his Myrmidons not to bear arms against the Trojans any
more, nor to dare henceforth to give assistance to the Greeks.

Meanwhile provisions were lacking in the Greek army which caused
115 a very great famine among them. For this reason Palamedes, at a
council attended by all the foremost men and officers of the Greek
army . . . . They all agreed in this, that they should send King
Agamemnon with many ships to King Telephus at Messa, in order to
bring the ships back loaded with the greatest amount of provisions,
120 so that all scarcity of supplies would be driven away from the Greek
army and the Greeks could rejoice in great plenty. Agamemnon
willingly received the orders of his commander and went without
delay to Messa with the aforesaid ships, and when by good fortune he
had landed there, King Telephus received Agamemnon with much
125 pleasure. At last when the ships had been loaded with a great amount
of provisions and edible things and things for human use, they
returned to the Greek army by a fortunate voyage, and were welcomed there with the greatest joy. Palamedes took the responsibility
of his command and ordered all the ships which had come with the

130   army to Troy to be looked to and repaired, so that they could be
      preserved safely on account of the work of restoring them, and so
      that they would have them more easily available for meeting their
      needs.

Here begins the twenty-fifth book, about the tenth battle and
the death of Deiphobus and King Sarpedon and Palamedes.

When the truce granted according to the treaty had elapsed, both
armies assembled for battle, and a grim battle was waged by both
sides. Deiphobus rushed boldly upon King Creseus of Agresta and
King Creseus met him effectively in the swift charge of his horse and
5   shattered his lance against him. Deiphobus thrust at him with a blow
of his lance and struck him so mightily that he hurled King Creseus
dead from his horse. Thus King Creseus ended his last days. The
Greeks were much discouraged by the death of King Creseus, and as
the Trojans were pressing manfully against them, the Greeks were
10 forced to flee and they gave themselves up to headlong flight.
      But Palamedes and Diomedes with twenty thousand warriors aided
the Greeks and met the Trojans, and with them in addition was the
valiant Ajax Telamonius. This Telamonius, rushing at once upon
Sinsilenius, a natural son of King Priam, wounded him so seriously on
15 the arm that from then on Sinsilenius was rendered unable to fight.
When Deiphobus saw this, he was completely enraged. He rushed
furiously upon Telamonius so that he threw him wounded from his
horse. Palamedes, seeking to avenge him, took a lance and rushed
upon Deiphobus and struck him so heavily that on account of the
20 great force he broke his shield and shattered the plates of his hauberk.
He had thrust his lance into Deiphobus' chest, and since the lance
broke, the shaft with the iron point remained in Deiphobus' chest.
      When Paris, however, Deiphobus' brother, who was then at that
place of battle, saw Deiphobus thus mortally wounded, he dragged
25 him with great effort away from the fierce troops, weeping copiously,
and was at pains to carry him into the city. After Deiphobus had
been brought there, he opened his eyes and looked at Paris, his
brother, and said to him: "Are you allowing me, my brother, to
descend into hell? I implore you earnestly to hasten speedily to my

30 slayer, before this shaft is pulled from the wound in my chest, and
that you will take great pains before I die that he who slew me will
fall at your hands." Paris, when he heard the words of his wounded
brother, in great anguish of grief left his brother dying and hastened
to battle, all covered with tears because of his grief, since he no
35 longer wished to live after the death of his brother. Accordingly, he
eagerly sought Palamedes between the lines of the fighting men, and
he came upon Palamedes struggling manfully against King Sarpedon.
For King Sarpedon had attacked Palamedes, and while he was trying
to kill him, Palamedes had rushed furiously upon this King Sarpedon
40 with his naked sword, with which he wounded him so seriously on
the thigh that he separated it from the groin. And at once King
Sarpedon fell down slain. Seeing what deadly destruction Palamedes
was inflicting upon the Trojans, with the result that he had already
compelled them of necessity to flee with great loss of life, Paris, with
45 his bow taut in his strong arms, watched with keen glance in what
place of his body he could injure Palamedes with most deadly effect,
and having launched a poisoned arrow, he struck him in the throat,
so that he killed him at once by piercing his jugular vein. For this
reason Palamedes fell headlong to the ground and died.
50   The Greeks cried out, they were in anguish, and they grieved on
account of the death of their great leader. Since they were stunned,
they left the field and entered precipitously into flight, and by fleeing
arrived at their camp. The Trojans pursued them at the point of the
sword with deadly intent. But in front of their tents, the Greeks
55 turned with hostility against the Trojans in an excess of fierce
courage, and opposing them, resisted them manfully. The Trojans
turned their attention to resistance and dismounted from their horses.
They began a grim struggle against the Greeks, pressing so furiously
upon them on foot that they rushed upon them in their tents and
60 delivered the tents to looting. They took many silver vessels away
from them and a great amount of gold and silver which they found in
their chests.
    Then Paris and Troilus arrived at the shore with thirty thousand
warriors, and they at once ordered that the Greek ships be set on fire.
65 Without delay, they set many fires in many Greek ships. The air close
to them was blackened with smoke by this and soon grew hot, while
those fires burst forth in larger flames with crackling sparks. The air

was lit up with the brightness of the flames and the neighboring
places glowed, so that the flames could be seen easily by those who
70 were on the walls of the city. But at this, Ajax Telamonius arrived on
the Greek side with a very large band of warriors, and with a very
stiff resistance, they began a defense against the Trojans. A mortal
combat ensued between them. The slaughter was very great, since
many bodies of the slain fell everywhere on both sides. Then all the
75 Greek ships which were crowded together in one mass would without
doubt have been burned up if Ajax Telamonius, who was performing
miracles in his own person, had not manfully resisted. And still more
than twenty of the ships were consumed by fire.

The Trojans prevailed there with such prowess that besides slaying
80 the Greeks, they wounded an infinite number of them. Many of these,
who could not stand the grievous pains of their wounds, withdrew
from the fighting of the battle in great danger from weakness. Among
them, Heber, son of the king of Thrace, who had been mortally
wounded by a lance and still had the shaft in his body, raced to the
85 tent of Achilles, who was then staying in his tent and had refused to
go out to battle that day on account of the love of Polyxena. Heber,
thus mortally wounded, reproached Achilles greatly for exerting
himself in this cruel way with regard to the destruction of his
countrymen, since he disgracefully allowed them to die, and on
90 account of great cruelty permitted and contributed to their fall in
battle, though he could aid and protect them by the assistance of his
prowess. Then Heber pulled the shaft violently from the wound, and
straightway Heber, with failing eyes, breathed his last in the presence
of Achilles. A short time afterward an attendant of Achilles came
95 from the battle and raced to Achilles' tent, and when asked by
Achilles how it was with the Greek army, his attendant said to him:
"Oh, how badly things have gone for our Greeks today, lord, on
account of the immense number of Trojans who are killing these
Greeks! For it is thought that of all the Trojans capable of fighting
100 who were in Troy, not one could have remained in it, since they all
came to this battle and thus oppressed the Greeks vehemently. For
this reason, my lord, since the Trojans are already wearied by great
exertion, if it were in your power to march to battle against them
now, you would from this acquire for yourself the memorial of
105 eternal glory. For simply through the entrance of your courageous

presence into battle all the Trojans would be vanquished at once, and on account of their weariness, they would not dare to raise their hands against your strength."

Achilles did not apply his mind to his attendant's words and did
110 not even out of kindness turn his eyes toward the dead Heber, but he pretended that he did not hear all that he saw and heard, in the way that one who is bound by the chains of love neglects everything. For it is the custom of all lovers, when blinded by the wounds of love, to avoid honor and glory, thinking they would displease their mistresses,
115 even if it happens that with great ignominy they refrain from the glory and good works.

Meanwhile the battle raged bitterly between the Trojans and Greeks, but when the day was already turning toward sunset, the battle ceased. Troilus and Paris, leaving the strife with their Trojans,
120 returned to their own city. Deiphobus, who was prolonging his end, was not yet dead when Paris and Troilus came together before him. In his presence they wailed and cried out in great suffering; they were so overcome by excessive grief that they wished ultimately to die with him. Deiphobus, however, with fluttering eyes and a voice
125 almost failing, inquired of Paris if he had killed his slayer. When he had been assured of his death by Paris, he ordered the shaft pulled out of his wound. And when it was pulled out, Deiphobus died immediately.

All the Trojans were crushed by very great grief at the death of
130 Deiphobus. Nevertheless, since it would be superfluous to tell of the griefs of King Priam, Hecuba, the sisters and brothers of Deiphobus, and in addition the laments and tears which were poured forth for King Sarpedon, it is omitted in this place. King Priam had the body of Deiphobus buried in a very costly monument, and so also the
135 body of the illustrious King Sarpedon. In the Greek camp, the lamentation over the death of Palamedes was very great, and when his corpse had been given over to burial, the Greeks assembled, and since they could not exist without the efforts of a general, they unanimously accepted the advice of Nestor and again elected Agamemnon
140 as general of their army and commander in chief.

On the following day, the Trojans, with their battalions in martial array, marched out to battle. The Greeks at once rushed upon them boldly. On account of this, a grim battle was waged between them,

from which followed great carnage because of the dead. But though
145 on that day the cloudy dark sky poured forth much rain, on the
other hand, the blood of many dead was poured forth as the battle
raged. Many of the Greeks fell among frequent blows of the sword—
more than of the Trojans. Then Troilus marched to battle in a very
great company of armed men. The Greeks were not able to withstand
150 him in any way and fled before him. As they fled through the
torrents of rain, they turned toward their camp. The Trojans pursued
them to their tents, but finally left them on account of the stormy
weather and returned to their city and were received in it. On the
following day a mortal combat began between them, and when the
155 battle was engaged in, as Troilus came to the fray, he killed many
Greeks, several of their nobles, counts, and barons, as well as officers.
Thus they fought that day until the shadows of night, and without
intermission for the next twelve days following. When the Greeks
could hold out no longer, on account of the many dead bodies,
160 through their messengers they sought from King Priam a truce of two
months in a confirmed treaty. They were granted this by him, and
the treaty was confirmed and sworn to.

During the period of the aforesaid truce, Agamemnon sent his
messengers to Achilles, that is, Duke Nestor, Ulysses, and Diomedes,
165 to move and induce Achilles to come to battle with the other Greeks
and not to allow his fellow Greeks to be cruelly slaughtered by their
enemies. When they came to Achilles, Achilles welcomed them with
the greatest pleasure. And when they were all sitting down together,
Ulysses first addressed Achilles and said: "Lord Achilles, was it not
170 your intention and that of all of us, that is, of so many kings and
princes, to leave our kingdoms and take ourselves in a strong force to
the kingdom of King Priam so that we might be able to deliver King
Priam and his subjects to death and bring his city of Troy down in
perpetual ruin? From whence comes this new purpose of yours, so
175 that, with your intentions changed to the opposite, you have changed
your behavior, after so many losses inflicted on us in this land by the
Trojans, after so much anguish and grief, since the Trojans have
delivered to violent death so many of our kings and nobles, have
pillaged our tents and given them over to looting, and consumed so
180 many of our ships by fire? Had we not already arrived at the hope of
victory through your mighty arm since you delivered the very brave

Hector to be destroyed by death, on whom depended the Trojans'
hope of safety and of victory? Now with Deiphobus dead, the brother
of Hector, is not all hope of safety completely removed from the
185 Trojans? Now do you, who have sought the glory of great reputation
in the might of your strength, wish to extinguish your reputation for
the great glory through contrary acts, so that you will allow even
your own people, whom you defended for such a long time by
shedding your own blood, to succumb to bitter death? May it please
190 you henceforth to keep the fame of your reputation alive and to
protect your people, who without the assistance of your might can
do nothing, to the extent that from now on you will bear your
victorious arms to battle against your enemies, so that we may obtain
a speedy victory from them, which through you we can hope for
195 with certainty." At this, Ulysses made an end to the aforesaid speech.
Achilles then replied to the words of Ulysses: "Lord Ulysses, if, as
you said, we have advanced to this land for the purpose which it
pleased you to declare in your speech, we can safely say that the
wind of great foolishness impelled us and the spirit of very great
200 stupidity took away our senses (since simply on account of the wife
of one king, that is, of Lord Menelaus, so many kings and princes
have subjected themselves to death), and that we die cruelly at the
hands of the Trojans in foreign regions. Would it not have been better
for the illustrious Palamedes to have died in his noble kingdom than
205 to have been delivered to death in a foreign province, and for our
other kings who, destroyed in battle, finished their lives outside their
own kingdoms? Obviously, since the chief people of the world and
likewise of the nobility are gathered together here, if it should happen
that they all die in this land, the world, lacking so many nobles, will
210 be replenished and repopulated by the low offspring of peasants. Did
not the very brave Hector miserably end his life in this war? So easily
may I, who have not such fortitude. Therefore, to beseech me or ask
me to proceed against the Trojans is lost labor. For it is not my
intention to engage further in mortal combats. I would prefer that my
215 reputation for valor be extinguished rather than my person. For even
if right conduct is praised sometimes, oblivion suddenly swallows
it up."
Nestor and Diomedes tried diligently enough to persuade Achilles
with their words, but they could in no way induce him to agree

220 either to their words or to the prayers of Agamemnon. He, however, suggested to them that it would be profitable to seek peace from the Trojans before many nobles perished and died in their battles. Nestor, Ulysses, and Diomedes accordingly went back to Agamemnon and reported to him in order all they had learned from Achilles. For this

225 reason Agamemnon ordered all the Greek kings and princes and officers of the army to assemble for a conference. When they all were met in one place, he made known the will of Achilles and his recalcitrance, how Achilles had absolutely refused, when asked by him and other Greek kings, to come to battle against the Trojans,

230 how he had urged that the Greeks return to their own country, and that they seek peace with the Trojans. "Let everyone of you, if it pleases you, reveal his wish as to what your intentions are concerning these things and what is to be done henceforth by us." Thus Agamemnon made an end to his speech.

235   Then Menelaus, who rose first to speak, said it was very wicked to seek peace with the Trojans, since with Hector and Deiphobus dead, the Trojans considered themselves more dead than alive, and it was certain from this that without the might of Achilles they were sure of victory from the Trojans. But Ulysses and Nestor were in marked

240 opposition to Menelaus, saying that it was not to be wondered if Menelaus desired war and was against returning, since his whole heart yearned for the recovery of his wife. For Troy could not be considered bereft of Hector and Deiphobus, since there was in Troy a second Hector, no less endowed with courage, that is, Troilus, who

245 harassed the Greeks no less than if Hector were alive, and there was there another Deiphobus, that is Paris, who was of no less courage than Deiphobus and continued to fight courageously. Hence they suggested peace by all means and a return after the achieving of the peace.

250   Then Calchas, the traitorous Trojan priest, almost raging, shouted out among the Greeks, saying: "Ah, noble heroes, what are you planning to do against the will and commands of the gods? For the gods have assuredly promised victory to you, as I understood without error from their mouths, and it would not be safe to mock the gods

255 or to oppose their orders. Take arms, therefore, against the Trojans, renew the contest more manfully against them, and let not your hand fail until you can achieve the hoped for victory from them, which the

gods have incontrovertibly decreed you will achieve." Accordingly, at
the words of the priest Calchas, all the Greeks increased their vigor
260 and unyielding spirit against the Trojans, not troubling about the
assistance of Achilles but just as if he were not at all among them.

*Here begins the twenty-sixth book, about the death of
Troilus and King Memnon, who were slain.*

The two months of truce given according to the treaty were already
passed when the Greeks, having drawn up their battalions for battle,
marched out manfully in order to fight. The Trojans, who had then
marched out to battle, came up swiftly against them, and a very
5 hard-fought battle was waged between them. Many corpses of the
slain fell here and there. Then Troilus marched to battle in a very
great company of warriors, and killed Greeks as he hastened to
avenge the death of his brother. Dares writes that on that day,
Troilus killed a thousand Greek knights. The Greeks fled before him.
10 For this reason, when the Greeks had been compelled to flee, the
Trojans pursued them to their tents at the point of the sword. But
night came and cut short the conflict.
    On the following day, the twelfth grim and hard-fought battle was
engaged in, since the Greeks, striving manfully after vengeance for
15 their men, pressed hard against the Trojans in the grim contest.
Diomedes was remarkably enraged against the Trojans, killed many
Trojans, wounded them, and hurled them down. But Troilus, who
saw Diomedes, whom he well knew, pressing upon the Trojans so
acrimoniously, rushed upon Diomedes in a rapid charge of his horse
20 with lance extended forward, and Diomedes boldly received him.
Diomedes, however, broke his lance against Troilus, although he did
not injure or wound him at all. Troilus had thrust at Diomedes so
strongly that he hurled him headlong from his horse and wounded
him seriously, so that he reached the ground half-dead. Troilus then
25 taunted Diomedes with opprobrious words for loving Briseida. The
Greeks, with great effort, dragged Diomedes half-dead from under the
feet of the horses and carried him to his tent on his shield. Menelaus,
however, when he saw Diomedes so grievously wounded and thrown
from his horse, spurred his own horse into a charge, and rushing

30 against Troilus, endeavored to throw Troilus from his horse. Troilus,
with the same lance with which he had wounded Diomedes (since he
had noticed that it was not yet cracked or broken), struck Menelaus
so that he cast him from his horse and gave him a deadly wound.
When his men had hurriedly dragged him from beneath the feet of
35 the horses, they brought him back to his tent on his shield.

Agamemnon, seeing that his men were almost failing in the battle,
rushed upon the Trojans with his men and forced many others to do
so. They harried them manfully and killed many of them. Troilus
rushed upon Agamemnon, hurled him from his horse, not without
40 wounding him, although it was not a deadly wound. Agamemnon
mounted his horse with the aid of his men, and since he feared the
loss of his officers on that day, when the battle was ended, he
demanded through his messengers a six months' truce from King
Priam. When King Priam had held a council about this, this king
45 granted them a truce, although it was not acceptable to many of his
faithful advisors that he should bind himself to grant such long truces.

Meanwhile Briseida, against the will of her father, went frequently
to see Diomedes as he was lying in bed on account of the wound
given him, with the result that although she knew he had been thus
50 seriously wounded by Troilus whom she had loved a while ago, still
she reflected upon many things in her mind. When she carefully
considered that no assurance remained to her of uniting herself to
Troilus, she, so variable and changeable, as is typical of women,
inclined her whole thought toward Diomedes and changed her love,
55 proposing in her heart not to put Diomedes off with further expec-
tations, but, as soon as he had reached convalescence, to do his will
completely, since she was entirely enflamed by his love and burned
hotly with blazing desire.

During the period of this truce, King Agamemnon went to Achilles,
60 accompanied by Duke Nestor, and Achilles received them with a
pleasant expression. Then Agamemnon exhorted him to come to
battle and not permit his Greeks to perish any more. Agamemnon
urged Achilles, but with hardened heart Achilles would not be moved
by any prayer. However, because Achilles was sincerely fond of
65 Agamemnon, he conceded that in the battle they could have his
Myrmidons without him, and Agamemnon and Nestor, as they rose,
thanked him greatly for this. Finally Agamemnon and Nestor, having
asked leave of Achilles, went back to their tents.

When the aforesaid truce had elapsed, Agamemnon with his men
70 girded himself for the fray. Achilles commanded all his Myrmidons to
arm. He approached them as they were arming, and after bestowing a
red badge upon each one of them, with tears falling, he gave them
permission to march out to battle. Then the Myrmidons, at a slow
pace, advanced to the battle, which had already begun. The Trojans
75 oppressed the Greeks amazingly in this battle, but the Duke of Athens
defended them manfully. Troilus, when he arrived, rushed upon him,
threw him from his horse, and wounded many of the Myrmidons
fatally. That day they fought until the shadows of night, but with the
coming of the darkness of night the fighting ceased.
80   On the following day, both sides girded themselves for the fray.
A very hard-fought battle was waged. King Philimenis and Polydamas
seized King Thoas and tried to lead him away captive. The Myrmidons
resisted them manfully, however, and snatched him from their hands.
Then Troilus hurled himself among them and wounded many of the
85 Myrmidons and laid many low. They, making a fierce attack against
him, killed his horse and strove to surround him. Then Paris hurled
himself manfully among the Myrmidons with his natural brothers,
pressed them hard, wounded them, and scattered them. He freed
Troilus, who at once mounted another horse. A mortal combat was
90 engaged in for the liberation of Troilus, in which the Myrmidons slew
Margariton, one of King Priam's natural sons. Troilus, wishing to
avenge his injury and the death of his brother, bitterly attacked the
Myrmidons, wounded many of them, and harried them considerably
in aiding Paris and his natural brothers. It was not easy to overthrow
95 the Myrmidons, since they were reknowned for great valor and were
very well trained in the art of fighting. For this reason, fearing the
great multitude of Trojans, they formed themselves into a fortress
and stronghold by pressing together in one unit, and even so could
not protect themselves without Troilus goading them unmerci-
100 fully, hurting and injuring them and frequently compelling some of
them to separate from the mass.
        Then King Agamemnon, Menelaus, King Telamon, Ulysses, and
Diomedes, who was then flourishing in full health, entered the battle
with their battalions. For this reason a grim battle was waged on both
105 sides. The Greeks oppressed the Trojans amazingly, and killed many
of them. But Troilus bore down where the Trojans were most fiercely
harassed. He killed Greeks, wounded and overthrew them, so that, as

if by the prowess of Troilus alone, the Greeks were turned to flight
and hastened precipitately, with great speed, to their tents. But Ajax
110 Telamonius marched to battle and approached the Trojans with the
courage and determination to fight hard. Then the Greeks regained
the field. This sixteenth battle was very deadly, however, since a great
many slain fell on either side. Troilus, who on account of his strength
had not ceased to press against the Myrmidons and all the other
115 Greeks, harried them with such determination that the bravest of the
Greeks were not able to prevail against his courage and ability. On
account of this, the Greeks again turned in flight and the Trojans
pursued them to their tents. There Troilus attacked them amazingly,
and on account of his very great courage in fighting, he took a
120 hundred of the Greek nobles, whom he led captive to the city. The
battle broke off and both armies separated.

The Myrmidons returned, wounded, to Achilles in camp. Several of
them reported to him that many of them had fallen that day in
battle, so that, when they had sought after corpses of the dead, they
125 found that more than a hundred of them had died. Achilles grieved
immoderately at the death of his men, and with the coming of night
he went to bed in great grief and anguish, and there, because he had
become very restless, he did not seek to close his eyes in the usual
rest of sleep. For he was occupied by the many thoughts that rose in
130 his mind, and he was disposed in his mind to enter the battle in order
to avenge his men. But his love of Polyxena was hostile to the
thought and opposed it with a fierce struggle. When he thought that
since he loved Polyxena more than himself, it was an effective argument against him that perhaps, if he rushed to arms, he would be
135 frustrated in his desire for Polyxena and would be deprived of the
joys he expected from her. He had now already impiously deceived
King Priam and his wife by going against his promise, since he had
promised them that he would help the Greeks no further and yet had
many times given them the assistance of his men.

140   Achilles had been absorbed for many days in turning over such
thoughts when the armies of the Greeks and Trojans at last prepared
for the seventeenth mortal combat. A grim battle raged between them
which was not stilled for seven consecutive days. In these days,
Achilles, forbidden by love, held to his purpose and by no means
145 went into combat. During those days many Greeks were killed. When

Agamemnon saw this destruction of his people, he proposed a truce
to the Trojans. The Trojans refused to grant it to him, except for as
many days in which the Greeks could bury their dead.

When these days were elapsed, the eighteenth mortal combat took
150 place between the Trojans and Greeks. After they had drawn up their
battalions, a grim battle was waged between them. For this reason,
when Menelaus and Paris joined in combat, both fell from their horses
on account of the power of their lances. Polydamas rushed upon
Ulysses with his naked sword and likewise Ulysses manfully defended
155 himself from him with his sword. Menesteus, duke of Athens,
approached Antenor and struck him so that he cast him down from
his horse. King Philimenis went against Agamemnon, whom he then
attacked in earnest, but King Telamonius aided him and threw King
Philimenis wounded from his horse. Antilochus, however, the son of
160 Nestor, rushed upon one of the natural sons of Priam, whose name
was Brunus de Gemellis, piercing him so powerfully with his lance
and wounding him so fatally that he fell dead to the ground.

The Trojans were very pained at the death of Brunus. When the
report of it reached Troilus, Troilus shed many tears, and rushed
165 upon the Greeks in fury, so that without doubt he would have forced
them to flee, if the Myrmidons had not manfully resisted him. On
account of this, Troilus left the others and turned toward the
Myrmidons. He hurled himself upon them courageously, wounded
them, threw them down, and killed many of them, so that the
170 Myrmidons, being unable to withstand the attack of Troilus, nor the
other Greeks the great number of Trojans, they all took flight
precipitately. Troilus and the rest of the Trojans pursued them to
their tents. There the Trojans inflicted severe wounds upon the
Greeks, and, dismounting from their horses, cut them down in their
175 tents, wounded them, and cruelly delivered them to death.

The uproar was very great among these tents, and the sounds of
lamentation echoed and reechoed through the air nearby. For this
reason the tumultuous confusion of these sounds reached Achilles
staying in his tent. Achilles inquired what was the cause of such a
180 confused uproar. Those fleeing from battle told him that the Greeks
had been vanquished by the Trojans and had been of necessity forced
back to their tents in order to avoid being slaughtered, but even there
they were not able to protect themselves, so that they were killed

there by the Trojans. "And you who trust you will be safe in your
185   tent will see at once more than fifty thousand Trojans who will not
permit you to live since you are unarmed, and who have already
delivered so many of your Myrmidons to death, and do not cease
now to deliver them ruthlessly to death, so that they may consider
themselves dead men for certain, unless someone rises powerfully to
190   their aid."
   At these words Achilles arose, almost infuriated, and his spirit
raged and he became heated with anger on account of his great fury.
He put aside his love of Polyxena, sought arms, armed instantly,
mounted his horse with speed, and just like a starving wolf among
195   the lambs, hurled himself eagerly against the Trojans. He rushed upon
them, scattered them, wounded them, and slew them, so that in one
short hour his sword was known among the combatants since it was
completely soaked in the blood of those slain by it, and was filling
and covering the ground with the corpses of the dead. After Troilus
200   saw this, he recognized the grim blade of Achilles and accordingly
directed his horse toward him. Similarly Achilles perceived him,
effectively intercepted him, and while one thrust at the other, Troilus
wounded Achilles so seriously that Achilles had of necessity to leave
the battle for several days, and he had to stay in bed for many days
205   because of this wound. Although Troilus was not seriously wounded
by Achilles, he did not experience the blow of Achilles without a
wound. Finally by both thrusts, both fell at the same time from their
horses. The combat on that day lasted from morning till night, and
with the coming of the shadow of night the combat was cut short.
210   The fighting lasted continuously for six days, during which many fell
in battle on either side.
   King Priam was overwhelmed by great grief because Achilles had
entered the battle against his promise. He now considered that
Achilles had spoken in order to deceive. He reproached the queen his
215   wife very much, because if he had placed his faith in Achilles' words,
he would have been involved in a very great disgrace. Polyxena also
grieved because already it had pleased her to have Achilles as a
husband. Achilles during the aforesaid six months was, by means of
beneficial medicine, restored to health from the wounds given him by
220   Troilus. He had, however, nurtured a raging passion against Troilus,
who had wounded him so seriously. For he said that the necessary

outcome would be that Troilus should die disgracefully by his hand.

When these things were accomplished, the period of the war arrived in which the nineteenth mortal combat was engaged in, and
225 with both armies joined and struggling among themselves, great slaughter was perpetrated on either side. Before Achilles entered the battle, he called his Myrmidons into his presence and explained to them his serious complaint against Troilus, and accordingly advised them by commands and entreaties how they should proceed in battle
230 against Troilus. When they were all joined together, they should apply themselves to no other aim than to endeavor to surround Troilus in their midst, so that they would be able to detain him irresistibly, and that they should not kill him when they had detained him, but should prevent him from fighting for as long as it should take Achilles
235 to reach them, although he would always be not far from them in battle. Then Achilles, when he had made an end to his speech, marched to battle, followed by his Myrmidons. Meanwhile Troilus entered the battle in a very great train of knights, and with great courage and daring he rushed upon the Greeks, threw them down,
240 wounded them and slew them, so that in a short time it happened that on account of his mighty courage the Greeks were forced to turn their backs and flee before the face of the Trojans, the sun at that time standing at midday, so that the Greeks hastened headlong to their tents as if vanquished. Then the Myrmidons, who were two
245 thousand warriors in number, hurled themselves boldly into battle, joined close together and not unmindful of the command of their lord. They set upon the Trojans with the point of the sword, and the Greeks regained the field and a grim combat was engaged in between them. The Myrmidons looked earnestly for Troilus among the
250 fighters, and they found him fighting boldly among the troops. Then they surrounded him on all sides and put him in their midst. But he killed many of them and wounded countless numbers of them fatally. There was no one of his men who could come to Troilus' assistance, and the Myrmidons killed his horse and wounded him many times
255 with their lances. They snatched his helmet violently off his head, shattering the hood of his hauberk with violence. On account of this, Troilus, with bare head, defended himself with failing strength from the Greeks. Then Achilles arrived, and after he saw that Troilus had his head unprotected and lacked the aid of all defense, he rushed

260 upon him furiously, and piling blow upon blow, cruelly cut off
Troilus' head with his naked blade and cast the head among the feet
of the horses; taking the body, however, with his own hands, he tied
it firmly to the tail of his horse and dragged it shamefully through
the whole army behind his horse.

265   But oh, Homer, you who have extolled Achilles in your book with
so many praises and commendations, what possible reason led you to
exalt Achilles with such great titles of honor, especially in that you
said Achilles slaughtered by his own might two Hectors, that is,
Hector and Troilus, his very brave brother? Clearly, although you

270 were led by fondness for the Greeks, from whom you are said to
have taken your origin, you speak not moved by reason at all but by
madness. Did not Achilles give over to a treacherous death the brave
Hector who had and will have no equal in valor, when Hector was
occupied with complete attention in taking from battle that king he

275 had captured, and had at that time thrown his shield over his back so
that he became, as it were, unarmed, and thought of nothing else but
taking the captured king away from the troops and consigning him as
a captive to his soldiers? Would not Hector, if he had perceived the
wiles of Achilles, have quickly put his shield back, and opposed

280 Achilles in his own defense, since he usually oppressed Achilles with
many setbacks? Likewise he was not ashamed to kill the very brave
Troilus, whom he slew not by his own strength but after he had been
attacked and conquered by a thousand other warriors; from him
Achilles could find neither resistance nor defense, so that he killed a

285 man more dead than alive. Was Achilles ever worthy of praise, whom
you have described as adorned with great nobility, who, with no
regard for honor, dragged at the tail of his horse the son of a very
noble king, a man reknowned for great nobility and valor, neither
captured nor conquered by him? Clearly if he had acted from

290 nobility, if he had been led by valor, he would have been moved by
compassion and would never have cruelly inclined to such vile deeds.
But he could not be moved to do such things which were not really
in him.

     Achilles was thus shamelessly dragging the body of Troilus, and as
295 soon as Paris, Polydamas, and Aeneas realized that Troilus was dead,
Paris swooned and almost died of anguish. The Trojans put forth
much effort to recover Troilus' body, but they could not regain it on

account of the great number of the Greeks, who greatly opposed his
recovery. King Memnon, however, moved by great grief at Troilus'
300 death, boldly went against Achilles, first saying these opprobrious
words to him: "O wretched traitor, by what cruelty were you provoked so that you tied such a very noble, such a valiant son of a
most noble king to the tail of your horse and did not shrink from
dragging him along the ground as if he were of the lowest rank?
305 Because of this you will not be able to withdraw further without
losing your life." And rushing at once upon Achilles in a swift charge
of his horse, Memnon, with a blow of his lance, wounded Achilles so
seriously in the chest that he could hardly remain upright, and
Memnon at once pulled forth his sword, and with fierce blows struck
310 Achilles so heavily upon the helmet he was wearing on his head that
Achilles, seriously wounded, fell half-dead from his horse to the
ground. On account of this the Trojans recovered the body of Troilus,
but not without the greatest effort of battle.

The Myrmidons lifted Achilles from the ground and caused him to
315 mount his horse, and after no great time, having regained his strength,
he entered the battle and furiously approached King Memnon. King
Memnon, however, intercepted him, and a grievous combat was
engaged in between them. But King Memnon harassed Achilles the
more resolutely. With the arrival of a great number of their battalions
320 fighting here and there, they were separated from each other. Since
the day was verging upon sunset, the combat ceased.

The Trojans and Greeks maintained a heated battle for seven days
continuously, until Achilles, healed of his wounds and eager for
vengeance on King Memnon, entered the battle on the seventh day.
325 He addressed his Myrmidons, commanded them strictly to surround
King Memnon in their midst and to hold him surrounded until he,
Achilles, reached them in order to take final vengeance on him. The
battle was waged in earnest and many fell dead. Achilles and King
Memnon assailed each other, both fell from their horses, and both
330 fought manfully on foot, until the Myrmidons rushed upon King
Memnon, surrounded him on all sides, and seized him, deprived of all
help of his men, since there was no one to aid him against the
Myrmidons. When Achilles saw him thus cut off by the Myrmidons,
he rushed upon him and slaughtered him with innumerable wounds.
335 Achilles was not able to accomplish this without serious danger to

himself, since King Memnon inflicted several serious wounds upon him, by which the blood poured from him down to his heels in excessive quantity; for this reason it was expected that he would die rather than live.

340   Notice, miserable Homer, that Achilles never killed any valiant man except by treachery, so that he is deservedly worthy of praise, if treachery is to be extolled by the titles of praise. Meanwhile, as the battle raged, Menelaus, Menesteus, Diomedes, and Ajax Telamonius, making an attack against the Trojans with their battalions, drove them
345   from the field, so that, taking flight suddenly, they hastened to the city and tried to enter it in the greatest danger, since the Greeks pursued them with the greatest determination, wounding and slaying countless numbers of them. The Trojans who could flee, however, entered their city and fortified the gates of the town with secure
350   bolts and locks.

Here begins the twenty-seventh book, about the burial of Troilus and the death of Achilles and Antilochus.

When the body of Troilus had been brought to the palace of King Priam, Priam grieved immoderately, Hecuba grieved, Polyxena grieved excessively, Helen grieved, and they spent mournful days in anguished lamentations. All the Trojans grieved who, since they saw themselves
5   deprived of the assistance of Hector, Deiphobus, and Troilus, considered that they could survive no longer. King Priam asked the Greeks for a truce, confirmed by a treaty, which the Greeks granted. During it, King Priam interred the body of Troilus in a rich tomb, and also had the body of King Memnon placed in a rich sepulchre.
10   Queen Hecuba was exceedingly anguished at the death of her sons, and examined ways by which she could finally avenge their death, so that she could deliver to death the tyrannous Achilles, who did not shrink from behaving cruelly toward her sons. At last, when she had summoned Paris to her, she addressed him secretly and with an
15   abundance of tears said to him: "Dearest son, you know how that ill-omened Achilles has delivered to treacherous death your brothers, my very dear children, depriving me, their miserable mother, of Hector and Troilus, who alone with you were the whole consolation

of my life. On account of this it would be meet and right that, as by
20 treachery he has bereaved parents by killing others' sons, so he should
suffer a like injury and die by treachery. For this ill-omened Achilles
often asked me to give him Polyxena my daughter as his legal wife,
and since I have placed him in the certain hope that she will be given
to him, I propose to dispatch a messenger to him, telling him to
25 come to me in the temple of Apollo in order to speak to me. I wish
that you, son, with a band of our faithful knights, would hide there
in secret, and that when he comes there you would rush upon him,
so that he will not be able to escape your hands and will consequently be killed there."
30   Paris, moved by the loving tears of his mother, likewise shed loyal
tears and agreed to do this. It was arranged that Paris, according to
what he had promised his mother, would lie hidden in the temple of
Apollo with twenty men who were faithful to him and exceedingly
bold. At once, by the messenger sent through Hecuba to Achilles, the
35 ill-omened Achilles, deceived by the ill-advised passion of love, which
deprives even wise men of their senses, came to the temple of Apollo,
accompanied by Antilochus, the son of Nestor. When they had arrived
there, Paris and his faithful men emerged from their hiding places
with drawn swords and rushed upon Achilles. Achilles was unarmed
40 except for a sword. With his mighty arm Paris hurled three spears
against Achilles with which he struck him fatally, while the other
knights rose against him. Achilles, however, having drawn his sword
and wound his cloak around his arm, rushed upon those rushing upon
him and killed seven of them. But at last Achilles and Antilochus
45 were dead in the temple of Apollo, wickedly killed by Paris. Paris
ordered the bodies of Achilles and Antilochus to be cast out to the
crows and dogs, but by the prayers and advice of Helen they were
merely cast forth from the temple of Apollo into the square, so that
they could be seen clearly by all the Trojans wishing to look at them.
50   The Trojans rejoiced over the death of Achilles, agreeing among
themselves that henceforth they could have no great concern about
the Greeks. Agamemnon sent messengers to Priam so that he would
order the body of Achilles to be delivered to the Greeks, and the
body of Antilochus to Nestor, as a sad comfort to his father, who
55 was immeasurably grieved. Priam agreed to this, and the Greeks
carried the bodies of both the dead men across to their camp. The

lamentation at the death of Achilles was very great among the Greeks, who thought and agreed among themselves that with Achilles taken away from them, there remained no hope of seizing the city. They
60 had Achilles placed in a tomb of great cost, asking King Priam to permit the tomb of Achilles to be placed in the city of Troy, and he conceded that they might build the tomb at the entrance of the Thymbrean Gate. It appears superfluous, however, to describe the costly appearance and fashion of the tomb.

65   Agamemnon, after this, ordered all the Greek kings and princes to be called together for a conference. When they had come and were in his presence, Agamemnon indicated to them in his speech that the majority of the army seemed to be discouraged at the death of Achilles. He inquired accordingly what would be the best choice: to
70 desist from the war, or to persist in the war with renewed strength, or to return to their own country. The opinions of the hearers were divided according to their different wishes; some approved of the war, others said the return was pleasing. At last they all agreed upon and heartily approved of one opinion—to continue the war, saying that
75 even if they lacked Achilles, they did not lack the promises of the gods that the Greeks would rejoice at the longed-for victory against the Trojans, and that the city of Troy would be entirely overthrown.

Ajax, rising in the midst of the kings, urged that even if Achilles had been taken from their midst, they should send for the son of
80 Achilles, who as a young man was being trained in arms by King Lycomedes, his grandfather, since Ajax had learned for certain that the Greeks could not obtain the victory from the Trojans without Achilles' son. When the Greeks had heard this advice, they were all in favor of it, and elected King Menelaus to go to King Lycomedes for
85 the son of Achilles, who was called Neoptolemus.

It was the time when the sun had already progressed so far in its course beneath the celestial circle of the zodiac that in that year it had entered the sign of Cancer, in which, according to the divine arrangement of stars, the summer solstice takes place. For these are
90 the longest days of the year. On the sixteenth day of the month of June, when the days are the longest in the year, as it was said, the Greeks and Trojans began the twentieth mortal combat, and when both armies had joined together, a very grim battle was waged between them. Then Ajax, carried away by some mad impulse,

95 marched to battle without armor and with uncovered head, and he
carried only a sword in his hand, thus indeed being without protection. The rest of the Greek princes, Diomedes, Menesteus, Menelaus,
Ulysses, and Agamemnon, having arranged their battalions well,
arrived at the place where the Trojans had made a stand. King Priam
100 had shrewdly arrayed his troops and phalanxes, and ordered and
commanded them to go out to battle against the Greeks. But oh,
with what terror were the Trojans smitten when they saw themselves
marching to battle without the leadership of the very brave Hector,
the wise Deiphobus, and the exceedingly bold Troilus! But because it
105 was necessary that the Trojans protect their lives, they put their lives
to the hazard of battle. On account of the killing of his brothers,
Paris went out to battle with many tears flowing in streams hidden
by his helmet and accompanied by an imperceptible lament. Then
Polydamas, King Philimenis, King Esdras, and Aeneas joined the fray
110 in a swift charge against the Greeks. Paris, with his battalion of
Persian men with bows and arrows, wounded many Greeks and killed
many. Diomedes rushed upon King Philimenis, and the king resisted
him mightily. The Paphlagonians, vassals of this king, killed many
Greeks, wounded them and threw them down, so that Diomedes and
115 the Greeks were not able to withstand their attack and were forced
to give ground for a great distance.

Menesteus, duke of Athens, rushed upon Polydamas, thrusting at
him so powerfully with his spear that he threw him from his horse.
Menesteus attacked Polydamas manfully with his naked sword,
120 inflicted grim blows upon him, and tried to kill him, which he would
have done had not the might of King Philimenis and his aid freed him
from Menesteus' hands.

Paris likewise wounded many of the Greeks and killed many of
them. Then Ajax rushed upon Paris' people with his sword. Some-
125 thing remarkable can be told about him: although he had then killed
so many Trojans in battle and was without armor, still he had escaped
unharmed by any wound. When he arrived at Paris' men, he sprang
among the Persians with naked sword and killed countless numbers of
them, so that all fled before him. Paris was unable to endure this; he
130 drew his very strong bow and shot a poisoned arrow against Ajax. It
struck him fatally between the spleen and the ribs, so that Ajax well
perceived that he would without fail die from that wound. But before

he fell in death, he searched for Paris amidst the troops, found Paris,
joined him and said: "Paris, Paris, you have cruelly slain me with
135 your arrow, but before I die and descend to the lower world, you
will precede and go before me. For it is necessary that you be
separated here and now from that unlawful love of Helen, for which
so many nobles have been slain." At once he struck him murderously
on the face so that he split his jaws in two parts and separated them
140 from his head. Paris immediately fell dead among the feet of the
horses. Ajax carried on no longer but breathed his last and died.

When the Trojans saw Paris dead, they recovered his body with
great effort and carried it into the city with much shedding of tears.
But Diomedes and Menesteus, pressing against the Trojans with a
145 great number of Greeks, compelled them to flee, although the sun
had already half declined toward night, and the Trojans entered the
city at the hazard of their persons and made the gates of the city fast
with firm bolts and locks. Agamemnon, at the coming of night,
ordered the siege to be reinforced, not far from the city but very
150 close, setting up tents and pavilions on all sides. Although the Trojans
had immensely high city walls, still all around the walls they placed
guards who were to keep constant guard on them.

On that same night, when the body of Paris had been brought into
the palace of King Priam with much shedding of tears, the lamenta-
155 tion was very great among the citizens, who considered that henceforth the road of complete desperation was clearly open to them,
since all the sons of the king, on whom their entire hope of defense
depended, had fallen slain. Would it be easy to reveal in speech the
sorrows and laments of their father the king, and much more, of the
160 unfortunate Queen Hecuba and of their sisters, and much, much more
of Helen, especially of Helen, who more than twenty times that night
was carried away almost dead from the body of Paris, wishing to die
with the dead man and not caring to live any longer? Because of the
greatness of the task, I have nevertheless neglected to describe her
165 lamentations in this place, although they contained the anguish of
great grief, and although they could move a very wicked man to the
sweetness of pity and to a feeling of sympathetic grief. In fact, King
Priam and Queen Hecuba were so amazed at Helen's excessive grief
and anguish that, with their own griefs almost forgotten, their griefs
170 were painfully increased by the griefs of Helen. And when they saw

Helen was wracked by such grief on account of the death of Paris,
they held her more dear than a daughter from then on. Need I say
more? The exceedingly rich tomb of Paris was prepared in the temple
of Juno, and its form and construction have only been set aside as a
175 means of getting on with the narrative. The body of Paris was
deposited in it and buried.

*Here begins the twenty-eighth book, about the arrival of
Penthesilea, queen of the Amazons.*

While two whole months went by, King Priam refused to open the
gates of the city. For this reason the Trojans, living behind closed
gates, spent the time in nothing but continuous groans and laments.
Meanwhile Agamemnon by his messengers many times requested King
5 Priam to order his people to go out to battle. King Priam refused
absolutely to do this, fearing the final destruction of his people, and
further, because King Priam had undoubted faith of obtaining without
fail the aid of the queen of the Amazons, who had already prepared
for the journey. For there was then in the eastern regions a certain
10 province called Amazonia, in which women lived alone without men.
The most powerful interest of these women in their youth was to
labor with weapons of war and to wage war, from which they were
able to obtain a reputation for valor and glory in fighting. Opposite
this province there was a certain large island which was very fertile
15 and pleasant, where only men lived for any length of time. It was the
custom of the women to go across to this island for three months of
the year, that is, April, May, and June, and to stay with the men on
that island. On account of this many of them became pregnant, and
when they were pregnant they returned to their own land. When the
20 child was brought forth, if it happened that a girl was born, they
kept her with them in the province, but if a male, they sent him
across to the large island when he became three years old. The queen
of this province at that time was a certain noble and exceedingly
aggressive young woman named Penthesilea, who was closely bound
25 to Hector in friendship on account of the exceeding merit of her
valor. When she heard that the Greeks were coming against King
Priam in a large army, she went, with a thousand young women who

could fight with great valor, to fight in Troy and help King Priam, because of her great love for Hector.

30   On account of this she entered the city of Troy with her company of young women, and she still did not know that Hector had died. After his death was made known to her, she became very troubled and passed many days in tears. At last she addressed King Priam with affectionate words, requesting him to order one of the gates of the
35 city to be opened on the following day, when all his men were prepared for battle. For she intended to gather at the battle with her women, so that the Greeks would be able to experience afterward what the right arms of the young women could do in battle. At the order of King Priam, therefore, King Philimenis with his Paphla-
40 gonians, Aeneas, Polydamas and the rest with their battalions, and Penthesilea with her women, went out to war through the Dardanian Gate, which King Priam had commanded to be opened.

The Greeks ran manfully up to them and received them powerfully with blows of their lances. A grim struggle was engaged in between
45 them. Menelaus rushed upon Penthesilea, but Penthesilea thrust at Menelaus so powerfully that she cast him down from his horse. She took his horse from him and consigned it to her women. Diomedes, however, violently attacked Penthesilea in the swift charge of his horse and with a blow of his lance. Penthesilea met him courageously.
50 Both thrust at each other with blows of their lances, but Penthesilea remained firmly on her horse. Diomedes was forced to sway at the blow of the attacker, likewise his horse. Penthesilea snatched Diomedes' shield from his neck and consigned it to one of her maidens. Telamon was not able to endure the things which were done
55 in battle by Penthesilea and urged his horse in a charge against her. Penthesilea met him manfully and threw him from his horse to the ground, and rushing among the Greeks, fought with them fiercely. Hence in a short time the Greeks recognized the power and courage of Penthesilea. She attacked Telamon with such powerful blows of
60 her sword that with the aid of Philimenis she captured him and started to send him to the city in captivity. After Diomedes saw this, he was stirred with great anger and hurled himself boldly against those detaining Telamon so that he freed him from their hands.

Then Penthesilea shouted to her women and collected them in one
65 place, and making an attack against the Greeks, persisted against them

so manfully that they were of necessity compelled to flee, fleeing
before the face of the young women who pressed upon them
incredibly. Penthesilea pursued the Greeks as they fled, in order to
kill them, and they reached the shore in their flight. There all the
70 Greeks would have failed at last had it not been for the illustrious
Diomedes, who brought about an amazing resistance to the Amazons.
They fought a long time until the coming of night made the fighting
cease. Then Penthesilea with her women, who had conducted themselves so marvelously in the battle, and King Philimenis with his
75 Paphlagonians, returned as it suited them to the city of Troy. There
King Priam gave affectionate thanks to Penthesilea for the deeds done
by her and made her many rewards and presents, offering her freely
all his goods, since King Priam believed that his griefs would be
relieved by her.
80   War was waged continuously for several days following, until
Menelaus, within two months, had gone to and returned from King
Lycomedes, and had brought to the Greek army Neoptolemus, the
son of Achilles, who was called by the other name of Pyrrhus, since
he had two names. The Greek kings and the others welcomed him
85 with the greatest honor, and the Myrmidons received him as their lord
and were made exceedingly joyful by his arrival. The Greeks at once
accorded Neoptolemus the honor of knighthood, and Ajax Telamonius
girded him with the sword belt, adding verbally that he had been
decked with the honor of knighthood by this sign so that he would
90 arise to avenge the death of his once illustrious father. Two of the
Greek princes placed the golden spurs on him with their own hands.
King Agamemnon immediately assigned to him all his father's arms,
tents, and other things. The Greeks spent several festive days joyfully
celebrating his knighthood.
95   Meanwhile the day of battle arrived. On both sides the battalions
were drawn up, they went to war, and a grim battle was waged
between them. Then Pyrrhus marched to battle in his father's armor,
rushed upon Polydamas, and attacking him with blows of his sword,
strove to deliver him to death forthwith. King Philimenis manfully
100 aided him by the might of his people. For this reason Pyrrhus had no
power to injure him then. Pyrrhus, having left Polydamas, approached
Philimenis, hurled him from his horse, and summoned his forces in
order to cut him off. The Paphlagonians subjected themselves to

obvious danger to free their lord, but the Myrmidons would not
105   permit them to do so. Polydamas rushed up with the Trojans,
endeavoring mightily to recover Philimenis, but he could not do this
at all on account of the resistance of the opposite side.

Meanwhile Penthesilea arrived at the battle with her women, with
the devices on their armor as white as snow, and they hurled them-
110   selves upon the Myrmidons, wounded them and threw them from
their horses. Ajax Telamonius approached Penthesilea and cast her
down from her horse. She, however, rose up boldly and went for
Telamonius on foot. She struck him so heavily with her bare blade
that Telamonius fell to the ground headlong, touching the ground
115   with the palms of his hands. By their great prowess in fighting, the
young women made Penthesilea, their lady, mount her horse. After it
was made known to her that Philimenis had been captured by the
Myrmidons, she at once hastened boldly with her maidens against the
Myrmidons. She wounded and killed them at the point of the sword
120   so that the Myrmidons were forced by her to retreat. Pyrrhus, seeing
the destruction of his Myrmidons, released Philimenis, whom he had
captured without injuring him, and shouting loudly at his men, spoke
thus to them: "Are you not ashamed to be killed thus disgracefully
at the hands of women? Strive with me to deliver them to death
125   suddenly at the point of the sword."

Penthesilea heard the threats of Pyrrhus but did not trouble herself
at all about them. When she had advanced closer to Pyrrhus so that
Pyrrhus could clearly understand her words, Penthesilea reproached
him much in her speech for the death of Hector, treacherously
130   brought about by his father, "for whose death not only women who
are able to fight, but indeed the whole world should arise, and we
whom they call women . . . The Greeks will suddenly feel our fatal
blows."

Pyrrhus was kindled with great wrath at these words, and on this
135   account urged his horse swiftly against Penthesilea. When Penthesilea
perceived him, she came to meet him in the swift charge of her horse,
and both thrust at each other in turn with blows of their lances.
Pyrrhus shattered his lance against Penthesilea, but he could not
unseat her from her horse. Penthesilea, however, thrust at him so
140   mightily with her spear that she threw him from his horse to the
ground. Pyrrhus rose quickly from the ground and hurled himself

upon Penthesilea with his naked sword, attacking her again and again
with many blows of his sword. Penthesilea in her fury hurled back no
smaller return with many blows of her blade. But the Myrmidons by
145 their prowess in fighting made Pyrrhus, their lord, mount his horse.
　　Then Agamemnon, in a very great train of knights, Diomedes with
his battalion, the duke of Athens with a great number of warriors,
and the other Greek kings and princes with their battalions, came
into the conflict. King Philimenis, freed from the hands of Pyrrhus,
150 delivered manifold thanks to Penthesilea, claiming that by her good-
ness his life had been saved. Then he collected his people in one place
and Penthesilea did likewise with her women. Polydamas, who had
with great effort escaped the feet of the horses after his fall, advanced
to battle in a very great host of armed men, so also Aeneas, so also
155 King Remus. When both armies were joined, a deadly battle was
waged between them. Pyrrhus pressed hard against the Trojans but
Penthesilea more resolutely against the Greeks. Pyrrhus rushed so
furiously upon Glaucon, the son of Antenor and brother of Polydamas
by another mother, that he killed him with blows of his sword.
160 Penthesilea approached Pyrrhus. Pyrrhus met her mightily. Both came
together in the charge of their horses, both fell from their horses but
both boldly remounted and both struggled with each other. When the
troops arrived, they were separated from each other. Polydamas was
exceedingly anguished at the death of his brother and cruelly
165 oppressed the Greeks to avenge the slaughter of his brother. He killed
many of them and injured them with many wounds. From this it
happened that on account of the courage of Polydamas and
Penthesilea as they often pressed upon them, the Greeks were forced
to flee. Polydamas and Penthesilea pursued them at the point of the
170 sword. Pyrrhus, Telamonius, and Diomedes all resisted them courageously and made the Greeks cease to flee, although they had already
fled some distance away. Since the day had already inclined toward
sunset, they ceased from combat. One continuous battle raged
between them for a whole month during which more than ten
175 thousand warriors fell for the last time on either side, and in the
interim Penthesilea lost many of her women.
　　With the arrival of the days following the passage of the one
month, a more determined battle was begun, and the battalions
assembled on either side and a mortal combat was engaged in between

180   them. Pyrrhus marched to battle and Penthesilea likewise on the
      other side. Both pursued each other with a deadly hatred and both
      came together in the fury of a mortal combat. Pyrrhus broke his
      lance against Penthesilea in the charge of his horse, but he was not
      able to remove her from her horse's saddle. Penthesilea, however,
185   thrust very resolutely at Pyrrhus with her spear. Although she did not
      cast him down from his horse, she broke her lance against him so
      that she wounded him seriously, and left the shaft of her lance in his
      body. On account of this the uproar was very great, and many Greeks
      rose against Penthesilea to avenge him, so that by superior strength
190   they burst the thongs of Penthesilea's helmet. Pyrrhus then, on
      account of the fury of his animosity, did not consider what would
      result from the fact that he carried the whole shaft of the spear in his
      body, and accosted Penthesilea, since Penthesilea then lacked her
      helmet and was completely exhausted by the forces rising against her.
195   When Penthesilea saw Pyrrhus coming swiftly against her, she believed
      she could strike him first. Pyrrhus arrived swiftly to strike her, and
      with the strength of his arms struck her so heavily between the
      shoulder and the top of her shield with his sword that he cut off her
      arm by the violence of the blow and severed it from its natural joint
200   at the shoulder. Penthesilea died and reached the ground headlong.
      Pyrrhus, in satisfaction of his vengeance, hacked her whole body to
      pieces. Then on account of the great amount of blood pouring from
      his wound, he was not able to hold himself upright and fell half-dead
      among the combatants. His men carried him on his shield to his tent.
205   Penthesilea's women were exceedingly moved at her death and
      deeply wished they might die. They accordingly yearned with all their
      hearts to avenge her killing. They rushed upon the Myrmidons, who
      lacked their protector, and killed an infinite number of them, and
      delivered to death more than two thousand of the other Greeks. But
210   what did the fall of so many Greeks profit the Trojans, since the
      Greeks rushed upon the Trojans with an infinitely huge multitude and
      killed countless numbers of them? For Dares writes that ten thousand
      Trojans perished then from the fury of the sword. For this reason
      both the remaining maidens and the remaining Trojans who could
215   escape by flight withdrew into the city, and they strengthened the
      gates with very strong bolts in many locks, since it was neither in
      their will nor in their power to leave by them in order to fight.

Here begins the twenty-ninth book, about the betrayal of Troy by Aeneas and Antenor.

When the Trojans were enclosed within the portals of their city, they were wracked with great grief, since henceforth they would not be cheered by any hope of having more assistance from which they could hope at all for their safety. Accordingly they devoted the time
5 to nothing except providing faithful and courageous guards for the city guard by which the city would be protected. For they knew that the immense height of the city walls kept all outside attacks away from them, and that for countless ages enclosed thus they could be safe if they did not lack provisions for their sustenance. They also
10 grieved with very great anguish over the death of Penthesilea, who, while she could, had defended them so manfully and annihilated so many of their enemies, and they grieved more strongly because they could not have her body in order that they in their grief might repay her by the proper funeral rites which are usually owed to dead
15 nobles. The Greeks with a multitude of armed men in close formation secured the outer gates of the city on all sides so that none of those who were staying inside had any freedom to go out by them.
    Some of the Greeks decided that the body of Penthesilea should be given to the dogs to be eaten. Pyrrhus, however, objected and said
20 that it should be given a suitable burial. Diomedes said that since so many Greek nobles had perished through Penthesilea, her body was undeserving of burial. At last it was settled that the body of Penthesilea should be cast into a large pond of water near the city of Troy.
25 While the Trojans were experiencing such great pain and sorrow, and were enclosed in the city, Anchises, with his son Aeneas, and Antenor, with his son Polydamas, began to plan how they could make their lives safe so they would not be lost to the Greeks, and if they could do it in no other way, to betray the city. On account of
30 this they decided among themselves to speak with King Priam so that this king would seek peace from the Greeks by restoring Helen to Menelaus, and honorably make restitution for the injury done by Paris on the island of Cythera.

But oh, how happily it would have turned out for Priam if the
35 Greeks had wished to accept such an agreement! For although Priam
had lost his sons, heroes of great valor, and had endured such losses,
if such an agreement had been accepted, he would have been able to
commit to perpetual safety himself, his wife Hecuba, his daughter
Polyxena, those of his natural sons who remained, the city of Troy,
40 and those who were then his subjects. Priam could have done this
long ago when it was requested by Agamemnon while the Greek army
was at Tenedos. From somewhere or other comes a proverb spoken
among the common people that only young agreements are good,
that is, those which are made in the beginnings, before the parties are
45 wearied by losses, expenses, and hardships. For after the injuries and
losses of life, who can incline himself to agreement who is better able
to obtain his wish by disagreement? Who could hold it certain that
the Greeks would wish to consent to such an agreement after their
great injuries, with so many of their nobles slain, and after they had
50 on this account been subjected to so many losses and setbacks, and
now especially, when they were placed in the manifest hope that they
would be victors in this present war, so that they believed that
according to their intent they would deliver all the Trojans to death
and the city of Troy to complete ruin? For this reason the counsel
55 of these men is conjectured to have proceeded solely from guile, so
that under the cover of treating for peace, these traitors could seize
the opportunity to betray their city, if they could save themselves by
no other way.

Desiring therefore to continue in the plan they had begun, Antenor
60 and Aeneas together spoke to King Priam about seeking peace with
the Greeks, in the presence of Amphimacus, the youngest of Priam's
natural sons, and in the presence of many nobles of the city. When
King Priam heard what Aeneas and Antenor were urging him to
negotiate concerning peace with the Greeks, he at once conceived in
65 his mind that what they were earnestly promoting did not proceed
from the zeal of loyalty or the sense of affection. After many prolonged sighs, he answered them with prudence, hiding, nevertheless,
the meditation of his mind. For he said to them that he wished to
take counsel for several days concerning this. They said, "If you say
70 you are going to examine a plan afterward, then hear ours, and if you
think it displeases you, you can follow another plan." The king said

to them: "I do not disapprove of your plan, but it pleases me to hear
it and to place my trust in it if it is good. If, however, it seems to
deviate from good, it should not displease you if I follow a better
75 one."

Then Antenor arose and spoke these words standing: "Lord King,
in your prudence you cannot disguise what great peril you and your
people are involved in. Your enemies, who are striving to destroy
your life and that of your people, are besieging the gates of your
80 city. Among them are more than fifty kings who desire nothing other
than to overthrow your noble city completely and that you and your
people may not survive. You do not have the power to enable you to
be victorious over them or even to be able to resist them, since you
have descended to such impotence that you are not freely permitted
85 to open the gates of the city, nor can you summon any defenders
whom it would interest to defend you and your land, since all your
sons, men conspicuous for great valor in battle, are dead, and also the
more powerful of your people. Are we and you to die thus closed in?
Of the two evils it would be good to choose the lesser evil. For this
90 reason it appears expedient for us and for you to seek peace from the
Greeks so that Helen, for whom so many nobles have been killed,
may be restored to Menelaus, since Paris, who had held her as his
wife, has ended his last day, and so that all the things which were
taken by Paris on the island of Cythera may be restored to the
95 Greeks."

Then Amphimachus, the natural son of the king, arose in strong
opposition to the words of Antenor, and disapproving of what he had
said, said to Antenor: "What hope of you can we and the king have
henceforth, since when you should hold your mind firm and your
100 feet unwavering in all firmness with regard to your king and city, we
now see you vacillate and direct your feet to ruin, and you, who
should with very steadfast loyalty live and die with us, now play the
turncoat and shamelessly try to persuade us that our king should seek
peace with the Greeks, much to his dishonor because of such a
105 defection, when you should support him in his weakness by the
strength of your integrity? Because this speech which you have been
eager to propose is harsh, twenty thousand men would rather lose
their lives than that it should happen that your speech would be
carried out, since it does not proceed from the zeal of loyalty but

110   from the error of detestable treachery." And so Amphimachus offered
      many other opprobrious words against Antenor.

        Aeneas endeavored to restrain Amphimachus with gentle words,
      saying: "At least we have no further hope of beginning an attack
      against the Greeks or of daring to open the gates of our city in a
115   hostile fashion against them. Henceforth we should seek another more
      practical way, which cannot be safely procured except through
      peace."

        At this King Priam was not able to moderate the disturbance of
      his mind; far from it, he was much stirred to anger against Antenor
120   and Aeneas and spoke thus to reprove them: "How can you behave
      toward me without shame for such bold cruelty and disloyalty? Truly
      on account of you I am pained and overwhelmed by the pangs of
      despair, since, whatever I have done or accomplished up to the
      present, I would not have proceeded against the Greeks if not at the
125   instigation of your advice. For when you had returned from Greece
      where you went to demand Hesione of the Greeks, did you not
      persuade me, Lord Antenor, to dispatch Paris to Greece to prey upon
      the Greeks in a hostile fashion? It would never have resulted from
      any boldness of mine to start a war against the Greeks when I
130   reposed in such great peace. But the advice from your false counsel
      and the constant stimulus of your speeches incited me to such
      boldness and daring. You, Lord Aeneas, when you went with Paris,
      were you not the chief agent of the plan for Paris to abduct Helen
      and bring her to this kingdom? You even aided him in person,
135   although if you had wished to dissuade Paris, Helen would never have
      seen the walls of Troy. Now after the slaughter of all my sons and
      after so many losses and setbacks, you rise up brazenly in council to
      ask me to sue for peace to the Greeks, who have finally ruined me so
      wickedly and so cruelly. Obviously such a plan is not to be followed,
140   because a snare is prepared for me so that I will end my life in the
      disgrace of great infamy."

        Aeneas, very much aroused to anger, uttered many haughty words
      against King Priam, and on account of this, Aeneas and Antenor left
      the king with very provoking words. Priam, overwhelmed by great
145   grief, burst into tears, since he perceived plainly and could reasonably
      fear that Aeneas and Antenor would deliver the city into the hands
      of the Greeks and would betray the city so that the Greeks would

then wickedly deliver him to death. For this reason, since he desired
to prevent them from carrying out their treacherous designs, he
150 secretly called his son Amphimachus to him and addressed him with
these words, saying: "Dear son, am I not your father and you my
son? Since we are united by ties of blood, let us resist while we can,
lest we be separated from each other by the destruction of death.
For I know that those two, that is, Antenor and Aeneas, intend to
155 manage so that the Greeks will kill us and betray the city to them,
and therefore it is not unjust that they should fall into the trap which
they have prepared for others. For I have decided that they should
both be killed before we are killed by the Greeks through them. If
this can be done conveniently, tomorrow in the evening when they
160 come to council, while the council is being held, I want you to
conceal yourself secretly in this palace together with some of our
loyal men hidden with you, where you and the others can rush upon
them at once and ruthlessly assassinate them."
   Amphimachus promised to carry this out faithfully and to keep
165 what they had discussed a closely guarded secret between them. Since,
however, there is nothing hidden which cannot be revealed, and
peasants claim that the earth spews forth and divulges secrets, it is
not known how knowledge of the plan which King Priam had made
for the death of the two reached Aeneas. Aeneas and Antenor at
170 once swore to the betrayal of the city, together with certain of their
accomplices, planning that if they happened to be summoned to
council, they would not go except with a large number of armed
men. Aeneas was very powerful in the city of Troy on account of
relatives and friends, and none of the citizens was richer than he, so
175 that he equalled the king in power, and so did Antenor. Trusting in
the large family of relatives, they strengthened their resolve to betray
Troy, since they had from the Greeks the frank assurance that they
and their relatives would be safe in their persons and property.
   Meanwhile King Priam commanded Aeneas and Antenor to come
180 to him to have a council concerning what was to be done about these
pressing matters, desiring to complete his intended plan at last. But
Antenor and Aeneas, as they had agreed between themselves, went to
King Priam with a great number of armed men. When the king saw
this, he commanded Amphimachus to desist from the assignment he
185 had given him.

On the following day, King Priam commanded all the Trojans to
assemble for a conference, and when they had come, Aeneas arose
and advised and urged them to negotiate a peace with the Greeks. All
the Trojans unanimously agreed to this. When the king opposed it,
190 Aeneas said to him: "Why do you resist, Lord King? Whether you
wish it or not, the peace will be negotiated and carried out, even if
you are unwilling." After the king saw that he could not oppose him,
he preferred to agree rather than to provoke his subjects to offense
by the error of opposition. On account of this he said to Aeneas:
195 "Do whatever you think ought to be done concerning this present
business, since whatever you do about it will appear acceptable to
me." When the plan had been divulged, Antenor was elected to go in
an embassy to the Greeks to negotiate a peace with them in all ways.
       When the conference was adjourned, the Trojans mounted the
200 walls of the city with olive branches as a sign of peace. Seeing this,
the Greeks returned visible signs of agreement. On account of this,
they let Antenor go down from the walls of the city. When he had
been received by the Greeks and presented to Agamemnon, King
Agamemnon discussed this whole business with the Greeks, the king
205 of Crete, Diomedes, and Ulysses. All the Greeks promised to hold
firm forever whatever things were to be done in this business by the
said three, with the fourth, Antenor, being joined to them. When
those men had been appointed on behalf of all the Greeks, they
promised by a solemn oath to do all things mentioned above. For this
210 reason, when these three with Antenor were withdrawn apart,
Antenor, filled with guile, promised to betray the city to them so
that they could freely do with it what they wished, as long as they
firmly assured him and Aeneas concerning their persons and those of
their relatives that they themselves thought should be selected, and
215 that they would give assurance to him and Aeneas concerning the
safety of all their possessions and the rest of their goods, so that they
might be freely released to them without loss or injury. The three
swore faithfully to Antenor to attend to this. This plot was to be
held secret until its effect was obtained, lest by chance, after this
220 business had been revealed, it would happen that its effective outcome would be impeded. Antenor earnestly advised them to consign
what had been said among them to the seal of silence. In order that
this plot might be better concealed and that it might be better

developed under some assumed appearance, Antenor besought the
225 Greeks to send King Talthybius with him to Troy, a man burdened
with age who would be more easily believed, who would pretend to
ask the will of the Trojans, whether the peace was pleasing to all of
them and what they wished to do for the Greeks in confirming the
aforesaid peace. Furthermore, Antenor asked that the body of
230 Penthesilea be granted him by the Greeks. The Greeks granted him
this with the greatest reluctance and after the efforts of many
entreaties. When they had taken leave of the Greeks, Antenor and
King Talthybius went to the city, entered it, and notified King Priam
of their arrival.
235 On the following day, when King Priam had called together the
citizens of the city of Troy for a conference to hear the embassy of
Antenor, he commanded Antenor to reveal in the common hearing of
all what he had negotiated with the Greeks. Antenor, wishing to
conceal the fabrications of his guile, craftily devised a long speech in
240 uttering his words, asserting by his words that the Greeks had great
power, and that they held firmly and lawfully to their promises. On
account of this, he introduced cunning arguments on behalf of the
Greeks concerning the maintaining of the treaties, none of which they
had broken. In addition, he mentioned the excessive weakness of the
245 Trojans and how they were reduced to nothing other than to lead
their mournful lives continually in continual tears and great anguish
of grief. He therefore tried very hard to convince them with his words
that henceforth it would be advantageous and sound to search
diligently for a way, and when it was found, to follow it diligently,
250 by which it would be possible to bring about an end to their lamentations and tears. He also added that it was not possible to arrive at
this with the Greeks except through very great quantities of gold and
silver, in reparation for the serious losses which they had endured on
that account. On account of this, in his speech he urged all of them
255 who had money, and especially the king himself, to open their hands
to relieve such great griefs, since according to the popular proverb it
is said, "It is better to adjust grievous injuries with purses of money
than to be troubled by continuous sorrows of heart." Since he had
not yet been able to learn the final wish of the Greeks, he sought and
260 recommended that Aeneas go with him to the Greeks, so that they
could both together elicit from the Greeks their final wish, and the

Greeks would be reassured and strengthened concerning the compliance with the things promised by Antenor. They all approved
Antenor's idea. For this reason Antenor and Aeneas went to the
265   Greeks, and Talthybius returned with them.

King Priam, when the conference had adjourned, went secretly to
his room, where he shed many tears in great pain because of his grief,
considering in his heart the treacherous wiles of Antenor and Aeneas,
and that he had lost all his sons, who were distinguished for such
270   great valor, and that he had endured such great injuries. "And what
is worse, it is now necessary for me to redeem myself from the hands
of those who caused me such losses, and that they, on the pretext of
this reparation, consume all the gold that I have accumulated for a
long time, so that at last, despoiled of all my goods, I shall sink into
275   the depths of poverty. And oh, would that I could be untroubled
concerning my life!" Thus King Priam did not know what he was
doing, since, forced by necessity, he had to pursue the wishes of
those who with all their strength were certainly yearning for the
complete destruction and loss of his life.
280   Helen, knowing that a peace was to be negotiated with the Greeks
and that Aeneas was to go with Antenor as an ambassador to the
Greeks, went secretly to Antenor under the shadows of night and
begged him earnestly to negotiate her peace and reconciliation with
Menelaus, her former husband, so that she might be able to obtain
285   the favor of peace from him only through his mercy and pity.
Antenor graciously offered to negotiate this for her. Helen left him
and went back to the royal palace.

Meanwhile, however, Glaucus, the son of King Priam, was
honorably interred, and it was arranged by King Philimenis, with the
290   consent of the Trojans, that the body of Penthesilea would remain
unburied until, when the peace had been negotiated, King Philimenis
would take this body to the kingdom of the Amazons, where it
would be interred as the body of a queen in her own kingdom and
in royal fashion.
295   Antenor and Aeneas, however, went to the Greek camp where
they negotiated more definitely concerning the betrayal of the city
with those three whom the Greeks had chosen. Concerning the
reconciliation of Helen with Menelaus, they obtained a firm promise
from him. On account of this, the Greeks decided that Ulysses and

300 Diomedes should go as ambassadors to Troy with Antenor and
Aeneas. When they entered the city the crowd rejoiced. For since
both were kings and very intelligent, they thought the peace would
be more easily accomplished by them.

On the following day in the morning, all the Trojans came to the
305 palace at the command of the king in order to hold a conference.
Ulysses arose then and in the course of his speech said the Greeks
sought two things from them, that is, the reparation of their losses by
a great amount of gold and silver, and that Amphimachus be perpetually exiled from the city without any hope of returning. Antenor,
310 with complete guile, had arranged this whole matter concerning
Amphimachus because he opposed his words when he with Aeneas
first told King Priam that peace with the Greeks should be sought.

Oh, how expedient it is for a wise man to have that concern for
himself so that in times of uprising and sedition he may not be the
315 spokesman before others and that he may place a guard on his
mouth! Amphimachus was lost because of his plea. Antenor would
not otherwise have procured the banishment of exile for him. But
God, who always avenges unjust anger, punishes men with the punishments they have procured for others. For Antenor also, by the
320 negotiation of Aeneas, was perpetually exiled from Troy, just as the
train of events in the present history will disclose.

Ulysses and Diomedes were together for a conference with the
Trojans in the palace of the king, when suddenly an amazing sound
came to their ears and many outcries like shouts were heard at the
325 entrance of the place where the aforesaid conference was being
carried on. On account of this, Ulysses and Diomedes were very afraid
and feared that the tumultuous crowd of people would rush upon
them and kill or injure them. Others thought it was the sons of the
kings who, on account of the exile of Amphimachus, were yearning
330 for the capture of the two royal ambassadors to the king, that is,
Diomedes and Ulysses. When they had diligently searched for the
cause of this sound and clamor, they could by no means perceive
what it had been. For this reason the conference was adjourned, and
all who had come to the palace of the king left it.

335   Antenor, however, took Ulysses and Diomedes aside to a remote
place where they could speak freely enough about the secrets of their
deceit. While these three were sitting alone, Ulysses said to Antenor:

"Why do you delay fulfilling our wishes, so that the thing promised
to us by you has not attained its result?" Antenor said: "The gods
340 know my will—that with Aeneas I watch for nothing other than that
our promises to you will be speedily fulfilled by us. The impediment
to our wishes, however, is a certain miraculous structure of the gods,
which, if it pleases you, I shall explain in my speech." Diomedes said
to him, "It is pleasing and acceptable to us." Antenor thus told them:
345 "It is certain and without doubt in this city that King Ilius, who first
founded Ilium in Troy, whence it was called Ilium from his name,
decreed that a large temple in honor of Pallas should be built in this
city. When its walls were all completed, and nothing remained to be
built except the roof, there descended from heaven a certain mirac-
350 ulous image and a thing of exceeding virtue. By divine intervention,
it affixed itself on the wall near the high altar, and it stayed there
always from then on, and no one was allowed to carry it away from
the place where it was, with the sole exception of its guardians, and
now of just one guardian, a priest, who guards it with very great
355 diligence. Its material, as it is reported by these guardians, is mostly
wood, but no one can learn what kind of wood it is, nor can it even
be known how it was made in the form in which it is. The goddess
Pallas, to whose beneficence the Trojans say it is due, declared what
virtue existed in the image, which is such that while the image is
360 inside the temple or within the walls of the city, neither the Trojans
nor the Trojan kings nor their heirs will ever lose this city. For this is
the very sure hope of the Trojans, on account of which the Trojans
live free of care and do not fear the destruction or ruin of their city.
The name of this image is called Palladium by everyone, because it is
365 believed to have been given by the goddess Pallas."

At this Diomedes said to Antenor, "If it is as you say concerning
the Palladium, our effort rests on a false hope, since we can neither
seize nor hold the city on account of the Palladium."

Antenor responded to him: "If you are wondering about the delay
370 and why our promises to you are not accomplished and fulfilled, this
is the only reason why they are delayed up to now. But since I have,
so far, negotiated with the guardian priest to give you the Palladium
in stealth, concerning which, in return for a large amount of gold
promised by me to this priest, we already have the certain pledge of
375 which we are absolutely certain, and as soon as the Palladium is

outside the walls of the city, I shall take care to dispatch it to you, and then your wish will be accomplished for certain in every respect."

Thus the aforesaid council among them was adjourned. Before their departure, however, Antenor said again: "Dearest friends, lest
380 this present council and our delaying be suspected, it is necessary for me to go to King Priam and tell him in a lie that our business is by its very nature secret, since I am negotiating with you about having certainty from you as to the amount which you intend to have from this king and his subjects." And when they had taken leave of each
385 other, Antenor went to King Priam.

Here begins the thirtieth book, about the capture and destruction of Troy and the death of King Priam, Hecuba, his wife, and Polyxena, his daughter.

When Ulysses and Diomedes had gone back to their camp, Antenor told King Priam to command all the citizens to assemble for a conference. After they had assembled, Antenor explained to them in the course of his speech that peace had been negotiated with the Greeks
5 to the effect that, in return for maintaining a lasting peace with them, the Trojans would give twenty thousand marks of gold and the same amount of silver and one hundred thousand loads of grain. On account of this it was arranged among them that, within the space of certain days, the aforesaid quantities should be collected and held.
10 When they had been handed over into their possession, guarantees of security would be offered faithfully by the Greeks, in confirmation of the peace to be observed inviolably by them.

While the Trojans were exerting themselves diligently to collect these amounts, Antenor went in the quiet of night to the priest
15 Thoans, the guardian of the Palladium, carrying with him a very great amount of gold of great weight. Antenor offered this to the priest Thoans, when they were both in a secret place, and said to him: "Here is such a great amount of gold that while you live you and your heirs will always have abundant riches. Take it for yourself and
20 give me the Palladium, which you guard, so that I may take it away with me. No one will be able to know by any means what we two have done. Just as you intend to avoid the reproach of the Trojans,

so do I, and I would prefer to die rather than that it could be
imputed to me by the Trojans that I was an accessory or agent in the
25 crime we have committed. I propose, if you do this, to transfer the
Palladium to Ulysses very secretly, and when it is afterward known to
be in his possession, the crime will be ascribed to Ulysses only. For it
will be said that Ulysses took the Palladium from the temple and we
two will be completely absolved from all danger of guilt."
30   Thoans the priest vehemently resisted Antenor's words for almost
the greater part of the night. But at last, before Antenor was deprived
of the opportunity of leaving freely by night, Thoans, ensnared by
greediness for gold, willingly agreed to Antenor's removing the
Palladium. Antenor immediately carried it out of the temple and sent
35 it immediately, that night, to the Greeks by his messenger, and it was
forthwith consigned to Ulysses. Afterward, by the report of rumor, it
was said publicly that Ulysses had removed it from the Trojans by his
shrewdness.
        But, O gods, from the fact that Thoans the priest chose to prefer
40 that his city should perish by treachery rather than that he should
lose the gold offered him, what place can be safe or secure if holiness
which should be incorruptible is corrupted? This is, of course,
nothing new in priests, in whom from ancient times avarice, the
mother of all vices, has fixed its roots and voracious greed its kernel.
45 For no crime can be so serious that for committing it priests will not
receive sudden blindness in the glittering of gold. They are the temple
of avarice and the refuge of greed.
        While the Trojans were collecting the promised amount of gold and
silver and grain, and were placing it in the temple of Minerva to be
50 preserved until the whole amount of it could be possessed, it pleased
them to celebrate the solemn festival of the god Apollo in this temple
with a great number of slaughtered animals. When these animals had
been placed on the altar and committed to the flames to be burned
in the allotted sacrifice, two miracles suddenly took place before
55 them. The first was that the fire could by no means be kindled for
the sacrifice, and just as it was attempted for the tenth time, the fire
suddenly died and dissolved into smoke, so that the Trojans could by
no means have a fire kindled for the sacrifice. The second miracle was
that when the entrails of the animals were prepared for the sacrifice,
60 a certain eagle, flying in the air over the altar, descended with a loud
clamor, and rushing upon the altar, carried away all the aforesaid

entrails in his greedy claws and took them to the ships of the Greeks.

The Trojans were very astonished at those things which they saw happening to them, and by analogy truly realized by the indication
65 of the first miracle that the gods were provoked to anger against them. But for the significance both miracles had, they earnestly demanded the advice of Cassandra. Concerning the first sign, she said that Apollo was angry at them "because his temple was profaned by you through the shedding of human blood, when Achilles was slain
70 there. But on account of this it is expedient for you to go to the tomb of Achilles and kindle a light there. From that light there will arise such a light of sacrifice as will never be extinguished by anything." This was done. Of the second miracle, Cassandra asserted to the Trojans that without doubt the betrayal of the city had been
75 negotiated among the Greeks. The priest Calchas, however, when asked about these signs by the Greeks, said the second miracle signified the capture of the city by them in a very short while.

Meanwhile, however, Calchas and the priest Chryses persuaded the Greeks that they should offer a sacrifice to Apollo. This was done at
80 once. After the sacrifice was performed, the priest Chryses advised the officers of the Greek army to have a certain large horse of bronze made in secret in the likeness of a horse so that they could crowd at least a thousand knights into it. "This horse will be made according to what I decree; for this is truly the will of all the gods. The horse
85 will be made by the great mastery and skill of the wise craftsman Apius. In it certain openings will be constructed, so skillfully designed that on the outside they will not appear to the sight of men, and through them, when it is the time and place, the aforesaid knights who had been crowded into the horse will be able to go out of it.
90 When this has been done and the thousand knights have been secretly placed in complete secrecy inside the finished horse, you will beseech King Priam to allow the horse, in honor of Pallas, to enter the city and her temple, pretending on this occasion that in order to fulfill a certain vow of ours you have promised this to the goddess, on
95 account of your having accomplished the removal of the Palladium from her temple." This horse was made according to the advice and design of the priest Chryses with the greatest exertion of laborers and without any pause, and it was finished and completed in the last year of the capture of this city.
100 The kings who came to Troy to help the Trojan king, about whom

it has been reported above, seeing what a despicable pact King Priam
had entered into with the Greeks, all left Troy with their forces, and
having left Priam, went to their own kingdoms. On account of this,
King Philimenis, who had arrived in Troy with two thousand knights,
105   left Troy with the two hundred and fifty remaining to him, and in
the company of the maidens with the body of Penthesilea. Of these
one thousand maidens only four hundred remained, and having
received their queen, they hastened through their journey in order to
reach their longed-for provinces.

110   On the morning of the following day, as it had been promised
falsely concerning the swearing of the peace, King Priam went out of
his city in a very great retinue of his people, and he, as well as the
Greeks, swore to uphold the peace firmly, according to the form of
the legal oath, in the sanctuary set up by the Greeks in the midst of
115   the fields outside the walls of the city. Accordingly, Diomedes first
swore that he would observe the peace inviolably as Antenor had
arranged between them. When the Greeks afterward broke the peace,
they said they were not perjurors because Antenor had negotiated the
betrayal of the city and a false peace. This is true, although it is said
120   in a proverb: "Who swears falsely, perjures falsely." In the same
manner as Diomedes had sworn, the rest of the Greek officers swore.
King Priam, with all his Trojans, was deceived and did not know it
was a false peace, but swore to it absolutely. When the oath had been
performed, since King Priam thought for certain that the oaths made
125   by the Greeks were without guile, he restored Helen to the Greek
kings and commended her to them with humble prayers that they
would not permit any possible injury to be offered her. The Greeks
promised this with feignedly joyous expressions.

Then the Greeks, desiring to carry out the plots of their wily
130   deception, asked Priam to order the bronze horse, which they said
they had made in honor of Pallas so that she would be favorable to
them on their return journey, to be brought into the city of Troy
and placed before the temple of Minerva, so that the goddess Pallas,
appeased for the theft of the Palladium by the offer of such a gift,
135   would allow them to sail safely with their ships in their return to
their own country without dangers of the sea. Although King Priam
did not reply in any way to the request, still Aeneas and Antenor
said it should be done, claiming that such a gift would be for the

perpetual and lasting honor of the city. King Priam unwillingly agreed
140   that Aeneas and Antenor should comply with the guileful deceptions.
Meanwhile, the Greeks had received the gold and silver promised
them by King Priam, and the loads of grain stipulated by them, and
had taken them to their ships and loaded them.

Then all the Greeks assembled in one place with the greatest
145   appearance of devotion, and with processions of their priests, and
with ropes and other necessary implements, dragged the horse and
brought it to the gate of the city. The gate was not large enough in
width and height for the horse to be conveniently brought in through
it. Accordingly, it was necessary to demolish enough of the wall and
150   the gate to bring in a horse of such great height and width. When this
was done, the citizens brought this horse into the city of Troy with
great joy. But it is not unusual for the utmost joy to be changed to
grief, and the Trojan citizens and their nobles, blinded by hidden
wiles, were taking to their bosoms not a horse, although the fates had
155   provided the horse, but rather their death. For the Greeks had introduced into the aforesaid horse a certain man named Sinon, to whom
the Greeks had given the keys, so that when the opportune time
came, he could open the doors constructed in the horse, and as soon
as he saw the Trojans were sleeping quietly in their lodgings, he
160   would light a signal fire for those who were outside the city, so that
the Greeks could conveniently enter the city and easily put the
sleepers to death.

On that same day, however, the Greeks, having found a deceptive
pretext, sent to Priam that they wished to leave Troy and go first to
165   Tenedos, where they decided to receive Helen secretly, fearing that if
they received her in Troy that perhaps an outcry in the Greek army
would be raised against her and that they would afterward deliver her
to death, and there would not be anyone then who could protect her
with his defense. These feigned words of the Greeks pleased Priam, as
170   he did not know they were feigned and thought them true. After
this, when the Greeks had embarked upon their ships and sailed away
from the Trojan shores, the Trojans saw them and became very
happy, while the Greeks reached Tenedos a little before sunset. There
they dined with great enjoyment, and when the darkness of night
175   arrived, they armed themselves in martial array and went toward the
city of Troy in great silence.

After Sinon saw that the Trojans had gone to sleep, he unlocked
the openings, got out of the horse, kindled the fire, and gave the
signal to the oncoming Greeks. When they had entered the city
180 through the broken wall of the gate, and the knights who were
crowded into the horse had left it, they rushed manfully against the
Trojans, who were sleeping tranquilly in their homes, and prompted
by no stirring of dread, were staying tranquilly in their lodgings
without any anticipation of hostile attack. Their doors were shattered
185 and beaten in everywhere by the Greeks; the Greeks entered their
houses in a hostile fashion, and whomever they found, without
respect for age or sex, they killed violently, exposing their precious
riches to rapacious looting, since they seized and plundered all their
precious things from them, so that before that day dawned more than
190 twenty thousand men had perished by the sword, and they had
ruthlessly plundered the temple of the city.

A very great uproar burst out everywhere from the dismal voices
of the dying, and King Priam, when he heard such a confused uproar,
realized at once that he had been betrayed by Aeneas and Antenor,
195 and arose anxiously from his bed with many tears, and when he had
put on what clothes he could in an instant, he descended headlong
from his chamber and went to the temple of Apollo, which was in
the palace, thinking that he would be put to death at once by the
enemy and that he could have no hope of living from now on. For
200 this reason he fell flat before the great altar, awaiting certain death.
Cassandra, made almost mad, fled alone and entered the temple of
Minerva where she lamented sadly the destruction of all her people.
The rest of the women remained in the palace of the king with much
weeping and grief.
205 When it was morning, in the dawning of light, the Greeks, under
the leadership of Aeneas and Antenor, the acknowledged betrayers of
their country, rushed into great Ilium and found there no defense by
the Trojans. On account of this, the Greeks put to death everyone
they discovered. Pyrrhus entered the aforesaid temple of Apollo,
210 where King Priam was awaiting his own death, rushed upon him with
his naked sword, and in the sight of the evil Antenor and Aeneas, his
guides, wickedly slew King Priam before the altar, so that the greater
part of the altar was drenched by the great shedding of his blood.

Hecuba and her daughter Polyxena fled, and they did not know

215 where they were fleeing. Still as they fled they met Aeneas. Hecuba
said to him in her raging fury: "Ah, wicked traitor, how could you
behave with such great evil and cruelty toward King Priam, from
whom you have received such great possessions and by whom you
have been exalted in great honor so that you could endure to guide
220 the murderers to him, whom you should have saved by your
protection? You have betrayed your country and the city in which
you were born and in which you were famous for such a long time,
so that you see its ruin and you do not shrink from looking at the
fires as it goes up in smoke. Let your evil heart at least deign to pity
225 this pitiable Polyxena, and let your wicked eye spare her, so that
among so many evils which you have done at least it can be attributed
to you that you accomplished this small amount of good, namely,
that you at any rate took measures to save her if you could before
she fell into the hands of the Greeks, who would slay her or dishonor
230 her shamefully." Moved by the words of Hecuba, Aeneas received
Polyxena from her and took her with him without anyone's knowledge, and consigned her to a secret place.

Ajax Telamonius took Andromache, formerly the wife of Hector,
from the temple of Minerva, and with her Cassandra, and led them
235 both away. Menelaus joyfully led Helen away from the royal hall in
which she was. The Greeks, persisting in their savagery, were eager to
overthrow Ilium altogether, and having set many fires in the city of
Troy, they exposed it to the devouring flames to be burned completely, on account of which all of Neptune's Troy was going up in
240 smoke. The great palaces were destroyed and perished, consumed
suddenly to ashes, except for the homes of the traitors, which by a
given sign were preserved unharmed from the fires.

When the whole city was almost completely overthrown, King
Agamemnon decreed that all the officers of the army should assemble
245 in the temple of Minerva. When they had assembled, Agamemnon at
once earnestly inquired of them concerning two things: the first, of
course, whether the pledge to those whose efforts had made the
Greeks victors and masters of the city, that is, to Antenor and
Aeneas, was to be observed; and the second, what should be the
250 means and what procedure should be observed in dividing the spoils,
riches, and treasures they had obtained in the city. The reply of the
Greeks was this, that the pledge to the Trojans, that is to Antenor

and Aeneas, the chief partisans, should be kept, since through them
the Greeks were made masters of the city, and that all of the riches
255 obtained in the city should be placed in common for distribution to
everyone according to the rank, merits, and efforts of everyone. Ajax
Telamonius added that Helen, through whom the Greeks had been
subjected to so many evils for such a long time, should be delivered
to death. Many of the kings adhered to his advice, and Agamemnon
260 and Menelaus were hardly able to defend Helen, since the majority of
the kings agreed unanimously upon the extermination of Helen. King
Ulysses, inclining to the contrary opinion, by means of his speeches
and his organized way of speaking, influenced the aforesaid kings so
much that when they had changed their opinion they all peacefully
265 consented to the liberation of Helen. Agamemnon then insisted
strongly in the presence of these kings and took care that the kings
would grant him Cassandra, the daughter of King Priam, as a reward
for his efforts.

Before the conference of those kings had dissolved, Antenor and
270 Aeneas went to him, explaining how Andromache, and Helenus, the
son of King Priam, had always dissuaded the Trojans from hating the
provocations and hostilities of the Greeks, and that by their manage-
ment the body of Achilles was freed and given funeral obsequies.
Hence they claimed that they were worthy to be freed from custody,
275 which was freely granted by the kings. Helenus however, and Andromache likewise, humbly prayed for the two sons of Hector, as an
uncle for his nephews and a mother for her sons, for their liberation.
The kings likewise agreed to this, as well as Pyrrhus, who was holding
them, although he had at first insisted that they be delivered to
280 death. They also decreed that from then on all the noble women who
had escaped the bonds of death be freely permitted to go away and
have free opportunity to stay or go according to their wishes.

Moreover, they themselves decided to leave Troy, but such a great
tempest at sea arose that they could not sail for a whole month. And
285 since the tempest at sea had not yet quieted, the Greeks eagerly
demanded of the priest Calchas the reason for their hindrance and
where such a lasting cause of such serious grievance came from.
Calchas told them thus: this had happened to them on account of the
infernal furies because the soul of Achilles slain in the temple of
290 Apollo had not yet been satisfied. A sacrifice to these gods should

therefore be made of her through whom he had endured death and
who until now had remained unpunished.

Pyrrhus then inquired diligently what had been done about
Polyxena, who was the motivating cause of the murder of Achilles,
295 since he determined she had not been killed or captured. They all
maintained together that she was alive. Agamemnon therefore
examined Antenor. Since Antenor refused questioning, Agamemnon
vehemently assailed him concerning the life of Polyxena and where
she was. Antenor, seeing that he was urgently pressed by Agamemnon
300 and the other Greek kings, and being so much a son of iniquity and
wishing to complete finally all his betrayals, displayed such pains and
efforts for several days that at last he recognized Polyxena hidden
secretly in a high chamber of an old tower. Antenor went to her and
took her away violently by force from the aforesaid tower, and
305 immediately presented her as a captive to Agamemnon. Agamemnon
at once handed her over to Pyrrhus.

Pyrrhus at once commanded her to be slain on the tomb of his
father. While Polyxena was led to the slaughter, the kings rushed
together and the people rushed together, and all grieved in common
310 and had pity and compassion upon her, on account of the appearance
of such beauty which was to perish without any reason of a crime
committed by her. They would have speedily freed her from Pyrrhus'
hands, if this would not, according to the pronouncement of Calchas,
have prevented all of them from being able to return to their own
315 countries, and while she was alive, no free opportunity of returning
could be open to them. Polyxena however, when she was placed
before Achilles' grave, with humble words several times disclaimed
responsibility for Achilles' death; on the contrary she said that she
had grieved excessively over his death, and that the kings and princes
320 of Greece, contrary to justice, were allowing an innocent maiden to
perish without guilt—not that she shrank from death, since her life
would be more painful than her death if a maiden of her nobility
were to allow the defenses of her chastity to be illicitly broken, and
if her chaste purity and modesty would be exposed to violation by
325 the hands of those less noble than she, and especially by those who
had with hostile intention cruelly slain her father and her illustrious
brothers. For this reason she said she preferred to die in her own
country rather than to go away to alien provinces to lead her life

during exile in grief and in the straits of poverty. "And so let death
330 come," which she said she received gratefully, while she was a virgin,
adding that of her free will she offered her virginity as a libation to
all the gods and to death.

At this, when Polyxena fell silent, Pyrrhus at once killed Polyxena
wickedly with his sword, before the tomb of his father, in the sight
335 of Hecuba, her mother; and when her body had been cut to pieces by
him, he moistened the tomb on all sides with a great amount of the
maiden's blood. When Hecuba saw Polyxena killed before her, she
was deprived of her senses and became crazed by a grief too great for
her sex. For this reason, completely abandoned to her madness, she
340 ran wildly here and there and bit whomever she could, as if she were
a dog, and threw stones at them, rushing now at this person, now at
another, and injuring the Greeks with stones in many ways. On
account of this she was excessively dangerous to the Greeks. The
Greeks, therefore, had her captured and sent her to be stoned by
345 men on the island of Aulis near Troy. She concluded her last day
overwhelmed by stones. The Greeks commanded a lofty and
distinguished monument for the body of Hecuba to be made where
they buried the body of Hecuba. The structure of this monument
appears today in that very place. The name which was then given to
350 that place on account of the memory of Hecuba is "the dangerous
place," which name even now is in common use there.

*Here begins the thirty-first book, about the exile of Aeneas,
about the banishment of Antenor from Troy, and about the
death of Ajax Telamonius.*

After the capture of the city of Troy, to the great peril of its citizens
and their wealth, when the Greeks had not yet been able to leave
Troy on account of the excessive storminess of the sea and weather,
Ajax Telamonius lodged a complaint against Ulysses before
5 Agamemnon and the other Greek princes. He said that although there
was a procedure to be followed in the distribution of the goods and
wealth obtained in the capture of the Trojan city, so that the
privileges of everyone should be observed according to worth, merit,
and effort, still, in the granting of the Palladium this procedure had

10 not been followed fairly because the Palladium had been granted to
Ulysses, who was not worthy of such a reward, "and I myself am
without it, who am much more worthy of it, since on account of the
immense efforts of my valor I often replenished in great fullness, with
a wealth of food supplies, the Greek army, when they were burdened
15 with excessive hunger. Many times, by my hardy strength, I caused
the army to carry on unharmed and to be kept safe from the enemy
when it was almost conquered by the Trojans. I killed King Poly-
mestor, to whose guardianship King Priam had entrusted his son
Polydorus, along with an infinite amount of treasure. When this
20 Polydorus had been killed by me, I brought all his treasure to the
Greek army, so that the army was always well supplied for its
expenses. I also slew the king of Phrygia and brought all his goods to
the Greeks. What is more, by my diligence and on account of my
powers, I added many kingdoms to the dominion of the Greeks,
25 namely, Gargari, Crepesis, Arisdia, and Larissa, and in addition the
kingdoms bordering on Troy and the places encroaching upon the
walls of the city itself, since there was then no one to help the
Trojans in any way and to furnish them with supplies in the way of
provisions. Furthermore, I accomplished many victorious deeds with
30 Achilles"—all of which things he mentioned separately in his speech,
though they are omitted here as rather superfluous. "But Ulysses,
lacking all valor of knighthood, seems to flourish and survive by the
eloquence of his speech alone, which has no strength except in
flattery and the deceptive art of speaking. If he has said we were
35 made lords of the city of Troy through him, this has not proceeded
from his valor or courage, but from his treacherous and deceiving
words, on account of which we labor perpetually under a taint of
infamy among all nations, namely, that we have conquered the
Trojans through the deceptions of maneuvering and through guile
40 when we should have vanquished them on account of your power."

    After Telamonius had made an end of his words, Ulysses replied
boldly to his words and said that he had defeated the Trojan army by
his valor and by his wise counsel and intelligence, and if he had not
been in the Greek army and exercising his intelligence greatly, Troy
45 would still be standing in its strength and glory, and its citizens would
still be in a position of strength. "Obviously, Lord Telamon, the
Palladium, among other things, was not obtained by the Greeks

through your courage, but rather by my diligent efforts. The Greeks
would never have known what the Palladium was, nor what was its
50 special power and virtue. I discovered, however, through my own
unaided investigation, that our capturing the city was delayed only by
the Palladium, since the Palladium had the virtue that Troy could not
be captured while the Palladium was within the walls of the city. For
this reason I went secretly to Troy and negotiated so diligently that,
55 when I possessed the Palladium, we gained control of the city." With
these things among others, Ulysses then made an end to his speech.

Ajax Telamonius, however, bitterly hurled many opprobrious
words against Ulysses, and Ulysses against him. On account of this
they became mortal enemies, Telamonius publicly maintaining that it
60 was necessary that Ulysses die at his hands. Since it pleased the kings
that it be decided by a judgment of Agamemnon and Menelaus which
of them should have the Palladium, Telamonius or Ulysses, they
decreed by their arbitration that the Palladium should be left wholly
to Ulysses, resigned, so to speak, to his control. They were so moved
65 perhaps because, in their opinion, Ulysses had, by his speech, freed
Helen from the danger of death at the hands of Telamonius and the
other Greek kings. Telamonius was thus aggrieved that such an
arrangement concerning the Palladium had been made against him by
Agamemnon and Menelaus without reason, since almost all of the
70 officers of the army firmly asserted that Telamonius was worthier
than Ulysses of having the Palladium. On account of this, Telamonius,
bearing a bitter feeling against Agamemnon and Menelaus, uttered
opprobrious words against them, asserting that henceforth he was
their mortal enemy. Because of the aforesaid reasons, the two brother
75 kings, and Ulysses with them, in a very great train of knights, took
care to guard themselves with the greatest caution.

After that day had passed, with the coming of the following night
and the rising of the dawn of the next day, by which the following
day shed its light from on high upon earth at daybreak, it was found
80 that Telamonius had been slain that night in his bed, his body hacked
in many places and pierced with many wounds. Accordingly a very
great uproar burst forth throughout the whole army, and all grieved
together over the death of Telamonius, and they attached the blame,
as if by a real belief, to Agamemnon and Menelaus, and especially to
85 Ulysses. Pyrrhus, who had cherished Telamonius with sincere affection,

uttered many threatening words against Ulysses and the other participants in the murder of Telamonius. For this reason Ulysses, fearing
for his life, left Troy stealthily with his ships on a certain night under
the exceedingly obscure darkness of that night, and committed him-
90 self to the deep sea, and left the Palladium with Diomedes, his friend.
Pyrrhus commanded that the body of Telamonius be cremated, and
when it had become ashes, Pyrrhus arranged that the ashes be placed
in and consigned to a certain gold vase, sealed by a protective barrier
of very clever design, so that it could be carried to the kingdom of
95 King Telamonius. Then Agamemnon and Menelaus, with those kings
favoring them, had themselves guarded with caution against Pyrrhus
and certain kings who favored Pyrrhus, since Pyrrhus was plotting
against them, and they likewise were plotting against Pyrrhus. But
Antenor by his negotiation restored a firm peace among them and
100 took care to invite all the Greek officers to a feast with great
solemnity. He surprised and delighted them with a great diversity of
foods, and besides he took care to honor them with the presentation
of many gifts.

The Greeks then pressed their claims against Aeneas, that is, that
105 he had broken faith with them, that he had broken the bond of his
oath in that he had concealed Polyxena, who was under sentence of
death, since she was the reason that the great Achilles had been
killed. Having consulted, therefore, they sentenced Aeneas to exile
and banished him from Troy forever. Since he could not oppose their
110 orders, he humbly begged the Greeks that they would at least deign
to grant him the twenty-two ships with which Paris had gone to
Greece, and since they badly needed repair, that they would favor
him with the time to repair them. This the Greeks freely granted, and
he was given the space of four months to repair them.

115 Meanwhile Antenor, not wishing to stay in Troy, got himself some
ships and of his own accord left Troy with a large number of Trojans.
But where they went and where they directed themselves the present
history does not reveal.

Aeneas, bearing a feeling of hatred against Antenor because he was
120 banished from Troy by Antenor's action, and Antenor was allowed
complete freedom to come to and go from Troy at his own free will,
prepared hidden snares for Antenor so that he could be banished
perpetually from Troy, and the means of coming and going in and

out of Troy would be completely removed from him. For this reason,
125 Aeneas called together all the Trojans who were remaining in Troy
for a council, and he addressed them thus, saying: "Friends and
brothers, since you have recently come by unpropitious fortune to
the present state in which you are, you see clearly that you will not
be able to lead your lives in safety without the advice of some
130 protector. It would therefore be sound for you to think soundly
about your leader, when I have gone. For, if those living near you in
manors and castles and other places know that you live without a
protector, they will rush upon you indiscriminately and will expose
you to the constant affliction of looting. It is therefore necessary for
135 you, as it seems to me, to send for Antenor and make him your king,
so that with his advice you may be able to protect yourselves in
safety against your rivals." The counsel of Aeneas pleased everyone.
On account of this they searched for Antenor through their messengers, and when he had been found, he went swiftly to Troy. Aeneas
140 wished to assail him at once in an armed band in order to injure him,
since now Aeneas was more powerful than Antenor in Troy. Hence,
the surviving Trojans who were in Troy humbly pleaded with Aeneas
so that he would cease from his undertaking, and that all their woes,
which had been allotted some kind of end in battles, would not be
145 renewed by civil and internal warfare among them. In reply to their
words, Aeneas spoke thus: "What man can be so softened by gentle-
ness and mercy that he can mercifully spare such a very evil man and
the constant author of treachery, by whose treacherous designs it
happened that Polyxena, the illustrious daughter of the king, an
150 innocent girl, came to be sacrificed so cruelly on the tomb of
Achilles? I am perpetually banished from your society, I who desired
to share the common grief of your tears as a partaker in them, and to
find means of consolation for the common anguish through which we
might be relieved of our great sorrows." At the words of Aeneas, the
155 Trojans, when they had deliberated in council together, decreed that
Antenor should be banished perpetually from Troy and that he
should never be allowed to come back to Troy, and permission was
given him to leave Troy immediately. This was carried out at once.
Antenor at once put out to sea with his ships and many of the
160 Trojan survivors, and sailed for a long time through foreign waters
until he fell into the hands of some pirates who rushed upon them

and killed some of them, inflicted wounds upon others, and finally
plundered them. When at last they were delivered from their hands,
they travelled along the surface of the sea until, blown by a favorable
165 breeze, they touched upon the shores of a certain province which was
called Gerbondia. In it there reigned then a certain very righteous and
merciful king called Oecides, who ruled this province with great
tranquility. Antenor, in a small company of men, disembarked in the
land of this king near the shore where a high cliff hung over this
170 shore. For this reason, having looked over the level ground of this
place, which stretched far and wide through the fields from the base
of the cliff, and through the groves, with many springs of water all
around, Antenor, attracted by the pleasantness of this place, planned
to found a city on the brow of this cliff. He founded it with the
175 surviving Trojans who had sailed with him and decreed it should be
called Corcyra Melaena. In a short time he had surrounded it with a
circuit of stout walls and had established many strong towers on
them along the periphery. After it was made known to the Trojans
who had remained in Troy that a city had been built in a safe place
180 which was fertile and pleasant, the majority of them went over to it
of their own accord. This city was fully populated by them and many
others besides. Antenor knew, from his great shrewdness, how to
submit himself to the aforesaid King Oecides, to whose rule this
province was subject, in such a manner that this king most graciously
185 received him and his city and all those Trojans. For this reason
Antenor was very exalted in the affection of the king, on account of
his zealous loyalty, and in this kingdom the king made him second
to him.

Cassandra, who had remained in Troy, wracked by many sorrows
190 on account of the stoning of her mother and the death of Polyxena,
her sister, spent many days in weeping, anguish, and lamentation. At
last, when she had dried the storms of tears and was relieved a little
of her sorrows, the Greeks who were intending to leave Troy asked
many things of her concerning their futures. Cassandra told them
195 many evils would befall them before they were welcomed in their
countries. She said to Agamemnon that he would be killed by those
of his own household, and just as Cassandra had prophesied to them,
so it happened to each of them as the present history will reveal in
order.

200   Two sons survived the secretly murdered Telamonius, who had
been borne to him by two queens, his wives. The first was called
Eantides, by Queen Clausca, and the other Antissacus, by Ethimissa.
These two, while they were children, were given to the care and
tutelage of King Teucer, so that he might bring them up until they
205   were grown and were ready to be knighted.
         Agamemnon and Menelaus demanded permission to leave the
Greeks. The Greek officers who were still in Troy hardly wished to
grant them this, because they suspected them of the clandestine
murder of Telamonius. Since Agamemnon and Menelaus were some-
210   what exonerated, because of the stealthy flight of Ulysses, by which
he made himself his own accuser, the Greeks with unwilling minds
gave them permission to leave. They left Troy and set out upon the
deep sea.
         It was the time after the grapes had been pressed, when autumn
215   had already fulfilled its changeable months upon the earth, and
encroaching winter coming in its slow and inevitable course had
already despoiled the trees of their leaves and had already enjoined
silence upon the sweet songs of the birds. Then, when the strength
and severity of the winds burst forth from their caverns in great puffs
220   and gusts, then, when the brightness was driven from the clear sky
and dark masses of clouds covered it, which, dissolved in floods of
rain, gave new fullness to the rivers and, by pieces of summer's
branches and logs falling between the banks, in their downward
courses everywhere scoured and stripped these banks, then ill-advised
225   heedlessness moved the hearts of the Greeks with the blind passion
of eagerness. (This eagerness compels the hearts of travellers wishing
to return to their own countries to become feverish with its fervent
heat so that, not paying attention to the perils of the route nor the
condition of the weather, they prepare for the journey they long to
230   make. On account of this it happens to many of them that as they
hasten ill-advisedly to return to their countries, when they are assailed
by unexpected impediments appearing in the way, they fall in the
midst of the journey, and the means of reaching their own country
no longer remain to them.) Since the wishes of the Greeks were
235   seized by this ardent desire to go back to their own countries, they
left Troy with their ships loaded with much wealth which they had
gained in various ways from the rich plunder of the Trojans, and

having seized upon a certain calm day in the depths of winter, they
took to the sea, and with raised sails spread to the gusts of wind,
240 they had a pleasant voyage for four whole days and nights. On the
fifth day about noon, while they were plowing the surface of the sea
through the Aegean Sea, in complete tranquility, the clear sky
suddenly became black, while the gathering clouds spewed forth
showers in a great amount of rain. The sky rumbled, with masses of
245 thunder clouds emitting terrifying sounds, and sudden flashes and
gleams of false fires among the darkness of the storm presented a
flickering light. Eurus, Notus, and Africus were released from the
caves of Aeolus and overturned the depths of the sea, and now the
violent gusts of the tempest raised the waves in swollen hills, and
250 now cleft them into deep gaps. And thus the ships of the Greeks,
exceedingly buffeted by the storm at sea, were carried now here now
there, in an uncertain course. The sails were rent and torn into many
pieces, the masts were broken with a great noise, and the yards,
separated from their masts by the violent wrenching, were shattered
255 in different pieces. When the guidance of their rudders, which had
been torn loose from the ships, had been forcefully removed, these
ships, while they wandered in jeopardy among the tossing waves, were
separated from each other when the coming of night doubled the
darkness, and they were set on fire in the midst of the waves by
260 thunderbolts rushing from highest heavens in threefold flames, and
when they were consumed, they perished amidst the foaming waves,
while the heavenly fires burned them and the water of the sea
drowned them. The Greeks sailing in them perished, and the ravenous
sea swallowed up the infinite wealth of the Trojans which they were
265 carrying in them.

Ajax Oileus had entered into the aforesaid tempest with thirty-two
ships, and when all his ships were burned and sunk in the sea, he
turned to the strength of his arms, and by swimming reached land
half-dead. Swollen by swallowing too much water, he could hardly
270 get himself to the shore, where he lay naked on the sand almost dead
until the light of coming day, expecting his death more than his life.
But when certain of his men arrived naked on the shore, having likewise escaped the devouring sea by swimming, they looked on the
shore for their lord, in case he had escaped. They found him lying on
275 the sand and warmed him with sweet words and speeches, since they

were not able to warm him again with clothes or by any other
assistance. Thus, as has been related, it happened to the imperilled
Greeks and to Ajax by the might of the goddess Minerva, who had
conceived a most bitter anger against Ajax and wished to take
280 vengeance against him and the others because they had violently
dragged Cassandra from her temple. For although it is said that the
actual performer should take the punishment, it is not unheard of
that on account of the guilt of one man alone, often a thousand
innocent men are imprisoned. Concerning the other Greeks and
285 leaders of the Greeks then leaving Troy and hastening to go back to
their own countries, who did not suffer the danger of the present
calamity—what happened to them will be plainly related in the
following book.

*Here begins the thirty-second book, about the shipwreck of
the Greek ships and about the death of Agamemnon.*

At this time there was in Greece a certain king named Nauplius, who
possessed in Greece a kingdom of great breadth and length. The site
of his kingdom was joined on the side of its northern region to a long
stretch of ocean, and had high cliffs on this side, around the bases of
5   which the rough sea surged, and it had many mountainous crags
bordering it on this side. King Nauplius had two sons at the time of
the Trojan War, of whom the firstborn was called by the name of
Palamedes, and the younger was called by that of Oectus. Palamedes
was esteemed on account of his great valor, since he was a very brave
10 and bold man in battle and distinguished by much fame as a knight
and horseman. He had gone in his might with the greatest splendor to
the Greek army, in a fleet of many ships with a train of many of his
knights, since no king in Greece had a larger kingdom nor such wealth
and riches. The Greeks made Palamedes the commander in chief of
15 the whole army when Agamemnon had been removed from the duties
of his leadership. This Palamedes finally breathed his last and died in
a conflict of battle, as was sufficiently explained above about all
these things and about him. But certain people who are pleased at the
ruin of others and who always glory in their own malice reported
20 otherwise to King Nauplius and his son Oectus concerning the death

of Palamedes in false inventions and in much feigning of secretly
instigated lies. For they said Palamedes had not perished in battle but
was wickedly killed secretly and stealthily by Ulysses and his companion Diomedes, at the advice of the Greeks. In order that firm
25 credence would be given to their lies, they made up lies about the
form and method of his killing, adding in their reports that Ulysses,
Diomedes, Agamemnon, and Menelaus had devised two false letters
which contained the information that Palamedes had negotiated with
the Trojans for the betrayal of the army, which had been settled with
30 him by the Trojans for a very great amount of gold, and they had
these letters tied to the side of the slain man. However, since they
pretended to know the amount of money promised, Ulysses had
arranged with a chamberlain of Palamedes to whom money was given,
so that he might take care to hide secretly under the head of
35 Palamedes' bed that money which the Trojans promised they would
give Palamedes for the betrayal of the army. When Ulysses had consigned this to him, this same chamberlain of Palamedes hid it secretly
under the head of his bed. This chamberlain went to Ulysses afterward and told him in secret that he had done what Ulysses had com-
40 manded, and Ulysses had him secretly killed on the spot. After these
letters had been found and read by the Greeks, they said the Greeks
conceived a feeling of suspicion against Palamedes. And when the
Greeks afterward went to Palamedes' tent to inquire diligently
whether this business of the gold was true, and when they had
45 searched through the head of his bed, they found the gold in it, and
the weight of it was what the aforesaid letters had reported. Hence,
when the Greeks were afterward confirmed in their belief of those
things which were contained in the letters, they wished to fall upon
Palamedes as the author of such a betrayal. Palamedes, boldly resist-
50 ing the aforesaid, then offered to defend himself by a mounted duel,
thus proving that he knew nothing of the crime and was ready to
justify his innocence by this battle. Since there was no one of the
Greeks who wished to advance against him to dispute his cause, when
his rivals saw that they could not injure him at all in this way,
55 Ulysses appeased the people with his speeches and took such pains
that when they were dissuaded from the false belief concerning those
things which had been mentioned against Palamedes, Palamedes was
then put in command of the army by Ulysses, so that he might

appear to be Palamedes' helper. These liars also added to their inven-
60   tions that not many days later, Ulysses and Diomedes addressed
      Palamedes secretly, asserting to him that they had been notified that
      there was a very great treasure hidden in an old well, which could
      undoubtedly be obtained by them, if he wished to be a participant
      with them, and they planned to go the following night to the well; if
65   it pleased him to go with them to get the treasure, it would be
      pleasing and acceptable to them. Palamedes, ignorant of their deceit
      and deceived concerning their trustworthiness, went with them at the
      coming of night to the aforesaid well, where there was a discussion
      among them as to who should descend first, and Palamedes offered to
70   descend. When he had taken off his shoes and cast aside his super-
      fluous garments, he boldly descended into the well. When they
      realized that he had reached the bottom of the well they at once
      buried him under a heap of stones and killed him, and they left him
      dead in the well, hastening to their tents in the silence of night.
75   Such was the mass of false lies to be believed about the death of
      Palamedes which overwhelmed the mind of King Nauplius his father
      and Oectus his brother. On account of this, King Nauplius and his
      son Oectus inquired very earnestly how they might effectively rise
      against the Greeks who had been in the army at that time, in order
80   to avenge the murder of their son and brother. They heard that the
      Greeks, who had of necessity to go past the boundaries of their
      kingdom, had assuredly set out upon the sea in the winter weather,
      in order to return to their own country. They accordingly com-
      manded their men to kindle fires on the peaks of the mountains
85   which were near the ocean on each night, so that, as the Greeks were
      going along, deceived by the darkness of night, they would think they
      were near land which they could go to safely and would incautiously
      turn aside there, and with spread sails they would rush with their
      ships against these mountains and crags, where the ships, ripped
90   asunder, would suffer shipwreck and would be lost irrevocably. This
      was done. More than two hundred Greek ships with their sailors were
      sunk in this shipwreck on these cliffs and crags. When the rest of the
      ships, which were following after those which had gone first, arrived
      at this place in the shadows of night, they heard the crashing of the
95   ships which were breaking against the crags and the doomed shouts of
      those who were dying in the sea, and they avoided this fatal place

and fled from it and put out upon the open ocean. With these,
Agamemnon, Diomedes, Menelaus, and certain others, whose story
will be told below, avoided this shipwreck.

100   Oectus, or Peleus (for he had two names), the son of King
Nauplius, striving particularly for the death or serious harm of
Agamemnon and Diomedes, inquired diligently in his mind how he
could injure them, if it happened that they went back safely to their
own countries. On account of this, he declared, through special letters

105 and a wise messenger to Clytemnestra, wife of Agamemnon, that it
was true and certain that her husband Agamemnon had taken one of
the daughters of King Priam as his wife, and that, loving her ardently,
he was bringing her with him to his kingdom so that he might make
her the queen of his kingdom and deprive Clytemnestra, the real wife,

110 of her kingdom and deliver her without fail to death. Hence, since it
would be expedient to forestall him before the time, he warned her
to make careful provisions for herself, so that she would not meet her
downfall. Clytemnestra believed the words of Oectus, and, giving him
humble thanks, kept silent counsel as to how she would protect

115 herself in safety from the reported plots of her husband.
    It happened that Agamemnon escaped safely from the perils of the
sea and reached his kingdom; and Clytemnestra, his wife, who had
already prepared for his treacherous murder, received him with a
feignedly joyous face. This Clytemnestra had, however, in the absence

120 of her husband, sinned against the law of the matrimonial bond.
Having put aside her modesty, she had defiled her marriage bed with
a man named Aegisthus. Clytemnestra had been enflamed by his love
to such an extent that she bore him a daughter, who was called
Erigona, to whom she had promised certainly to give the kingdom,

125 although Aegisthus was not of royal birth nor honored by the noble
rank of duke or count. It is certain among lascivious women that
when they fall into wantonness of their bodies, they never desire to
join with anyone who would be better than or equal to their
husbands, but they always descend to a lower person. Since they have

130 become careless of their honor, they do not shrink from doing base
deeds in their own right, but they only do these things with base
fellows, since they would think it a crime if they did these things
with men better than their husbands and themselves, or of higher
rank in the world. Even the nobility and wealth of the one

135 committing adultery with them do not absolve them from the crime
     so that they would not join infamy to adultery, and so that they
     would not afflict an innocent husband with the disgraceful stigma of
     a rival. Clytemnestra made arrangements with her beloved Aegisthus
     in such a way that on the first night that Agamemnon came, while he
140 was sleeping soundly in bed, Aegisthus rushed upon him and cut his
     throat. A few days after he was dead and his body given to burial,
     Clytemnestra took Aegisthus as her husband and made him king in
     her kingdom of Mycenae.

     Agamemnon was survived by a certain son whom Clytemnestra had
145 borne him; his name was Orestes, and at this time he had not yet
     attained the years of manhood. King Talthybius, his kinsman, fearing
     that Aegisthus would kill him stealthily, took him away secretly and
     sent him to Idomeneus, king of Crete, who was likewise his kinsman.
     Although he was joined to Orestes by a remote relationship, still
150 Idomeneus and his wife, Queen Tarrassis, welcomed him with joyful
     hearts and showed no less feeling of affection to him than to their
     daughter, named Clymena, their future heir in the kingdom, who was
     in the years of her childhood, not yet ready for marriage.

     This same Oectus, son of King Nauplius, went to Egea, the wife of
155 Diomedes, and in the same way in which he influenced the mind of
     Clytemnestra to believe that her husband was bringing with him one
     of the daughters of King Priam, in the same way he influenced Egea.
     Egea was the daughter of Polynices, king of the Argives. When he
     died he was survived by Egea and a son named Assandrus. Hence,
160 after the death of their father Polynices, Egea and Assandrus divided
     the kingdom of the Argives between them, and one part of it went to
     Egea and the other part to Assandrus, her brother. With her part of
     the kingdom, Egea took Diomedes for a husband. While her brother
     Assandrus was going with Diomedes, his brother-in-law, to the Greek
165 army against the Trojans, they arrived at Brecia before they reached
     the Greek army, and they proposed to stay there several days to
     refresh themselves. King Telephus, lord of this province, feeling dis-
     pleasure at their stay, attacked them with a great number of his
     armed knights. Because of this, since they had of necessity to defend
170 themselves, Assandrus killed many of King Telephus' knights. King
     Telephus, being unable to bear the destruction of so many of his
     men, took a certain lance on which there was a very sharp point and

fatally wounded Assandrus with it, so that he fell dead from his
horse. When the death of his relative Assandrus was made known to
175 Diomedes, he hurled himself furiously among the men of King
Telephus, killed many of them, and at last dragged the body of
Assandrus by force from under the feet of the horses and with many
tears brought it to his men. This was the truth of the matter concerning the death of Assandrus, brother of Egea. But Egea was not
180 convinced of this; on the contrary, it was asserted to her that
Assandrus had been killed at the desire of Diomedes, so that when he
was dead, his half of the kingdom would go to Diomedes' wife, Egea,
by whom he would be sole lord of the Argives. Egea, however, who
loved her brother Assandrus no less than she did herself, who would
185 have preferred to have lost her half of the kingdom than to have been
deprived of her brother, became ill-disposed toward Diomedes, her
husband. Hence, both because of this reason and because of the
words of Oectus, son of King Nauplius, she arranged with her Argive
men so that she would by no means receive Diomedes, and Egea
190 henceforth condemned him to exile, refusing to let him stay in his
kingdom any longer. Hence Diomedes was forced into exile and did
not know where to turn. At last, at the dictates of fortune, he went
to Salamis, where King Teucer, brother of the former Telamonius,
lived as lord of that province. But having already heard some time
195 ago that Diomedes had conspired with Ulysses in the death of his
brother Telamonius, he ordered him captured. But by stealthy flight,
Diomedes escaped and fled from the hands of King Teucer.
    When King Demophoon and King Athamas arrived in their king-
dom, they were forced into exile from their kingdoms in similar
200 fashion. They came to Carthacius, where King Nestor received them
joyfully. There these two kings proposed to go to their kingdoms in
an armed band and to attack their subjects with a powerful force and
to kill them all, if fortune favored, delivering to an especially cruel
death those who were the agents in these uprisings. Nestor did not
205 approve of their plan; on the contrary, he persuaded them to send
their messengers to their kingdoms with flattery and promises of great
freedom. From this it happened that after a few days, when their
subjects had adopted a spirit of reconciliation, they received their
kings into their kingdoms with willing hearts.
210   Aeneas, however, had remained at Troy to have his ships refitted,

and while he was there, the city suffered many hostile invasions from
the inhabitants of the neighboring places, who were striving to prey
upon the Trojan survivors. Aeneas took counsel with them so that,
since he could not be with them longer for their defense, they would
215 send for Diomedes, a very valiant man. Since Diomedes was enduring
exile then, so that he could not be received by his people, he would
gladly come to their guidance and assistance. The Trojans sent for
Diomedes, who, having collected aid wherever he could, went to Troy
with great speed. He found the Trojans almost besieged, and Aeneas
220 still there. They greeted each other warmly, and both prepared for
battle; and when they had drawn up the Trojans who were skilled in
battle, they marched out to combat with them in an armed band.
They fought continuously for seven days. Diomedes did many things
among them on account of his personal valor; he killed many of the
225 adversaries of the Trojans, captured many of them, and whoever
happened to be captured by him he at once had hanged from a
gallows as if they were the worst thieves and pirates. On the eighth
day he rushed upon them manfully with much skill in warfare, so
that he surrounded them on all sides, with the result that they could
230 not escape from his hands. For that reason he commanded that they
all be hanged from the gallows and that they be fastened to crosses in
the manner of thieves. When the remaining neighbors from the
adjacent manors and castles had heard that those who had attacked
the Trojans had been taken by such a bitter death, they were exceed-
235 ingly terrified and ceased altogether to harass the Trojans. After this,
the Trojans enjoyed a very great peace, if in their afflictions it could
be called peace.

Meanwhile Aeneas, having refitted his ships, embarked upon these
ships with many of the surviving Trojans and his father Anchises, and
240 prepared for the exile to which he had been condemned by the
Greeks. Hence, he set out with his ships upon the deep ocean, and
since he did not know at all what habitation the fates had decreed
for him where he might place his family gods, he touched upon many
places, troubled by the many perils of the sea. But by the will of the
245 gods he entered the ocean with his ships, and he sailed for a long
time through foreign seas until he reached Italy and went to Tuscany.
The present history does not tell about the particular adventures of
Aeneas, however, and how it turned out for him after his departure

from Troy and what happened to him after he ceased to voyage, that
250 is, from the time when he came to Tuscany. But he who wishes to
have knowledge of these things should read Virgil in the *Aeneid*.

After knowledge reached Egea, wife of Diomedes, that Diomedes
had been welcomed by the Trojans and had manfully attacked their
enemies, she feared that Diomedes might perhaps collect his forces
255 and attack her and injure her and her subjects, since he had been
harmed so much by them. Because of this, when she had consulted
with the Argives, she decided to send for Diomedes and to tell him
that he could return safely to his kingdom. When he had his wife's
message, he rejoiced greatly and swiftly returned to his own kingdom,
260 where Egea his wife and all the Argives received him with sincere
hearts and the greatest joy.

The rest of the Greeks who had refused to receive their kings
returning from Troy, led by remorse, humbly sought them and
restored them to the dignities of their kingdoms. After they had
265 reached their kingdoms, with earnest thoughts they rebuilt the cities
and places which had collapsed in their absence and took pains to
restore them to better condition.

*Here begins the thirty-third book, about Orestes avenging the
death of Agamemnon, his father, and about the death of
his mother and the recovery of his kingdom.*

Orestes, the son of Agamemnon, whom Idomeneus had received in
order to bring up on account of the fear of Aegisthus, was already a
young man and had completed twenty-four years when Idomeneus
distinguished him with the honor of knighthood with very enjoyable
5 festivities. When he had been made a knight, Orestes, since his age
and time were ripe for the recovery of his kingdom and he intended
to avenge the murder of his father, earnestly demanded that
Idomeneus give him the aid of the knights of his kingdom. Idomeneus
freely consented and assigned a thousand very valiant knights to him,
10 whereupon Orestes sought and awaited the assistance of many, so
that in a short time he had obtained a thousand more knights, and
with the two thousand knights, he boldly entered the city of Trozen.
The lord of this city was King Forensis, as he was named, who for a

long time had been a close friend of Agamemnon and very hateful to
15 Aegisthus. The principal reason for this hatred, that is, why King
Forensis nourished such deadly enmity against Aegisthus, was this:
King Forensis had contracted the marriage of one of his daughters
with Aegisthus, and Aegisthus had turned away from the daughter of
King Forensis on account of the love of Clytemnestra, and had sent
20 her a notice of repudiation. On account of this he offered himself
with a joyful heart, and asked Orestes to take him with him in his
company against Aegisthus, and he determined to go with three
hundred knights to serve Orestes and to destroy Aegisthus. Orestes
was very grateful to him for this.
25   It was the time when the sun had already entered the sign of
Taurus. Then, when the meadows were green and the fragrant blossoms bloomed on the trees, the roses blushed among the green briers,
and the nightingales warbled with sweet melody in sweet songs, then
when it was the month of May, which is the leader of all the months
30 and their delightful foster son, then both Orestes and King Forensis
and their army joyfully left the city of Trozen and hastened to
Mycenae. Since the inhabitants of Mycenae did not wish to receive
them, the army of Orestes surrounded that city in a grim siege.
Orestes received an answer from the gods to proceed safely against
35 Aegisthus. He was granted the victory against Aegisthus, and it was
acceptable to the gods that he take vengeance upon his mother with
his own hands. Although Clytemnestra was in this surrounded city,
Aegisthus went to gather fierce knights to aid the city, and with them
he hoped to provide sure protection for the city. Orestes, however,
40 having certain information about the route by which Aegisthus could
return with his troops, for this had been reported by his scouts,
decided to crowd many knights together on all sides along the passes
of the routes by which he could return, so that they could intercept
Aegisthus as he returned. Every day Orestes harrassed the city with
45 continuous attacks, and because this city had not been fortified ahead
of time for its defense against attacks upon it, it was weakly defended
by its citizens. Hence it happened that its citizens, being unable to
withstand the nightly and daily onslaughts, ceased altogether to fight
on the fifteenth day of the siege, and the city was taken by Orestes'
50 army. Orestes entered the city in a great company of knights.
     When he had drawn up the knights in a garrison at the gates so

that no one could enter or leave by them, he hastened to the royal
palace of his late father, where he found Clytemnestra, his mother.
He commanded that she be seized at once and held fast in custody,
55 and so also with all those who had conspired in the death of his
father, King Agamemnon, and who were the chiefs of the party
opposing his rebellion. On that very day, while Aegisthus was
speeding to the aid of the city with his knights, he fell into the hands
of Orestes' knights who were waiting for his return. They rushed
60 upon him and his companions, and having engaged in battle, captured
Aegisthus, killed all his knights, and brought Aegisthus to Orestes
with his hands tied behind his back. On the following day Orestes
commanded his mother, Clytemnestra, to be brought forth naked
with her hands tied. Orestes rushed upon her then with unsheathed
65 sword and cut her breasts from her body with his own hands and
killed her with many blows of his sword. When she was killed he
commanded that her naked body be dragged on the ground out of
the city and decreed that it was to be devoured by the dogs and
birds. On account of this she long remained unburied until the dogs
70 and birds had consumed all her body except the bones. He commanded that Aegisthus be drawn naked through the whole city and
hanged from the gallows, and in the same way he decreed that all the
others he had captured should be put to death after being drawn
through the city and hanged from the gallows. Need I say more?
75 When the city of Mycenae had been purged by Orestes of all the
wicked, disloyal, and evil people, it could be said that the death of
Agamemnon was fully avenged by the deaths of so many and also by
the death of Clytemnestra, who was killed on account of the dishonor shamefully done by her to her husband, and the injury offered
80 to her son in the many things in which Clytemnestra had sinned. For
she was guilty of homicide, since she had had such a man and such a
great king as the illustrious Agamemnon killed while he slept under
her protection, and she had done injury to her husband and son by
disgraceful adultery, and had violated both nature itself and behavior
85 befitting noble women. Hence it was right that on account of so
many evils she should have met with much evil, especially through
him upon whom she had inflicted so many evils with the marks of
dishonor.
Meanwhile Menelaus, who had escaped the many perils of the sea,

90 reached Crete with Helen, his wife, where he heard the report of his
    brother Agamemnon's death and of the revenge taken by Orestes.
    Menelaus accordingly became seriously angry at Orestes for the awful
    vengeance which he had exercised against his mother. The nobles as
    well as the people from the greater part of the city came there to see
95 Helen, for whom the Greeks had suffered so many woes. At last,
    when favorable winds were blowing, Menelaus left Crete with Helen,
    and enjoying a fortunate voyage, he reached the port of Mycenae
    where he expressed his hatred and anger toward Orestes, telling him
    that he should not succeed to the kingdom of his father because he
100 had executed such an awful vengeance upon his mother, and that it
    could be called impiety rather than vengeance. Hence it happened
    that, when all the Greek kings had gathered in Athens, it seemed to
    the majority of them that Orestes was unworthy of the throne of his
    father Agamemnon, since he had killed his mother with such cruel
105 impiety, and that he was therefore worthy of exile. Orestes in his
    defense alleged that whatever he had done against his mother had
    been executed by the order and will of the gods. The duke of Athens,
    however, offered himself against anyone to prove in behalf of Orestes
    that Orestes was worthy to be lord of the kingdom of Mycenae, and
110 that what he had done to his mother had been accomplished by the
    will of the gods. Since there was no one who wished to offer himself
    against him in the aforesaid duel, these kings, having consulted in a
    solemn council, exonerated Orestes of any complaint, crowning him
    with solemnity in the kingdom of his father. When he had taken leave
115 of them, he reached Mycenae, with the duke of Athens, who had
    accompanied him out of affection, and he was received there with the
    greatest rejoicing. And so Orestes sat on the throne of his father,
    crowned with the diadem, and felt ill will against his uncle Menelaus.
    But when the duke of Athens had left Orestes, King Idomeneus of
120 Crete went to Mycenae and negotiated peace and concord between
    Menelaus and Orestes, so that Orestes took as his wife Hermione,
    daughter of King Menelaus and Helen, that is, his first cousin, and the
    festivities of the marriage between them were celebrated with
    solemnity. Erigona, the daughter of Clytemnestra and Aegisthus, born
125 of a disgraceful union, hanged herself with a noose, being disturbed
    by excessive grief because she had learned that Orestes, her half
    brother, had been established on the throne of his kingdom.

Not many days afterward, Ulysses came to Crete with two mer-
chant ships which he had bought for a price. For he had lost his
130 ships, and whatever he had had been taken away by the forays of
pirates, and especially because he had fallen into the hands of the
people of Ajax Telamonius who had seized him and had taken away
whatever they found in his possession, and had intended to hang him
on the gallows. But Ulysses, by the quickness of his wits, had escaped
135 from these people's noose, although he was poor and destitute and
had no possessions. For although he had escaped from the hands of
the people of Ajax, and while he believed that he had been removed
safely from misfortune, he fell subsequently into the hands of King
Nauplius, who pursued Ulysses with an implacable hatred on account
140 of the death of his son Palamedes. The cleverness of Ulysses was very
great, and by it he escaped safely with his life from the hands of
King Nauplius. The present history does not reveal by what ingenuity
or by what subtle and clever argument Ulysses escaped capture by the
people of Ajax and from the hands of King Nauplius, but only that
145 from these causes he came poor and destitute to King Idomeneus.
King Idomeneus, however, wondered at the great poverty of Ulysses,
although he received him favorably, and sought to discover from him
his misfortunes and the circumstances of his disasters, and asked him
to report them to him in order and in detail. Ulysses willingly agreed,
150 and in order to satisfy the king's request, he reviewed the misfortunes which had befallen him and explained them in order in the
telling of his story.

He spoke thus about these things: "It is true, Lord King, that after
the capture of Troy, in which capture I undoubtedly took a great
155 part, I put out to sea with my ships loaded with much wealth from
the riches of Troy, including a great quantity of gold and silver and
with a company of many of my attendants, and voyaging prosperously for several days I first arrived safely at a port which is commonly called Ismara. There I disembarked with my men to refresh
160 ourselves and there I lingered out of danger for some days, since no
one offered to molest me and my men there. Then I departed from
this port, and with a favorable breeze caressing me, I arrived safely at
the port which is called Lotophagos, where likewise I lingered for
some days with my men. When the deceiving winds seemed to
165 promise favorable weather to me, I left the port and sailed with good

fortune for almost the next three days. Then unexpectedly a storm of
winds grew strong, and the sky from being clear suddenly became
dark, and buffeted me about in an uncertain voyage, now here, now
there, subject to the very great devastation of the storm. Finally the
170   storm forced me to turn aside very unwillingly toward Sicily, where I
suffered many troubles and hardships. For in Sicily there were two
brother kings, of whom one was called Laestrygon and the other
Cyclops. These two kings attacked me and my men. Seeing my ships
filled with such riches, they delivered them by violence to be looted,
175   and whatever they found in them they carried away from them with
a great number of their armed knights. And what was worse, in
addition, their two sons came, very valiant and exceedingly fierce
knights, of whom one was called Antiphates and the other Polyphemus.
They rushed upon my knights, killed a hundred of them, captured me
180   and Elpenor, one of my companions, and thrust him and me into
prison in a certain castle. This Polyphemus had a sister, a beautiful
young woman, and after Elpenor had seen her, he was enflamed with
desire for her, and, ensnared in her love, became completely dis-
tracted. Polyphemus held me captive in Sicily for six months. At last
185   he had pity on me and freed me and Elpenor. Afterward Polyphemus
bestowed on me many favors and honors. But Elpenor exerted himself so much in the vehemence of his love that during the night he
carried Polyphemus' sister, whom he loved, away from her father's
chamberlain, and took her with him. When this came to the notice of
190   her family, they were deeply distressed. On account of this, that
night Polyphemus again burst upon me and my men with a very great
company of knights, and when they had made the attack against my
men, Polyphemus' men recovered his sister. At last Polyphemus
rushed upon me, and while I was persisting in defending myself, I
195   struck out one of his eyes, and with my companions who remained
alive, I went back to my ships, and with them I left Sicily that night.
Then when I had followed a direct course, the wind forced me to the
island of Aulis, although I was unwilling.

"On this island there were two young women, who were sisters
200   and very beautiful, the rulers of this island, who were considered very
learned in the arts of necromancy and exorcising. These sisters so
strongly captivated whatever sailors fortune attracted to this island,
not so much by their beauty as by their magic enchantments, that

those who entered the island became forgetful of all other responsi-
205 bilities and had no hope of being able to leave it, to such an extent
that if the sisters found them rebellious to their commands, they at
once transformed them into beasts. One of these sisters, that is, the
one who was more learned in this knowledge, was named Circe, and
the other, Calypso. Fortune led me into the power of these two
210 sisters, one of whom, that is, Circe, almost crazed by love for me,
mixed her potions, and with the wiles of her enchantments charmed
me so that I did not have the ability to leave her for a whole year.
During that year Circe became pregnant and conceived a son by me,
and this son, whom she bore, grew and became an exceedingly fierce
215 hero. I took care, however, concerning the plan for my departure.
Circe clearly perceived this and was angry, and thought to detain me
by her magic arts. I, who was likewise very erudite in this art,
destroyed all her devices by contrary operations and made them
completely vain. Because art was thus deluded by art, my more
220 effective arts prevailed over the contrary contrivances of Circe so
much that I, with all the companions who were then with me, left
Circe in great distress.

"But what did that departure profit me? For when I had committed myself to the sea, the wind drove me to the land of Queen
225 Calypso, who so ensnared me and my men with her arts that she
detained me with her for more time than I would have wished. Still
my stay with her was not too tedious, on account of the beauty of
this queen, for which she was wondrously esteemed, and on account
of the gentle disposition which I found in her and with which she
230 attempted to please me and my followers. At length it happened that
by the exercise of my intelligence, I departed from her safely,
although with the greatest pains and difficulty, since my arts could
barely repel her arts.

"Then by sailing with my followers I arrived at another island, in
235 which an oracle was held sacred, which by the permission of divine
might gave true and certain answers to those who asked. I eagerly
asked this oracle many things, and among them I sought with deep
concern to know what happened to our souls after they had left our
bodies. I received certain answers to all that I asked of it then, except
240 to the part about souls, concerning which I could obtain from it no
certain response.

"When, therefore, I had left this oracle, blown upon, as I believed, by a favorable breeze, the wind compelled me to cross a certain place full of many hazards. I had arrived upon the sea where the Sirens,
245   who are very great sea monsters, roam the ocean. Above the waist they are of feminine shape with the faces of girls, but below the waist they have the appearance of fish. They reveal in singing marvelous voices of marvelous melodiousness, in such sweet tunefulness of chanting that you would think they surpassed the heavenly
250   harmony in the sounds of their music, so that miserable sailors, having reached them, are captivated by the great sweetness of their songs and lower the sails of the ships, let the oars rest on the sea, and refrain from sailing completely. This singing makes the minds of the miserable men so delirious that the miserable men hearing it are
255   divested of the troubles of all other responsibilities, and the sweetness of the sound soothes their ears so much that they straightway become as if forgetful of themselves and do not desire food or nourishment, while a certain drowsiness steals upon their minds, by which they are made to sleep soundly. When the Sirens perceive that they are asleep,
260   they at once overturn their ships, which lack the guidance of rudders, and sink them with a shipwreck, so that the sailors in them, because of their luckless sleep, are shipwrecked and drowned. I fell among these Sirens, and lest my companions be likewise overwhelmed with me in the error of sleep, by my arts I so firmly stopped their hearing
265   and mine that I and my companions, hearing nothing at all of their song, attacked them and killed more than a thousand of them, so that we could go across their place in safety, freed from the danger of them.

"Then during our sailing, an unlucky chance drove us between
270   Scylla and Charybdis, and since these perilous whirlpools extend for fifteen miles, I lost more than half my ships there in the devouring sea. On account of this, my companions sailing in them were shipwrecked and perished in the devouring sea.

"When I had pulled away from the midst of the devouring sea with
275   the other half of my ships, I arrived at Phoenicia by sailing, where I found a tyrant of a remarkable race, who, rushing upon me and my followers, killed the majority of my men with the sword, and only a few of them survived. The men of this nation took from me all the goods which I had with me then in the ships, seized me, and shut me

280 and those who remained with me in a grim dungeon. At length, the
gods willing, they freed me and those whom they had shut up with
me, but they did not restore any of my possessions. For this reason,
reduced to the most extreme poverty, I have circled the world and
have at last reached this land, poor and needy, as you see. Behold, I
285 have reported to you all my fortunes after I left Troy, and how I was
reduced to poverty." Thus Ulysses made an end of his report.

King Idomeneus, when he had heard Ulysses' words, had great
compassion for him, by reason of his nobility and his exertions, and
as long as it pleased Ulysses to stay in Crete, the king honored him
290 with a great abundance of goods. At last when it pleased Ulysses to
leave Crete, the king gave Ulysses two ships, well supplied with all
necessities, with which he could conveniently sail to his own kingdom. He also gave Ulysses many gifts, silver and gold, which would
be plenty for him until he should reach his own country. At Ulysses'
295 departure, however, Idomeneus asked him to go to King Antenor,
who desired very much to see him.

Ulysses, when he had taken leave of Idomeneus, embarked upon
his ships and went to King Antenor, who received him with great
pleasure and with a happy expression. Ulysses was very acceptable to
300 him on account of his great eloquence and the great quickness of his
wits. Then he reported to Ulysses certain rumors concerning his wife
Penelope, plagued by so many princes and preserving her honor
unharmed, and of certain others who had invaded his land and were
staying there boldly against the will of his wife. There his son,
305 Telemachus, having learned of his father's arrival, came to him and
confirmed by his report all the rumors which his father had learned.
For this reason Ulysses asked King Antenor to accompany him to his
kingdom with a company of his knights. Antenor freely agreed to this
and accompanied him with his knights.
310 When they had enjoyed a fortunate voyage, Ulysses took so much
precaution that they reached the city at night, and when the knights
had landed, he invaded the homes of the traitors at night, where he
killed all he found sleeping so that none of them escaped. With the
arrival of day in the clear brilliance of its splendor, he went to his
315 palace with King Antenor. There the king himself was welcomed with
great pleasure, and oh, how happy Penelope was made at the sight of
her lord, whom she had longed anxiously to see for such a long time!

The citizens rushed together and hastened with great joy to see their
king whom they had awaited for such a long time; they offered him
320 many gifts and exceedingly grand presents, and Ulysses was greatly
honored in his kingdom. He arranged with King Antenor that
Telemachus should take Nausicäa, the daughter of King Antenor, as a
wife. The nuptials of Telemachus were accordingly celebrated with
many joyful festivals. King Antenor returned happily to his kingdom,
325 and Ulysses rested at last in the glorious condition of his kingdom,
with exceeding peace and quiet.

*Here begins the thirty-fourth book, about Pyrrhus and his
death.*

Because up to this point the present history has said nothing about
Pyrrhus, the son of Achilles, after he left Troy, we now direct our
pen to the telling of his adventures. Pyrrhus on his father's side had
King Peleus for a grandfather, since from this Peleus and his wife,
5   Thetis, was begotten and born Achilles, the father of this Pyrrhus,
whom Achilles had begotten by Deidamia, the daughter of King
Lycomedes. Pyrrhus had two grandfathers, King Peleus on his father's
side and King Lycomedes on his noble mother's side. King Lycomedes
was the son of King Acastas, the great-grandfather of the aforesaid
10   Pyrrhus, still living then, although he was senile. Acastus held Pyrrhus
and all his father's family in hatred. The present history does not
relate the reason for his hatred. King Acastus, Pyrrhus' great-grandfather, expelled Peleus, Pyrrhus' grandfather, from the kingdom of
Thessaly, so that Acastus forced him to be exiled, and placed his
15   snares to murder Pyrrhus so that he would not escape his hands.
     Pyrrhus, however, after he had left Troy and subjected himself to
the hidden dangers of the sea, endured many perils on the sea and
cast into the sea the greater part of the things which he had carried
off with him, and with his ships almost dashed to pieces, he reached
20   Molossia, where he had his ships, which had been battered by the
stormy weather, reinforced by necessary repairs. There he also learned
how King Acastus, his great-grandfather, had cast King Peleus, his
grandfather, forth from the kingdom of Thessaly, and how he had
been devising plots against Pyrrhus. Pyrrhus grieved over such an

25 enormous loss to his grandfather but more over the loss to himself,
since King Lycomedes, the maternal grandfather of this Pyrrhus and
the son of King Acastus, had brought him up from his earliest years.
   Meanwhile, King Peleus, cast out of his kingdom by King Acastus,
could not safely appear in public, for fear of King Acastus and his
30 sons (since King Acastus had two other sons and a daughter named
Thetis; one of his sons was called Philistenes and the other Menalipus). Peleus accordingly made provision as to where he might hide
until Pyrrhus, his grandson, came back from Troy and could assist
him in his danger. For he knew that Pyrrhus would come back from
35 Troy over the sea with his ships. About eight miles from the city of
Thessaly there was an ancient building near the sea, and between the
city and this building there were woods to which the kings of
Thessaly used to come very often to hunt, since many wild animals
for hunting abounded in them. This ancient building had been com-
40 pletely deserted for a long time, since its situation was in a very
remote place, and none of the structure appeared above ground.
There were many caves in it hidden under ground, in which one
could hide safely, since the entrance to the way down, surrounded
and overgrown by many thorny thickets and wild cliffs, was
45 unknown. The way down from this entrance to the lower depths was
easy, that is, by steps built in it, although at the top of the opening
there was a pit hidden by the thickets, in the middle of which the
entrance had its opening. Peleus decided to hide in this building.
While he was hiding there, he often went out of it, and arriving at the
50 shore of the sea, scanned its surface with his glance to see if Pyrrhus
was coming back with his ships.
   Pyrrhus, after he had repaired his ships in Molossia, intended to
sail straight to Thessaly in order to take vengeance, if he could,
against King Acastus, his maternal great-grandfather, for the banish-
55 ment of Peleus, his paternal grandfather, and to protect himself from
Acastus if he could forestall him by the obstacle of an attack. So that
he might do cautiously what he intended, he took care to send two
attendants, that is, Crispus and Adastrus, clever spies, to Assandrus, a
citizen of Thessaly for a long time, who was loyal to Peleus and this
60 Pyrrhus, so that through him he might be informed about everything.
When they came to Thessaly, they were carefully instructed about
everything by Assandrus, and, returning swiftly to Pyrrhus, they

faithfully reported to him everything they had seen and what they
had learned from Assandrus' report. Pyrrhus at once embarked upon
65 his ships in order to set out for Thessaly. But when he thought to
have a successful voyage, a storm at sea rushed upon his ships and
lasted for almost three days. At last, by the favor of the gods, it
happened that he reached a certain port called Speliades with his
ships, although the fury of the winds had not yet subsided. This port,
70 however, was only eight miles distant from the city of Thessaly and
was near that ancient building where King Peleus was hiding. Pyrrhus,
wearied by the tiring voyage, landed, and while he hastened to go on
foot to the nearby woods, a miraculous chance of fortune led him to
the opening of the aforesaid entrance to the building mentioned
75 above. Being unable to see it because it was covered with overhanging
grass, he fell into it and placed his feet upon the highest and first
step of those steps by which one descended below, and while he was
looking at the steps, he wanted very much to see what was beneath.
Accordingly, when he arrived at the bottom of this place, behold,
80 King Peleus rushed forth from his hiding place, recognized his grandson, in whose appearance he thought he could see Achilles, since
Pyrrhus resembled his father very much in appearance. Peleus
embraced Pyrrhus affectionately, and mournfully and tearfully kissed
him. Finally he explained to him how he was imperilled by King
85 Acastus, keeping back his own cause for complaint. Pyrrhus grieved
but kept all things quietly in his mind. Grandfather and grandson
went up above, and Pyrrhus' retinue came to him. It was immediately
made known to Pyrrhus that Philistenes and Menalipus, the sons of
Acastus, had arrived in these woods in order to hunt. When he heard
90 this, Pyrrhus at once stripped off his clothes, and having obtained for
himself a certain old, dirty garment, torn in many parts, he put it on,
girded on a sword, and having taken leave of his companions,
hastened alone to the woods. Pyrrhus had not wandered far in the
woods when he met the sons of King Acastus, who asked Pyrrhus
95 from what place he might be, from what place he had come, why he
had come, and where he was going. Pyrrhus answered them that he
was from Greece and that he had wished to return from Troy to his
country with his companions in a certain ship. But such a great storm
at sea had arisen against them, that after many dangers and hardships,
100 they had suffered a shipwreck not far from the shore, so that five

hundred sailing in them lost their lives in this unexpected shipwreck. "Nevertheless, I alone escaped, whom the lofty waves have cast up on the shore half-dead. Almost drowned in their foam, while it crashed on the land and while it descended upon the surface of the land

105 along the shore, I reached shore by means of a swelling of the waves crashing along the land. There, after I had spit out much of the salt water I had swallowed from the sea, I was relieved in some degree and was at last almost fully restored to my former health after many distresses. Since I have lost in the shipwreck all that I had with me,

110 I have become poor and beg for my bread from door to door until I reach my own home. You, however, if you have not eaten and if you have brought anything to this wood to be eaten, kindly favor me with some of it." They said to him: "Stay with us." Meanwhile, a deer, wandering with slow steps, appeared before them, and Menalipus at

115 once separated himself from his brother to pursue it, leaving him alone with Pyrrhus. When Menalipus was very far from them, intent on pursuing the fleeing deer, Philistenes, his brother, dismounted from his horse in order to rest, and Pyrrhus immediately rushed upon him and killed him. Then when his brother Menalipus returned from

120 the pursuit of the deer, Pyrrhus rushed upon him with unsheathed sword and immediately slew him. Thus Pyrrhus cruelly killed his two uncles, the brothers of Thetis, his grandmother. When he was returning from slaughtering them, he met Cynaras, one of King Acastus' household. Pyrrhus asked him where Acastus was. He told him

125 Acastus was near. Pyrrhus at once cruelly gave Cynaras over to death with his unsheathed sword. He hurried quickly to the ships, where, in a serious frame of mind, he put on his handsome clothes, and, leaving the ships, went to meet King Acastus. He said to Pyrrhus: "Who are you?" Pyrrhus answered King Acastus thus: "I am one of King

130 Priam's sons who was taken into captivity by Lord Pyrrhus." When King Acastus, not knowing that he was Pyrrhus, said to him: "Where is Pyrrhus?" he said: "He has landed, very wearied by the tossing of the sea, and for the sake of rest has gone to that pit," which he pointed out to him with his extended right hand. At once Pyrrhus

135 drew out his sword and was about to kill Acastus. Then Thetis, the wife of King Peleus, immediately appeared to him there, she who was the daughter of King Acastus, the mother of Achilles, and the grandmother of Pyrrhus, and she said to him: "Dear grandson, what are

you about to do? Am I not your grandmother? Have you not bereft
140   me of my two brothers, your uncles, and do you now intend to
bereave me of King Acastus, who is my father and your great-
grandfather?" At once Thetis, by embracing him strongly, seized the
arm with which he was holding the sword in his hand, so that he
could not raise it for a blow against King Acastus. Pyrrhus said to
145   her: "King Acastus, your father, cast King Peleus, your husband, from
his kingdom. Did he not injure you in this? But let Peleus come, and
if he wishes to spare Acastus I will spare him." Peleus came and
asked Pyrrhus not to deliver King Acastus to death, since King
Acastus was afflicted enough by the death of his two sons, and his
150   life was worse to him than death. Hence peace and goodwill were
restored between Acastus and Peleus, who had disagreed with each
other for a long time. Then they all sat down, that is Thetis, King
Acastus, Peleus, and Pyrrhus, and began to negotiate concerning the
kingdom. King Acastus, who then had control of the kingdom as its
155   king, said to them: "I am broken down by excessive old age and
henceforth the duties of the kingdom are of little concern to me. I
have lost my sons who would have been able to have the rule of the
kingdom. Therefore, there is no one else upon whom the kingdom
should devolve by right except Pyrrhus, my dearest grandson, and
160   accordingly I strip myself of this kingdom and willingly grant it to
this Pyrrhus." He at once covered Pyrrhus with the fringe of his
garment. Peleus said to Acastus: "And I yield all right I have to it
and transfer it to him, because this has always been my greatest
desire and wish, that Pyrrhus should hold the scepter of the kingdom
165   of Thessaly." All arose from that place then, and mounted their
horses and arrived in Thessaly. For this reason Pyrrhus commanded
his ships to sail into Thessaly. When they had come to Thessaly, King
Acastus commanded all the people of Thessaly to take the oath of
loyalty and to pay homage to Pyrrhus. They were very happy about
170   the rule of Pyrrhus, and on account of this performed the oath to
Pyrrhus with great joy. On the following day King Acastus and Peleus
crowned Pyrrhus as king of the kingdom of Thessaly. Pyrrhus sat
upon the throne of his kingdom, crowned with the diadem. It
happened afterward that the kingdom of Thessaly was exalted above
175   all the other kingdoms of Greece thanks to King Pyrrhus, and King
Pyrrhus preserved it in the greatest peace until the extreme end of
his life.

When Idomeneus, king of Crete, died, two sons survived him, that is, Merion and Laertes. But Merion only lived a short time after the
180   death of his father, and died, and left the kingdom to Laertes, his brother, and was buried with the usual honors in Crete. To Telemachus, however, the son of Ulysses, and to Nausicäa, his wife, the daughter of King Antenor, was born a son named Deiphobus.

The story now returns to Pyrrhus, to tell of his adventures and
185   how and when Pyrrhus ended his last days. King Acastus, immoderately torn by grief at the death of his sons, commanded the bodies of his sons to be brought to Thessaly, and there they were buried, at the command of King Pyrrhus, in their very costly monuments. The fates, however, who, when they have placed men in the highest felicity,
190   prepare hidden snares by which they make them fall from the height of felicity into unexpected ruin, reveal to them these things which are pleasing but which will afterward produce ruinous injuries. When Pyrrhus had been given the highest rank in the kingdom, he was captivated by the desire of fervent love for Hermione, the daughter
195   of Helen and Menelaus and wife of Orestes. On account of this, endeavoring to satisfy his will, he abducted Hermione by stealth from Orestes, and by stealth brought her to the kingdom of Thessaly from Mycenae, once the kingdom of Agamemnon, in which Orestes was reigning. He joined her to him in matrimony. Orestes accordingly
200   grieved that such a disgrace should have happened to him, but he had not enough power to attack Pyrrhus in his kingdom. He kept silent and considered in his mind, however, the future events by which the means of vengeance would be fully prepared for him. And it happened that Pyrrhus decided to go to the island of Delphos to give
205   thanks to the god Apollo and to the other gods for the great victory accomplished by the dead Achilles, his father, against the cruelly slain Paris. On account of this, Pyrrhus prepared for the journey in his magnificence, and went to the island of Delphos, leaving in his palace along with his wife Hermione, Andromache, formerly the wife of
210   Hector, with hers and Hector's little son whose name was Laomedon, although she was pregnant by Pyrrhus. Hermione sent to Menelaus, her father, after the departure of Pyrrhus, saying that she was grievously injured by her husband Pyrrhus, who was madly in love with Andromache alone and cared little or nothing for her, and she
215   asked Menelaus to hasten to come to Thessaly and kill Andromache and her son Laomedon. Menelaus hastened to Thessaly at the words

of his daughter Hermione, where, having put aside all honor of his
noble rank, he rushed upon Andromache. But Andromache hastily
took her son Laomedon in her arms and having escaped by headlong
220 flight, went into the streets, where, crying out loudly, she tearfully
implored the aid of the people against Menelaus, so that the people
would not allow her to be killed with her little son. The people
rushed immediately to arms, and in an armed band looked for
Menelaus, so that Menelaus, stupefied by fear of the people, went
225 back to his own country. Orestes, however, hearing that Pyrrhus had
arrived at the island of Delphos, went there in a large company of
knights and attacked Pyrrhus in a powerful troop, and killed him
with his own hand. And Pyrrhus died, and was buried at once on that
island. Orestes, however, recovered his wife and took her back to his
230 kingdom. Peleus and Thetis, departing from Thessaly, took
Andromache who was pregnant by Pyrrhus, along with her son,
Laomedon, to the city of Molossia, where Andromache gave birth to
a son whom she had conceived by Pyrrhus, and whose name was
Achilleides. This Achilleides grew up and crowned his brother
235 Laomedon king of Thessaly, since he himself had renounced it,
although the kingdom rightly belonged to him, and he also desired
and commanded, on account of his love for his brother, that all the
Trojans who were captives in Greece should enjoy complete freedom.
      The history adds this besides. It was told in the twenty-fourth and
240 twenty-fifth books how Achilles, at the death of Troilus, tied the
body of Troilus to the tail of his horse and dragged it despicably
through the whole army, and how Memnon, in order to recover it,
manfully attacked and hurled Achilles from his horse and gave him a
deadly wound so that he was carried back to the camp half-dead, and
245 how Achilles killed him, when he had cut him off by his Myrmidons,
not by his military prowess but by treachery; and how afterward
King Priam had Memnon buried magnificently next to Troilus. Now
the present history tells that the aforesaid King Memnon had a sister
of wonderful beauty, who came openly before everyone to the
250 monument of Memnon, commanded it to be opened, and took the
bones of Memnon from it and deposited them in a golden vase for
preservation. She straightway vanished from the sight of those present, with the aforesaid vase, just like a shadow, so that she was never
afterward seen in that place. Some said she was a goddess or the
255 daughter of a goddess, or one of those whom people call fairies.

Here begins the last book, about the death of Ulysses.

The pen of the present history, omitting other matters for the present, is now sharpened to tell about the death of Ulysses. For this reason, it tells and narrates that Ulysses was sleeping one night in his bed, and while he slept he saw the following vision in his sleep. For it
5 seemed to him he saw an apparition of a handsome young man of such amazing beauty in appearance that the apparition did not appear to be human but rather divine, because of the exceeding beauty of its appearance. It also seemed to him that he desired exceedingly to be able to touch that apparition and to enfold it firmly in his
10 embrace, but that it avoided his embraces and seemed to him to gaze upon him from afar. Afterward it seemed to come nearer to him and asked Ulysses what he wanted. But he said: "I want us to come together so that I may perchance recognize you." Then the apparition said to Ulysses: "Oh, how painful and bitter is this request of yours!
15 For you ask me to join you. But oh, how unfortunate that union would be! For it is necessary that one of us die from such a union." Then it seemed to him that that apparition bore a lance in its hand, and on the up of this lance there seemed to be a turret ingeniously constructed of fishes. Then it seemed to him that the apparition
20 wished to leave him. It said to him: "This is the sign of the wicked separation which will be between us two in the future." Ulysses was then released from his sleep, and wondered greatly about the vision in his sleep; he inquired much in his mind as to what the dream meant. At last with the dawning of day he sought for soothsayers
25 and seers, and commanded them to come to him. When they had come and he had related the substance of his dream, they said that by the significance of the dream it was plainly prophesied that Ulysses would be delivered to exile or death by his son.
    For this reason, Ulysses in extreme terror had his son Telemachus
30 seized, and ordered him to be held in safe custody. He himself chose a place where he could stay without fear in the loyal company of some of his retainers. He walled this place with high strong walls, to which no one could have access except by a certain drawbridge. He also decided that no one could approach him unless he was one of
35 his retainers mentioned above.

It happened that Circe had long ago borne Ulysses a son, named Telegonus, whom no one except his mother Circe knew was Ulysses' son. Telegonus attained fifteen years of age and eagerly asked his mother whose son he was and if his father lived and where he stayed.

40 For a long time his mother refused to reassure him about his father. Finally, since Telegonus had tormented his mother so often with his inquiry about his father that she was wearied by his tormenting, she revealed and disclosed to her son that Ulysses was his father, and she carefully instructed him concerning the location of the kingdom

45 where Ulysses was staying. Telegonus was made very happy by his mother's report. Nevertheless, he was bursting with the sole and single desire to see his father, and he burned in his heart with the desire to go to him. And so, having taken leave of his mother, who asked him to return speedily, Telegonus prepared for the journey, and exerted

50 himself so much to make progress in his day's journeys that he reached Achaia, where he ascertained where the place was in which Ulysses was staying, and he went to that place. When he arrived there in the morning of a certain day of the moon, he found the guards of Ulysses at the entrance to the bridge, and he asked them gently if

55 they would allow him to go freely to Ulysses. They refused, wishing to observe the command of their lord. Telegonus stood before them with humble prayers, but they used their strength to repulse him and attacked him unjustly and violently. Hence Telegonus, since he did not wish to endure the injuries offered to him, rushed upon one of

60 the aforesaid guards, and having closed in combat with him, struck him so powerfully on the vertebrae of the neck that since his neck vertebrae were shattered, he breathed his last at once. By manfully attacking the other guards, this one's companions, Telegonus cast them from the bridge and hurled them headlong into the moat. The

65 uproar became very great. Hence many, rushing to arms, rushed upon Telegonus, exerting themselves to kill him. But Telegonus, having made an attack against one of them who had approached him, violently snatched from him the sword which he had in his hand, and rushing upon the others, killed fifteen of them with his naked sword

70 and was himself seriously wounded by them. When the uproar grew louder, Ulysses rose at the sound of the uproar, thinking that some-one of the household of Telemachus, who was being detained by Ulysses' attendants, had attacked them, to kill or wound them in

order to free Telemachus. Hence he was angry and hurried with a
75 spear which he carried in his hand to the place of the uproar, where
he saw his men killed by this young man who was unknown to him.
He saw him, and to avenge the murder of the slain men, hurled his
spear at him so that he struck him. And yet he did not hurt him
much with it. Telegonus, however, since he did not know that the
80 man was Ulysses, seized the spear which Ulysses had hurled against
him and which had fallen to the ground, and returned it with a more
severe attack against Ulysses, who had impetuously hurled the spear,
so that Telegonus mortally wounded him, piercing his ribs by this
wound. For this reason Ulysses fell to the ground, wounded by this
85 blow, being unable to hold himself upright, like one who feels that
death is near. His bodily strength failed in him, and since he had
almost lost his speech, in babbling words he inquired who Telegonus
was. While Ulysses was recalling to his memory the fatal vision of his
dream, Telegonus, at the question of Ulysses, inquired of those in
90 attendance who it was who asked about him. They told him it was
Ulysses. When he heard this, Telegonus exclaimed in anguish, saying:
"Woe is me! I came to see my father so that I might enjoy living
with him, and now I have become the cause of his death." And at
once because of excessive grief, he fell to the ground as if half dead.
95 At last, rising from the ground, with torn garments, since he was
unarmed, he struck his face with his fists and tore his blond hair
from his head. He turned to fall at the feet of Ulysses, and said with
sobs and tears that he was Telegonus, the unfortunate son of Circe,
"whom you, Ulysses, my father, unfortunately begot by her. If you
100 die, dear father, may the gods grant that I die with you and not
allow me to live after you." Ulysses recognized him as his son by
Circe, soothed him in the very great weakness of body in which he
was, and commanded him with broken words to refrain from tears
and grief. He sent for his son Telemachus, and he, when he came,
105 sought to rush upon Telegonus, as if he were eager to avenge his
father's murder. But Ulysses by such words and gestures as he could
restrained Telemachus so that he would not attack him, but on the
contrary would hold him dear as his brother. Ulysses was brought to
Achaia almost dead, where he lived for only three days and died after
110 the third, and was buried with royal honors in Achaia.
After his death, Telemachus took over his father's kingdom as

king. He cherished Telegonus, his brother, with much honor, kept
him with him for a year and a half, and made him a knight with very
great honor. He wished him to stay longer, but Telegonus, requested
115 by letters from his mother, unwillingly left his brother, in order to
please his mother. At his departure, Telemachus honored him with
presents and gifts and all the things which would contribute to the
magnificence of his return journey. Telegonus accordingly departed
from his brother Telemachus, and each of them shed many tears.
120 After his departure, he safely reached his mother on the island of
Aulis. His mother was overjoyed at his return and arrival, since she
was concerned about her son on account of the great dangers from
the fates which had turned out to be so unpropitious, as she had
foreseen by her art. Not many days afterward, Circe became mortally
125 ill. Violently overwhelmed by this illness, she finished her last day.
Telegonus accordingly was received as king and lived happily in his
kingdom for sixty years. Telemachus reigned in Achaia seventy years,
and the kingdom of Achaia expanded very much under his very
strong government. Ulysses, on the other hand, had lived ninety-three
130 years and died happily in his kingdom.
    In this place Dares brought the work at hand to an end, and so
did Cornelius. The rest accordingly is from the book of Dictys. It
may be allowed that Dares the Trojan will have brought his work to
an end with the capture of Troy, and did not afterward proceed
135 further in his book; the rest, up to the end, is from the book of
Dictys, who wished to make Dares' work complete. If, therefore,
anything is found to be added to this work, it is to be believed that
it is not from the truth of the work but rather from the fiction of
the work.
140 Nevertheless, Dares and Dictys, who were present in the war at the
time of the Trojan War, are found to agree for the most part in the
material of their works and are found to disagree in few things. They
both agree that Antenor and Aeneas were the agents in the betrayal
of Troy. However, Dares said that Polydamas, the son of Antenor,
145 went to the Greeks at night, and he negotiated that night with the
Greeks concerning the method of the capture of the city, so that he
provided that they could come to Ilium at a signal given by him.
Dares also said that the Greeks entered Troy at night, and said that

150 they did not enter through the walls broken by the arrival of the
bronze horse made by the Greeks, since he made no mention of
this horse, but he said they entered through the Scaean Gate, one
of the gates of the city of Troy. On the top of this gate a certain
marble horse's head was constructed and placed, although Virgil
agrees with Dictys about the bronze horse. Dares said that Antenor
155 and Aeneas with Polydamas welcomed the Greeks at this gate, and
furthermore afterward granted entrance to them, and through them
great Ilium was captured that night, and Neoptolemus, son of
Nestor, was first brought into it. Dares said also that Aeneas hid
not only Polyxena but also her mother, Hecuba, with her, and for
160 this reason he was condemned to exile. He said nothing of the death
of Hecuba.

At the end of this work, however, he added this: the war was
fought ten years, six months, and twelve days; that eight hundred and
six thousand warriors came from Greece to Troy; there were six
165 hundred and seventy-six thousand Trojan warriors who fought to
defend the city. He said also that Aeneas was exiled with two
hundred ships, and that Paris had gone to Greece with them. Twenty-
five hundred Trojans followed Antenor. The rest followed Aeneas.
The Greek and Trojan officers on both sides, and who were killed
170 and by whom, are these, as this same Dares wrote: Hector killed King
Archilogus, King Protesilaus, King Humerus, King Patroclus, King
Ortomenus, King Pallamon, King Pheypus, King Prothenor, King
Dorius, King Xantipus, King Leontus, King Merion, King Polixenus,
King Pollibetes, King Cedius, King Fannus, King Epistrophus, and
175 King Alpinor. Paris killed King Palamedes, King Antilochus, Achilles,
and Ajax. Ajax killed this Paris, since both died from the wounds
each gave the other. Aeneas killed King Amphimacus and King
Nereus. Achilles killed King Euphenius, King Ligonius, Troilus, King
Iponeum, King Euforbius, King Memnon, King Austerus, King
180 Plebeus, Hector, and King Neptholonus. Pyrrhus killed Penthesilea,
King Priam, and his daughter Polyxena. Diomedes killed King
Antiphus, King Esterion, King Prothenor, and King Optonemus.

These are the epitaphs of Hector and Achilles.

This is Hector's and the first verse would have been sufficient since
185 it is very brief and includes everything. It goes thus:

Epitaph of Hector

Here lies Hector, protector of the Trojans, fear of the Danäi,
Hector, the bravest of youths, the defender of his country. He was a
second wall for his wretched fellow citizens. He died, conquered by
190   the impetuous spear of Achilles, and at the same time the hope and
security of Phrygia died. The savage Aeacides dragged him around his
walls, which the youth had protected with his hands. Oh, what sorrows that day brought to Priam! What tears it gave to Hecuba, what
tears to Andromache! But the unhappy father buried him, stolen
195   away and ransomed by gold, and weeping, piled up the earth.

Epitaph of Achilles

I am the very renowned offspring of Peleus and Thetis, whose
courage has allowed him to have a famous name. Many times I have
laid the enemy low with victorious arms, and I alone put many thou-
200   sands to flight. But my greatest glory was the slaughter of great
Hector, who had often depleted the Argolian riches. When he was
slain, he paid the price and I was avenged. Pergama then fell by my
sword. I shall be borne above the stars with great praise, although,
killed by deception, I fell on hostile ground.

205   However, I, Guido delle Colonne, have followed the aforesaid
Dictys the Greek in all things, because this Dictys made his work
perfect and complete in everything for the pleasure of the learned, so
that they might have true knowledge of the present history and might
take more delight in it. And I would have decorated this history with
210   a more beautiful style by means of richer metaphors and figures of
speech and through occasional digressions, which are the artistry of
this style; but frightened by the magnitude of the task, lest I prolong
this work by a long narration on the pretext of a more decorated
style, and during this long period something untoward would happen
215   to me, in accordance with human weakness or change of purpose, on
account of which I would have desisted from the work and the work
would not come to an end, and would lack the advantage of being
complete . . . . I persisted so much that, with the gracious favor of
the Holy Ghost, I finished and completed this work in its entirety
220   within three months, that is, from the fifteenth of September of the

first indiction until the twenty-fifth of the following November,
although long before, at the insistence of Lord Matteo da Porta, the
venerable archbishop of Salerno, a man of great learning, I had composed the whole first book of the present work, and no more. For
225   after the removal from our midst of him who was the stimulus and
impetus for me to take up the present work, I ceased to carry it out,
since there was no one whom I might worthily please with it. I considered, however, the failure of the great authors, Virgil, Ovid, and
Homer, who were very deficient in describing the truth about the fall
230   of Troy, although they composed their works in an exceedingly
glorious style, whether they treated them according to the stories of
the ancients or according to fables, and especially that highest of
poets, Virgil, whom nothing obscures. And lest the truth remain
unknown, I have labored for the effective completion of this present
235   work.

      The present work was happily completed in the year of the
Incarnation of Our Lord 1287, in this same first indiction. Here ends
the Book of The Fall of Troy. Thanks be to God!

NOTES

Works frequently cited are referred to by an abbreviated form of the author's name or, occasionally, by title and can be found in the bibliography following the notes. Page references to Griffin's edition of Guido are in parentheses; page references to this translation are in square brackets. The number or numbers at the beginning of each entry in the Notes refer to lines in the translation.

Prologue

10 valiant. For "strenuis," d. pl. of *strenuus,* literally "active" or "vigorous." However, Guido uses this word, along with the noun *strenuitas,* over and over again, either as stock attributes, or to translate Benoit's *pro* or *hardi,* or the noun *valor.*

17 transcribed. For "transsumpserunt," 3rd pl., perf. indic. of *transsumere,* which Griffin glosses as "transformed," but this does not seem to fit the next use of the word. See note to *Prologue,* line 44.

38-40 read Latin . . . books written in Latin. For "grammaticam legunt . . . in libris grammaticalis." Even in classical times, "grammar" meant philology or the study of language as well as grammar proper; in the Middle Ages, the term came to mean the literary language, Latin, as opposed to the vernacular. See Lewis and Short, s.v. *grammaticus;* and Niermeyer, s.v. *grammatica.*

40 [were related]. Constans (VI:326), in discussing this passage, inserted "[*narrata sunt?*]" and remarked in a footnote that the words were lacking in the version of the *Historia* he was using. Since Griffin does not list them among the variants, we have to assume that they were not part of the original and that this is one of the many incomplete sentences the work contains. Unless some such verb is supplied, "ea que" [the things which] lacks a predicate.

44 transcribed. For "transsumpta," p. part. of *transsumere,* agreeing with "ea" [those things]. For *transsumere,* Du Cange gives "transcribere" [transcribe] and Niermeyer, "to copy." See introduction, pp. xviii-xix.

46 an agreement as with one voice. See introduction, p. xviii.

47 Cornelius. See introduction, pp. xii and xix.

57-58 Magna Graecia . . . Italy . . . Romania. As can be seen by his statement at the beginning of Book I, Guido must mean that Greece is called Romania and Italy is called Magna Graecia, but the phrase "quam apellamus hodie Romaniam" (p. 5) is separated by three lines of text from "Greciam" and follows directly upon "id est Ytaliam." Of course "quam" can just as well agree with "Greciam" as with "Ytaliam," but the arrangement of the sentence works against this. In his *Troy Book,* Lydgate, while disparaging Cornelius and preparing to eulogize Guido, says that among the things Cornelius omitted was the fact

> . . . þat Grece is called Gret Ytaille,
> and the lass, as bokys verrefye,
> Is named now the londe of Romanye.

> Prologue, 334-36

As indicated in Griffin's index of proper names, Romania designates the Eastern Empire. Guido applies the term only to Greece and the Greek islands, which were, of course, part of the Eastern Empire, and this is consistent with contemporary usage. See R. L. Wolff, "Romania: The Latin Empire of Constantinople," *Speculum* XXII (January 1948): 1-34. Wolff points out that "though the word Romania [to mean the Eastern Empire] was known to the chroniclers and historians of South Italy, it was by no means standard usage until after the Fourth Crusade, when the Latin conquest and foundation of the Latin Empire—*Romania* par excellence—gave the term so great a vogue" (p. 21). Guido prides himself on his knowledge of the correct technical term (cf. his discussion of the constellations used in navigation [*Book One,* lines 206-12] and his list of the craftsmen to be found in Troy [*Book Five,* lines 158-69]), and his stating that "today" Greece is called Romania suggests that he is aware of the novelty of the expression.

On the other hand, Guido's lack of comment about the term Magna Graecia shows that the classical designation for the ancient Greek colonies in Sicily and on the Italian peninsula was still current in the Middle Ages. Sicily had been under the control of Byzantium until the Arab conquest in the ninth century, and even in Guido's day there were Greek-speaking communities, so that a Greek version of the statutes of Frederick II had to be prepared, and the governor of Messina had the Greek title of *strategoto*. Frederick II, however, identified himself with Rome; he had the titles Caesar and Augustus and reduced the authority of the Byzantine church. See Denis Mack Smith, *A History of Sicily*. 2 vols. *I: Medieval Sicily, 800-1713* (London: Chatto and Windus, 1968), pp. 53-60.

Since Guido had probably been a member of Frederick's court and held a judgeship which was the result of Frederick's reform of the legal system along Roman lines, it is not surprising to find him attempting to dissociate Sicily from Greece. Moreover, there apparently was some sort of tradition, based on the designation "Magna Graecia," that Italy was the Greece that fought against Troy. Not only does the author of the *Prose Roman* claim that Greece included mainland Greece and the islands, the lands around the Black Sea, Sicily, Calabria, Apulia, and Maremma, and locate Peleus' city in Italy, but Guido himself mentions the theory that Peleus may have come from Abruzzi, and in talking about the Greeks' supply base at Mysia ("Messa"), states that "Messa" may be Messina since it is known that Sicily had once been subject to Greece. Guido is not convinced that this was at the time of the Trojan War, but as a careful historian, he gives the opposing views.

Book One

1 **the aforesaid Romania.** As mentioned in the preceding note, this statement that Thessaly is one of the provinces of Romania indicates that Guido uses the term "Romania" to designate Greece, not Italy.

2 **Thessaly.** Benoit states that Peleus and Aeson lived in Penelope (for Dares' Peloponnese). As Constans points out (VI:236), Benoit might have known the story of Jason and Medea as given in *Metamorphoses* VII and *Heroides* XII; Guido follows Benoit for the most part, but it is clear that he also knows the Ovidian material, since he adds details taken directly from it. Since Ovid calls Jason "Thessalian," Guido rightly concluded that Jason came from Thessaly.

4 **Peleus.** As Griffin points out in his index, both Benoit and Guido

have made one character of Dares' Pelias, uncle of Jason, and Dares' Peleus, who fought with the Greeks at the first destruction of Troy.

10-11 **the city of Thetis.** Thetis is probably Chieti, an important city in Abruzzi, which in ancient times was called Teate or Theate Maruccinorum. The association of the city with Thetis is probably accounted for by the spelling, since, unlike cities in southern Italy which have Greek gods or heroes for their patrons, Chieti was outside the region settled by the Greeks. In the same way, the author of the *Prose Roman* thought that the ancient designation for Naples was "Penelope" (p. 5), not Parthenopolis, and he associated this with the "Penelope" Benoit gave as Peleus' city. Of course, as will be seen later in the catalogues of the Greek and Trojan allies, there was a good deal of confusion in the transmission of proper names, and in many cases a writer with some vague knowledge of classical figures may have put down a form that was familiar to him without really knowing whether it was a person or a place.

16-25 **Ovid's account of the Myrmidons.** Benoit does not mention the Myrmidons, and Guido is here following *Met.* VII:614-60. Ovid's ". . . adspeximus agmine longo/grande onus exiguo formicas ore gerentes" (624-25) ["we spied . . . ants in a long column bearing heavy loads with their tiny mouths"—Loeb] probably inspired Guido's "innumerabilium formicarum discurrentibus aciebus" (p. 5), since as a military term *agmen* is practically synonymous with *acies.* The passage follows Ovid's story of Jason and Medea which Guido was consulting to augment what he found in Benoit.

25 **the legend of the blessed Matthew.** Since Guido, as he tells us in his epilogue, wrote this first book at the suggestion of Matteo da Porta, archbishop of Salerno, he may very well have had access to the archbishop's library which undoubtedly contained all sorts of saints' legends, the legend of Saint Matthew being an obvious one for him to have had. The reference to the Myrmidons and Thessaly indicates that this legend is that found in a Latin version of the apocryphal *Acts of Andrew and Matthew in the City of the Anthropophagi.* The Latin differs from the earlier Greek in making the companion of Andrew Matthew, not Matthias, and in giving the place of their missionary activities as Mirmidonia, to which Andrew comes from Achaia. This Achaia was originally not that in Greece but the one in Scythia; however, in later versions of the story, the more familiar Greece replaced Scythia. See George Philip Krapp, ed.,

Andreas and the Fates of the Apostles (Boston: Ginn and Company, 1906), pp. xxvii-xxix, lxi-lxvii.

31 **govern himself.** For "seipsum . . . regere"; the real force of this is that Aeson could hardly govern himself, let alone the whole kingdom, with perhaps a play on the idea that he has lost almost all control of his faculties.

31-33 **Aeson's resigning** the government of Thessaly because of extreme old age would seem to be Guido's invention, suggested, perhaps, by the account in *Met.* VII:159 ff. of Medea's restoring Aeson's youth. See 37-40.

38 **young man.** Griffin's text has "anniculus" [yearling] but "juvenis" [young man] is listed among the variants. Guido may have written *anniculus* or *agniculus* [lambkin], recalling the episode in which Medea changes a ram into a lamb in order to demonstrate her powers of rejuvenation and trick the daughters of Pelias into killing him (*Met.* VII: 297ff.).

62 **tattling rumor.** For "loquax fama," another Ovidian echo—a stock epithet, in fact. Cf. *Met.* IX:37, ". . . cum Fama loquax processit ad aures . . . tuas" ["when tattling Rumor came on ahead to your ears"—Loeb]. See also notes to *Book Seven,* line 101 and *Book Eight,* line 3.

77 **poison-breathing serpent.** For "quendam draconem squamis orridum." Cf. "ecce draco squamis crepitantibus orrens" (*Her.* XII:101, variant reading) ["behold! . . . all a-bristle with rattling scales"—Loeb]. In Ovid, both in *Met.* VII and *Her.* XII, the dragon's teeth which Jason sows are given him by Aeëtes, and he does not fight the dragon but lulls it to sleep. Guido follows Benoit, who may have been thinking of the fire-breathing dragon and the warriors produced from its teeth in the Cadmus story (*Met.* III:1-139), but Guido uses the lines from Ovid at appropriate places in his paraphrase of Benoit.

83-85 **fraternal combat . . . reciprocal wounds.** For "fraternum bellum inter se committentes, qui se per mutua vulnera perimebant." Cf. *Met.* VII:141: "terrigenae pereunt per mutua vulnera fratres" ["the earthborn brothers perished by each other's wounds"—Loeb].

91 **great mass of treasure.** For "cumulum thesauri magni." The translation uses the variant reading which gives "magnum" for the text's "magni."

93 **magical practices.** For "artes mathematicas," Griffin's gloss.

105-6 **proclaim . . . widely acclaimed.** For "in celebriori ciuitate

Thesalie solempnem curiam celebrare . . . ," literally "in the acclaimed (or celebrated) dominion of Thessaly to proclaim (or celebrate) a solemn assembly." Guido is fond of verbal echoes, as can be seen in the repetitions of "glory" and "glorious" in Peleus' speech to Jason, *Book One,* 110ff.

158-82 **certain persons . . . "Argo."** Cf. Benoit, 913-917. See also Du Cange, s.v. *Argis:* "Navis sic dicta ab *Argo* qua Jason Colchidem navigat" [a ship so called from the *Argo* in which Jason sailed to Colchis], which may indicate that the term was fairly current.

167-84 **Exploits of Hercules.** Benoit (805-10) simply says that Hercules had suffered a great deal, done many marvelous deeds, killed many a "felon," and set up the boundaries where Alexander found them. The story of Hercules was so well-known in the Middle Ages that Guido would not have needed a specific source for the details he adds; it is interesting, however, that these details are given in the same order as in *Met.* IX:182-85, the beginning of Hercules' speech summarizing his labors.

178 **poisons.** For "acchonitis," literally, "aconite plants," as in *Met.* VII:404-19, when Medea uses aconite in preparing the poison with which to kill Theseus; and Ovid tells the story of the origin of the aconite plant from the flecks of foam scattered about by Cerberus when Hercules dragged him away from Hades. According to Lewis and Short, s.v. *aconitum,* the word was used to denote any strong poison, and Guido uses it to describe the poisonous breath of the dragon that Jason killed.

183 **Pillars of Hercules at Gades.** In classical mythology, the mountains of Calpe and Abyla on either side of the Straits of Gibralter were called the Pillars of Hercules, because Hercules was supposed to have created them; but the term had very early come to refer to some actual pillars, the ruins of a temple to Hercules on the island of Gades off the western shore of Spain, at what is now Cadiz. In both cases, the pillars were held to mark the boundaries of the known world.

184 **Alexander.** Suggested by Benoit's statement that Hercules ". . . les bones iluec ficha/Ou Alixandre les trova" (809-10). In the medieval Alexander romances, Alexander reaches the boundaries of the Eastern world in India, and there finds the Pillars of Hercules, actually statues to Hercules and Dionysos. Despite the popularity of this story (in addition to the tenth century version of the Archpriest Leo's *Historia de Preliis,* there were apparently several French versions in existence at the time Benoit was writing), Guido does not seem to have known it. He does know, however,

that the boundaries of the world are marked by the Pillars of Hercules and he may even have known Quintus Curtius' *History of Alexander,* in which Alexander plans that after subduing the East, he will go across Africa and then "direct his course to Gades—for the report had spread abroad that the pillars of Hercules were there—then to visit Spain . . . and . . . Italy" (xii: 17-19—Loeb). The rest of Guido's statement about him is sufficiently general to be a recollection of what was common knowledge about a famous historical figure. See George Cary, *The Medieval Alexander,* edited by D. J. A. Ross (Cambridge: Cambridge University Press, 1956, reissued 1967), pp. 27, 29-31, 38, 43-44, 71-74.

196 **Strait of Seville or Sebta.** For "strictum Sibilie . . . siue Secte," with variant readings of "Sibille" or "Sibile" and "Secce" or "Setta." This is, of course, the Strait of Gibraltar, here identified by the principle Spanish and Moroccan cities on either side, Sebta being the Arabic name for Ceuta, a town now held by Spain on the coast of Morocco opposite Gibraltar. According to Moore (p. 123), Dante uses the terms Strait of Seville or Strait of Spain as well as Strait of Morocco, and Guido's usage is similar if he means that the strait is called both the Strait of Seville and the Strait of Sebta. It is more likely, however, in view of his apparent confusion of the Moroccan town of Safi with Cadiz, that he thinks that Sebta is the Arabic name for Seville. Isidore of Seville says the town of "Septe" overlooks the Strait of Gades, and that its name is derived from the fact that it is located on seven mountains ("montibus septem," *Etym.* XV:73).

198 **Safi.** For "Saphy." Griffin's gloss: ". . . possibly connected with *Safi,* the Moorish city in Morocco. . . . Guido applies the name to Cadiz." Safi is located on the Atlantic coast of Morocco, at about the same distance from Sebta (Ceuta) as Cadiz is from Seville.

209 **North Star.** For "stellam . . . Tramontanam." According to Du Cange, s.v., "Tramontana" is an Italian name for the north wind, since a wind from across the mountains, *(trans montana),* would be, from the Italian point of view, a north wind. The word is thus applied to the North Star, as in the commentary on the *Sphere* of Sacrobosco by Cecco d'Ascoli in a passage discussing the North Star and the Septentriones (Lynn Thorndike, *The "Sphere" of Sacrobosco and Its Commentators* (Chicago: University of Chicago Press [1949]), p. 363).

211 **sailors . . . name the Big Bear the Greek.** The source of this is Isidore of Seville, who, in talking about the stars used in navigation says

of Arctos: "nomen est Graecum, quod Latine dicitur ursa. . . ." [the name is Greek and means "bear" in Latin] (*Etym.* III:71:6). Guido, however, read this as, "the name is 'the Greek,' which is called 'the bear' in Latin."

212 **the Dragon is the master** . . . For "Anguem dicunt esse magistrum." As Griffin's punctuation indicates, this is an incomplete sentence, and hence it is impossible to tell whether Guido meant to suggest that "master" is another name for the constellation or even if "master" is the sense he intended. Lewis and Short, s.v. *magister* give "pilot" as one of the meanings, and Guido may be commenting on the use of the constellation in navigation.

216 **"You see . . . new constellations . . ."** This is a quotation from *Met.* II:515-17 and 527-28, the Loeb translation, although for the first line, "Nuper honoratas summa, mea vulnera, celo," Guido substituted *viscera* [inner organs] for *vulnera* [wounds]. The idea is roughly the same and both require a figurative translation.

222 **Simois.** For "Simeonta." Griffin's gloss: "river *Simois* (made a port by Dares, Benoit, and Guido)."

Book Two

24-43 **The settling of Europe by the Trojan exiles.** This idea was such a commonplace in the Middle Ages that perhaps one need not look for a direct source for Guido's version. Some of the details, however, are so similar to what Otto of Freising has to say on the same subject that it is tempting to think that Guido is here following, if not Otto himself, at least one of his derivatives.

In chapter 25 of Book I of *The Two Cities,* Otto disposes of the rape of Helen and the fall of Troy in five lines and then goes on to say "that in consequence of this all the race of Romans had its origin from Aeneas . . ." (Mierow, p. 14). Otto next describes the origin of the Franks, in far greater detail than does Guido, including the fact that the country was named for Francus, and continues with the settling of Venice by Antenor. Chapter 26 begins with the lament, "But such great disasters pursued the victors that in connection with so pitiful a revolution of fortune there is room for doubt as to which side succumbed to an evil fate" (Mierow, p. 145), which precedes the comments on the wanderings of Ulysses and the settling of Apulia by Diomedes, with the story of the Diomedian birds.

It is true that, as Guido himself says, the story of the Diomedian birds is to be found in Isidore (*Etym.* XII:7.28-29) as well as in Ovid (*Met.* XIV:483-511), in which it is Venus, not Circe, who turns the men into birds. While Isidore is also a likely source for the story of the founding of Sicily by Sicanus and Siculus, and France by Francus (cf. *Etym.* IX:2:85, 101, 102), as Gorra noted (p. 137), still the details are different, and it is typical of Guido to embellish one source, say Otto, with another, in this case Isidore, especially when the embellishment has to do with Sicilian history.

Neither Otto nor Isidore gives this version of the founding of Britain, which originated with Geoffrey of Monmouth, and it would be amusing if Guido's knowledge of it may lend support to the tradition that he had gone to England in the retinue of Edward I. See Gorra, pp. 102-3, and E. Faral, *La Légende Arthurienne* (Paris: 1929), I:170-82.

28 **Julius.** In the *Aeneid* and the *Metamorphoses* the name is Iulus and he is Aeneas' grandson. See Lewis and Short, s.vv. *Iulus* and *Julius*.

182 **the knowledge of that jewel.** For "eius margarite scientia." Du Cange, s.v. *margarita scientiae,* literally "pearl of science," glosses the phrase as a term for philosophy, and Griffin lists this construction among the variants. If this is the correct reading, the phrase would have to be translated as "the pearl of knowledge by reason of which she was the more distinguished." Since Du Cange gives only one instance of the phrase, it may be only coincidence that Guido uses the two words in conjunction; on the other hand, he may have learned it as an elegant rhetorical expression, and this is also true if he means "margarita" to apply to Medea. This latter interpretation is concurred in by the author of the Middle English *Gest Hystoriale,* an alliterative poem based on Guido, in which the following lines occur at this point:

> þere was no filosofers so fyn found in þat lond,
> Might approche to þat precious apoint of her wit.

(400-401)

The words "þat precious" obviously translate *eius margarite,* as "wit" translates *scientia.*

183 **art of magic.** For "ars mathematica." See note to *Book One,* line 93.

185-90 **Medea's magic.** This is based on Benoit (1217-27) who was probably inspired by the passage in the *Metamorphoses* in which Medea, praying to Night, Hecate, and Earth, acknowledges the help of these divinities in doing these things, while asking them to help her restore Aeson's youth. Guido has already referred to this episode [*Book One,* lines 36-40], and here he adds to Benoit's rather brief account the details of the storms, earthquakes, and, especially, eclipses (*Met.* VII:192-208).

194-226 **Digression on eclipses.** While the curious term "fifteener" *(quintamdeciam)* is from Isidore of Seville, and the reference to Dionysius the Areopagite seems to show some knowledge of Dionysius' Epistle to Polycarp, it has been pointed out by Wigginton (p. 91) that this passage has many details which appear to come from the last chapter of a thirteenth century textbook of astronomy, the *Sphere* of Iohannes de Sacrobosco, which in at least one manuscript was attributed to Ptolemy. For purposes of comparison and a clearer picture of Guido's method of using his sources, here follow the relevant portions as translated in Thorndike, pp. 113-17 and 140-42:

> It should be noted that the sun has a single circle in which it is moved in the plane of the ecliptic, and it is eccentric . . . .
>
> Every planet except the sun has three circles, namely equant, deferent, and epicycle. The equant of the moon is a circle concentric with the earth and in the plane of the ecliptic. Its deferent is an eccentric circle not in the plane of the ecliptic—nay, one half of it slants toward the north and the other toward the south—and the deferent intersects the equant in two places, and the figure of that intersection is called the "dragon" because it is wide in the middle and narrow toward the ends. That intersection, then, through which the moon is moved from south to north is called the "head of the dragon," while the other intersection through which it is moved from north to south is called the "tail of the dragon." . . .
>
> . . . But, since in every opposition—that is, at full moon—the moon is not in the head or tail of the dragon or beneath the nadir of the sun, it is not necessary that the moon suffer eclipse at every full moon.
>
> When the moon is in the head or tail of the dragon or nearly within the limits and in conjunction with the sun, then the body of the moon is interposed between our sight and the body of the sun. Hence it will obscure the brightness of the sun for us, and so the sun will suffer eclipse—not that it ceases to shine but that it fails us because of the

interposition of the moon between our sight and the sun. From these
it is clear that a solar eclipse should always occur at the time of
conjunction or new moon. . . .

From the aforesaid it is also evident that, when the sun was
eclipsed during the Passion and the same Passion occurred at full moon,
that eclipse was not natural—nay, it was miraculous and contrary to
nature, since a solar eclipse ought to occur at new moon or there-
abouts. On which account Dionysius the Areopagite is reported to have
said during the same Passion, "Either the God of nature suffers, or the
mechanism of the universe is dissolved."

205-6 **seven successive signs . . . "fifteener."** In *Etym.* III:54, Isidore
lists the seven forms the moon takes in waxing and waning—bicorn, half,
etc.—and comments that the half-moon comes seventh and twenty-second
in the moon's cycle, from which it can be deduced that the full moon is
the fifteenth form, and in III:59, he says that it is the "quinta decima
luna" [fifteenth moon] that suffers eclipse, hence Guido's use of the
term "quinta decimam lunam" for the full moon.

221 **Dionysius.** Dionysius' remark, which is given as translated in
Thorndike, is in fact a Byzantine emendation to the account of the
Crucifixion in Dionysius' Epistle to Polycarp; actually it was his companion, the sophist Apollophanus, who, when Dionysius expressed wonder
at the darkness, said that the eclipse indicated disturbances among the
gods. See Maurice de Candillac, *Oeuvres Complètes du Pseudo-Denys
L'Aréopagite* (Paris: Aubier, 1943), pp. 1-11, and especially p. 11, n. 6;
and S. Dionysius Areopagiticum, "Polycarpo summo sacerdoto." *Epistolae
Diversae,* VII, J. P. Migne, ed. *Patrologia Latina* (Paris: 1863), CXXII:
1179-80.

230 **Sabaoth.** As Griffin's gloss indicates, this is Guido's (or possibly
a scribe's) error for Gabaon; the reference is to Joshua 10.12, where God
makes the sun stand still at Gabaon so that Joshua can finish his battle.
This miracle is also mentioned in Dionysius' Epistle to Polycarp.

268-69 **proper and improper events.** For "congruos et incongruos."
Actually Guido may simply mean that he will include the rough with the
smooth, but in view of the fact that he goes on at once to show Medea
becoming enamored of Jason and considering how to manage an affair
with him, it looks as if he means to make some sort of moral judgment
here, not to mention titillating his readers.

289-90 **she softly forced . . . ivory teeth.** An attempt to improve upon

Benoit's "Belement dist entre ses dents" (1861) which occurs at a later point in the story.

291-96 Medea's rationalizations. As Gorra pointed out (p. 128), this is similar in tone to *Met.* VII:69-73:

> But do you call it marriage, Medea, and do you give fair-seeming names to your fault? Nay, rather, look ahead and see how great a wickedness you are approaching and flee it while you may (Loeb).

333 modesty. Translated from the variant, "et honestate" instead of the text's "honeste," an adverb, which would mean that Guido is saying that since her father had given her permission, Medea is behaving modestly or fittingly in speaking to Jason, but this does not seem to fit the generally critical tone of the passage.

Book Three

29 setting signs . . . awake! For "signa cadentia sompnos nullatenus suadere," an echo of Virgil's ". . . suadentque cadentia/sidera somnos . . ." ["the setting stars invite to sleep"—Loeb] (*Aeneid* II:9).

45 made a short speech of greeting. For "salutis pandit oraculum," a rather odd expression, since *pandit oraculum* should mean "revealed the oracle (or prophecy)" and is so used later on when Andromache tells Priam and Hecuba about her dream: "Andromacha . . . pandit sue oraculum visionis" (172 [*Book Twenty-one,* line 55]). It is possible that Guido understood *oraculum* as a diminutive of *ora* [speech], (n. pl. of *os* [mouth]), since he uses a similar expression in describing Ulysses' and Diomedes' rude behavior to Priam: ". . . non sunt regem ipsum alicuius salutationis oraculo venerati" (107) [*Book Twelve,* line 120] where the sense must be "did not even honor the king himself with the slightest speech of greeting." The *Gest* poet, who is often quite faithful to the Latin, says Medea "mowthet" [whispered] (686).

62 according to the power. Griffin's variant readings indicate that several of the scribes felt something was lacking from this sentence; one of them added *potencia,* which suggested this translation.

67-94 Jason's perfidy. This digression is not in Benoit, and Guido seems to be expanding what he found in Benoit and the *Metamorphoses* with details from, and certainly the tone of, *Heroides* XII. Compare "Sed

O deceptiua viri falacia! . . . et senem patrem irreuerenda reliquerit, thesauri sui cumulo spoliatum, et paternos sedes deserens .propter te elegit exilium, preponendo natalis soli dulcedini prouincias alienus?" (24) with Ovid's "Quantum perdidiae tecum, scelerate, perisses/Dempta fovent capiti quam mala meo!" and "Proditus est genitor, regnum patriamque reliqui/Munus in exilio quodlibet esse tuli" ["How much perfidy, vile wretch, would have perished with you, and how many woes been averted from my head! . . . I betrayed my sire, I left my throne and my native soil; the reward I get is leave to live in exile"—Loeb]. (*Her.* XII, 19-20, 109-10).

96-111 **Medea's ability to foresee the future.** This is the orthodox view of soothsayers and others who claimed to be able to predict the future; cf. Canto XX of the *Inferno*.

110-11 **it is of God . . . times.** For "cum solius Dei sit, in cuius manu sunt posita scire tempora temporum et momenta," probably an echo of Acts I:7: "Non est vestrum nosse tempora vel momenta quae Pater posuit in sua potestate" ["It is not for you to know the times or the moments, which the Father has put in his own power"—Douay].

145-85 **The charms Medea gave to Jason.** In Ovid, Medea assists Jason simply with an ointment, which would make him invulnerable for one day, and with magic herbs. Benoit has added the silver image—perhaps on the analogy of religious medals—the liquid to be poured into the bulls' mouths, and the ring. Guido makes the stone in the ring an agate because he knows that it is an antidote to poison.

157-70 **The properties of the agate.** Some of this information was to be found in medieval lapidaries, a typical one being that cited in another connection by Gorra (p. 129, n. 1), the medieval French *Lapidaire de Berne*. The entry on the agate states that it is found near the River Achates in Sicily, that it protected King Pyrrhus in many a tournament, that it is an antidote to poison for those who carry it with them, and that it makes people feel friendly toward the wearer, which is how Aeneas gained the love of Dido. See Leopold Pannier, *Les Lapidaires Français du Moyen Age* (Paris: F. Vieweg, 1882), pp. 112-13.

167-70 **Virgil . . . agate.** The quotation is from *Aeneid* I:312: ". . . ipse uno graditur comitatus Achate" ["then, Achates alone attending, himself strides forth"—Loeb]. Guido's version of this line, "Graditur fido comitatus Achate" (26), is interesting because it shows he remembers the epithet "fidus" for Achates, even if he thinks Aeneas' trusty friend

Achates is his trusty agate amulet. Gorra (p. 129) quotes passages from two of the French lapidaries to show that Guido was not the first to have made this mistake, and it is even possible that he was following a lapidary or other work on stones in which the line from Virgil is quoted as he renders it.

296-307 **Isidore** (*Etym.* XVI:3:1-4) does not say that emeralds are to be found in India, but he does comment on the soothing effect of their color upon the eyes, so that jewellers rest their eyes by looking at emeralds, and he also comments that large emeralds reflect images just as mirrors do. A hazy recollection of these facts in combination with the notion of a green agate being an antidote to poison probably accounts for Guido's statements here. Furthermore, there is the added confusion that on the subject of jet, *gagates,* which is found by a river of the same name, Isidore says that it is used to drive off serpents (*Etym.* XVI:4:3).

325-30 **earthborn brothers . . . reciprocal wounds.** For "Durum ergo committitur prelium inter fratres terrigenas . . . cum multis et mutuis uulneribus inter se deciderint interempti" (30). Another echo of *Met.* VII:141, cited in note to *Book One,* line 83.

379-85 **Later adventures of Jason and Medea.** Cf. *Book Three,* lines 85-94, part of the long, moralizing apostrophe to Jason which is roughly parallel to this one to Medea. In neither passage does Guido show very specific knowledge of what happened to them, although the verbal echoes suggest that he knew about Medea's tricking the daughters of Pelias into killing him.

Book Four

9 **Danaë.** For "Dampne," as Griffin points out. Though Leda is listed among the variants, it is impossible to tell whether the confusion of Danaë and Leda is Guido's mistake or his copyists'.

13-14 **"Jupiter . . . egg."** The unknown author of this statement is probably also the source of the information that Jupiter lay with Danaë in the likeness of an egg. Jupiter's remark, " 'ouo quia Tyndaris exit ab ouo,' " with its play on the two meanings of *ovo,* "I rejoice" and "egg," sounds like a fragment of an epigram, perhaps not a finished product but simply an academic exercise. There may even be a faint reflection of Horace's statement about beginning a story of the Trojan War "ab ovo."

15 **Tyndaris in Sicily.** Tyndaris is today called Capo Tyndaro, and it is right where Guido says it is. As in the case of Thetis and Chieti, this is another example of the association of a figure of classical mythology with a city. Helen, and Clytemnestra too, for that matter, were called Tyndaris from their father's name being Tyndareus, but the city was probably named for Castor and Pollux, both of whom were called Tyndarides and were worshipped as deities, especially by sailors; hence their association with a seaport is logical. Helen, too, was worshipped, but her influence was not so beneficent. See Rose, pp. 230-31 and 278-79.

20 **Epistle of Canace.** As Griffin points out, Canace is an error for Oenone, and the latter appears among the variants. The letters *O* and *C* are easily confused; Oetes (Aëtes) appears as Cetes in some of the manuscripts and in the Middle English translations. The lines quoted are from *Her.* V:91 and 129, Loeb translation.

55 **It was the time.** Because of like details, this passage has been suggested as one of the sources for the opening lines of the *Canterbury Tales,* although, as Robinson points out (p. 651), this kind of description is so conventional that any number of similar passages can be found, including Guido's own descriptions of summer at the beginning of *Book Seven* and in *Book Twenty-seven* just before the twentieth battle, and of winter, toward the end of *Book Thirty-one,* as the Greeks sail for home. The details are Guido's in the sense that they do not appear in Benoit, who has a simple pastoral evocation of spring.

Book Five

55-65 **Priam's sons.** As Griffin's variants show, the manuscript he says has "on the whole better readings" (p. xiii), completes this list with the following account of Ganymede and Polydorus:

Moreover Virgil writes that two other sons were borne that King Priam by that Hecuba; one named Polydorus, whom Priam, as soon as he sensed that the Greeks, having formed an army, intended to come against him, sent, while he was still a child in years, to a certain king, his friend, with a great quantity of gold to be kept by him until King Priam could be sure of the outcome of the war (but that king, ensnared by a wretched desire for gold, when he sensed it would not turn out favorably for King Priam, ordered that his throat be cut and he be buried near a certain shore); the second, truly, was named Ganymede whom Jupiter loved; having stolen him away in Sicily, he carried him up to heaven and made him his cupbearer in the place of Hebe, the daughter of Juno, when she had gone off. Hence Virgil: "honours paid to ravished Ganymede."

The story of Polydorus is found in *Aeneid* III:43-56 and that of Ganymede in *Met.* X:155-61, but without the mention of Hebe or Sicily. The quotation is from the *Aeneid* I:28, given in the Loeb translation. Two of the other manuscripts also quote this line.

67 **Creusa.** Virgil mentions Creusa twice as Aeneas' wife but does not tell who her parents were. Benoit calls Priam's eldest daughter Andromache, but Guido feels this is wrong, since Andromache is Hector's wife and Hector, of course, is Priam's eldest son.

75-82 **Priam's natural sons.** Benoit gives the names of Priam's bastards in two places at the beginning of his description of the second battle, and although some of Guido's names are different, he is following Benoit, but arranging his material more logically.

100-82 **The description of the second Troy.** While Guido has added some details of his own, it is from Benoit that he gets the size; the arrangement of the walls, towers, palisades, and ditches; the richness of the materials; the covered passages; the fact that Ilium is built on solid rock; and the throne room with the dais and altar to Jupiter. Benoit was deliberately striving for an effect of exotic splendor, and one would expect that Guido would consider these details unhistorical. However, when one realizes that what was exotic to a twelfth-century Frenchman was quite familiar to a thirteenth-century Sicilian, one can see why Guido follows Benoit so faithfully. He had probably seen palaces fully as sumptuous as Priam's, and even today in Sicily there are buildings constructed during the Norman occupation, a hundred years before Guido's time, in which Byzantine, Arabic, and Romanesque architecture mingle, and mosaics, colored marbles, and lacy stonework abound. It is even possible that Benoit's description was inspired by what he knew of Sicily. Two twelfth-century descriptions of Palermo, which are cited in translation in Celia Wærn, *Mediaeval Sicily* (London: Duckworth and Company [1910], pp. 52-80), though of a later date than the *Roman*, indicate what Benoit could have seen or heard about. The first is by an Arab traveler and the second by Hugo Falcandus, who is also the author of a history of Sicily.

Since Guido could have seen these same sights, neither of these accounts is likely to have been used by him; besides, he almost certainly could not read Arabic and his phrasing is quite different from that of Falcandus. (See Hugo Falcandus, *La Historia o Liber de Regno Sicilie e la Epistola ad Petrum Panormitane Ecclesie Thesaurium di Ugo Falcando,* edited by G. B. Siragusa, Rome: 1897, pp. 177-84.)

1. ... A stupendous city, like Cordova in her architecture, her buildings are all of cut stone, a clear river divides her in two, four springs well up alongside . . . .

One of the most noteworthy of the monuments . . . is the "Church of the Antiochene". . . The inner walls are gilded, or rather are all one sheet of gold, with panels of marble in colours, of which the like was never seen, all inlaid with little pieces of mosaic of gold, framed in foliage in green mosaic; above there is an order of gilded glass windows, that dazzled the eyesight with the brightness of their rays. . . . This church has a belfry, supported on columns of marble in various colours and surmounted by a cupola which rests on other columns . . . .
2. But at the other end . . . is situated the new palace, with great industry and marvellous skill built of square-hewn stones outwardly enclosed by a wide circle of walls, and inwardly striking for the splendour of gold and many gems. . . . Nor must one forget the noble workshops where the blocks of silk are drawn out into threads of many colours and adapted to woven stuffs of many kinds. . . . the Royal Chapel with a pavement of sumptuous workmanship, walls decorated below with sheets of precious marbles and above with little square stones, some gilt, some of many colours. . . . The highest summit, further, is adorned with a ceiling of very elegant woodwork, with marvellous variety of painting, and here and there with the splendour of gold.

Thus disposed and ordered, this palace, full of every kind of delight and charm, like unto the head above the rest of the body, rises above the rest of the city . . . .

Three principal streets . . . divide [the city] . Of these the one in the middle, the Via Marmorea, occupied by things for sale, runs from the

upper part of the Via Coperta [covered way] in a straight line to the
Arab Palace . . . .

But who can ever sufficiently admire the marvellous buildings of
this illustrious city, the suave abundance of the springs that well up
here and there, the loveliness of the trees, ever green, or the aqueducts
that plentifully minister to the wants of the citizens?

109 **in the name of Neptune.** The idea that Troy was consecrated to
Neptune is not in Benoit and may have been suggested to Guido by the
episodes in the *Aeneid* in which Neptune aids the Trojans, as well as by
the fact that in *Aeneid* III:3, which he quotes later [*Book Thirty*, line
239], Troy is called "Neptune's Troy." It may also be his rationalization
of the legend of Neptune's building the first Troy.

111 **it took three days. . . .** For: "Fuit autem huius secunde Troye
ambitus longitudinis trium dierum et latitudinis coequalis." Guido has
expanded upon Benoit's statement that "tres jornees senz devise/Durot et
mout plus la porprise" (3027-28), probably feeling that a three days'
journey in each direction is what Benoit meant by "three days . . . and
more," especially since Benoit has said earlier (2995-96) that there never
had been such a large city. It is interesting that *ambitus* is an exact translation for *porprise*, the *enceinte* or outermost wall enclosing a castle or
city (Constans, V, s.v. *porprise*), as well as being the term for the actual
motion of going around something.

130-31 **a deep trench with hidden pitfalls.** For "obscuris hyatibus
profundo uallo." Since the trench (*vallum*, Griffin's gloss) is some distance
from the city walls, it cannot be the moat, and the pitfalls (*hiatus*,
literally "opening," but used by Guido for any kind of trench, including
the trough of the waves) are probably camouflaged. The *Gest* poet, however, takes "obscuris hyatibus" to mean "dark waves," and accordingly
renders the phrase as "With depe dikes and derke doubull of water"
(1566). Nevertheless, it should be noted that the primary meaning of
vallum is an earthen rampart set with palisades (Lewis and Short, s.v.),
and that Benoit's term, "terrier," has the same meaning. Lydgate,
apparently translating the phrase as "a high wall with concealed openings,"
thinks this refers to the machicolation, the slots in the floor of the
parapet through which boiling oil and such were poured down upon the
attackers in the moat ("Maskowed withoute for sautis and assay"—*Troy
Book*, II:580), but this kind of fortification was not in use in Guido's
day. See the *Cambridge Medieval History*, VI:780.

133 **Within.** The text has "infra" [lower than], but "intra" is listed among the variants and makes better sense.

136-38 **They assert . . . sixty cubits.** Not in Benoit.

152 **carters.** For "quadrigarii," and so glossed in the *Medieval Latin Word List,* though Du Cange suggests "fabricatores quadrigii," [makers of carts].

156-57 **spindlemakers . . . anvil.** The translation makes use of the variant, "ferro incude" [from iron on the anvil], from the Strassburg edition, instead of the text's meaningless "ferreo inferro." The fact that there are several other readings indicates that the phrase gave trouble to the scribes.

162 *pantalargae.* For "pantalarge," n. pl. of *pantalarga,* which Griffin glosses as "perhaps jack-of-all-trades, ingenious workman," indicating that like *gynaecarius* [163] and *argyroprata* [167], it is a word of Greek origin. See introduction, p. xxv.

163 *gynaecarii* **called weavers.** Sicily was famous for its silk industry, which had been introduced by the Arabs and promoted by the Normans and later by Frederick II. In both the Norman and imperial palaces, beautiful fabrics were produced by the women in the seraglios, the *gynaecia,* though by Guido's time there were also commercial weaving establishments and the term was applied to them. Guido apparently thinks of *gynaeciarius* as the technical term for a male worker in a textile workshop. See Griffin's glossary, s.v. *ginecarius;* Niermeyer, s.v. *gynaecium;* and Wærn, pp. 130 ff.

167 *argyropratae.* For "argiroprate," n. pl. of *argiroprata,* which Griffin glosses as "money changer."

170-82 **Xanthus . . . Aeneas.** Guido may have observed the Roman cloacae, or he may have read a description of them like that in Pliny (XXXVI: 15:24). Isidore's reference (XV:2:25) is too brief to be very suggestive. Pliny states that seven rivers flow through artificial channels beneath the city, and that sometimes when the Tiber floods, it backs up into these channels, and if Pliny is Guido's source, either direct or indirect, this may account for Guido's believing that the Tiber itself was diverted through these channels. The cloacae would have appeared incredibly ancient to a medieval writer, and it would be natural for Guido to suppose that they had been built by Aeneas; in fact, the idea may not have been original with him. Once this assumption had been made, the idea that there must have been a similar sewage system in Troy follows logically.

183-87 **Priam's colonizing of Troy.** Benoit says that people from all around were attracted to Troy because of its beauty, but Guido, perhaps remembering the way Frederick II forced the relocation of thousands of Sicilians, puts it this way. See note to *Book Thirteen,* lines 115-32.

187 **various diversions.** Guido's statement that these pleasures were invented in Troy comes from his misinterpreting Benoit's comment that all pleasures were to be found in the new city:

> Onques ne fu riche maistrie
> N'afaitemenz ne corteisie,
> Dont l'om eüst delit ne joie,
> Quil ne trovassent cil de Troie:
> Echec e tables, gieu e dez . . .

(3179-83)

193-94 **comedy devised in Sicily.** This notion is as old as the *Poetics,* but Isidore makes the same assertion in his description of Italy, after his account of Sicily's founding by Sicanus and just before his statement that the achates stone is named for the River Achates (*Etym.* XIV:6:34).

195 **May festivals.** For "maiuma." Griffin's gloss, following Du Cange, suggests "licentious festivals."

208 **in the shape of a sphere.** Domed roofs which were almost spherical were a feature of Sicilian architecture, and there is one on the Palace Chapel in Palermo, which, as described in the account given by Hugo Falcandus quoted in the note to *Book Five,* line 100, was located at the highest point of the city.

220-23 **Not thus . . . bases.** The "thus" refers to the marble decoration, and what Guido apparently means is that the piers of the windows were of marble like the walls, but that these piers were not heavy or thick, since the windows were largely of crystal; however, putting the negative clause first makes the sentence unclear.

225-41 **Priam's hall.** Although hardly anything remains of the Royal Palace in Palermo, the similarity of what is described here to what still exists in the Palace Chapel—wooden coffered ceiling, mosaic floor, marble walls—tempts one to think that Guido has in mind the Royal Hall of the Palace. See Wærn, *op. cit.,* pp. 123-26.

Book Six

85 **it will be meet and right.** "Dignum ergo erit et iustum . . ." This is probably an echo of the response in the Preface of the Mass to the Sursum Corda, "Dignum et justum est," and the translation is from the Anglican Book of Common Prayer in order to give the liturgical feeling which a modern literal translation does not. The phrase is repeated at *Book Twenty-seven,* line 19. It is interesting that in both instances an action which is neither suitable nor just is being suggested. It is also possible, of course, that the phrase is simply a cliché and should be translated, "it is fitting and proper;" in either case the irony is obvious.

353 **Panthus and Euphorbus.** Actually, Panthus was the father of Euphorbus, but Dares apparently misunderstood Ovid's "Panthoides Euphorbus eram" (*Met.* XV:161), and Benoit followed him. Guido makes the same mistake, although in the next line he refers explicitly to the passage in Ovid and may even have read it.

Book Seven

57 **Cunestar.** As Griffin's variants indicate, this is a corruption of Benoit's "Clitemnestre" (4239), which comes from Dares' statement that Castor and Pollux were taking their niece, Hermione, to Clytemnestra ("ad Clytemnestram," 11,24). Benoit certainly thought they were going to a city, but it is impossible to tell whether or not Dares knew that Clytemnestra was another sister of Castor and Pollux.

63-66 **Cythera . . . Citrius.** Since Guido, like Benoit, calls the island "Cytherea," an adjectival form, it may be that *Citrius* is an error for *Cyprius* [belonging to Cyprus], since Cyprus was also associated with the worship of Venus. It should be noted, however, that the *Prose Roman* states that Cythera is "l'ille qui est apelee Cetri" (60.10).

75 **festival of Venus.** Dares and Benoit agree that the great temple was to Venus but that the festival was in honor of Juno, and that Paris sacrificed to Diana. Benoit adds, "A la troïen maniere" (4243).

173-230 **the description of Helen of Troy.** This description is not in Benoit; Guido is drawing upon the stockpile of conventional attributes of beauty and enlarging upon them with legalistic literal-mindedness. This kind of description is a traditional device of rhetoric, in poetry as well as

in prose, and it goes back to the Alexandrian Greeks and the Roman
elegiac poets. Cicero, in *De Inventione,* had established eleven categories
of persons, and Horace, in the *Ars Poetica,* had said that a description
should be appropriate to the type of person, but the medieval rhetori-
cians codified these suggestions and established that a description should
begin with the physical appearance and proceed to the clothes, and that
in describing the physical traits, the writer should start with the hair and
proceed to the forehead, the eyes, cheeks, nose, lips, and so on. In
Matthieu de Vendôme's *Ars Versificatoria* there is a description of Helen
of Troy as an example of this kind of catalogue, and it includes most of
the items Guido mentions: the golden hair and how it is bound up, the
eyebrows, which in Matthieu are dark, the eyes like stars, the cheeks in
which red and white are blended, and the like. See Edmond Faral, *Les
Arts Poétiques du XIIe et du XIIIe Siècle* (Paris: E. Champion, 1924),
pp. 75-81, 129-30.

216 **a necklace composed of several strands.** For "linealis ordo . . .
murenarum," which Griffin glosses as, "perhaps a compound necklace in
parallel chains."

224-26 **Helen's bosom.** The word here translated as "nipples" is
"pilas," literally "anything round" like a ball (Lewis and Short, s.v.), and
"culminated" is for "cacuminavit," literally, "came to a point."

If Guido means that Helen's contours were revealed by a low-cut rather
than a form-fitting garment (as his following remark about the "hidden
parts" suggests, shocking though this would be in the thirteenth century),
the idea may have come to him from *Her.* XVI:249-250, in Paris' Epistle
to Helen, in which he mentions that once her tunic had been loose
enough to show her bare breasts. This is made the more likely by the
fact that Benoit gives no details of Paris' courtship of Helen, while some
of Guido's touches are reminiscent of Ovid. See next note. However, as
Wigginton points out (pp. 101-104), Guido's treatment of the whole
abduction episode is strikingly similar to that of Joseph of Exeter.

231-64 **The courtship of Paris and Helen.** While the meeting of the
lovers' eyes and exchange of glances is in Benoit, as is the fact that they
have an opportunity to speak briefly, the furtive signals are Guido's
addition and seem to be suggested by several passages in *Her.* XVI; cf. "et
modo per nutum signa tegenda dabam" ["and again I would nod, making
signs I should have kept hid"—Loeb] (258) and "Iuppiter his gaudet,
gaudet Venus aurea furtis;/haec tibi nempe patrem furta dedere Iovem"

["Jove's delight, and the delight of Venus, are in stealthy sins like these; such stealthy sins, indeed, gave you Jove for a sire"—Loeb] (291-292). Cf. also *Her.* XVII, Helen's Epistle to Paris, especially lines 74-90, in which Helen reproaches Paris for having made such signs as drinking from her cup, signalling with his fingers or glances, and writing her name and "AMO" in wine on the table.

Book Eight

4-5 **came to the ears.** For "aure sinuadit," which could be translated "insinuated [itself] into his ear," but is probably a misprint for "aures inuadit" and is so translated. The words are run together in the 1489 Strassburg edition, but the 1353 manuscript in the Harvard University Library has "aures inuadit" (f. 24, which is misplaced and should have come between ff. 34 and 35).

81-127 **The shipwreck of Castor and Pollux.** As Wigginton (p. 84) demonstrates, Guido is here supplementing Benoit's brief and vague description of the Twins' end with the account of their being made stars and worshipped as gods from Joseph of Exerter's *De Bello Trojano* III:427ff.

Although Benoit did not include Castor and Pollux among the Greek leaders who came at the summons of Agamemnon and Menelaus, but, like Joseph and the author of the *Prose Roman,* said that they set out from Lesbos, still Guido, with his attention turned to his supplementary sources, says that "certain people" say that Castor and Pollux went off on their own.

Guido's statement that the sign of Gemini in the zodiac was named for them is probably based on *Etym.* III:71:23-32, in which Isidore explains the names of the signs of the zodiac. Since he says that when the sun comes into the sign of Cancer in June, the days are getting shorter and the sun is going backward like a crab, and that the sun is in the signs of Pisces and Aquarius during the rainy winter season, one would expect that this would be Guido's authority for the fact that the sun stays in the sign of Gemini two days longer than in the other signs. But such is not the case, at least in the edition of Isidore as we have it now; perhaps this was a gloss.

138 **The scar between Helen's eyebrows.** In both Dares and Benoit

this is a beauty mark; Dares, "ore pusillo" (12.17); Benoit, "seing," (5135).

152 **Tantalus.** This should be Patroclus, whose portrait appears at this point in both Dares and Benoit. Perhaps Guido's text of Benoit was corrupt at this point; in any case, the name does not appear again.

154 **truthful.** For "veridicus." Perhaps a misreading of Benoit's "a la verté dire" (5176), which is simply a tag to fill out the line, equivalent to modern French *à vrai dire* or English "to tell the truth."

171 **licentious.** Guido's addition.

181 **joined eyebrows.** See note to line 194.

194 **Briseida's joined eyebrows.** Robinson (p. 834) points out that this trait is mentioned by Dares, Joseph of Exeter, Benoit, and Guido, but that only the last two, like Chaucer, regard it as a flaw. He also states that in ancient Greece, joined eyebrows were a sign of beauty, and sometimes of a passionate nature.

196-97 **pliable because of great compassion.** For "multa fuit pietate tractabilis," suggested by Benoit's "simple e aumosniere e pitose" (5278), which, like all the other qualities he attributes to Briseida, except her inconstancy, typify her as an ideal courtly heroine. The conjunction of *tractabilis* with *pietas* shows that Guido is well aware of the courtly connotations of *pité,* the compassion the lady may show toward her lover's sufferings, and that *pietas* goes back to "pitose" rather than "aumosniere" [charitable].

233 **he was pleased to maintain a certain reserve toward them.** This may have prompted Chaucer to make his Troilus somewhat diffident as a lover; in contrast, Benoit states that Troilus had often endured the pangs of love (5436).

234 **another Hector.** Root (p. 440) and Robinson (p. 818) have pointed out that this is probably the source of Pandarus' remark that Troilus is "Ector the secounde" (*Troilus,* II:158), since there is no such statement in Benoit, and Joseph of Exeter had said he was second to none (*De Bello Trojano,* IV:61).

Book Nine

1ff. **The catalogue of heroes.** As Griffin's variants indicate, in the enumeration of the allies, the names and numbers were dreadfully garbled by the scribes. Some of the forms are close to those in Dares, some to those in Benoit, and this has been used to prove that Guido was following Benoit here (Gorra, pp. 113-115; Constans, VI:318-321), or else that he was following Dares (Chiàntera, pp. 223-228). Because medieval writers using Guido reproduced what he had, it has seemed best to use his forms of the names, except in the case of the major characters.

Book Ten

19 **to rebel.** For "elevare calcaneum," literally, "to raise the heel." Du Cange, s.v. *calcaneum,* gives "rebellare" [to rebel] for both *calcaneum erigere* and *calcaneum levare.*

79-100 **Delphos ... Delos.** Delphi is a city and Delos an island, but both contained an oracle of Apollo. Isidore says Delos is both an island and a city (XIV:6:22). Benoit, following Dares' "Delphos," has "Delfon" (5789), and Guido of course regards him as the more reliable source, although in approved historical fashion, he adds the information from Isidore for comparison.

85-95 **Isidore ... *ortygiae.*** Except for the statement that there is a temple to Apollo on the island, these details are paraphrased from Isidore, XIV:6:21-22.

95-100. **Apollo.** As Gorra pointed out (p. 134), this information is from Isidore, VIII:11:53-54.

101 **pythonesses.** From Isidore, VIII:9:21.

103-4 **First Book of Kings.** The reference is to Saul's visit to the Witch of Endor: "... Est mulier pythonem habens in Endor.... Divina mihi in pythone, et suscita mihi quem dixero tibi" (I Kings 28:7-8), which the Douay renders as, "There is a woman that hath a divining spirit at Endor.... Divine to me by thy divining spirit, and bring me up him whom I shall tell thee." Isidore mentions the story in VIII:9:7, raising the question as to whether it was really the soul of Samuel whom the woman raised, or an illusion produced by Satan.

111-17 **deaf and dumb gods ... error.** From Isidore, VIII:11.4.

129-35 **The end of idolatry during the Flight into Egypt.** The fact that Guido mentions the Gospel, may indicate that not only does he have in mind the story of the Flight into Egypt in Matt. 2:12-21, but also the following passage from the apocryphal gospel of the so-called Pseudo-

Matthew (translated in M. R. James. *The Apocryphal New Testament,*
Oxford: The Clarendon Press, [1924], p. 75):

> XXII.   .... they arrived at Hermopolis and entered a city called
> Satinen, and had to lodge in a temple where there were three hundred
> and sixty five gods.

> XXIII. When Mary and the child entered, all the idols fell and Isaiah's
> word was fulfilled. "Behold, the Lord shall come upon a light cloud
> and enter into Egypt, and all the *gods* made by the hand of the
> Egyptians shall be moved before his face.

This story also appears in the *Historia Scholastica* of Petrus Comestor
(Migne, *PL,* vol. 198, col. 1543) which Guido cites later in the passage:

> On account of the warning of the angel, Joseph fled into Egypt with
> the child and his mother until the death of Herod. And when the Lord
> entered into Egypt, the idols of the Egyptians fell down, following
> Isaiah who said, "the Lord will ascend upon a swift cloud and will
> enter into Egypt and the idols of Egypt shall be moved. (*In
> Evangelium,* Ch. X)

Both here and in the text the translation of Isaiah is the Douay.

136-39   **the Jews ... statues.** From Isidore, VIII:11:8.

136-245 **The origins of idolatry.** As Gorra observed, much of this is
taken from Isidore, VIII:11, but as will be seen, it is not always in the
same order as in Isidore, and it is interspersed with quotations from
Petrus Comestor, Bede, the Bible, and the legend of Saint Brendan. In
view of this fact, and of the fact that one of the quotations from Isaiah
and the citation of Bede are to be found in the *Historia Scholastica,* it is
possible that Guido is following another source which contains all these
references, and which of course he does not name, any more than he
names Benoit.

It is interesting that the *Prose Roman* also has a digression on idolatry
at this point, and so does Joseph of Exeter (IV:221-37), as Wigginton
points out (p. 77), but these are little more than the orthodox criticisms
of the credulousness of the pagans for believing in oracles.

139-41   **They are called pagans ...** "Dicuntur autem gentiles quia
semper sine lege fuerunt, et ita semper fuerunt, ut geniti fuisse
perhibentur, ydolis principaliter servientes." Compare Isidore, VIII:10:2-3:

"Gentiles sunt qui sine lege sunt, et nondum crediderunt. Dicti autem gentiles, quia ita sunt ut fuerunt geniti, id est, sicut in carne descenderunt sub peccato, scilicet idolis servientes et necdum regenerati" [Gentiles are those who are without the law, and they did not yet believe. They are called gentiles because they are just as they were generated (born), that is, just as they descended into the flesh in sin, namely serving idols and not yet regenerated (reborn)].

142-55 **The worship of Baal.** While some of this could be derived from Isidore, the more direct source seems to be the *Historia Scholastica* (Migne, *PL,* vol. 198, col. 1090):

When Bel had died, Ninus, as consolation for his grief, made himself an image of his father, towards which he showed such reverence, as it would spare whatever things had recourse to it. Therefore men of his kingdom began to pay divine honors to his image; from their example many rich people dedicated images to their dead, and thus from the idol to Bel, the rest took their origin, so that they took the general name of idols from his name. For as Bel is said by the Assyrians, so other nations say, according to the idioms of their languages, some Bel, some Beel, some Baal, some Baalim. Furthermore, they make derivatives of his name, some saying Beelphegor, some Beelzebub.

158 **Saturn.** Cf. *Etym.* VIII:11:23: "A Babylonian idol is Bel, which means 'old.' For this Belus was the father of Ninus, the first king of the Assyrians, whom some people call Saturn, which name is worshipped among the Assyrians and Africans, wherefore the god is called Bal in the Punic tongue. Among the Assyrians, Bal for some reason of their rites is called both Saturn and Sol."

158-70 **Legend of Saturn.** This is not given in Isidore.

170-83 **Cult of other pagan gods.** This could come from two separate passages in the *Eytmologiae;* the first from Book III:71, which Guido drew upon in discussing the stars used for navigation [*Book One,* line 210] and the second from the beginning of Book VIII:11:

. . . The Romans consecrated them [the planets] with the names of their gods, that is, of Jupiter, Saturn, Mars, Venus, and Mercury.

Those whom the pagans claimed to be gods are reported to have been men . . . and they began to worship them after death, as Isis in Egypt, Jupiter in Crete, Juba by the Moors, Faunus by the Latins, Quirinus

by the Romans. And in the same way, Minerva at Athens, Juno at
Samnos, Venus at Paphos, Vulcan at Lemnos, Liber at Naxos, Apollo
at Delos.

184-251 **Demons and the Devil.** Despite Guido's earlier statement
that the answers given by the oracle were made by "unclean spirits," the
transition from pagan gods to demons, Lucifer, and the Fall may seem a
bit abrupt, but it should be noted that the same line of discussion is used
by Isidore (*Etym.* VIII:11:5-7). After the list of gods and their places of
worship, cited above, Isidore goes on to say that the pagans were deluded
by demons into worshipping statues of the famous men they had wished
to honor (*Etym.* VIII:11:4-7). Then follows a digression as to whether
the first idol was made by Ishmael or Prometheus (8), after which Isidore
proceeds to a further discussion of various idols and then to the etymologies of the words "idol," "idolatry," and "demons" (9-16). His statement
that the demons are the "prevaricating angels whose prince is the Devil"
(17) probably prompted the passage on Lucifer in Guido, and leads to the
explanation of the word "devil" [*diabolus*]: "In Hebrew, the Devil is
called [one] flowing downwards, because he scorned to stay in the quiet
of heaven but fell, sinking to earth downwards on account of the weight
of pride" (18). Guido uses this, and then omits the Greek and Latin
etymologies, the discussion of the Antichrist, and the discussion of the
various names under which the Devil is worshipped (19-26), except for
the information about Baal (23), and this leads into the explanation of
Behemoth and Leviathan (27):

> "Behemoth" from the Hebrew speech signifies "beast" in the Latin
> language, because he fell from the heights to earth, and for his punish-
> ment was made a brute beast. The same is the Leviathan, that is the
> serpent of the waters, because he engaged in deviousness in the churn-
> ing sea of this world. Moreover, Leviathan means "[something] added
> to them." To whom, indeed, if not to the men in paradise to whom he
> once offered the sin of lying, and increased or extended it up to
> eternal death by daily persuading?

This last comment, which is all that Isidore has to say about the Fall,
probably suggested the more extended discussion in Guido.

187-201 **Lucifer.** In W. H. Kent's article on the Devil in the *Catholic
Encyclopedia* it is pointed out that the passages quoted from Ezechiel and

Isaias were those upon which the tradition of the revolt of the angels was based, and the passage from Luke shows that this tradition was fully established by New Testament times.

188-91 **"The cedars . . . beauty"** Ezech. 31:8. Guido quotes the Vulgate almost exactly, except in the last clause he qualifies the tree as "pretiosum" [precious], and this has been added to the Douay translation.

193-94 **"I will place . . ."** Paraphrased from Isaias 14:13-14, " '. . . I will sit in the mountain of the covenant, in the sides of the north. I will ascend above the height of the clouds, I will be like the most high' "– Douay.

197-98 **"How have you fallen . . ."** For "Quomodo cecedisti, stella matutina, de medio lapidum ignitorum?" Cf. the Vulgate (Isaias 14:12): "Quomodo cecidisti, Lucifer, qui mane oriebaris?" ["How art thou fallen from heaven, O Lucifer, who didst rise in the morning?"–Douay.]

200-201 **"I saw Satan . . ."** For "Vidi . . . Sathanam quasi fulgur de celo cadentem." Cf. the Vulgate: "Videbam satanam sicut fulgur de coelo cadentem" (Luke 10:18), which has the same sense as the Douay translation used here.

207-208 **"crooked serpent . . . dragon."** For "serpentem tortuosum, et cum sit immense magnitudinis dictus est draco." Cf. Isaias 27:1: "In die illa visitabit Dominus in gladiosuo duro . . . super Leviathan serpentem tortuosum, et occidet cetum, qui in mari est." ["In that day the Lord with his hard . . . sword shall visit . . . Leviathan the crooked serpent and shall slay the whale that is in the sea"–Douay.]

209 **"This great and spacious sea . . . This dragon . . . therein."** For "Hoc mare magnum et spaciosum. . . Draco iste quem formasti ad illudendum ei." Cf. Psalm 103:25 and 26: "Hoc mare magnum et spatiosum. . . Draco iste, quem formasti ad illudendum ei." ["This great sea which stretcheth forth its arms. . . This dragon which thou hast formed to play therein"–Douay.] In Guido's context, and probably in others long before him, *illudere* must have been taken in the sense of "to deceive" (Niermeyer, s.v.).

212 the *Apographia* of **Saint Brendan.** Griffin's gloss: "designation of the *Vita Sancti Brendani.*" According to Carl Selmer, ed., *Navigatio Sancti Brendani Abbatis* (Notre Dame, Ind.: University of Notre Dame Press, 1959), p. x, there were two biographical traditions with regard to St. Brendan; the monastic, which produced the *Vita,* and the popular, which produced the *Navigatio.* Owing to the tremendous popularity of the

latter, many versions of the *Vita* included the *Navigatio,* and it is this kind of conflate *Vita* which appears in Carl Plummer, ed., *Vitae Sanctorum Hiberniae* (Oxford: The Clarendon Press, 1910; reprinted 1968), pp. 98-151.

It is the *Navigatio* which contains the well-known episode in which the saint's companions begin cooking breakfast on an island which turns out to be a large fish that swims away, but not before St. Brendan saves them. Guido does not seem to be referring to this, however, but to the fight of two sea serpents, one of which spews water, the other, fire. The first beast is described as being "mire magnitudine" [of amazing size], and when the second comes at St. Brendan's prayer to fight the first, the Saint comments, "See, my sons, the greatness of omnipotent God and observe the obedience which the creature shows to the Creator. . . ." After the fight, the second beast is described as going back "to whence it came." (See Plummer, p. 123.) These details are probably behind Guido's reference to the story.

227   **"Now the serpent. . . ."** Genesis 3:1, Douay translation.

231   **as Bede writes . . . Genesis.** Cf. *Historia Scholastica* (Migne, *PL,* vol. 198, col. 1072): "He chose also a certain kind of serpent, as Bede says, [one] having a girl's face . . . , and moved its tongue for speaking, without, however, its being aware, just as he speaks through fanatics and those who are possessed without their being aware." The detail about the serpent having a girl's face is not in Bede's commentary on Genesis (*Bedae Venerabilis Opera,* Pars II, Opera Exegetica, "Libri Qvatvor In Principium Genesis," ed. Ch. W. Jones, Turnhout, 1968, I, iii, 1, p. 59).

250-51   **"For all the gods. . . ."** Psalm 95:5, Douay.

Book Eleven

83   **Diana . . . the mistress of journeys and roads.** Diana was the goddess of roads, but not journeys, through her being associated with Hecate, when she was called Diana Trivia [of the three roads] because Hecate's rites were celebrated at crossroads—places connected with magic and the underworld. See Rose, pp. 120-22.

84-85   **propitious . . . in the tenth or eleventh house.** In astrology, the heavens are divided into twelve houses which correspond to the signs of the zodiac and which govern various human activities favorably or unfavorably, depending on which planet is in which house. The moon in the tenth house, for instance, would mean a rise in fortune, rank, or position, and in the eleventh would have to do with friendship and family relations. See Vivian E. Robson, *A Student's Textbook of Astrology*, London, 1922, p. 31.

98 **Sarranabo**. In saying that this name is not given by Dares, Guido means, of course, that it does not occur in Benoit. Nor is it in any other book Guido is thought to have made use of. Benoit does, however, in summing up the Greeks' achievements on the way to Troy, mention "Tenedon et Lauriëntel" (6066). See Constans, VI:319-21, note 1.

Book Twelve

232 *Liber Authenticarum*. For "libro *Autenticorum*." As Du Cange, s.v. *Authenticae* indicates, this is the Latin version of Justinian's *Novellae*, the supplement to the *Corpus Juris Civilis;* "rubric" was the usual term for the title of a law. The title here referred to is Title II of the Fifth Collection, "The name of the emperor shall be placed at the head of all public documents, and the date shall be written plainly in Latin characters." In the preface to this title, after explaining why documents must be clearly dated, Justinian goes on,

> . . . For whoever studies the events of past ages, and the ancient history of the government, will learn of Aeneas the King of Troy, Prince of the Republic, from whom We are said to descend; and if he turns his attention to the second epoch, when the Roman name attained great lustre among mankind, he will ascertain that Romulus and Numa founded the government . . . .
> If he should consider the third epoch, namely, that of the Empire, he would read of the Great Caesar and the Pious Augustus, and would find that the government which now is so powerful was rendered immortal by the acts of these sovereigns. . . .
>
> Justinian, *The Civil Law*, translated by S. P. Scott
> (Cincinnati: The Central Trust Company, 1932), XVI, 213.

240-41 **the *Aeneid* not finished.** Guido may think the *Aeneid* is unfinished, but he probably means that, as in the traditional biography of Virgil, he died before he could finish revising his poem. See the introduction to the Loeb Virgil, I:x-xi.

Book Thirteen

11 **Messa.** Benoit: "Mese" (6521); Dares: "Mesiam" for "Mysiam" (21, 1 and note). Mysia is in Asia Minor between the Hellespont and the Aegean, and is a logical place for the Greeks to have had a supply base.

25-37 **Messa was Sicily.** Difficult as it is to realize today, medieval Sicily was extremely fertile and prosperous, and the port of Messina was as thriving as Guido says. See Mack Smith, I:30-31, 55-57.

The Isidore-like etymologizing on the name comes from the fact that Messina is *Messana* in Latin, and the word for crops here is *messes.*

74-75 **vanquished . . . with clasped hands.** For "victum vinctis manibus," literally, "with bound hands," but there has not been time for Teuthras' hands to be bound. Guido probably means that the hands are clasped in petition, and he is undoubtedly playing with the sounds of "victum" and "vinctis."

117-32 **Hercules . . . Herculea . . . Terra Nova.** Herculea (Latin), or Heracleia (Greek), is a city on the southern coast of Sicily, modern Agrigento. There are ruins of several temples there, including one to Hercules (Helen Hill Miller, *Sicily and the Western Colonies of Greece* [New York: Scribner, 1965], pp. 118-129), and it is no wonder it was called the Place of Pillars, or that, as in the case of the temple to Hercules at Gades, the columns came to be thought of as pillars of Hercules.

That "barbarians" (that is the Arabs, who during their occupation of Sicily in the ninth and tenth centuries had irrigated and cultivated intensively) had once made the land habitable explains why Frederick II saw the possibilities in it, and he actually founded two settlements in the area. The one that Guido calls Terra Nova is obviously the one at Agrigento, at which Frederick had a quay built and which was populated by people brought in from other areas. The actual Terranova, today called Gela, as it was when it was a Greek colony, is some forty miles east of Agrigento. See Mack Smith I:8, 58-59, and T. L. Kington, *History of Frederick the Second,* London, 1862, I, 456.

150 **Teuthras' epitaph.** As Wigginton notes (p. 91), this was probably suggested by the similar epitaph in Joseph of Exeter (IV:491-92):

> Duke Teuthras, the glory of the plains of Mysia,
> having met Achilles,

Suffered death by the sword, the defender of his
ancestral sceptre.

185 **Dares Phrygius.** Refers of course to Benoit who lists Priam's
allies at this point (6658 ff.). The names are garbled, as usual, and the
forms here are usually as given in Guido.

191 **Dares . . . says nothing about their kingdoms.** Dares says that
these three came from "Zelia" (22.15), which Benoit renders as "De
Sezile," but among the variants are listed several which do not look like
place names, including "De Sez en il ont" (6667 and notes).

208-10 **The arms worn by King Remus' men.** The specific color of
the mens' arms is the sort of detail that Benoit usually delights to give
and Guido ignores; here Benoit had simply said that they all wore the
same colors so they could be recognized by their king (6720-27).

214-22 **Pannonia.** These details are in Benoit, except for the fauns
and satyrs and for the fact that the knights were skilled in the use of
lances; Benoit says that they did not carry lances but steel-pointed arrows
and Turkish bows (6760-65).

245 **two kings whose names are not given.** Benoit does give their
names: "Vint reis Fion et reis Edras" (6887), but the line may have been
missing in Guido's manuscript.

Book Fourteen

297-320 **The Greek encampment.** Benoit concentrates on silken
pavilions and gold standards, in contrast to Guido's more sober preoccu-
pation with palisades and sentinels. He may be reflecting what he felt as a
citizen of Messina during the siege in which the "untrained townsmen" of
Messina held off the forces of Charles of Anjou for three months until
Peter of Aragon came to claim the kingdom. See the *Cambridge Medieval
History* VI:199.

Book Fifteen

66 **the arms . . . were green or yellow, without any device.** Compare
Benoit,

> D'or bruni ert sis escus toz;
> N'aveit nul autre teint desoz,
> Mais de porpre ert coverz desus
> E entaillez par granz pertus.
>
> (7815-19)

84-87 **Phylon's chariot.** In Benoit (7885-912), the chariot is made of boiled elephant hide painted in various colors, while the shafts, wheel rims, and axles are of ivory; Guido has combined these details.

Benoit also says that the chariot is pulled by two dromedaries, and although this detail did not appear in any of the manuscripts used by Griffin, the fact that it was originally in Guido's account is indicated by its appearance in the *Gest Hystoriale*, as well as in a seventeenth-century translation which Griffin cites in his note to this passage.

113-14 **Hector's horse.** Dares, of course, says nothing about Hector's horse, but Benoit, although he does not comment specifically on the horse's "size, boldness, beauty, and other marvelous virtues," states that it was given Hector by a fairy who had loved him in vain (8023-33).

165-66 **Merion and Idomeneus.** As Griffin's variants and index to proper names indicate, these are not Idomeneus of Crete and his ally, who appear a few lines further on as leaders of the eleventh battalion. Benoit, who invented the entire passage, gave the names as "Merion" and, in at least one manuscript, "Ypomenès," though "Ydomenex" is listed among the variants (8179, 8182, and notes). It is possible that "Merion" was originally something else or that Benoit, not remembering that in Dictys, Meriones is the son of Idomeneus, gave the name to another Greek warrior.

172 **Seguridan.** As Griffin points out, Guido misread Benoit's description of Prothenor, "mout furent prou et segurains" (8197, note—the text has "li forz, li proz, li segurains"), and thought that "segurains" was another knight.

373-77 **Dares writes about him ...** Dares does not mention Celidis (Schedius) at this point, but Benoit gives the story about the Queen of "Feminea" and cites Dares as his authority for Celidis' great beauty (8839-40).

510 **in the Turkish style.** Griffin's gloss for "de Turcia." Benoit usually describes bows as "ars turqueis" (in 9494, for instance), and Guido accordingly describes the archers of Huners as fighting in the Turkish fashion.

635 **as Dares writes.** Dares does say this (24, 23-24), and Benoit repeats it, citing his authority:

> Ço dit l'Estoire de verité
> Que après ço qu'om l'ot navré
> En ocist plus que devant:
> Milliers, si com jo truis lisant . . .

(10099-102)

Book Eighteen

49 **Deucalion.** Guido could have found the story of Deucalion and Pyrrha and the flood in *Met.* I:245-415, or *Etym.* XIII:22:4.

Book Nineteen

134 **Briseida's grief.** This is much more exaggerated than Benoit's description, and, as Lumiansky points out (p. 730), the artificiality of the rhetoric reduces the situation to absurdity and makes Briseida seem insincere.

161-73 Guido's moralizing on the deceitfulness of women has its source in Benoit; compare this passage with lines 13437-56 and 13471-94 of the *Roman,* especially:

> A femme dure dueus petit:
> A l'un ueil plore, a l'autre rit.
> Mout muënt tost li lor corage.

Book Twenty-one

3-14 Benoit devotes some three hundred lines to the Chamber of Beauty, and although Guido retains the chief details, his comment shows his attitude toward his material.

Book Twenty-two

35-94 Hector's burial. The details are all suggested by Benoit, who, however, has much more emphasis on jewels and colors. In the *Roman,* the figures on the four columns represent two old men and two young men, not angels, and each is of a different precious stone, while the columns are of still another material. The details of the preservative apparatus are also slightly different; Benoit has two vases at Hector's feet and a system of pipes.

Book Twenty-three

95-109 Polyxena's grief. As in the case of Briseida's grief, this is greatly expanded from Benoit, and is clearly an exercise in rhetoric.

110-28 Achilles' love for Polyxena. The classical story of the slaughtering of Polyxena at the tomb of Achilles gave rise to the notion that he had been in love with her, and Rose (p. 235) cites Dictys as one of the earliest reporters of this, but the details in Dictys are slightly different from those in Dares, who is Benoit's source here.

115 arrow of Cupid. For "sagitta cupidinis," which could be translated as "arrow of desire," but Guido undoubtedly means Cupid since Benoit, without referring to arrows, personifies love as Amors throughout the passage (17540 ff.).

Book Twenty-six

53 so variable and changeable. For "tamquam varia et mutabilis, sicut est proprium mulierum." This echoes Virgil's ". . . varium et mutabile semper/femina" (*Aeneid* IV:569-70).

249-64 Death of Troilus. Guido has intensified the violence, by way of leading up to his diatribe against Homer for extolling Achilles. Dares does not specify that Troilus was killed treacherously, and in Benoit, although he is greatly outnumbered, he fights valiantly until his horse is killed and he falls with it. At that point, Achilles arrives, strikes off his helmet, cuts off his head, and then drags the body at the tail of his horse. Benoit may have been trying to glorify Troilus while blackening Achilles' character, or he may have misunderstood Dares' statement that Achilles, having killed Troilus, began to drag his body from the battle (33), presumably in order to plunder it, and thought that Achilles was dragging the body around in order to mutilate it. Furthermore, both Benoit and Guido, remembering Virgil's description of Troilus' dead body being carried back to Troy in its driverless chariot could have thought that Achilles was dragging Troilus' body as he had Hector's: "Troilus . . . ill-matched in conflict with Achilles—is carried along by his horses, and, fallen backward, clings to the empty car, yet clasping the reins; his neck and hair are dragged over the ground, and the dust is scored by his reversed spear" (*Aeneid* I:474-478—Loeb).

Book Twenty-eight

54 **Telamon.** For Telamonius. Guido gives two accounts of the deaths of Ajax Telemonius and Palameded because Benoit, in conflating Dares and Dictys, gave both their versions. See Constans, V, s.v. Aïaus[1] and VI:259.

201-2 **hacked to pieces.** For "per frustra truncauit," actually "hacked in vain." But Griffin's sidenote says "cuts . . . in pieces" (217), which would be *per frusta,* as in the 1489 Strassburg edition. Lydgate (IV:4340-41) says she was hacked "in pecis smale."

Book Thirty

15 **the priest Thoans.** Benoit: "Thoans le prestre soverain" (25617, and note). As Griffin states in his index, Benoit did not realize that Dictys' Theano was a woman.

81 **a bronze horse.** See note to *Book Thirty-five,* lines 150-54.

239 **all of Neptune's Troy** . . . For "tota Neptunia fumat Troya" (234). Cf. Virgil: "omnis humo fumat Neptunia Troia" (*Aeneid* III:3).

243 **the traitors . . . by a given sign were preserved.** . . . Not in Benoit or Dictys; Guido may know the tradition, cited by Rose (p. 234), that the Greeks favored Antenor because of his disapproval of the abduction of Helen, and that they advised him to hang a panther skin outside his door so his house would not be plundered.

337-51 **Hecuba's madness and death.** Benoit had been following

Dictys fairly closely, but where Dictys states that the place at which
Hecuba was buried was called "Cynossema (The Tomb of the Bitch)"
(V:16–Frazer) in Abydos, Benoit says it was called "Engrès," that is,
"fierce" or "violent," and that it was in "Aulide" (variant of "abidie,"
26570 and note). It will be noted that Guido follows Benoit exactly,
including the statement that the name is still current.

Book Thirty-three

163 **Lotophagos.** As Griffin points out, s.v. *Calastofagos,* this is the
acc. pl. of *Lotophagi,* "Lotus-eaters," which Benoit made a port.

198 **Aulis.** For Aeolus, as in Dictys and Benoit.

257 **food or nourishment.** For "esum neque cibum," though Griffin
gives "potum" ("drink,") as a variant for *cibum.*

298 **Antenor.** For Alcinous. Benoit: "Alcenon" (28951).

Book Thirty-four

98 **a certain ship.** For "quadam navi," though the plural should have
been used since a few lines later, "five hundred sailing in them lost their
lives."

Book Thirty-five

18-19 **a turret all ingeniously constructed of fishes.** For "quedam
turricula tota ex piscibus artificiose composita." The ultimate source of
this strange statement is Dictys VI:15 where Telegonus, on his way to see
Ulysses, carries "a spear whose point was the bone of a sea bird, the
turtle-dove, which was the symbol of Aeaea, where he was born" (Frazer,
p. 129). Benoit apparently conceived of this symbol as a kind of standard
so that there is at the tip of Telegonus' spear,

> Un signe de peisson de mer,
> Por certe chose demostrer,
> Dont il esteit, de quel contree,
> En semblance de tor ovree ...   (30021-24)

That the sign of the fish has been made in the semblance of a tower can probably be accounted for by Dictys' "turturis," gen. sing. of *turtur,* "turtle-dove," being confused with *turris,* "tower," either by Benoit or by the scribe of his Dictys manuscript. Guido translates Benoit quite literally, but transfers the spear from Telegonus to the apparition, probably considering a tower made of fishes, or even images of fish, to be the kind of marvel that is appropriate to a dream.

The number of variants suggests that the scribes found these lines obscure, and it is interesting to note that Lydgate expands the passage—as he frequently does—so that the spear is hung with a blue banner painted with fish and a gold crown (V:3020-24), while the *Gest* poet gives the apparition a sword with a pan of fish on the point (13826-27).

130 **happily.** For "feliciter," perhaps a mistake for *infeliciter* [unhappily].

131-204 **The problem of Dares,** "Cornelius," and Dictys, and Guido's possible use of them, is discussed in the introduction, pp. xvii-xx. It should be observed that, except as noted, Guido's summarizes Dares almost exactly.

150-54 **the bronze horse.** In the extant Dares (40), Polydamas tells the Greeks to enter by the Scaean Gate, "the one whose exterior was carved with a horse's head" (Frazer, p. 165), but makes no mention of the horse's being marble. Dictys, who said the horse was made of wood ("ligno"), does agree with Virgil; in *Aeneid* II:16, the horse's ribs are interwoven with planks of fir ("abiete") and *abiete* might easily be confused with *aereum,* "bronze."

163-64 **Dares** (44): "The number of Greeks who fell . . . was 866,000; the number of the Trojans 676,000" (Frazer, p. 168).

166-67 **Dares:** "Aeneas set sail with the twenty-two ships that Alexander had used when going to Greece" (Frazer, p. 168). Two hundred ("CC") is listed as a variant in Meister's edition of Dares, p. 52.

170-82 As Meister points out in the introduction to his edition of Dares, catalogues like this often appeared at the end of manuscripts of *De Excidio;* the one he gives (pp. viii-ix) is similar to this but not identical.

186-204 **The epitaphs.** If these are not Guido's work, or culled by him from some collection—and neither possibility seems likely in view of the fact that Hector's death is here given in the Homeric version and the terms Aeacides, Argolian, and Pergama are not used elsewhere by Guido—

then it is quite likely that like the catalogue, they were in Guido's manuscript of Dares.

237 **indiction.** A period of fifteen years, sometimes a fiscal period, and often used in dates; in fact it is so ordered in the Justinian title Guido had cited at *Book Twelve,* line 232.

BIBLIOGRAPHY

Works Cited in the Introduction and Notes

Atwood, Elmer Bagby. "English Versions of the Historia Trojana." Ph.D. dissertation, University of Virginia, 1932.

Bede. *Bedae Venerabilis Opera, Pars II, Opera Exegetica,* "Libri Qvatvor in Principium Genesis." Edited by Ch. W. Jones. Turnhout: Brepols, 1967.

Benoit de Sainte-Maure. *Le Roman de Troie.* Edited by Léopold Constans. Société des Anciens Textes Français, 6 vols., Paris: Firmin Didot et Cie., 1904-1912.

Cambridge. Harvard University Library. Latin 35, 1353. *Liber de Casu Troie* [by Guido delle Colonne].

Cambridge Medieval History. See Prévité-Orton, Schipa, Thompson.

Cary, George. *The Medieval Alexander.* Edited by D. J. A. Ross. Cambridge: Cambridge University Press, 1956, reissued 1967.

Chaucer, Geoffrey. *The Book of Troilus and Criseyde.* Edited by Robert Kilburn Root. Princeton: Princeton University Press, 1945.

Chaucer, Geoffrey. *The Works of Geoffrey Chaucer.* Edited by F. N. Robinson. Boston: Houghton Mifflin, 1957.

Chiàntera, Raffaele. *Guido delle Colonne.* Naples: Le Monnier, 1955.

Constans. *See* Benoit de Sainte-Maure.

Constans, L. and Faral, E., eds. *Le Roman de Troie en Prose.* Paris: E. Champion, 1922.

Contini, Gianfranco, ed. *Poeti del Duecento,* 2 vols. Milan: Riccardo Ricciardi, 1960. Vol. I:104-6.

Curtius, Quintus. *History of Alexander.* Translated by J. C. Rolfe. Loeb Classical Library. London: W. Heinemann, 1946.

Dares. *Daretis Phrygii De Excidio Troiae Historia.* Edited by Ferdinand Meister. Leipzig: B. G. Teubner, 1873.

Dictys. *Dictis Cretensis Ephemeridos Belli Troiae Libri.* Edited by Werner Eisenhut. Leipzig: B. G. Teubner, 1958.

Dionysius Areopagiticus. "Polycarpo summo sacerdoto," *Epistolae Diversae,* VII. In J. P. Migne, *Patrologia Latina,* CXXII:1179-80. Paris: 1863.

Dionysius Areopagiticus. *Oeuvres Complètes du Pseudo-Denys L'Aréopagite.* Translated by Maurice de Candillac. Paris: Aubier, 1943.

Du Cange, Charles de Fresne. *Glossarium Mediae et Infimae Latinitatis.* Niort: Firmin Didot, 1883-1887.

Falcandus, Hugo. *La Historia o Liber de Regno Sicilie e la Epistola ad Petrum Panormitane Ecclesie Thesaurium di Ugo Falcando.* Edited by G. B. Siragusa. Rome: Forzani e C., 1897. Pp. 177-84.

Faral, Edmond. *La Légende Arthurienne.* Paris: H. Champion, 1929.

Faral, Edmond. *Les Arts Poétiques du XIIᵉ et du XIIIᵉ Siècle.* Paris: E. Champion, 1924.

Frazer, R. M., Jr., trans. *The Trojan War: The Chronicles of Dictys of Crete and Dares the Phrygian.* Bloomington: Indiana University Press, 1966.

Gest Hystoriale. See Panton and Donaldson.

Golubeva, Olga. "The Saltykov-Shchedrin Library, Leningrad." *The Book Collector* (Summer, 1955): 99-109.

Gorra, Egidio. *Testi Inediti di Storia Trojana.* Turin: C. Trevirio, 1887.

Griffin. *See* Guido delle Colonne.

Guido delle Colonne. *Historia Destructionis Troiae.* Edited by Nathaniel Edward Griffin. Cambridge: The Mediaeval Academy of America, 1936.

Isidore of Seville. *Isidori Hispalensis Episcopi Etymologiarum sive Originum Libri XX.* Edited by W. M. Lindsay. Oxford: The Clarendon Press, 1911.

James, Montague Rhodes, trans. *The Apocryphal New Testament.* Oxford: The Clarendon Press, 1924.

Joly, Aristide. *Benoit de Sainte-More et le Roman de Troie, ou les Métamorphoses d'Homère et L'Epopée Gréco-Latine au Moyen-Age.* 2 vols. Paris: F. Vieweg, 1870-1871.

Joseph of Exeter. *De Bello Trojano,* in *Dictys Cretensis et Dares Phrygius*

De Bello Trojano . . . Accedunt Josephi Iscani De Bello Trojano Libri Sex. London: Valpy, 1825.

____. "The Text of Joseph of Exeter's *Bellum* Troianum," ed. Geoffrey B. Riddehough. Ph.D. dissertation, Harvard University, 1950.

____. *The Iliad of Dares Phrygius.* Translated by Gildas Roberts. Cape Town: A. A. Balkema, 1970.

Justinian. *The Civil Law.* Translated by S. P. Scott. 17 vols. Cincinnati: The Central Trust Company, 1932. Vol. XVI.

Kantorowicz, Ernst. *Frederick the Second.* Translated by E. O. Lorimer. New York: Ungar, 1957.

Kent, W. H. "Devil," *The Catholic Encyclopedia.* Edited by Charles G. Herberman, Edward A. Pace, Conde B. Pallen, Thomas J. Shahan, and John T. Wynne. 15 vols. New York: Robert Appleton Company, 1907-1914.

Kington-Oliphant, T. L. *History of Frederick the Second.* London: Macmillan and Co., 1862.

Krapp, George Philip, ed. *Andreas and the Fates of the Apostles.* Boston: Ginn and Company, 1906.

Latham, R. E. *Revised Medieval Latin Word List.* London: Oxford University Press, 1965.

Laud Troy Book. See Wülfing.

Lewis, Charlton T., and Short, Charles. *A Latin Dictionary.* Founded on Andrews' edition of *Freund's Latin Dictionary.* Oxford: The Clarendon Press, 1951 [first edition, 1879].

Lumiansky, R. M. "Structural Unity in Benoit's *Roman de Troyes*," *Romania* LXXIX (1958): 410-24.

____. "The Story of Troilus and Briseida According to Benoit and Guido." *Speculum* XXIX (1954): 727-33.

Lydgate, John. *Lydgate's Troy Book.* Edited by Henry Bergen. Early English Text Society, E. S. 97, 103, 106, and 126. London: 1906-1935.

Mack Smith, Denis. *A History of Sicily.* 2 vols. London: Chatto & Windus, 1968. Vol. I: *Medieval Sicily, 800-1713.*

Medieval Latin Word List. See Latham.

Mierow. *See* Otto, Bishop of Freising.

Miller, Helen Hill. *Sicily and the Western Colonies of Greece.* New York: Scribner, 1965.

Moore, Edward. *Studies in Dante.* Third Series. Oxford: The Clarendon Press, 1903.

Niermeyer, J. F. *Mediae Latinitatis Lexicon Minus.* Leiden: E. J. Brill, 1954–.

Otto, Bishop of Freising. *The Two Cities.* Translated by Charles Christopher Mierow. New York: Columbia University Press, 1928.

Ovid. *Heroides and Amores.* Translated by Grant Showerman. Loeb Classical Library. London: W. Heinemann, 1914.

Ovid. *Metamorphoses.* Translated by Frank Justus Miller. Loeb Classical Library. London: W. Heinemann, 1916.

Pannier, Léopold. *Les Lapidaires Français du Moyen Age.* Paris: F. Vieweg, 1882.

Panton, George A. and Donaldson, David, eds. *The "Gest Hystoriale" of the Destruction of Troy.* Early English Text Society, 39 and 56. London, 1869-1874.

Petrus Comestor. *Historia Scholastica* in J. P. Migne, *Patrologia Latina* CXCVIII. Paris: 1855.

Pliny. *Natural History.* Translated by H. Rackham. Loeb Classical Library. Cambridge: Harvard University Press, 1938-1962.

Plummer, Charles. *Vitae Sanctorum Hiberniae.* Oxford: The Clarendon Press, 1910. Reprint, 1968.

Prévité-Orton, C. W. "Italy, 1250-1290." In *The Cambridge Medieval History.* Planned by J. B. Bury. 8 vols. Cambridge: Cambridge University Press, 1911-1936. Volume VI: The Victory of the Papacy, edited by J. R. Tanner, C. W. Prévité-Orton, and Z. N. Brooke, pp. 166-203.

Prose Roman. See L. Constans and E. Faral.

Robinson. *See* Chaucer, *The Works of Geoffrey Chaucer.*

Robson, Vivian E. *A Student's Textbook of Astrology.* London: C. Palmer, 1922.

Root. *See* Chaucer, *The Book of Troilus and Criseyde.*

Rose, H. J. *A Handbook of Greek Mythology.* London: Methuen, 1928.

Rossetti, D. G., trans. *Dante and His Circle: With the Italian Poets Preceding Him.* London: Ellis and White, 1874.

Sacrobosco. *The Sphere. See* Thorndike.

Schipa, Michelangelo. "Italy and Sicily under Frederick II." *The Cam-*

bridge *Medieval History,* 8 vols. Cambridge: Cambridge University Press, 1911-1935. VI: 131-65.

Selmer, Carl, ed. *Navigatio Sancti Brandani Abbatis.* Notre Dame, Ind.: University of Notre Dame Press, 1959.

Thompson, A. Hamilton. "Military Architecture." *The Cambridge Medieval History.* 8 vols. Cambridge: Cambridge University Press, 1911-1935. VI: 773-84.

Thorndike, Lynn, trans. and ed. *The "Sphere" of Sacrobosco and Its Commentators.* Chicago: University of Chicago Press, 1941.

Virgil. *Aeneid.* Translated by H. Rushton Fairclough. Loeb Classical Library. London: W. Heinemann, 1918.

Wærn, Cecilia. *Mediaeval Sicily.* London: Duckworth & Co., 1910.

Wigginton, Waller B. "The Nature and Significance of the Late Medieval Troy Story: A Study of Guido delle Colonne's *Historia Destructionis Troiae.*" Ph.D. dissertation, Rutgers University, 1964.

Wolff, R. L. "Romania: The Latin Empire of Constantinople," *Speculum* XXII (1948): 1-34.

Wülfing, J. Ernst, ed. *The Laud Troy Book.* Early English Text Society, 121-122. London, 1902.

Young, Arthur M. *Troy and Her Legend.* Pittsburgh: University of Pittsburgh Press, 1948.

INDEX

The following index is greatly indebted to the index of proper names in Griffin's edition of the *Historia,* particularly in the identification of minor figures whose names either appear in more than one form or are given to several different characters. Griffin, in both his index and textual notes, traces the evolution of the names from Dares and Dictys to Guido. He also lists every proper name in the Latin text. In this translation, however, the index is limited to the major figures and, in the case of those that appear frequently, to their more important actions. The topics treated in Guido's digressions are found under the entry *Historia Destructionis Troiae.* Except for references to the Introduction, which is paginated in roman, all index entries refer to book and line numbers in the translation rather than to pages. Whenever the same name is used for two or more individuals in Guido's text, one is distinguished from another by the use of superscript numbers.